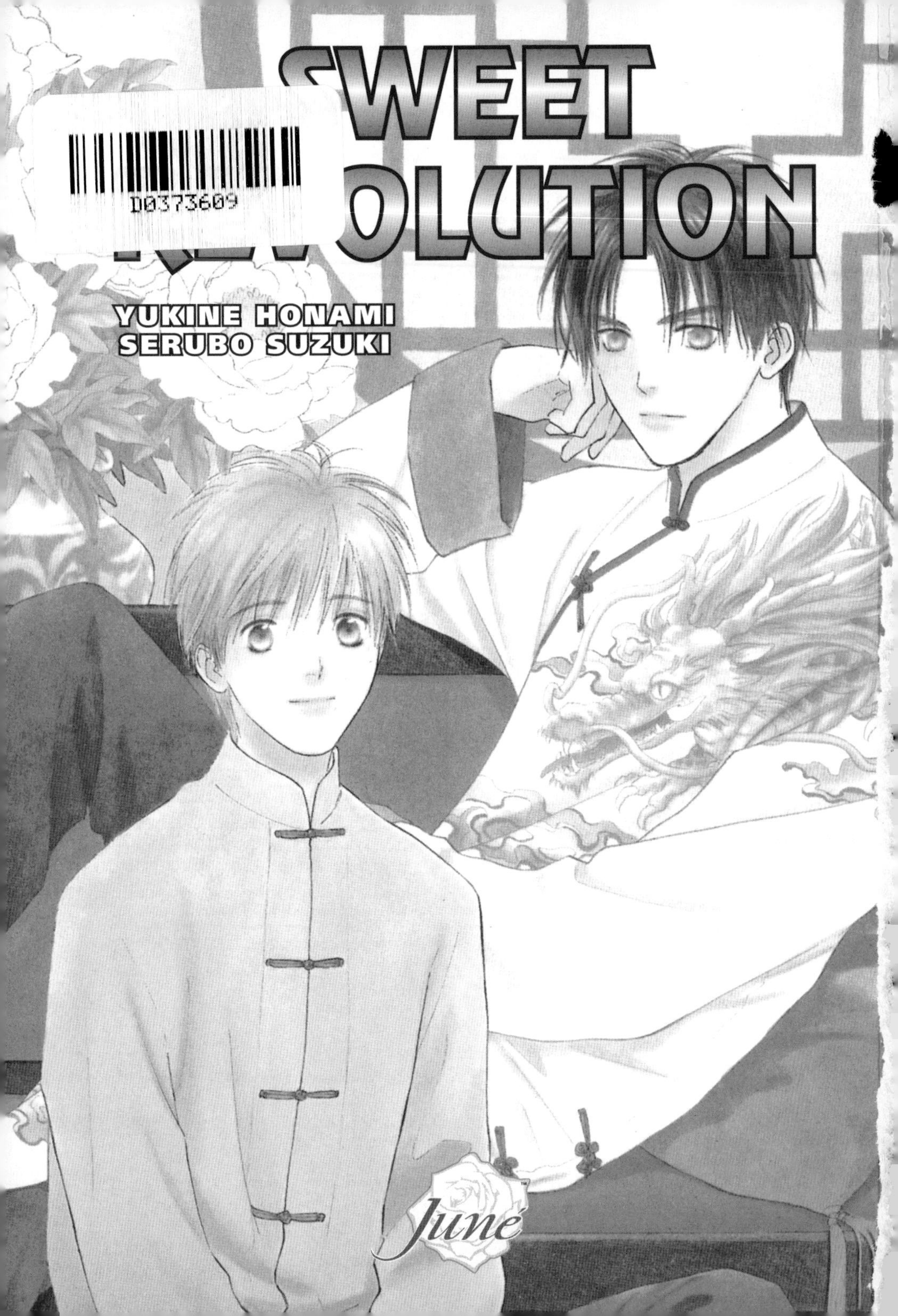
SWEET
OLUTION
YUKINE HONAMI
SERUBO SUZUKI
Juné

SWEET REVOLUTION

Translation	Sachiko Sato
Lettering	Replibooks
Graphic Design	Wendy Lee
Editing	Bambi Eloriaga
Editor in Chief	Fred Lui
Publisher	Hikaru Sasahara

English Edition Published by
DIGITAL MANGA PUBLISHING
A division of DIGITAL MANGA, Inc.
1487 W 178th Street, Suite 300
Gardena, CA 90248

www.dmpbooks.com

First Edition: February 2006
ISBN: 1-56970-910-6

3 5 7 9 10 8 6 4 2

Printed in China

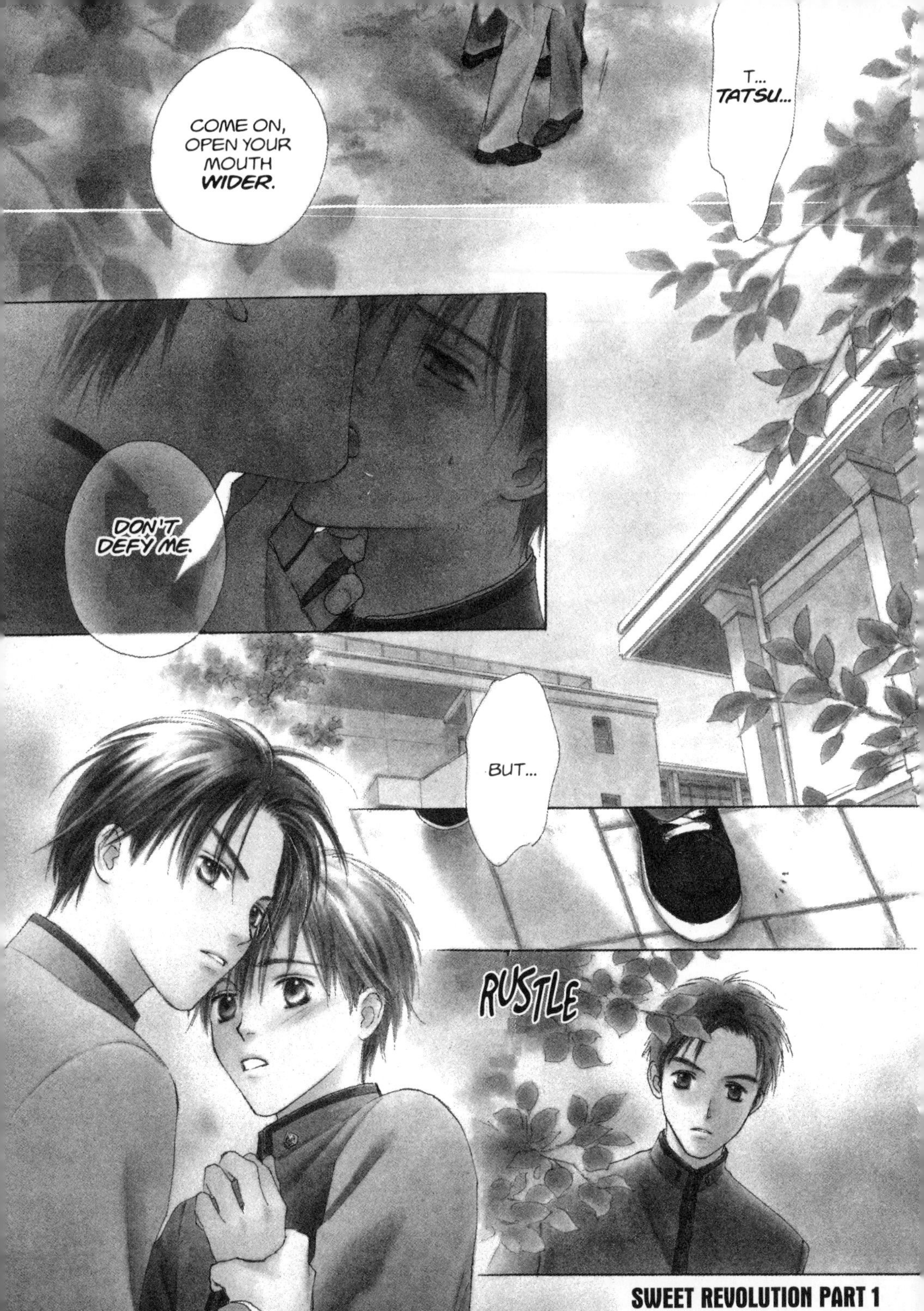
T... TATSU...
COME ON, OPEN YOUR MOUTH WIDER.
DON'T DEFY ME.
BUT...
RUSTLE

SWEET REVOLUTION PART 1

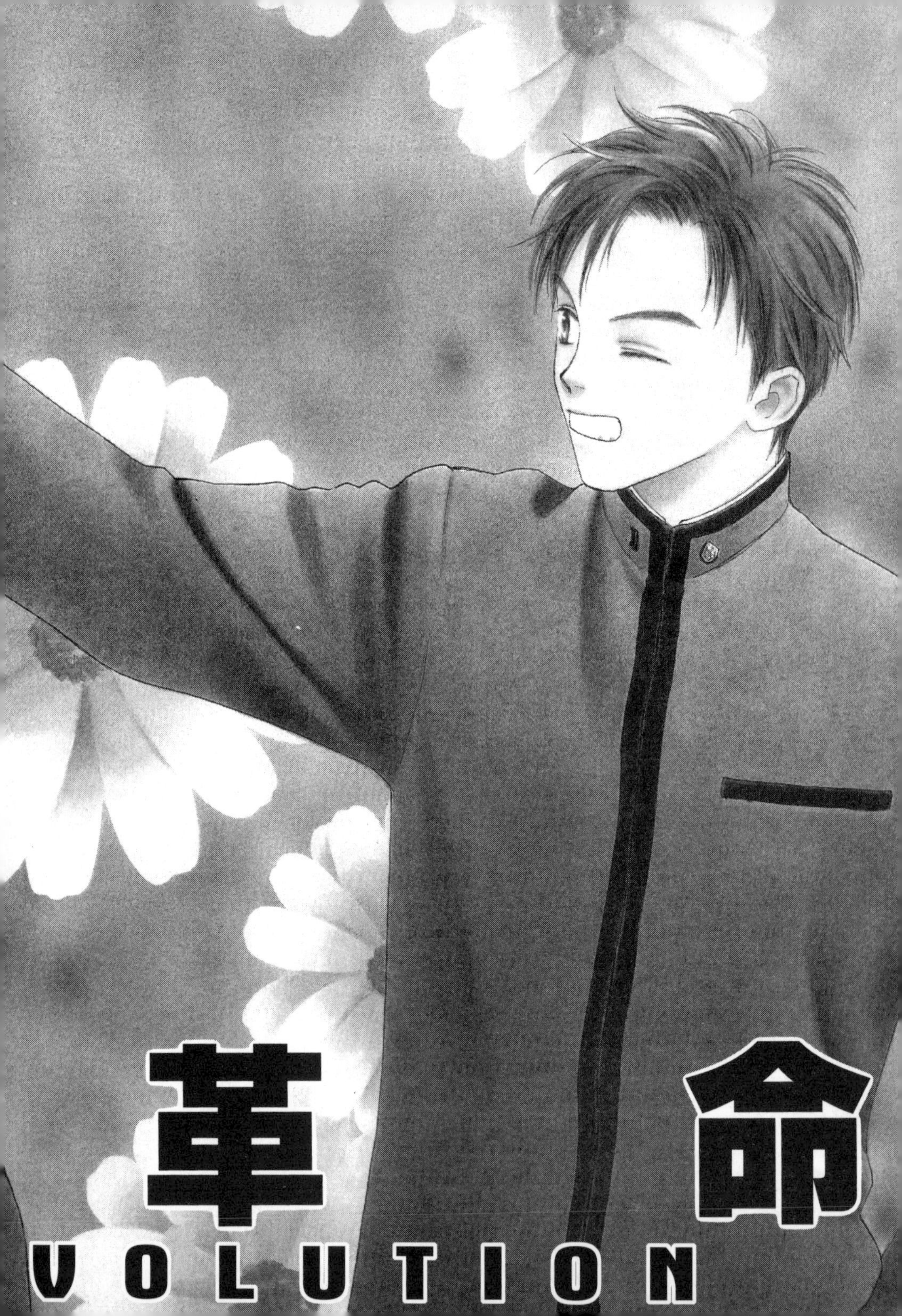
革命
VOLUTION

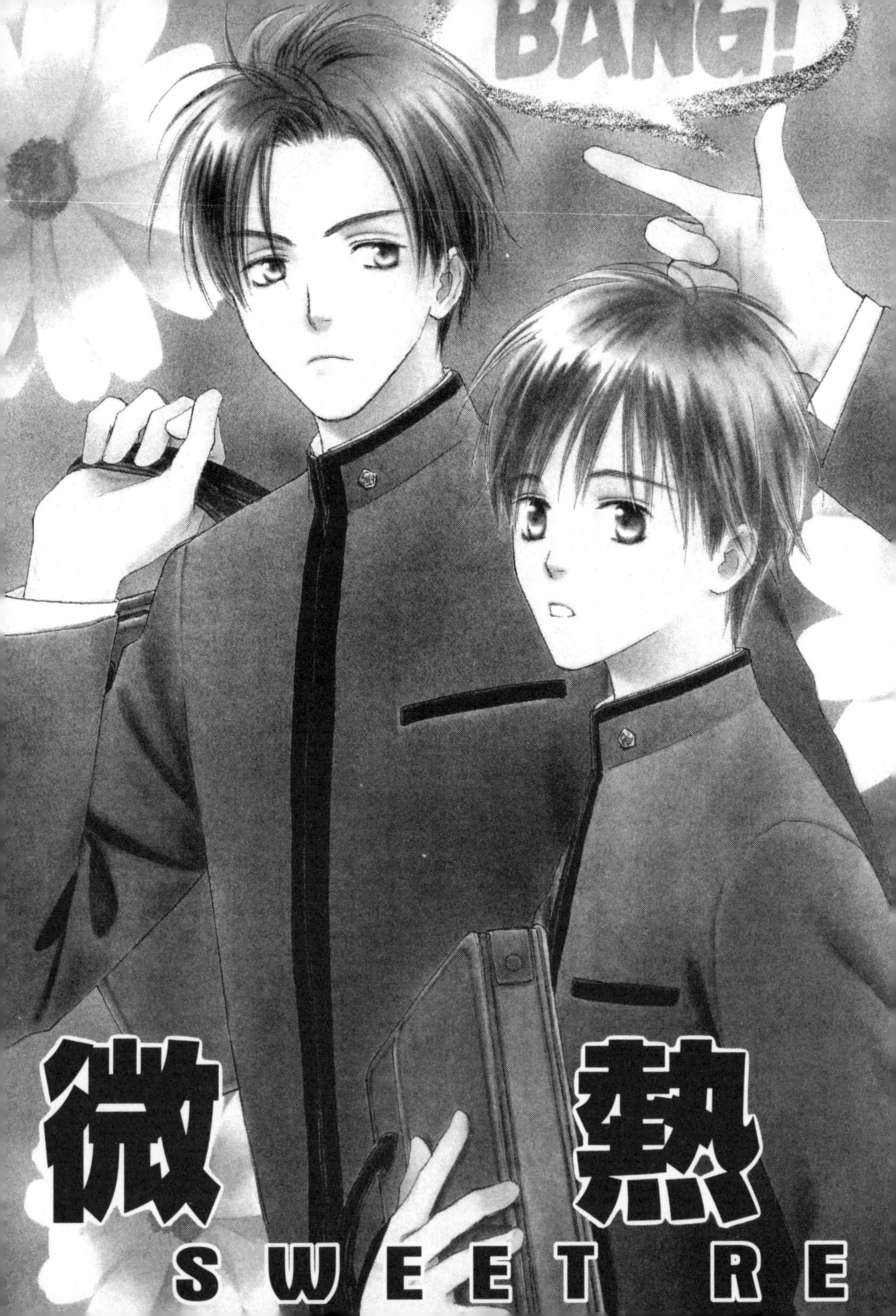
BANG!
微熱
SWEET RE

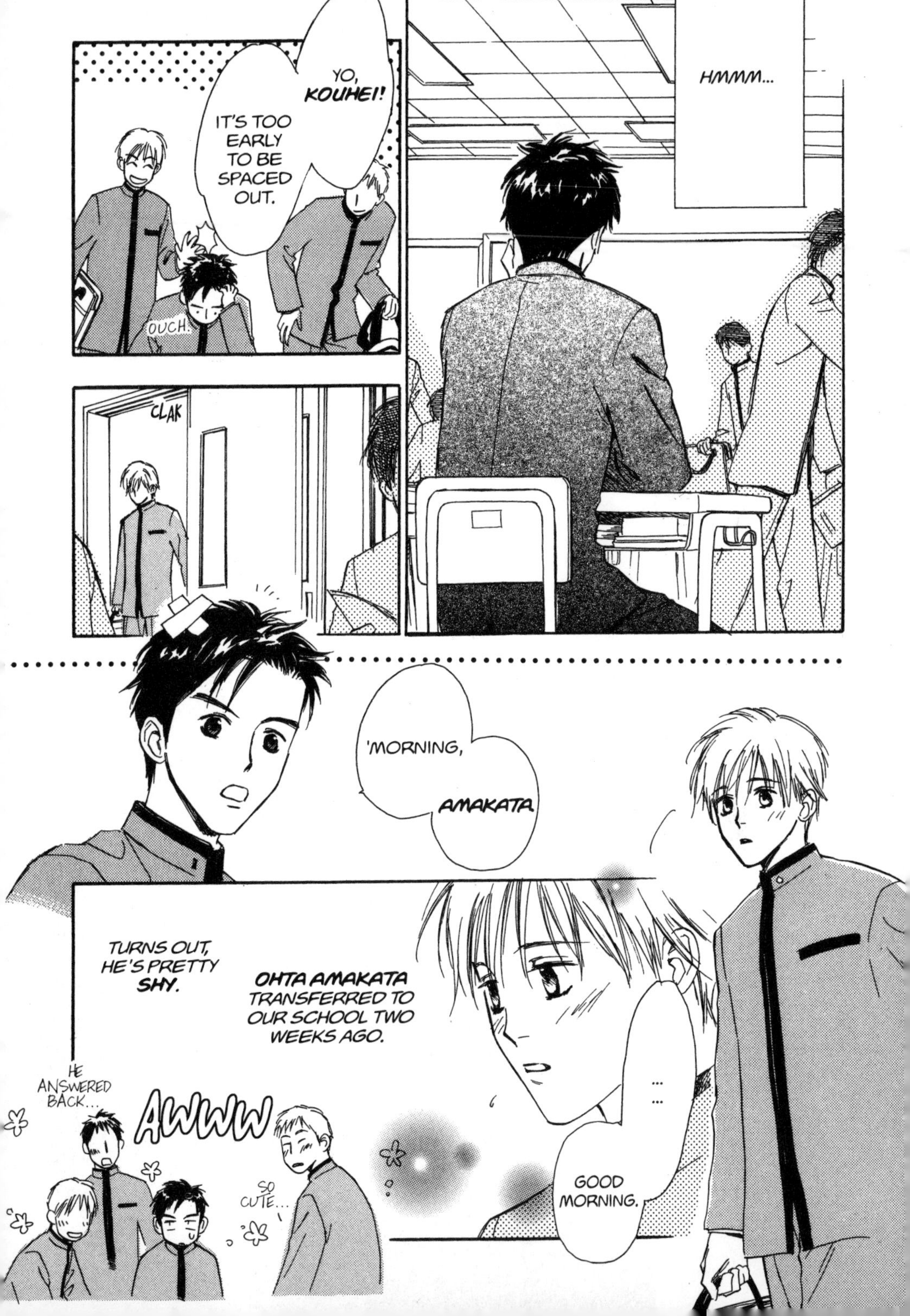
HMMM...
YO, KOUHEI!
IT'S TOO EARLY TO BE SPACED OUT.
OUCH.
CLAK
'MORNING,
AMAKATA
...
...
GOOD MORNING.
OHTA AMAKATA TRANSFERRED TO OUR SCHOOL TWO WEEKS AGO.
TURNS OUT, HE'S PRETTY SHY.
AWWW
HE ANSWERED BACK...
SO CUTE...

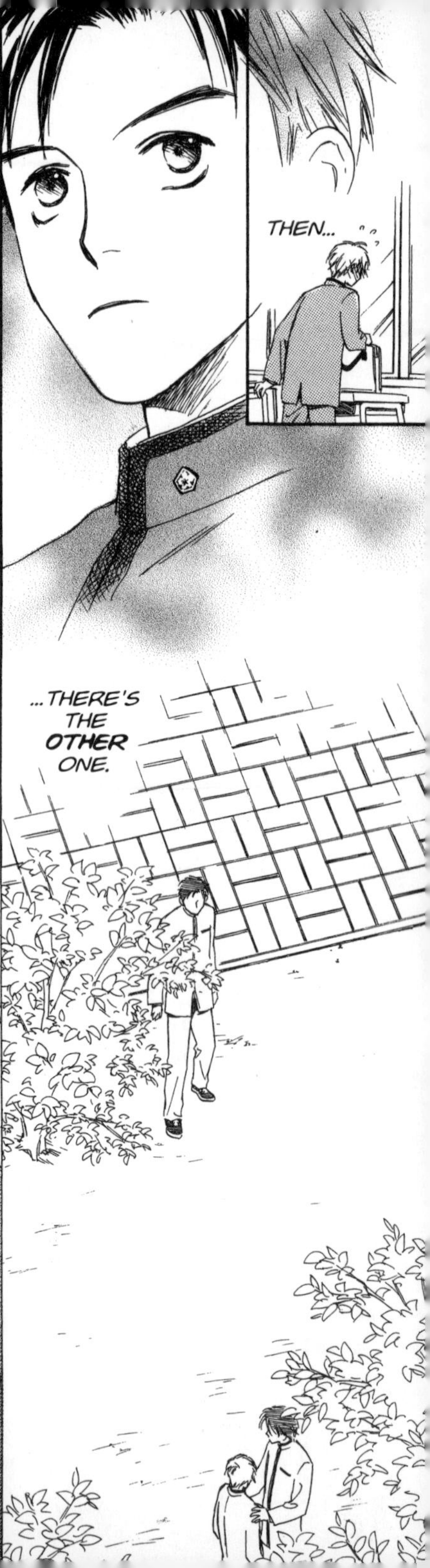
THEN...
...THERE'S THE OTHER ONE.

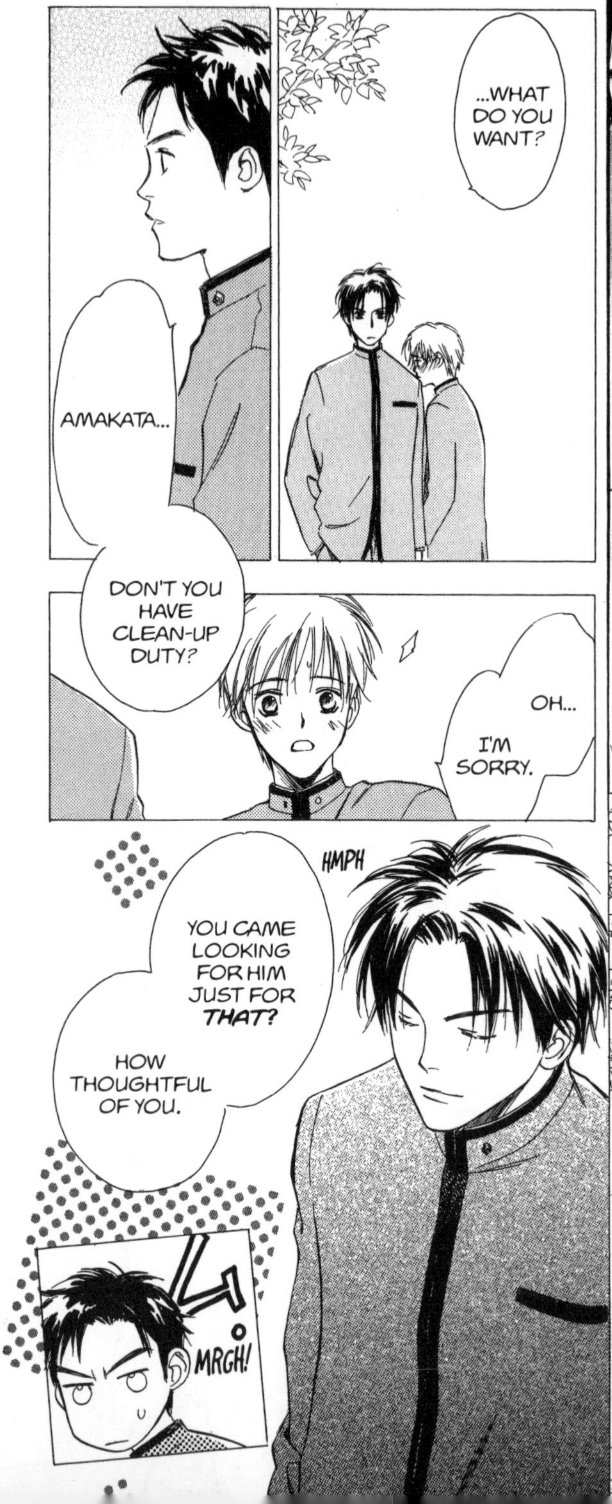
...WHAT DO YOU WANT?
AMAKATA...
DON'T YOU HAVE CLEAN-UP DUTY?
OH... I'M SORRY.
HMPH
YOU CAME LOOKING FOR HIM JUST FOR THAT?
HOW THOUGHTFUL OF YOU.
MRGH!

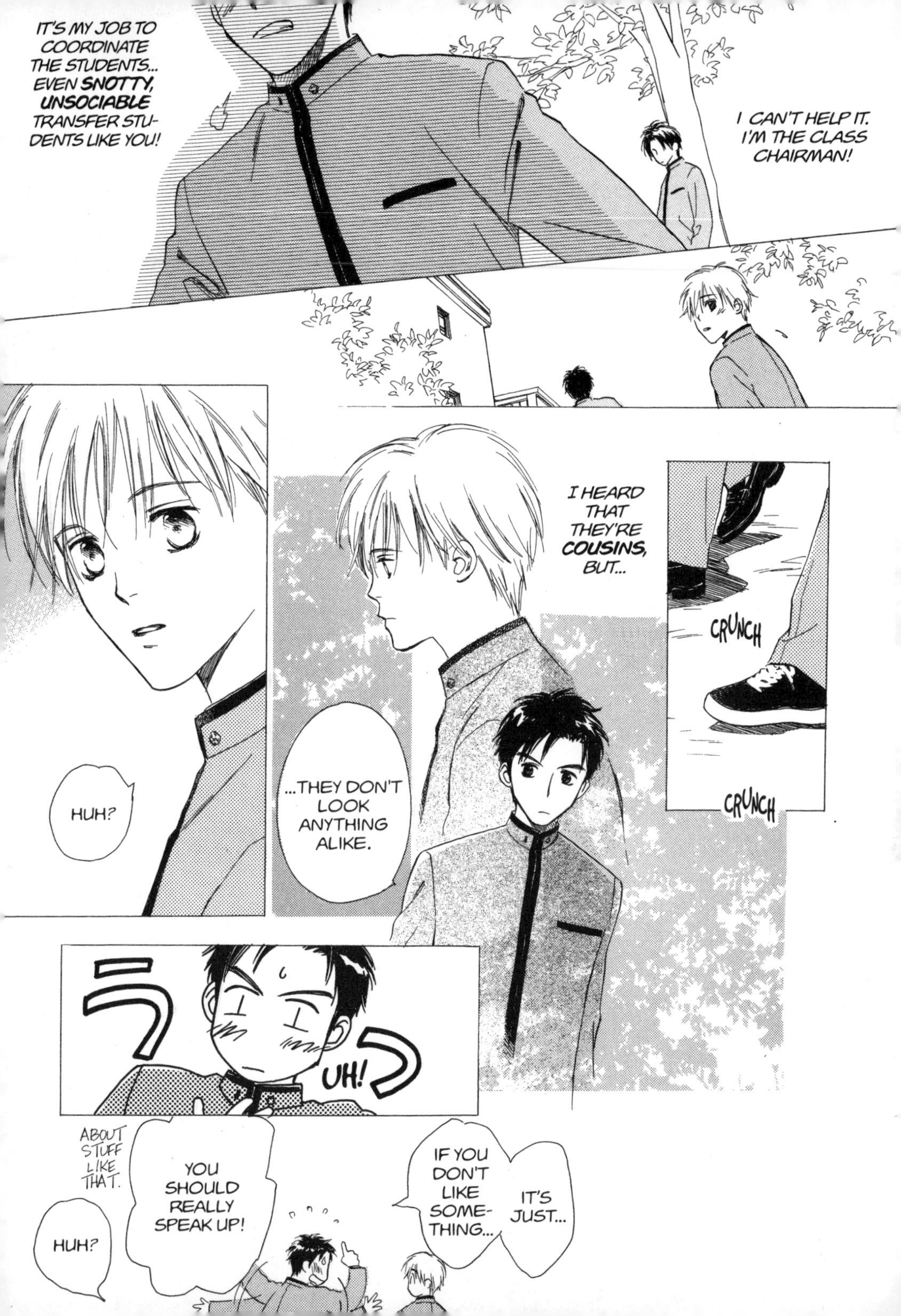

I CAN'T HELP IT. I'M THE CLASS CHAIRMAN!
IT'S MY JOB TO COORDINATE THE STUDENTS... EVEN **SNOTTY, UNSOCIABLE** TRANSFER STUDENTS LIKE YOU!
CRUNCH
CRUNCH
I HEARD THAT THEY'RE **COUSINS,** BUT...
...THEY DON'T LOOK ANYTHING ALIKE.
HUH?
う
UH!
IT'S JUST...
IF YOU DON'T LIKE SOMETHING...
YOU SHOULD REALLY SPEAK UP!
ABOUT STUFF LIKE THAT.
HUH?

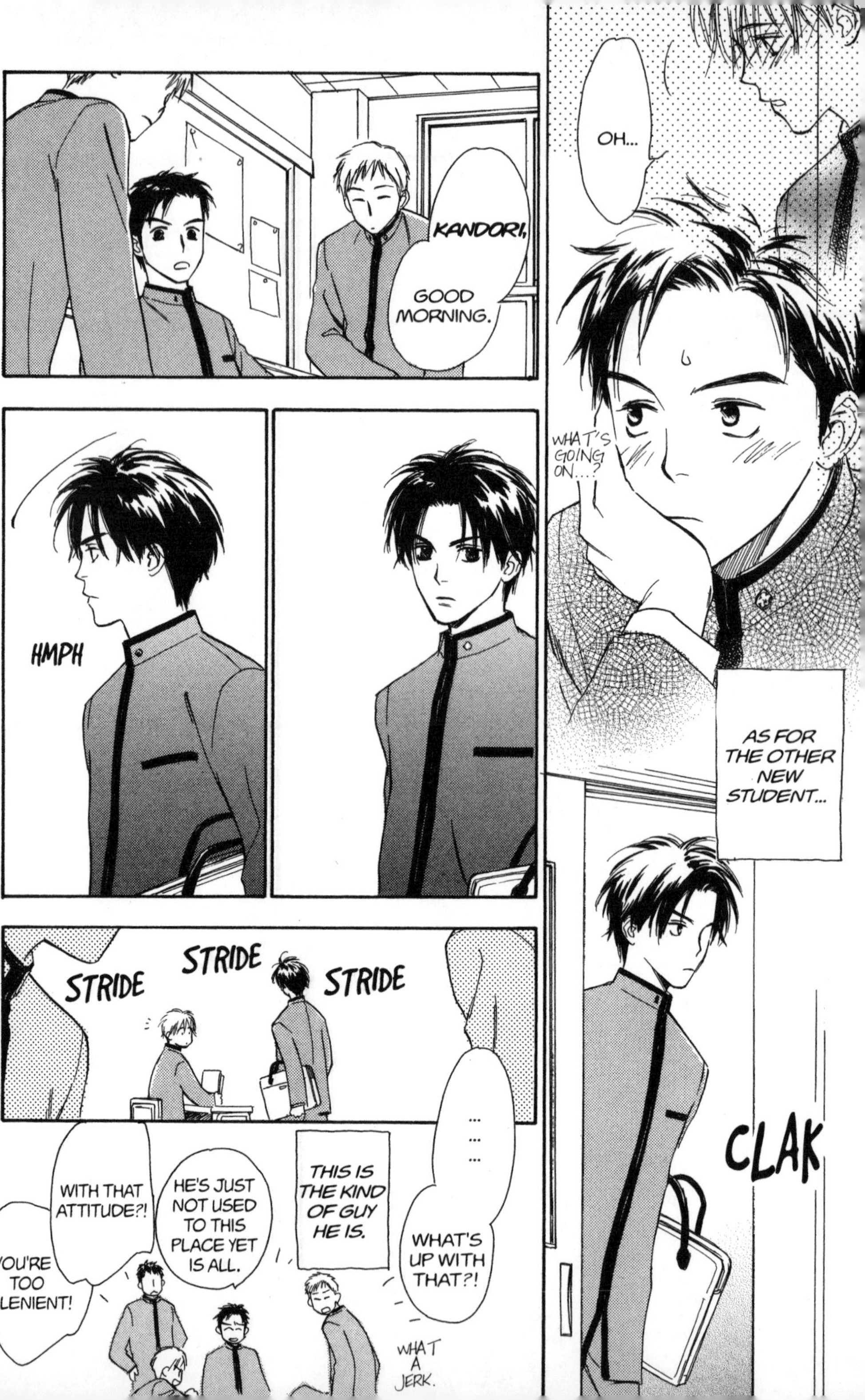
OH...
WHAT'S GOING ON...?
AS FOR THE OTHER NEW STUDENT...
CLAK
KANDORI,
GOOD MORNING.
HMPH
STRIDE
STRIDE
STRIDE
...
...
...
WHAT'S UP WITH THAT?!
WHAT A JERK.
THIS IS THE KIND OF GUY HE IS.
HE'S JUST NOT USED TO THIS PLACE YET IS ALL.
WITH THAT ATTITUDE?!
YOU'RE TOO LENIENT!

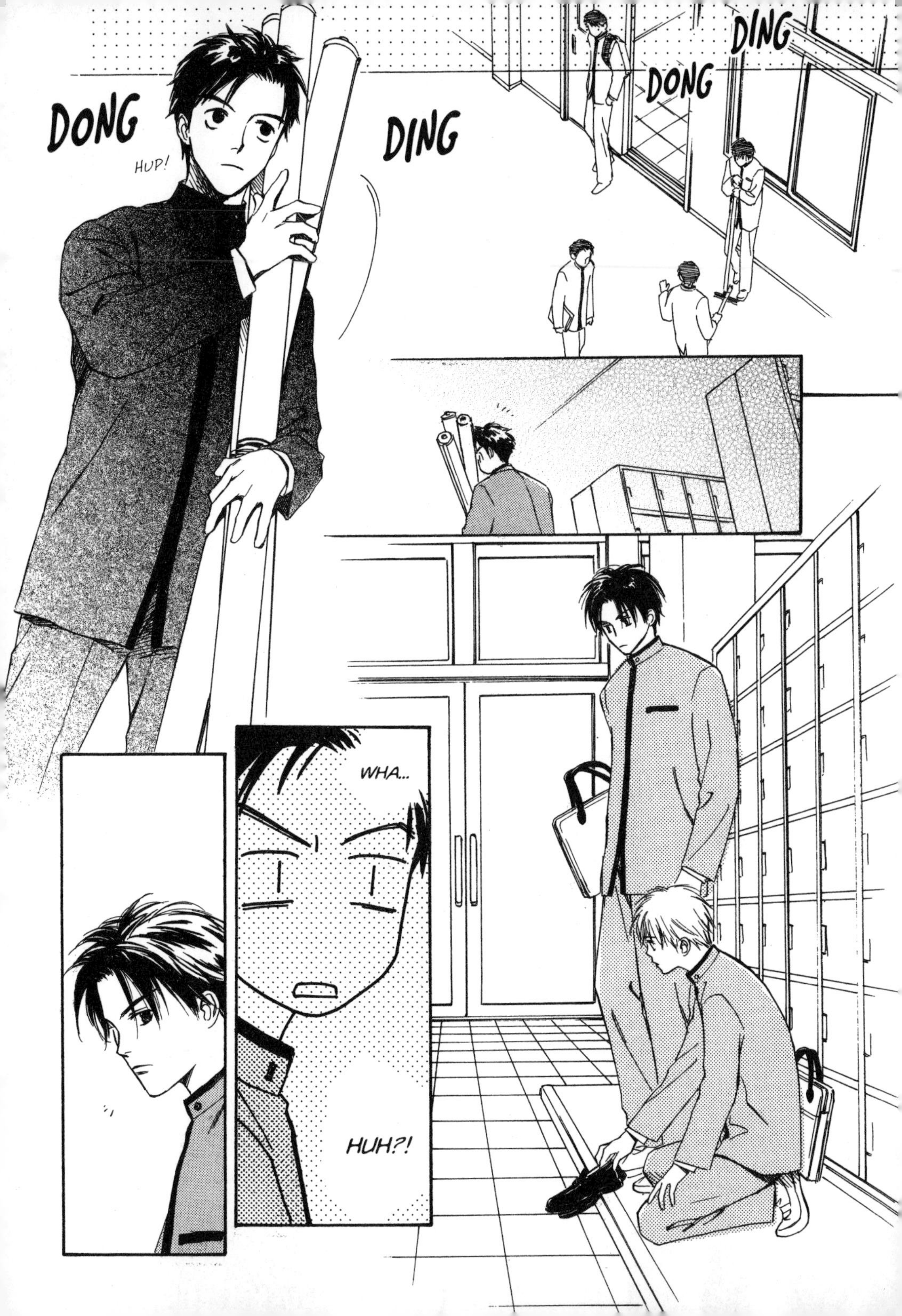
DING
DONG
DING
DONG
HUP!
WHA...
HUH?!

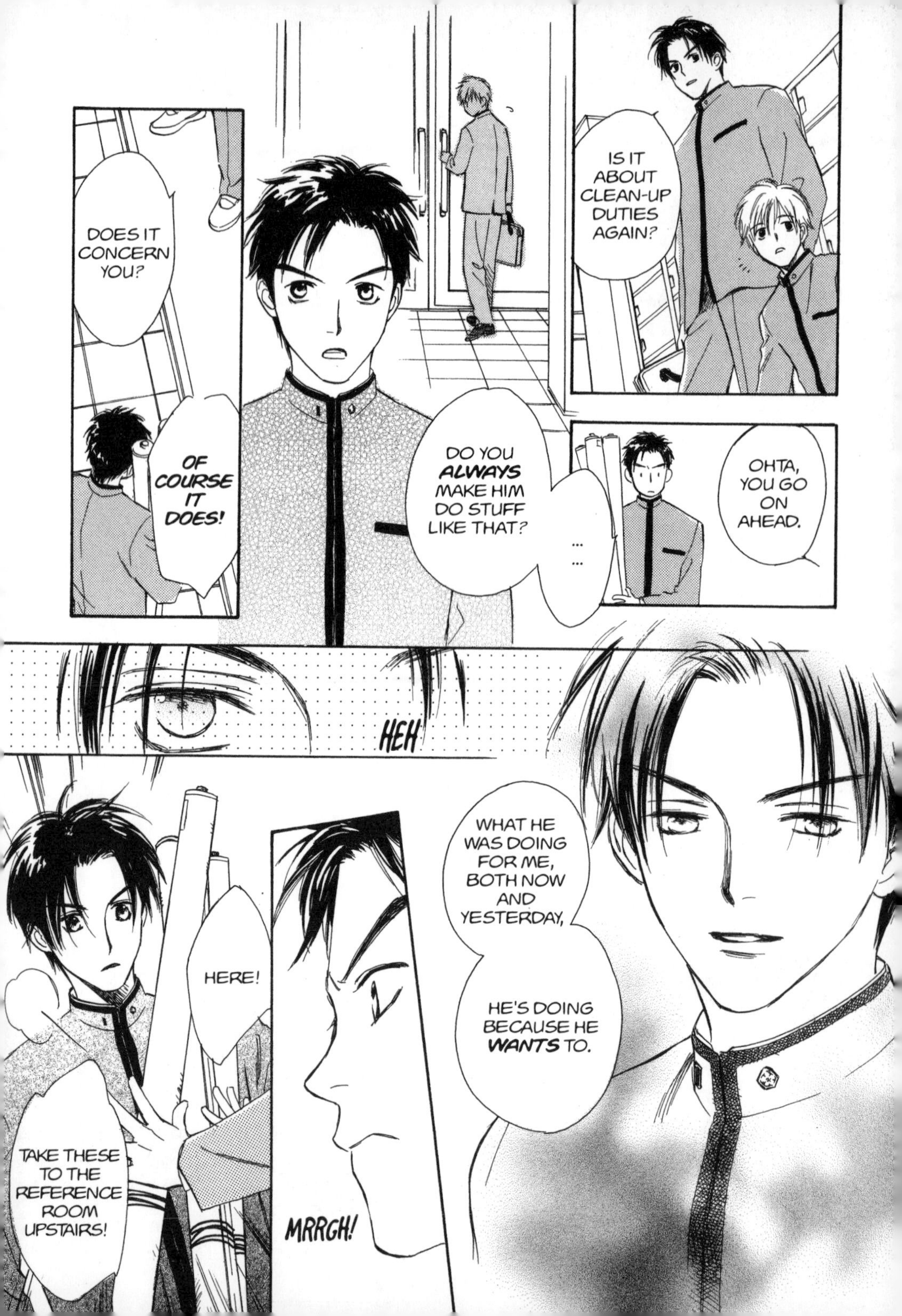
IS IT ABOUT CLEAN-UP DUTIES AGAIN?
OHTA, YOU GO ON AHEAD.
DO YOU ALWAYS MAKE HIM DO STUFF LIKE THAT?
... ...
DOES IT CONCERN YOU?
OF COURSE IT DOES!
HEH
WHAT HE WAS DOING FOR ME, BOTH NOW AND YESTERDAY,
HE'S DOING BECAUSE HE WANTS TO.
MRRGH!
HERE!
TAKE THESE TO THE REFERENCE ROOM UPSTAIRS!

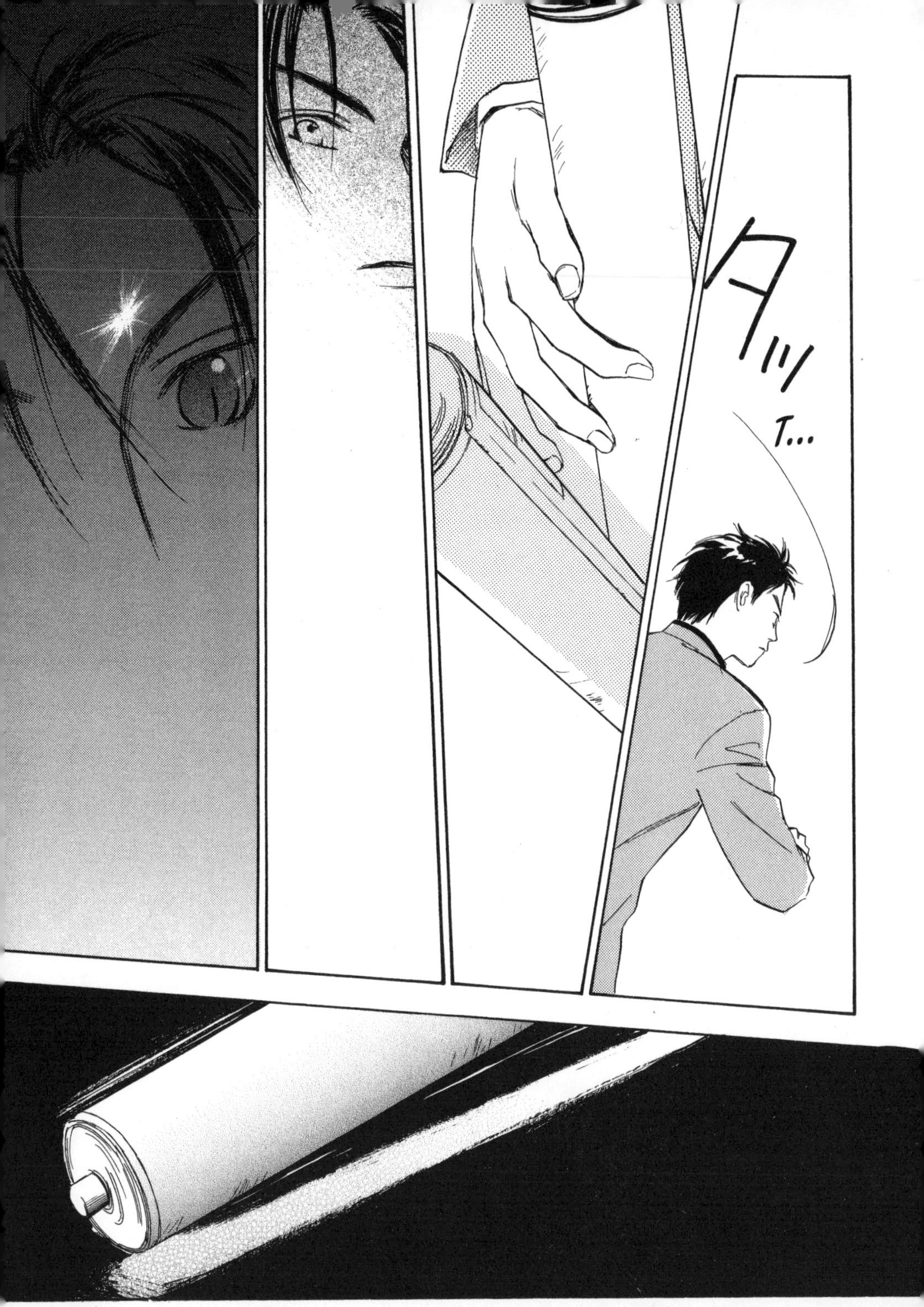
タッ
T...

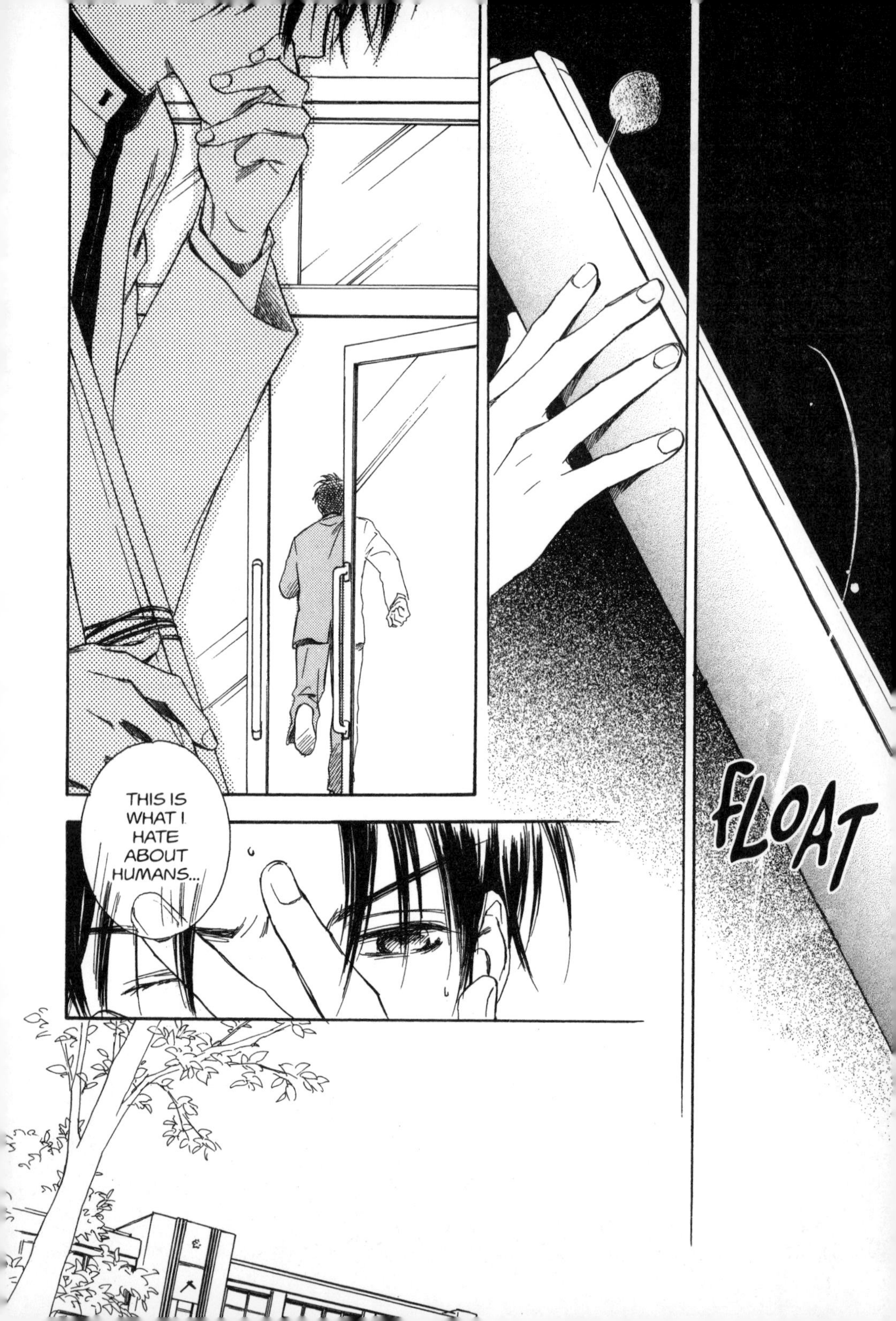
FLOAT
THIS IS WHAT I HATE ABOUT HUMANS...

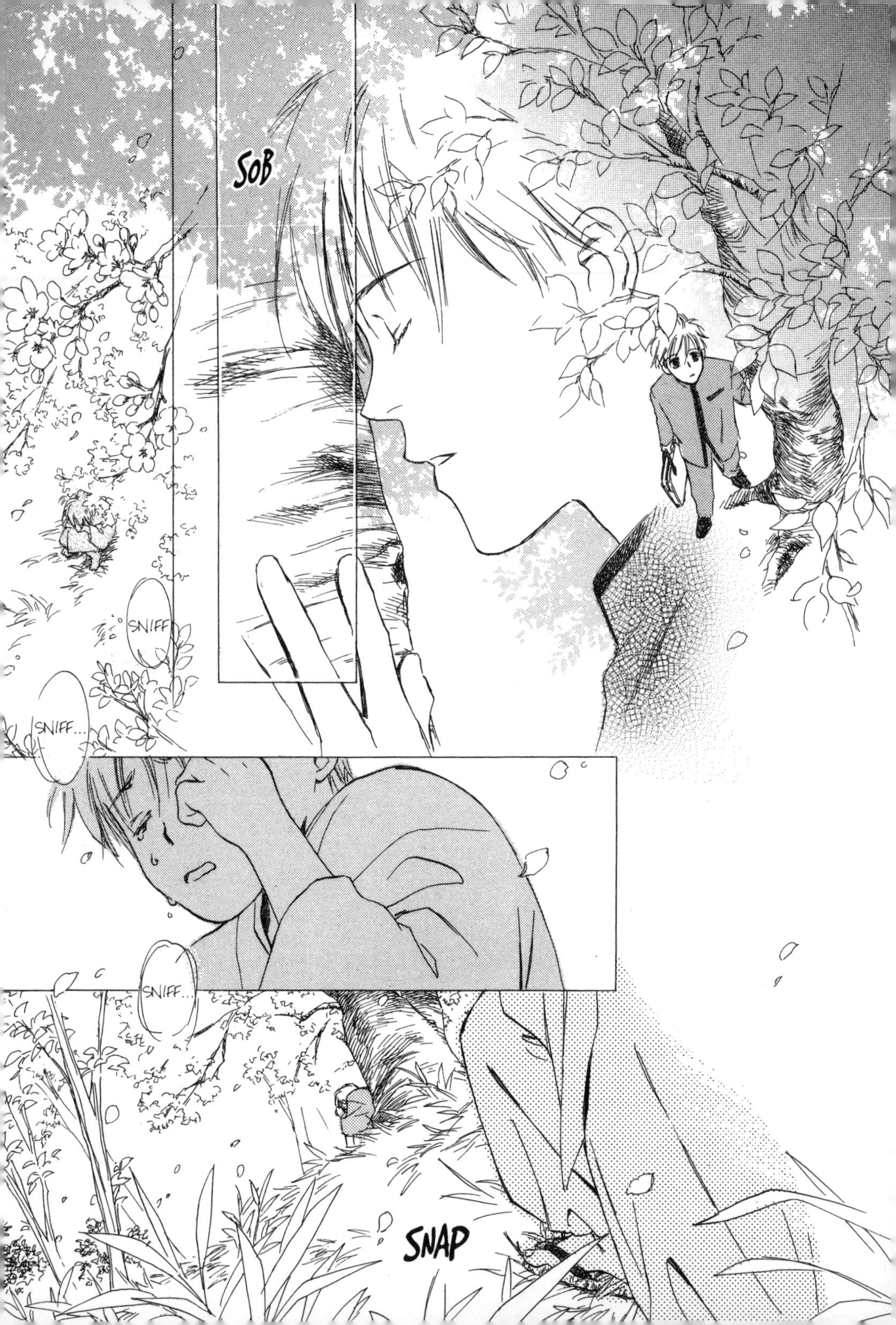
SOB
SNIFF
SNIFF...
SNIFF...
SNAP

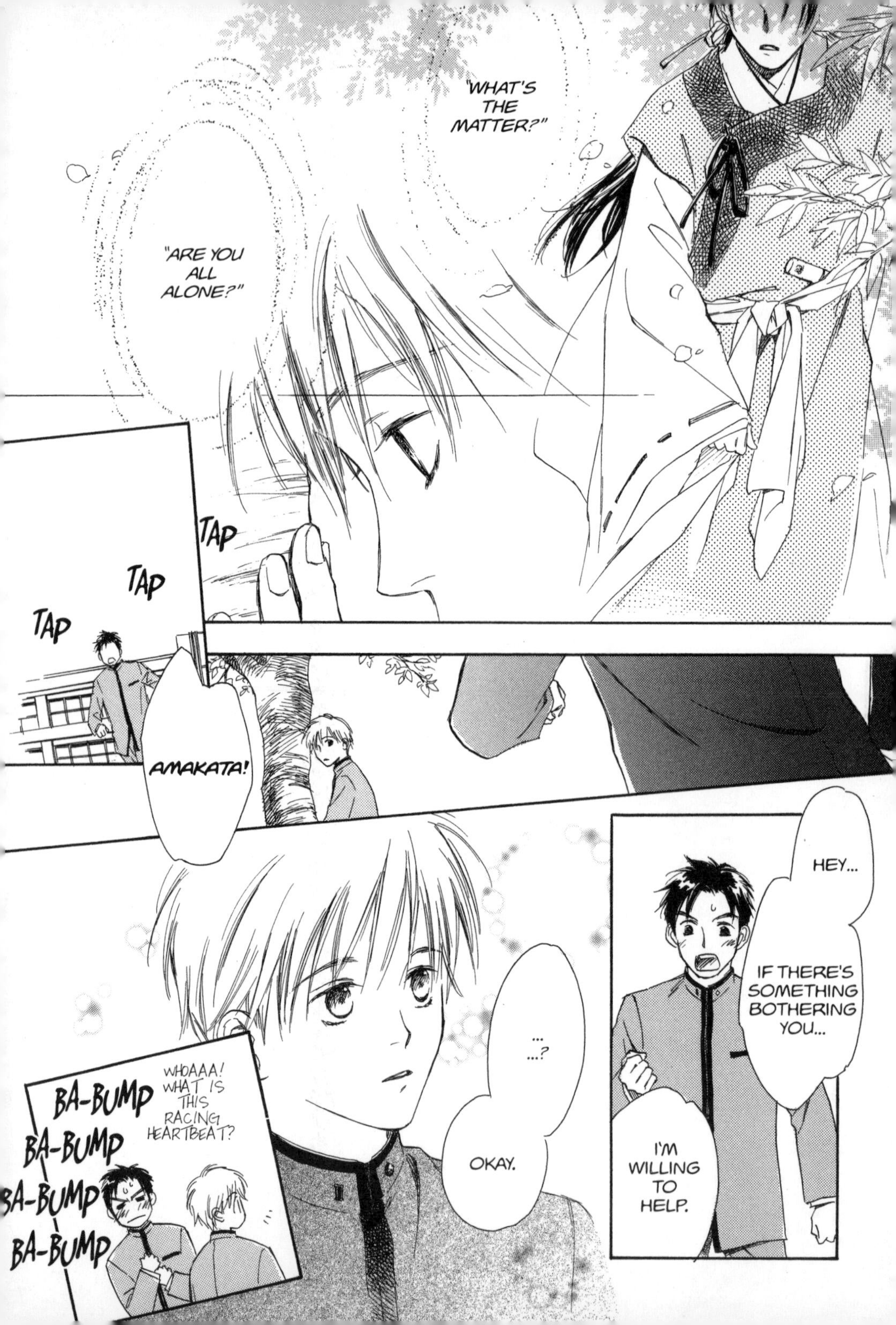
"WHAT'S THE MATTER?"
"ARE YOU ALL ALONE?"
TAP
TAP
TAP
AMAKATA!
HEY...
IF THERE'S SOMETHING BOTHERING YOU...
I'M WILLING TO HELP.
... ...?
OKAY.
BA-BUMP
BA-BUMP
BA-BUMP
BA-BUMP
WHOAAA! WHAT IS THIS RACING HEARTBEAT?

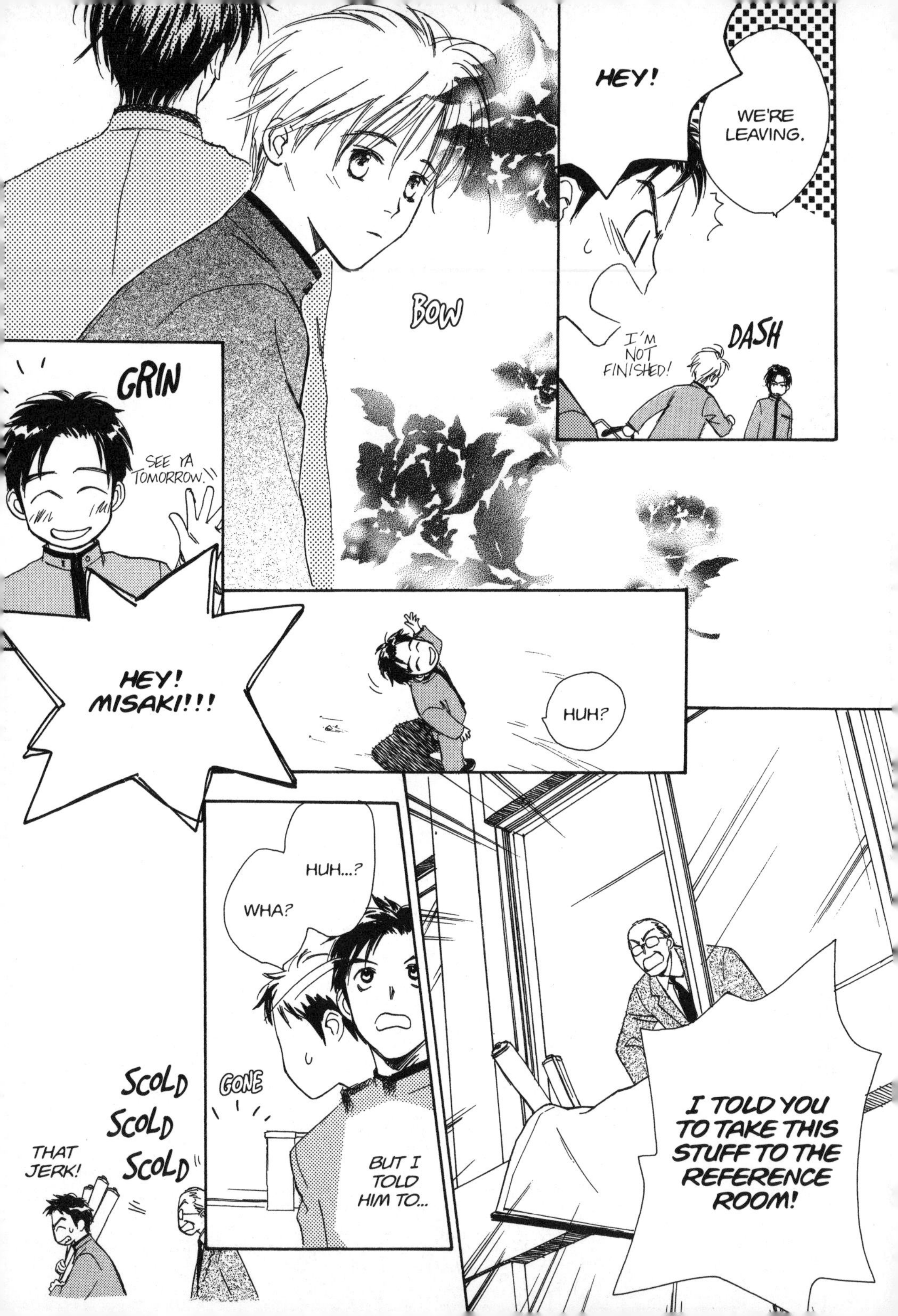
HEY!
WE'RE LEAVING.
DASH
I'M NOT FINISHED!
BOW
GRIN
SEE YA TOMORROW.
HEY! MISAKI!!!
HUH?
I TOLD YOU TO TAKE THIS STUFF TO THE REFERENCE ROOM!
HUH...?
WHA?
GONE
BUT I TOLD HIM TO...
SCOLD
SCOLD
SCOLD
THAT JERK!

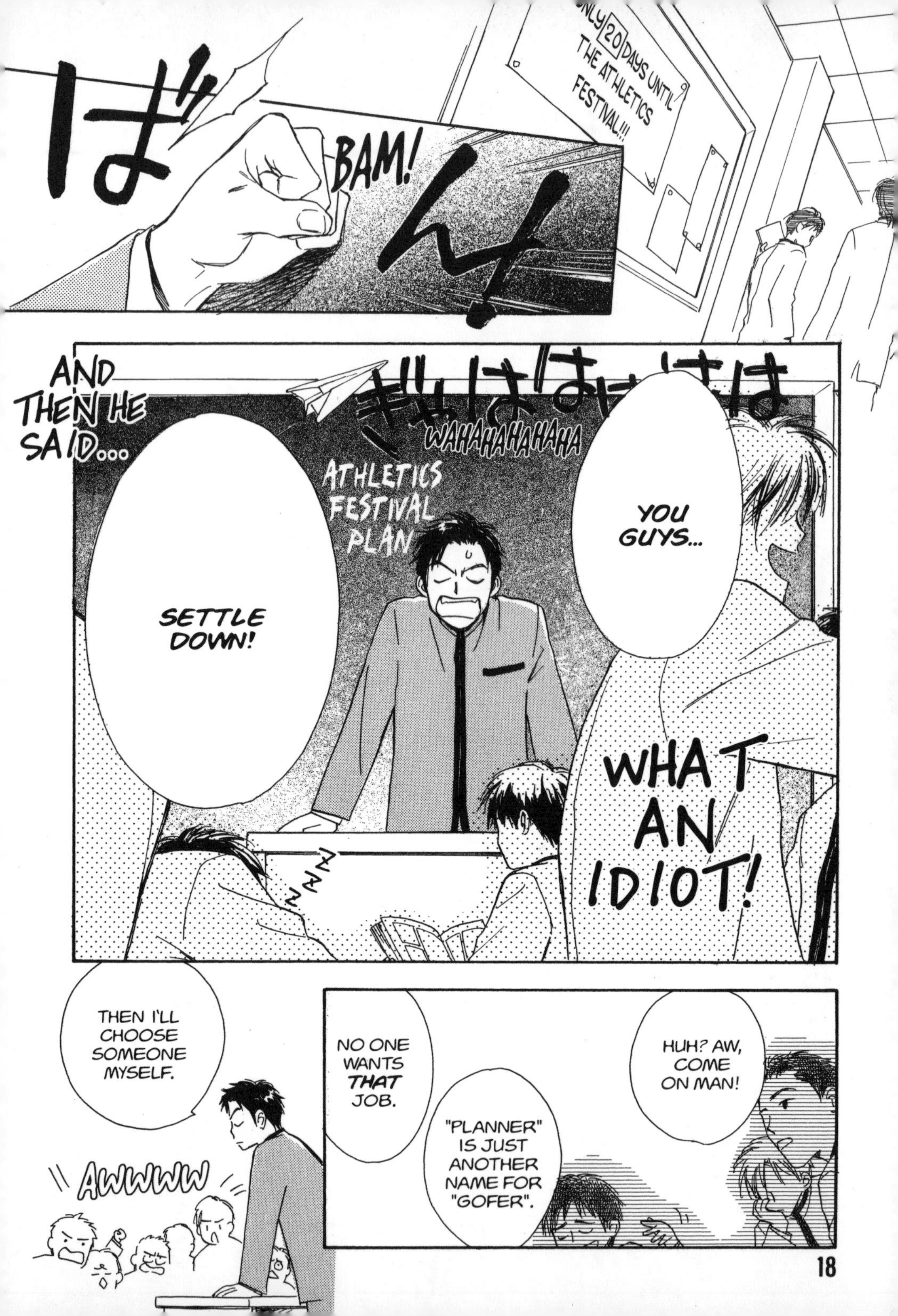
ONLY 20 DAYS UNTIL THE ATHLETICS FESTIVAL!!!
ばん
BAM!
AND THEN HE SAID...
YOU GUYS...
SETTLE DOWN!
WAHAHAHAHAHA
ATHLETICS FESTIVAL PLAN
WHAT AN IDIOT!
HUH? AW, COME ON MAN!
NO ONE WANTS THAT JOB.
"PLANNER" IS JUST ANOTHER NAME FOR "GOFER".
THEN I'LL CHOOSE SOMEONE MYSELF.
AWWWW

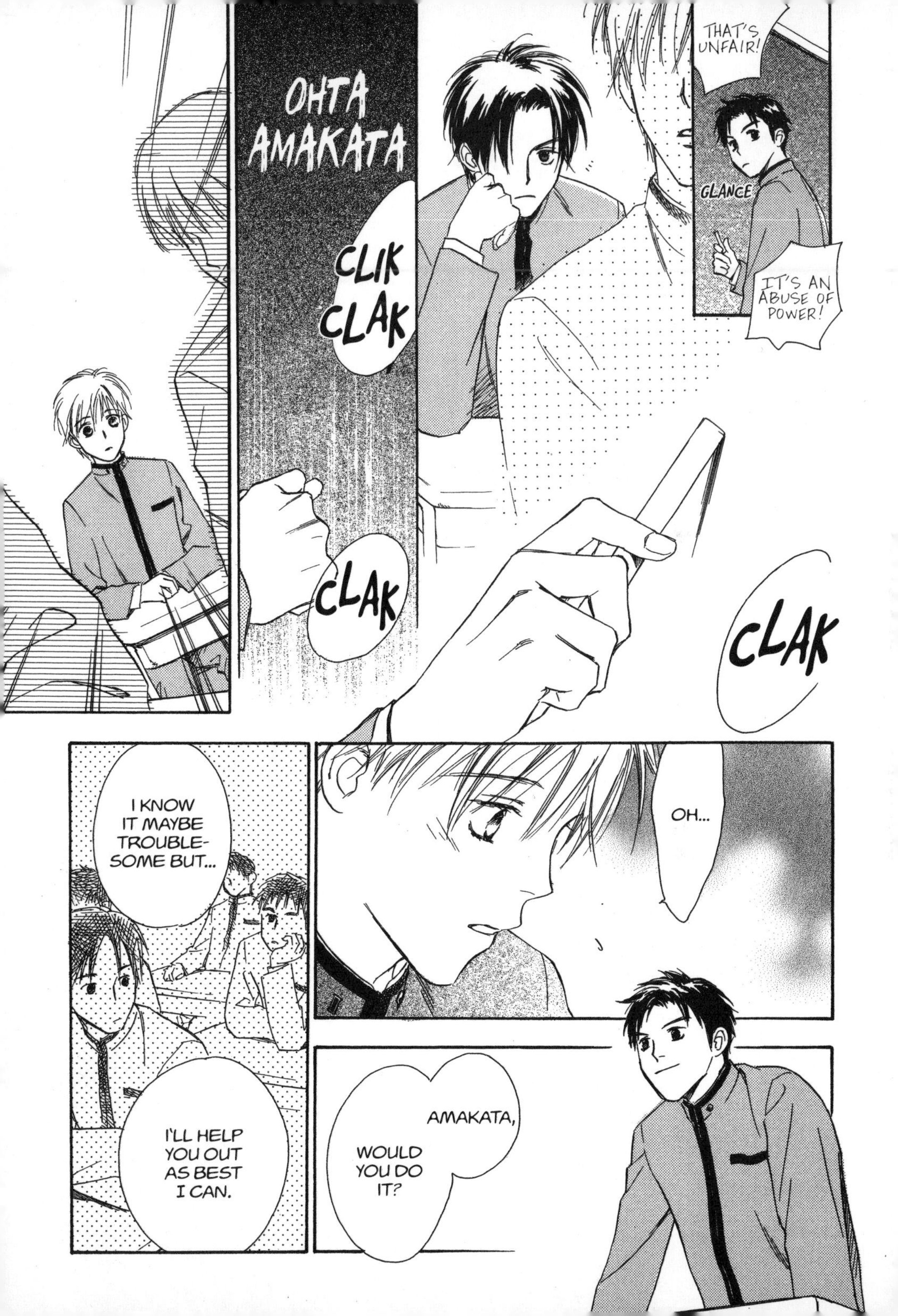
THAT'S UNFAIR!
GLANCE
IT'S AN ABUSE OF POWER!
CLAK
OHTA AMAKATA
CLIK CLAK
CLAK
OH...
AMAKATA,
WOULD YOU DO IT?
I KNOW IT MAYBE TROUBLE-SOME BUT...
I'LL HELP YOU OUT AS BEST I CAN.

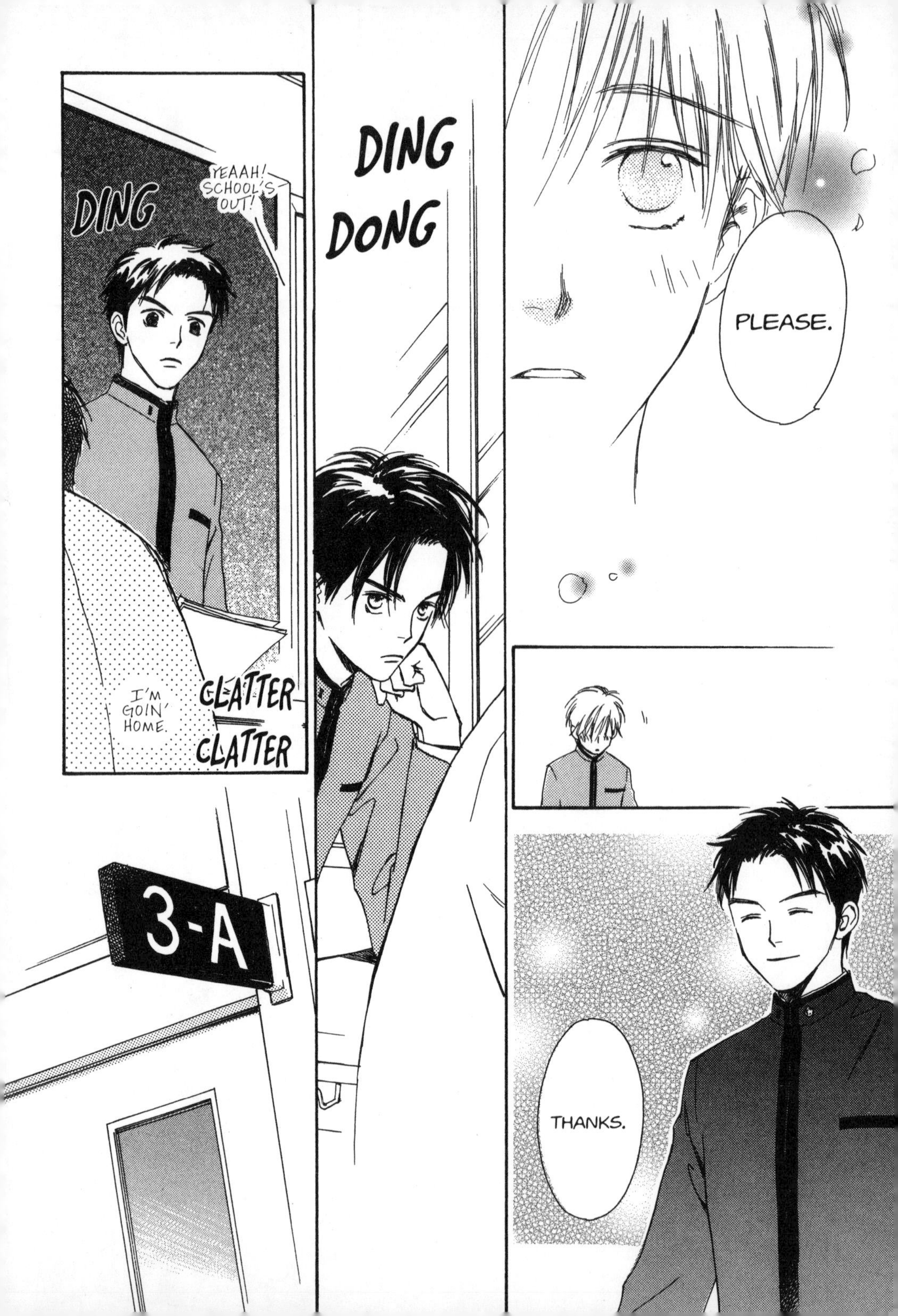
PLEASE.
THANKS.
DING
DONG
DING
YEAAH! SCHOOL'S OUT!
CLATTER
CLATTER
I'M GOIN' HOME.
3-A

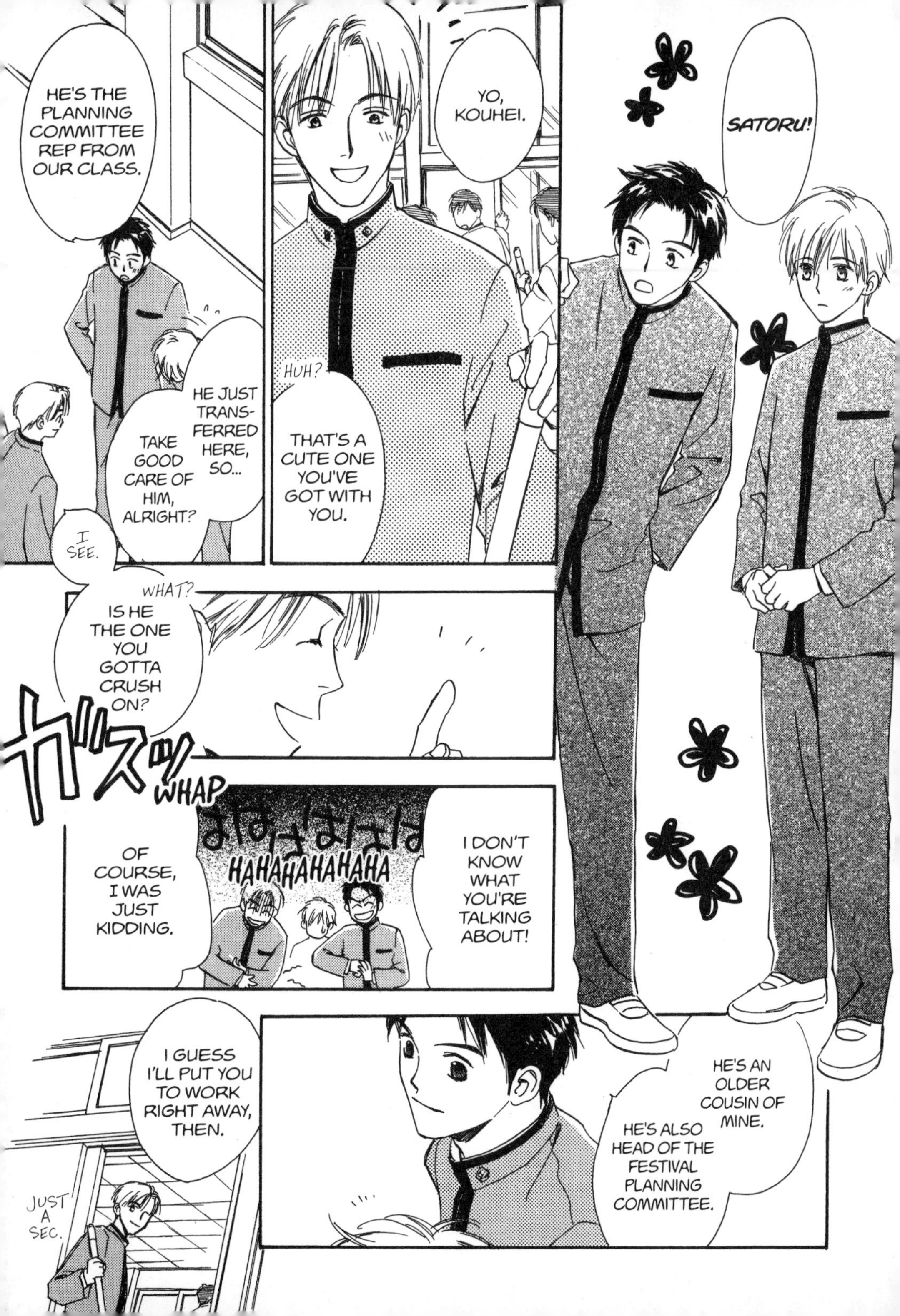
SATORU!
YO, KOUHEI.
HUH?
THAT'S A CUTE ONE YOU'VE GOT WITH YOU.
HE'S THE PLANNING COMMITTEE REP FROM OUR CLASS.
HE JUST TRANSFERRED HERE, SO...
TAKE GOOD CARE OF HIM, ALRIGHT?
I SEE.
WHAT?
IS HE THE ONE YOU GOTTA CRUSH ON?
ガスッ
WHAP
HAHAHAHAHAHA
I DON'T KNOW WHAT YOU'RE TALKING ABOUT!
OF COURSE, I WAS JUST KIDDING.
HE'S AN OLDER COUSIN OF MINE.
HE'S ALSO HEAD OF THE FESTIVAL PLANNING COMMITTEE.
I GUESS I'LL PUT YOU TO WORK RIGHT AWAY, THEN.
JUST A SEC.

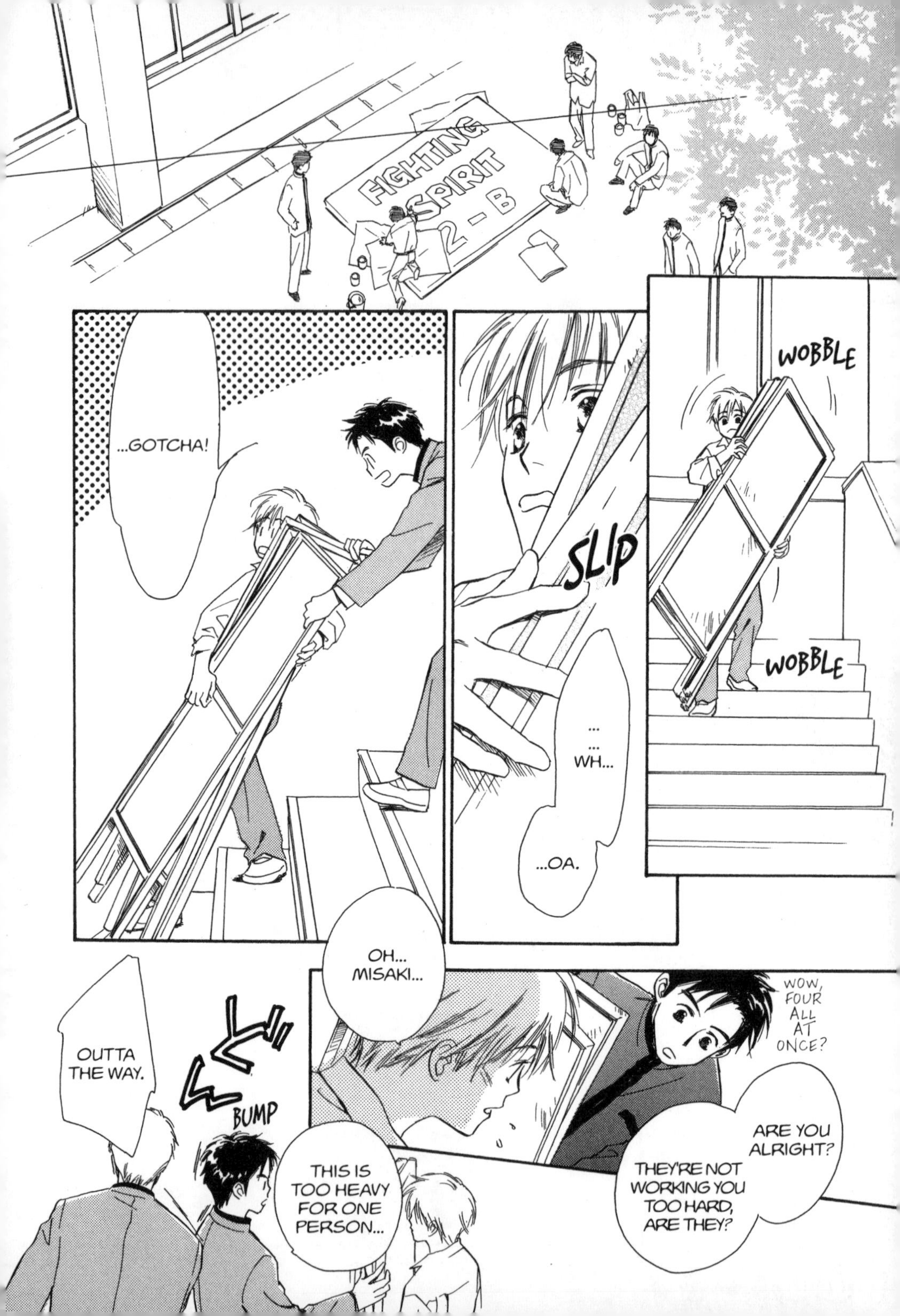
FIGHTING SPIRIT 2 - B
WOBBLE
WOBBLE
SLIP
...
...
WH...
...OA.
...GOTCHA!
OH... MISAKI...
WOW, FOUR ALL AT ONCE?
ARE YOU ALRIGHT?
THEY'RE NOT WORKING YOU TOO HARD, ARE THEY?
OUTTA THE WAY.
BUMP
THIS IS TOO HEAVY FOR ONE PERSON...

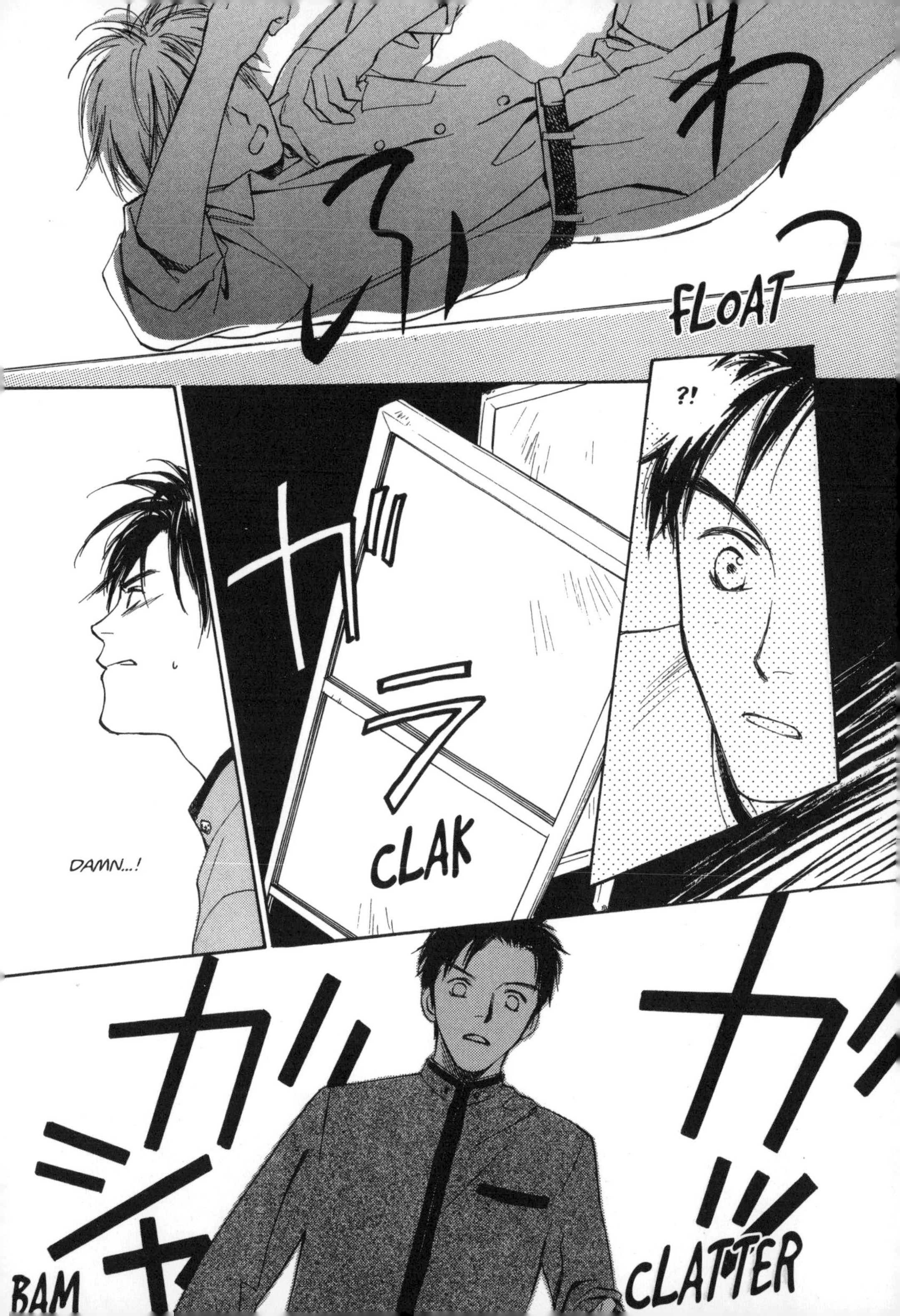
ふわっ
FLOAT
?!
ガラ
CLAK
DAMN...!
ガッ
CLATTER
ガシャ
BAM

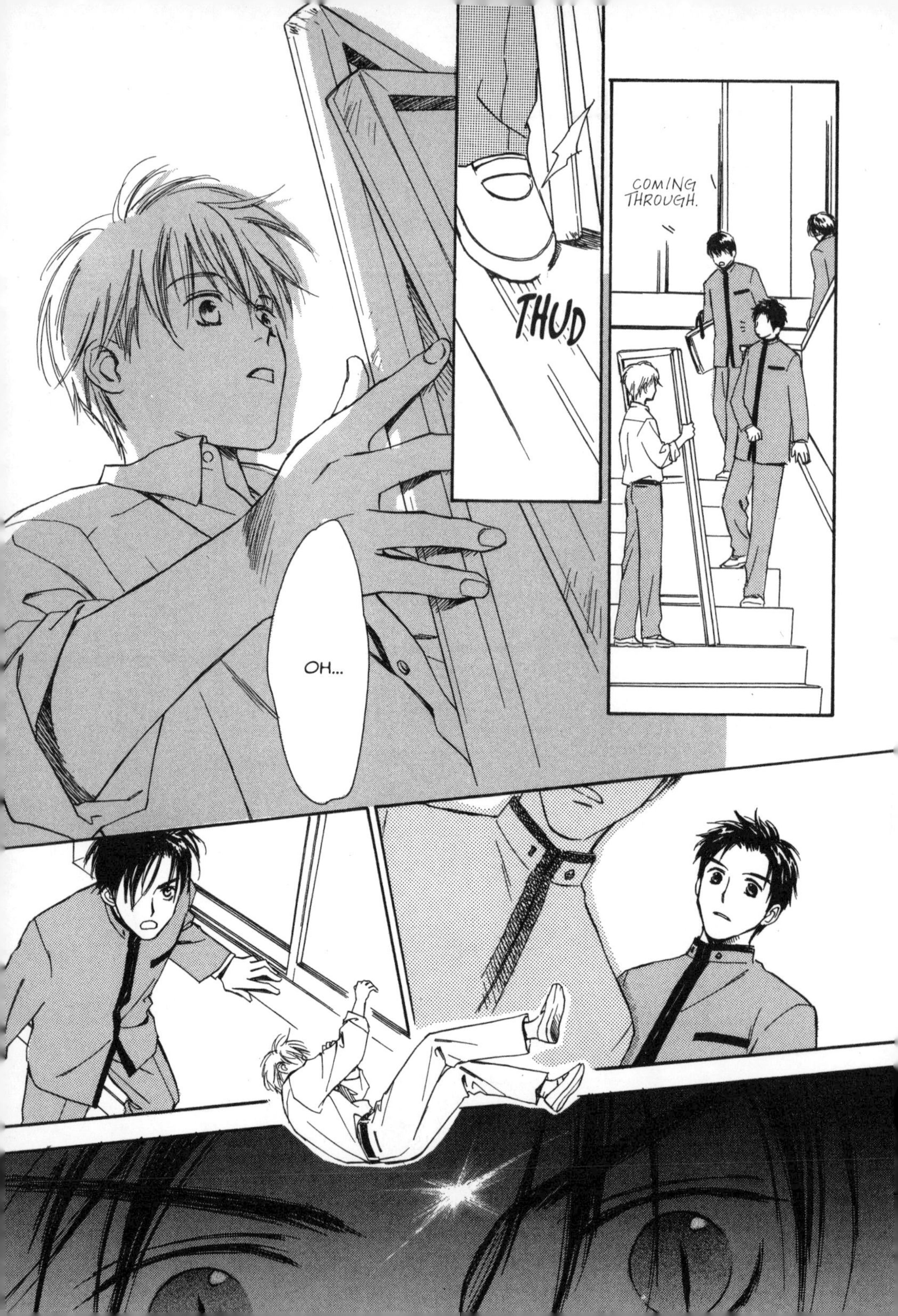
COMING THROUGH.
THUD
OH...

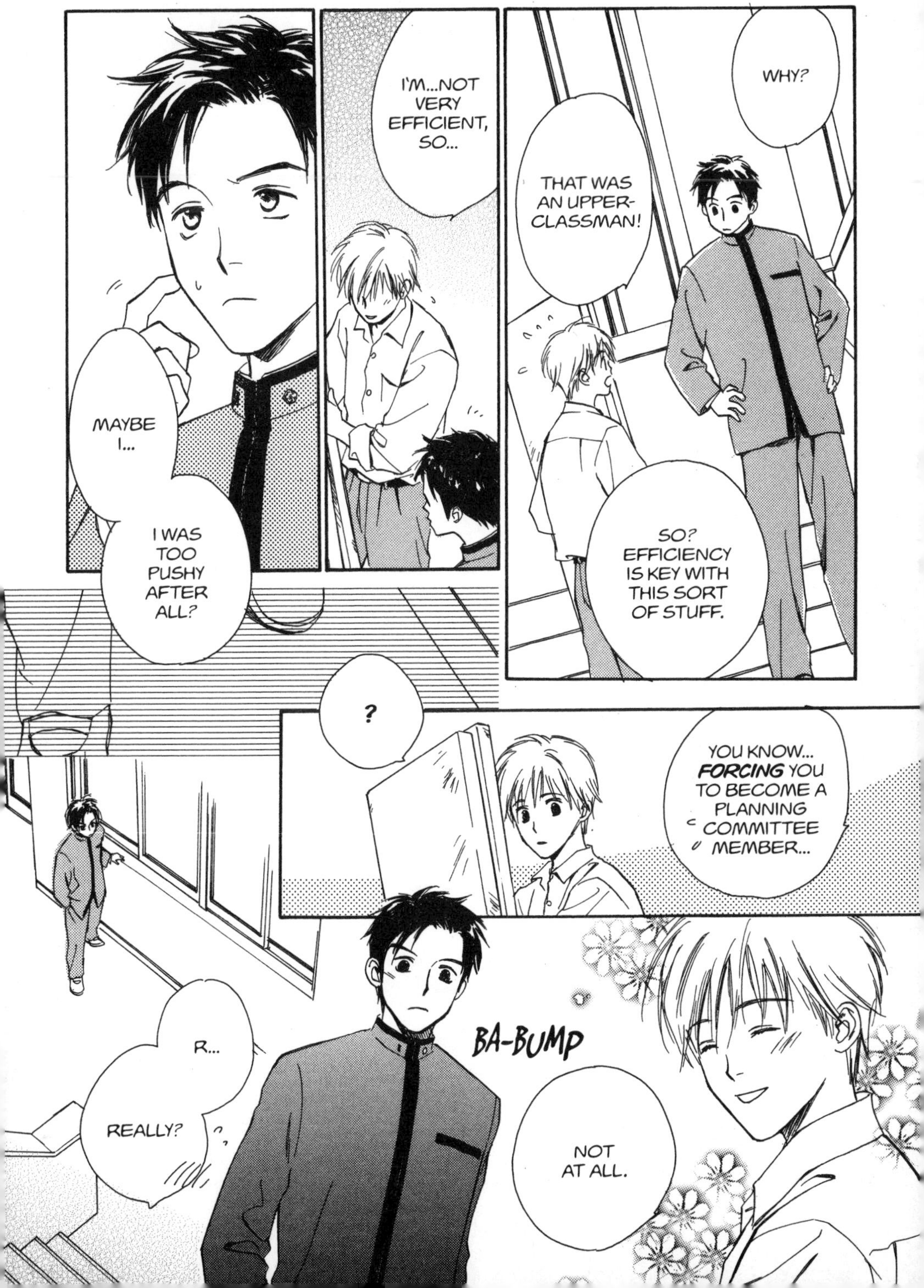
WHY?
THAT WAS AN UPPER-CLASSMAN!
SO? EFFICIENCY IS KEY WITH THIS SORT OF STUFF.
I'M...NOT VERY EFFICIENT, SO...
MAYBE I...
I WAS TOO PUSHY AFTER ALL?
YOU KNOW... **FORCING** YOU TO BECOME A PLANNING COMMITTEE MEMBER...
?
NOT AT ALL.
BA-BUMP
R...
REALLY?

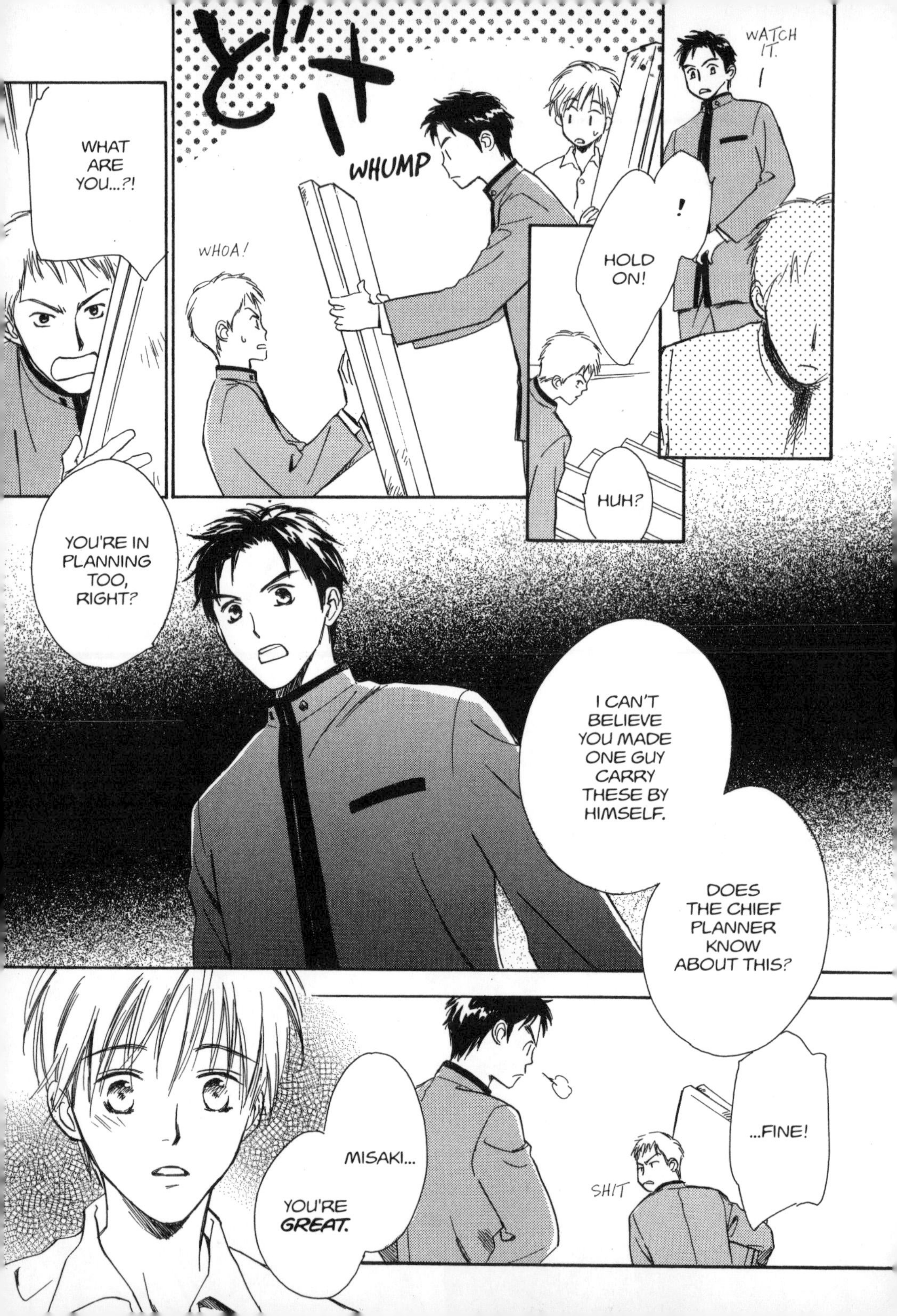
WATCH IT.
!
HOLD ON!
どけ
WHUMP
WHOA!
HUH?
WHAT ARE YOU...?!
YOU'RE IN PLANNING TOO, RIGHT?
I CAN'T BELIEVE YOU MADE ONE GUY CARRY THESE BY HIMSELF.
DOES THE CHIEF PLANNER KNOW ABOUT THIS?
...FINE!
SHIT
MISAKI...
YOU'RE **GREAT.**

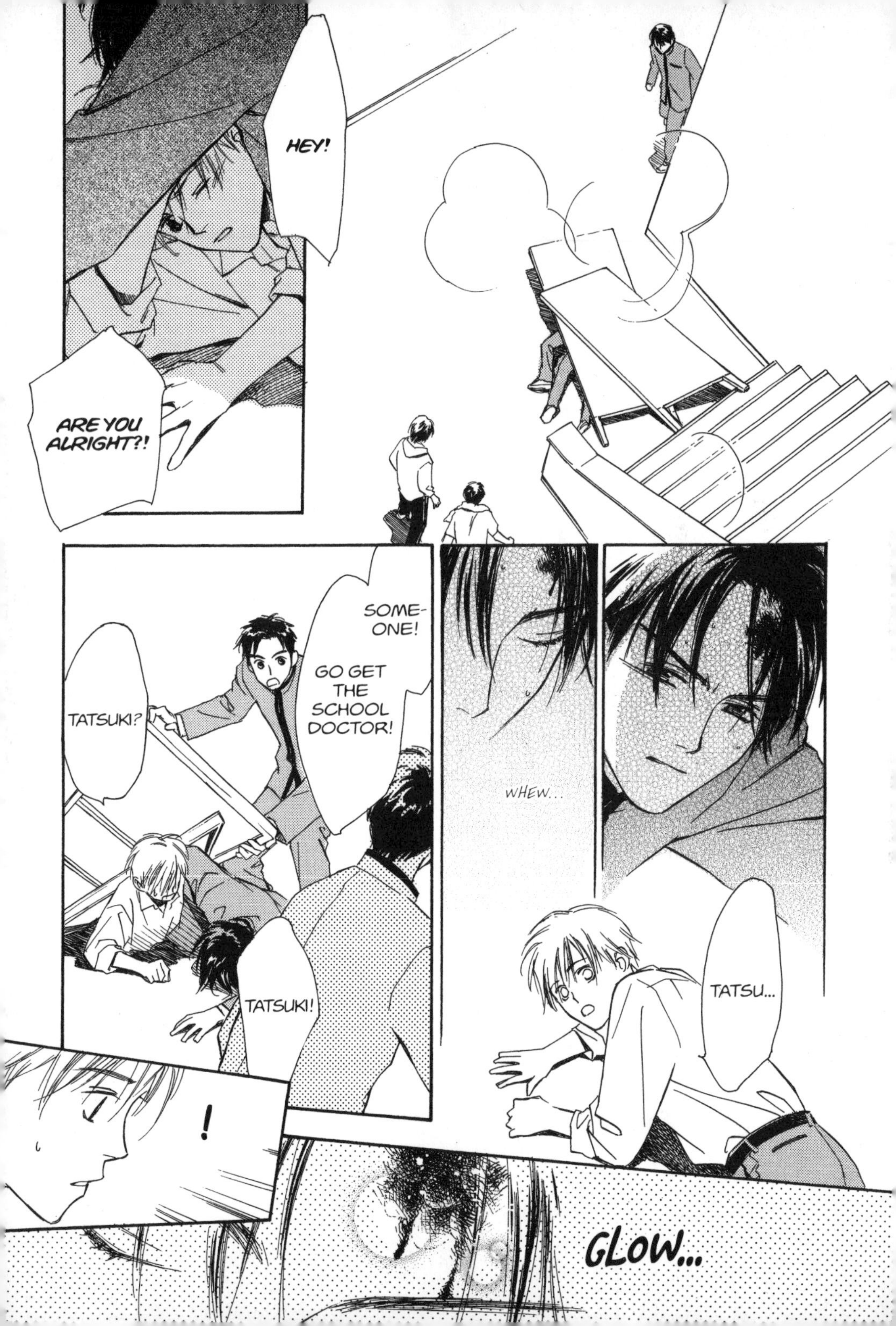
HEY!
ARE YOU ALRIGHT?!
WHEW...
SOME-ONE!
GO GET THE SCHOOL DOCTOR!
TATSUKI?
TATSUKI!
TATSU...
!
GLOW...

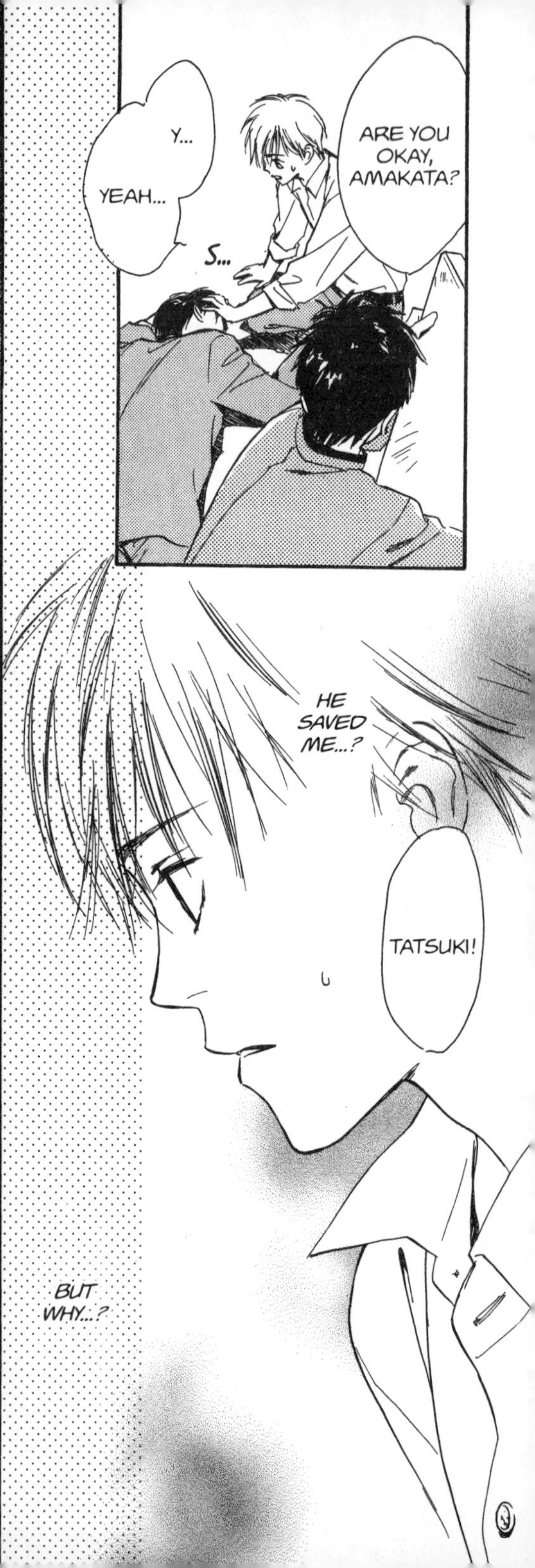
ARE YOU OKAY, AMAKATA?
Y...
YEAH...
S...
HE SAVED ME...?
TATSUKI!
BUT WHY...?
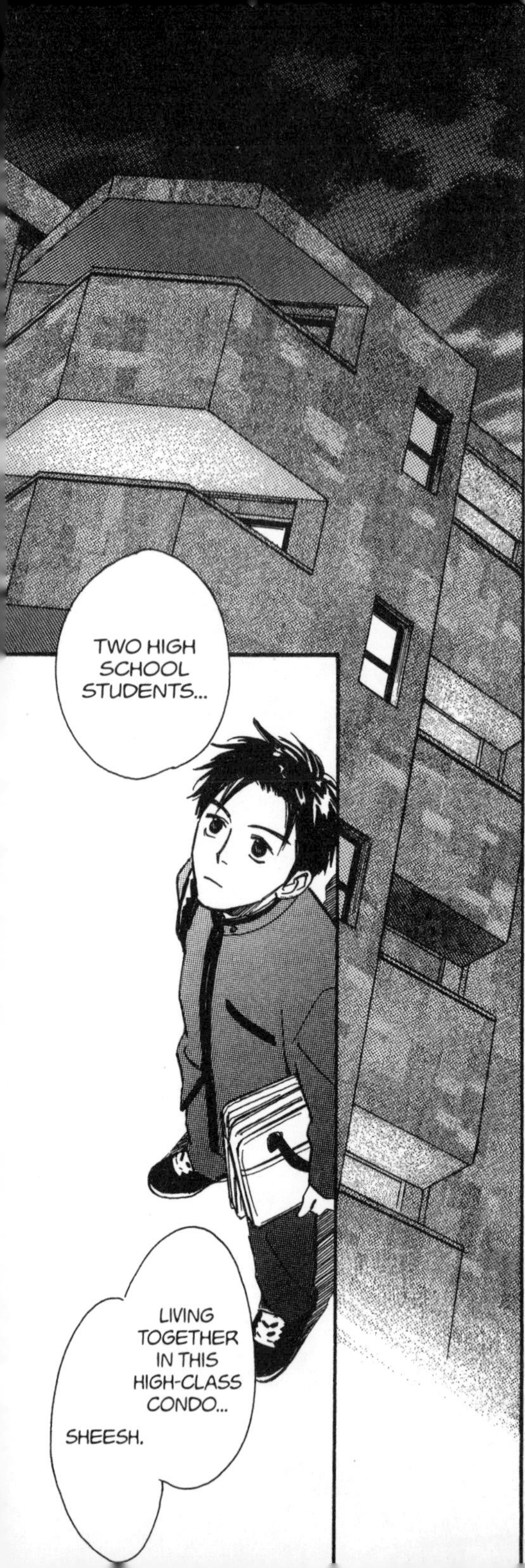
TWO HIGH SCHOOL STUDENTS...
LIVING TOGETHER IN THIS HIGH-CLASS CONDO...
SHEESH.

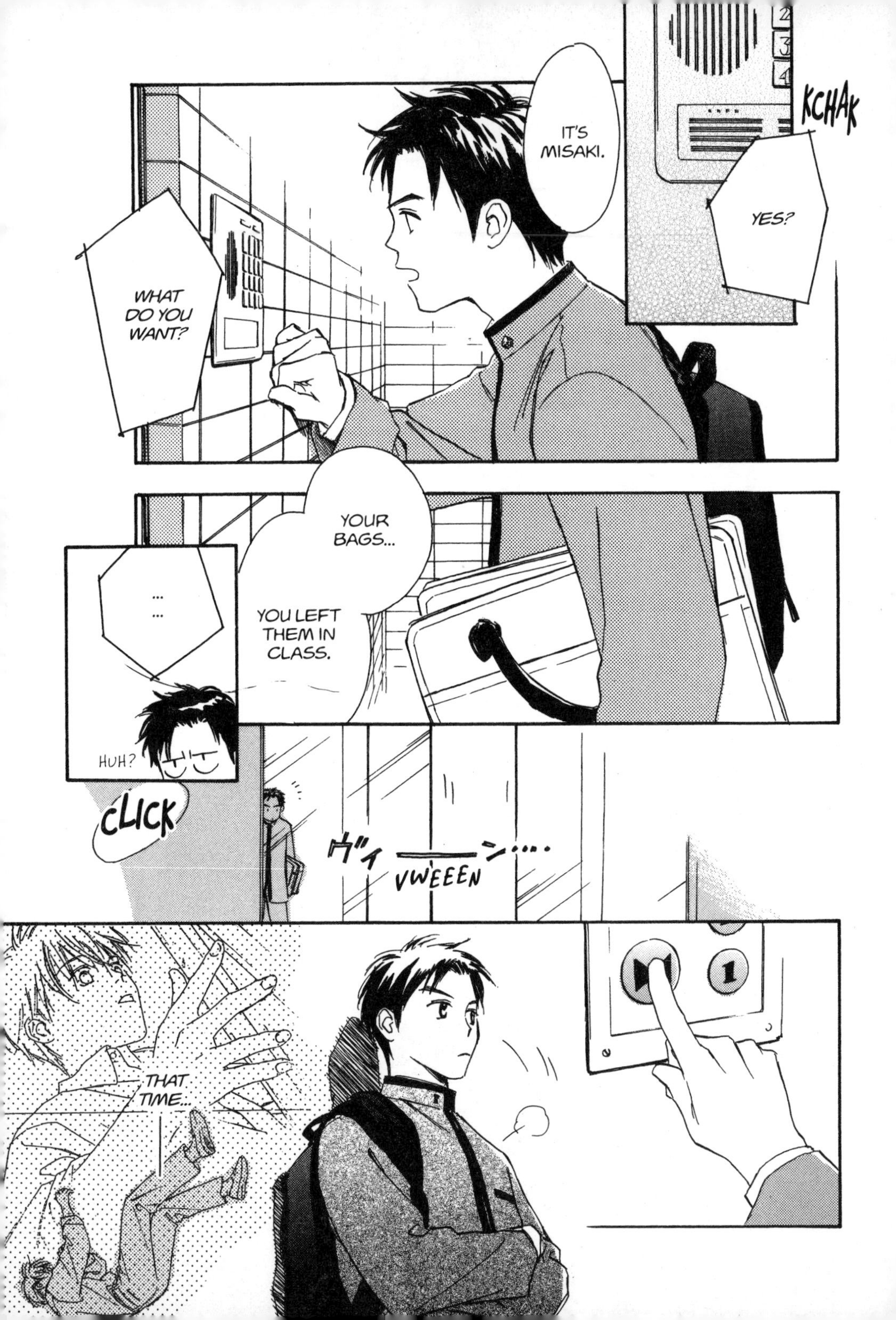
KCHAK
YES?
IT'S MISAKI.
WHAT DO YOU WANT?
YOUR BAGS...
YOU LEFT THEM IN CLASS.
... ...
HUH?
CLICK
ヴィーン・・・・
VWEEEN
THAT TIME...

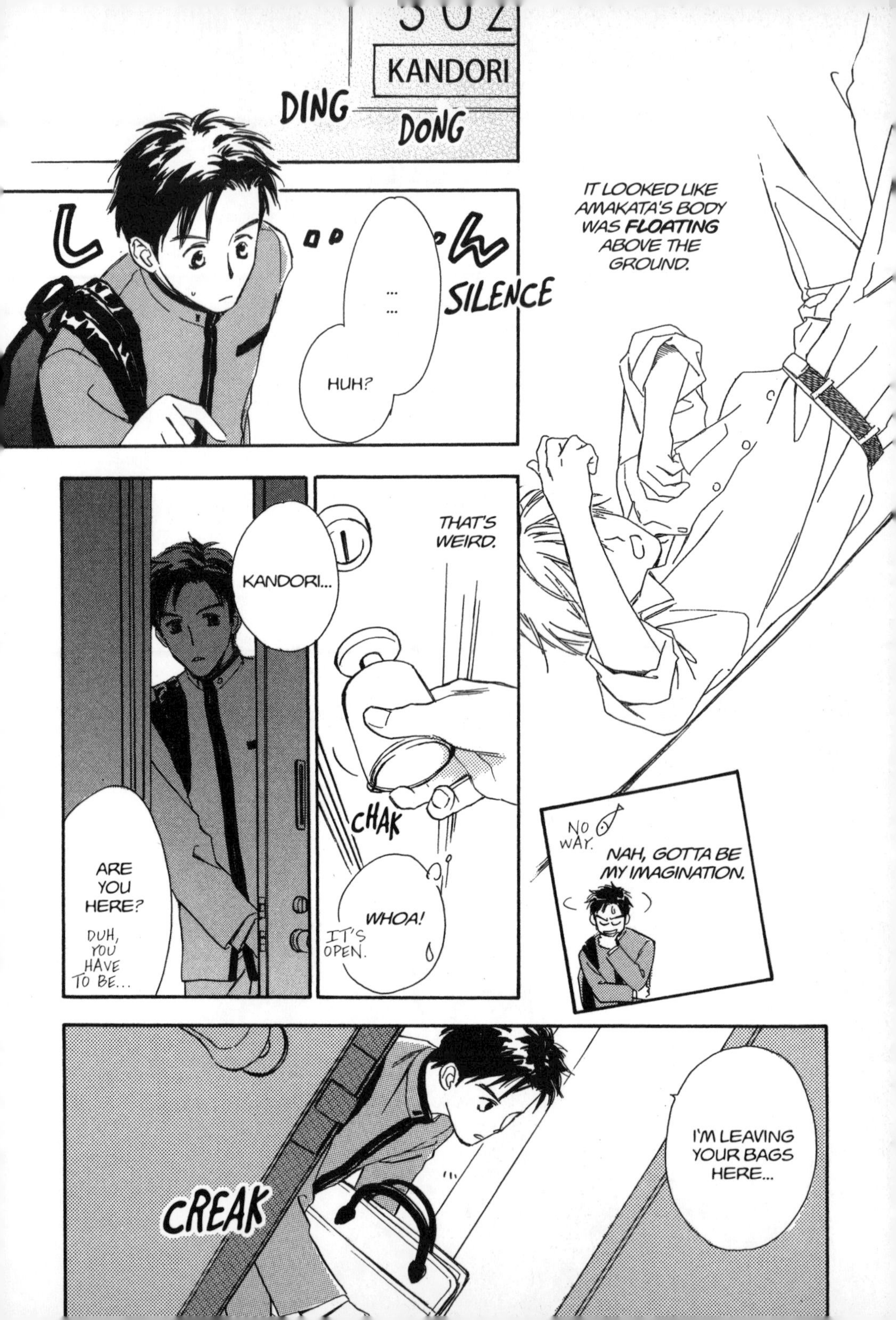

IT LOOKED LIKE AMAKATA'S BODY WAS **FLOATING** ABOVE THE GROUND.
302
KANDORI
DING
DONG
SILENCE
... ...
HUH?
THAT'S WEIRD.
CHAK
WHOA!
IT'S OPEN.
KANDORI...
ARE YOU HERE?
DUH, YOU HAVE TO BE...
NO WAY.
NAH, GOTTA BE MY IMAGINATION.
I'M LEAVING YOUR BAGS HERE...
CREAK

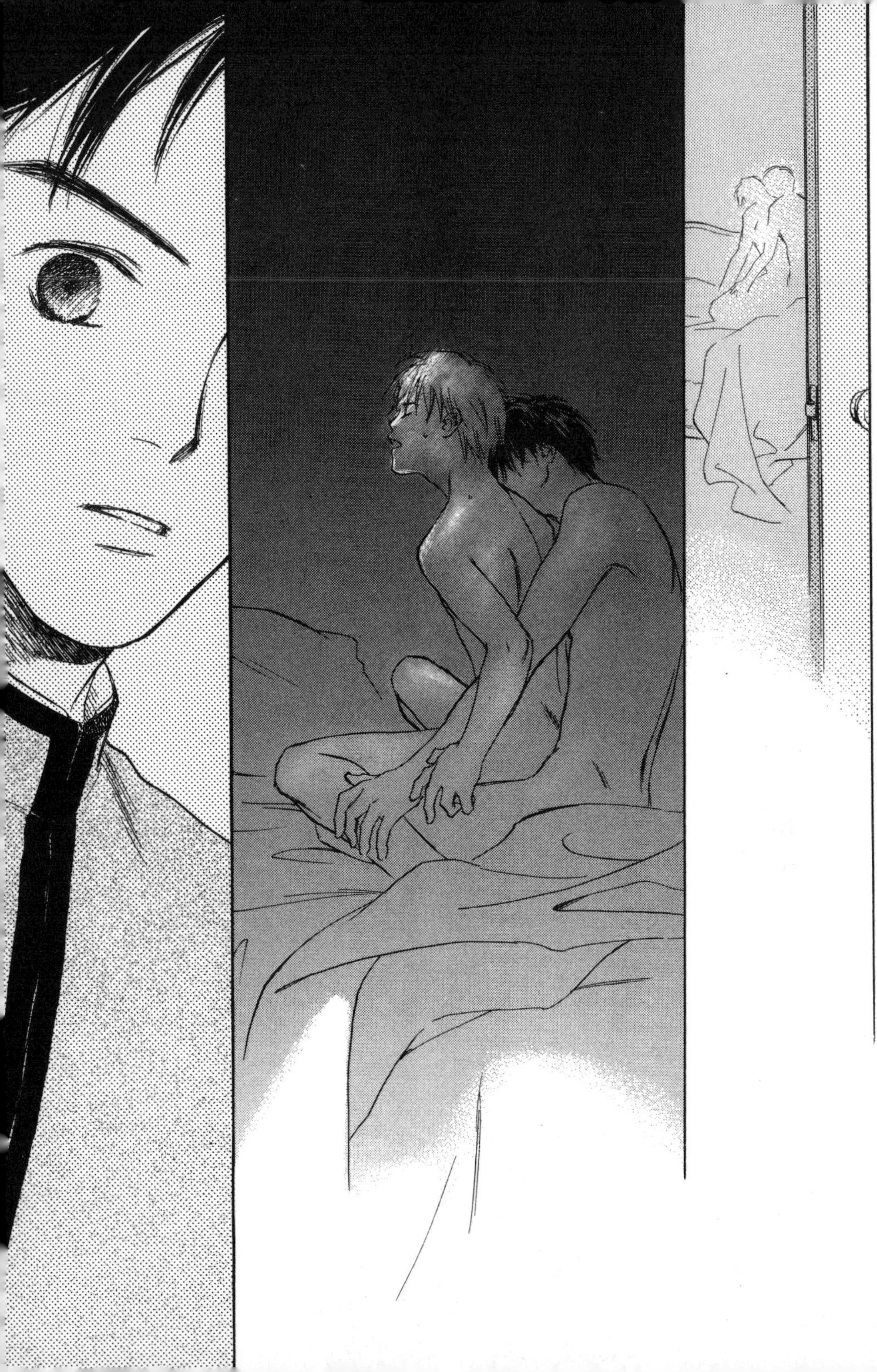

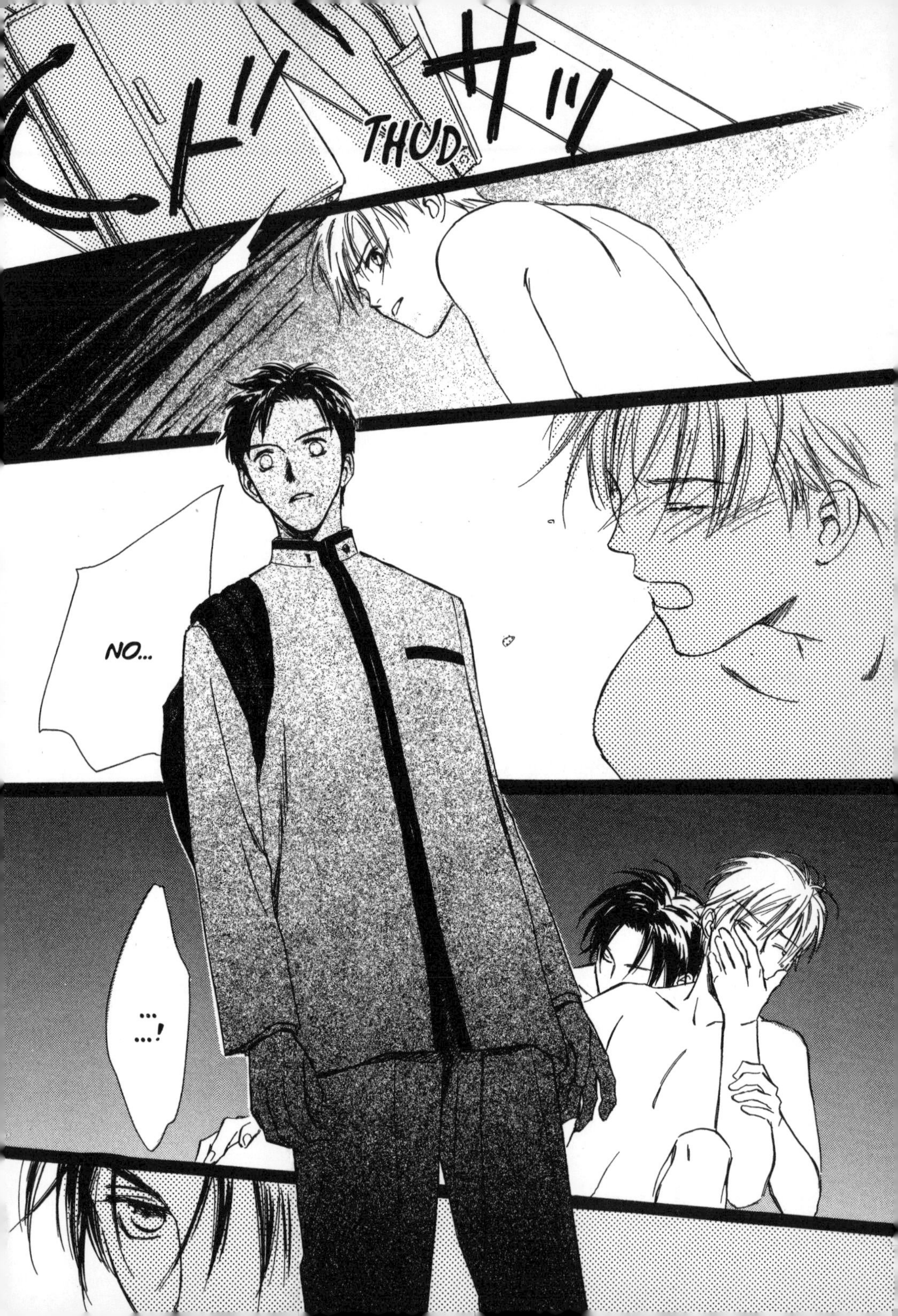

ドサッ
THUD
NO...
...!

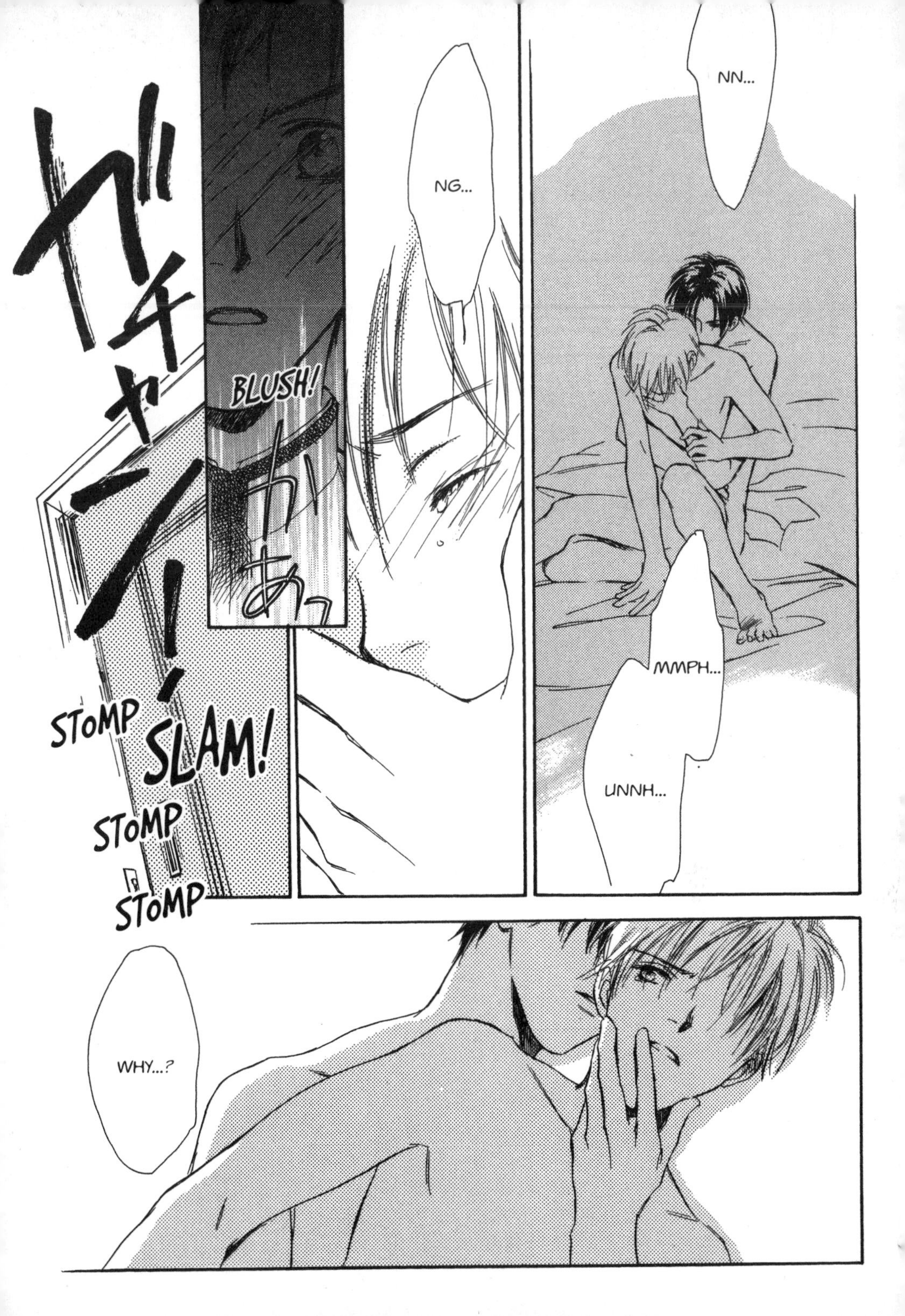
NN...
MMPH...
UNNH...
NG...
BLUSH!
かぁっ
ガチャン!
SLAM!
STOMP
STOMP
STOMP
WHY...?

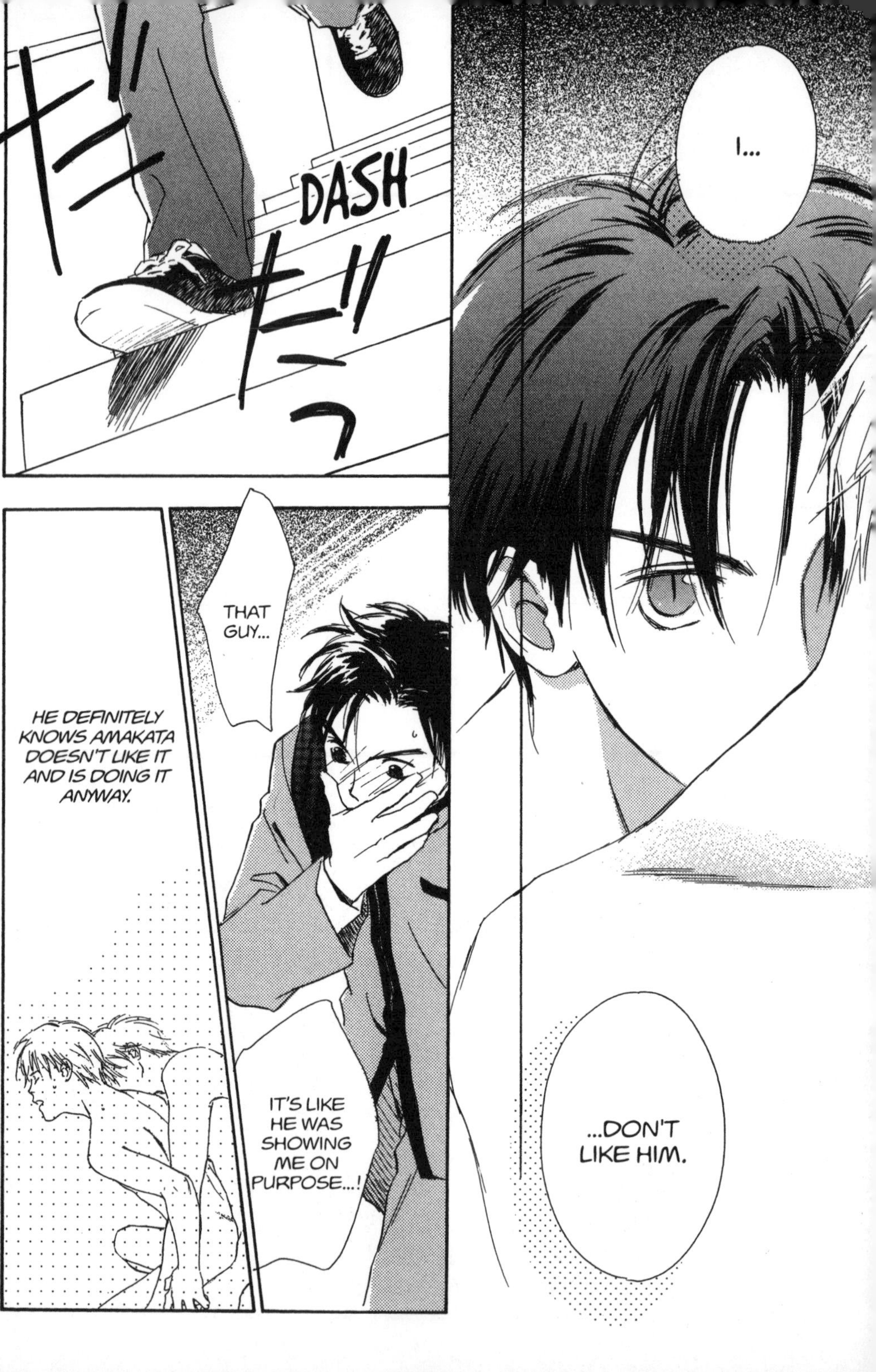
I...
...DON'T LIKE HIM.
DASH
THAT GUY...
IT'S LIKE HE WAS SHOWING ME ON PURPOSE...!
HE DEFINITELY KNOWS AMAKATA DOESN'T LIKE IT AND IS DOING IT ANYWAY.

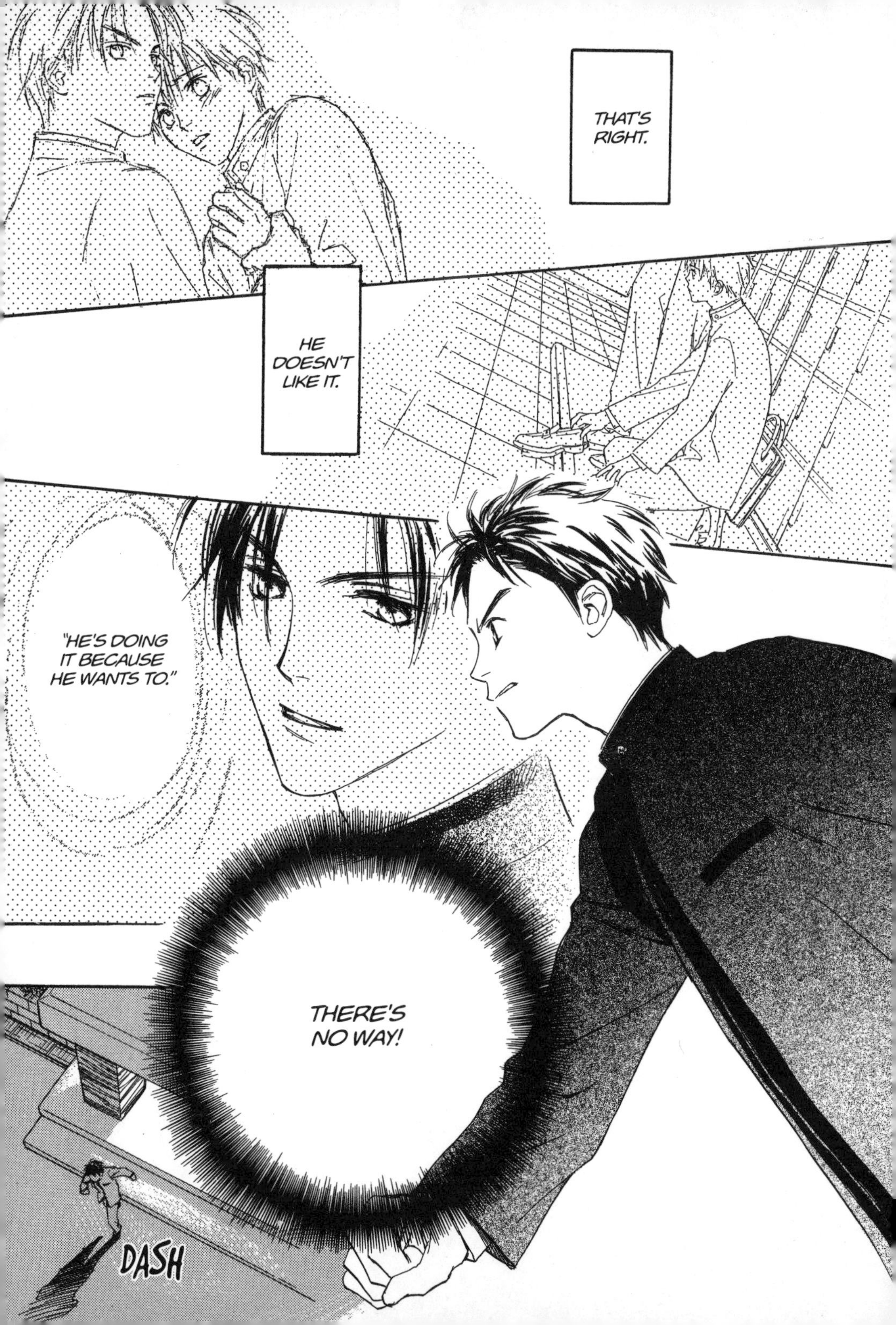
THAT'S RIGHT.
HE DOESN'T LIKE IT.
"HE'S DOING IT BECAUSE HE WANTS TO."
THERE'S NO WAY!
DASH

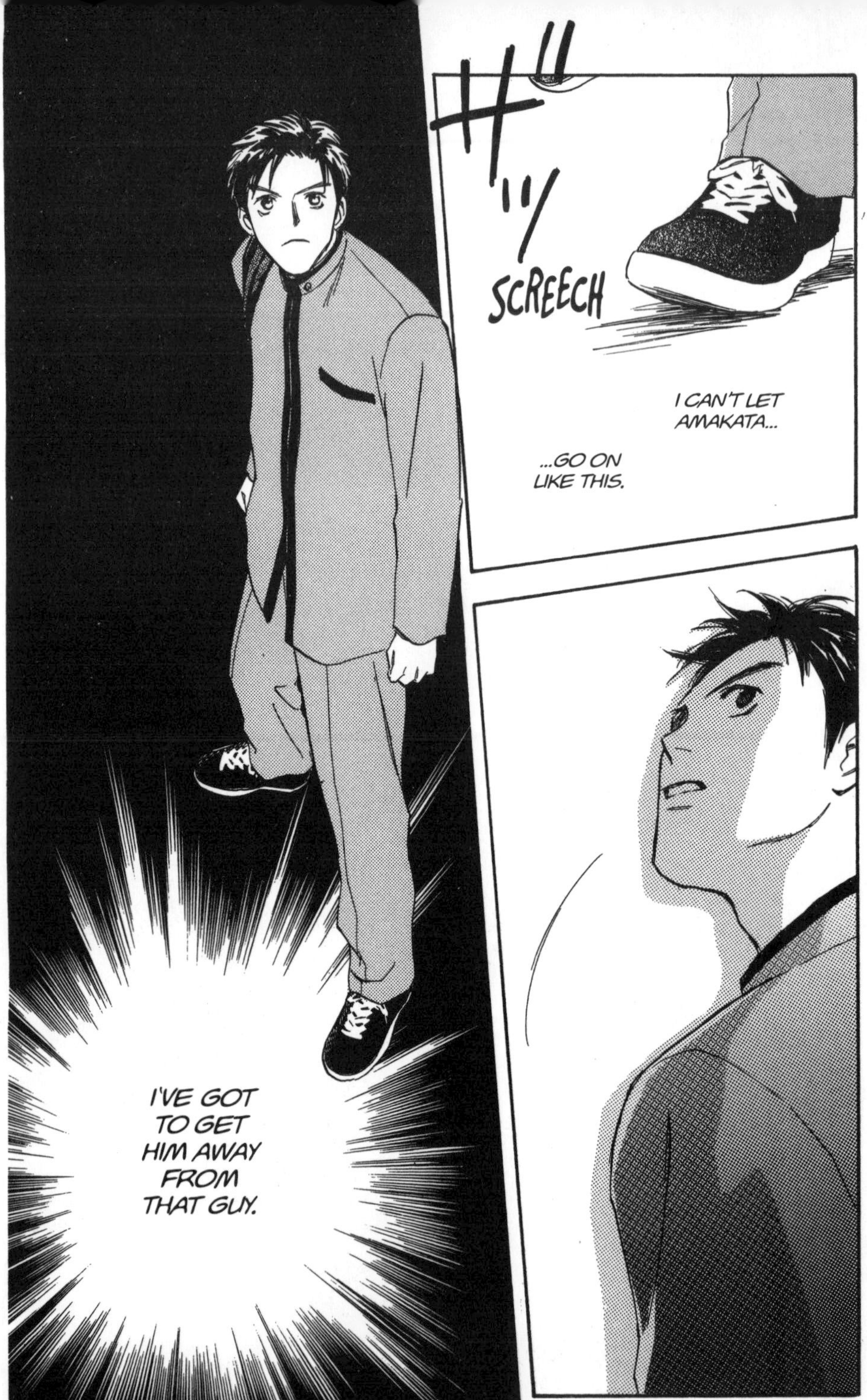
ザッ
SCREECH
I CAN'T LET AMAKATA...
...GO ON LIKE THIS.
I'VE GOT TO GET HIM AWAY FROM THAT GUY.

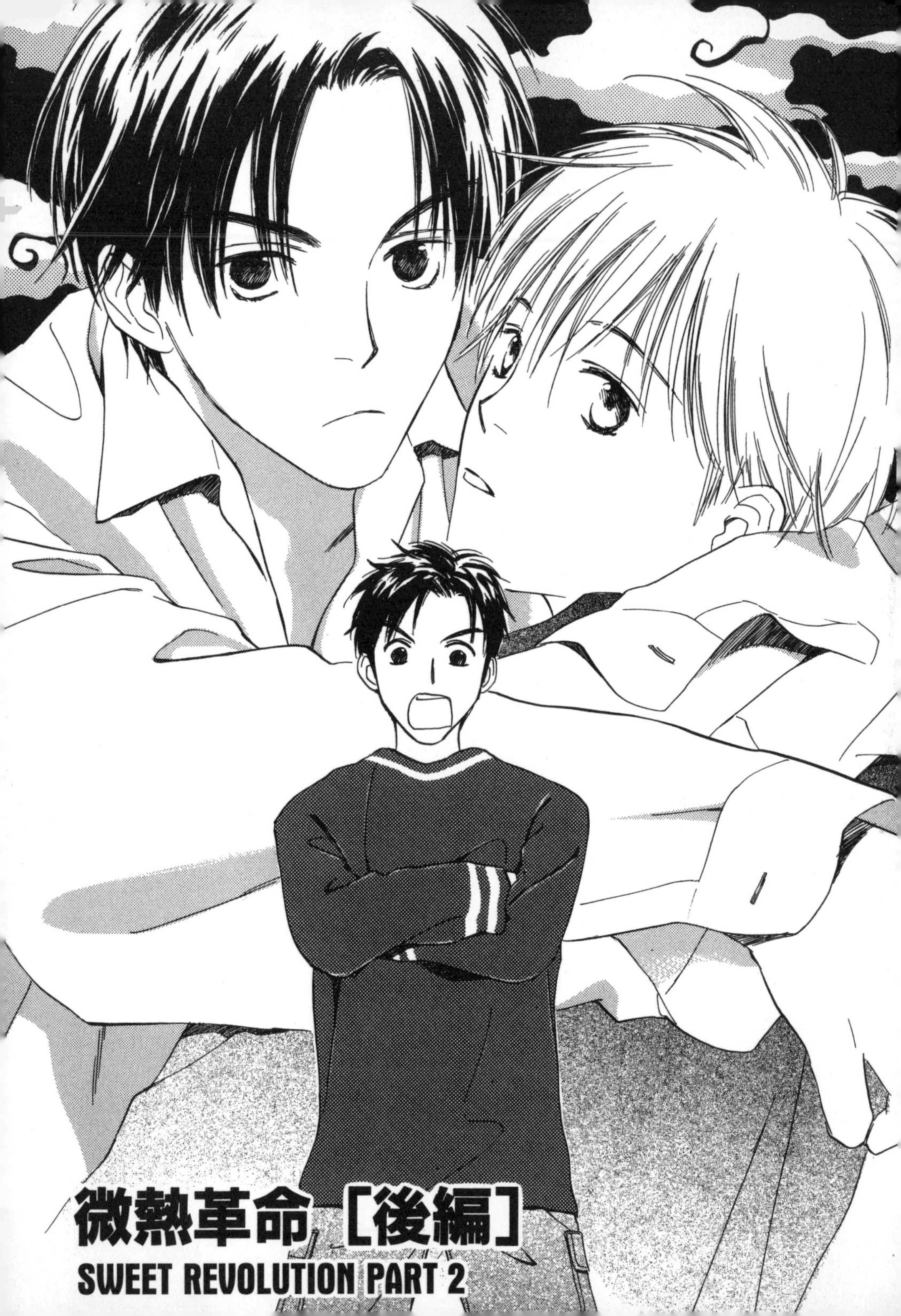

微熱革命［後編］

SWEET REVOLUTION PART 2

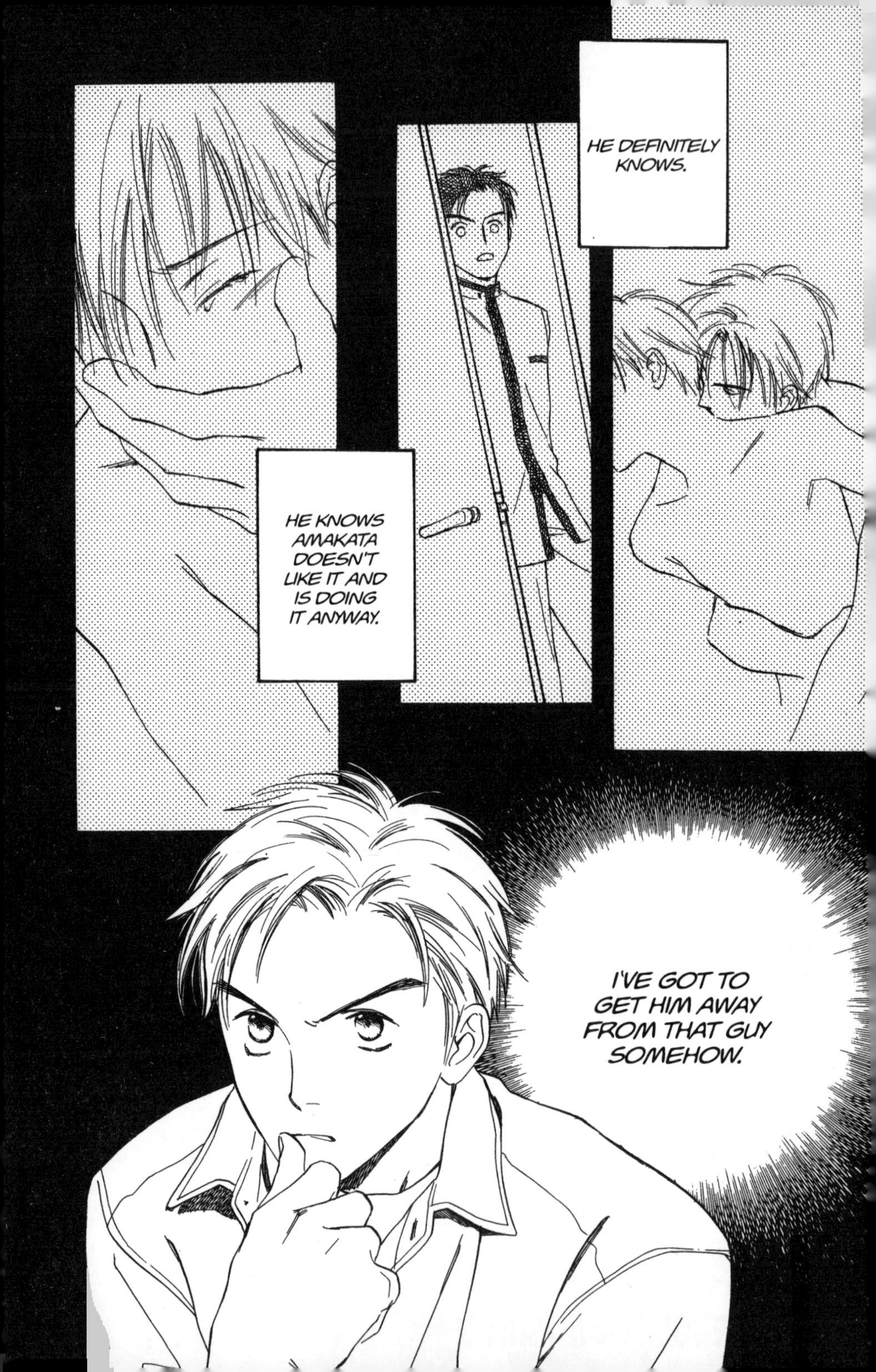
HE DEFINITELY KNOWS.
HE KNOWS AMAKATA DOESN'T LIKE IT AND IS DOING IT ANYWAY.
I'VE GOT TO GET HIM AWAY FROM THAT GUY SOMEHOW.

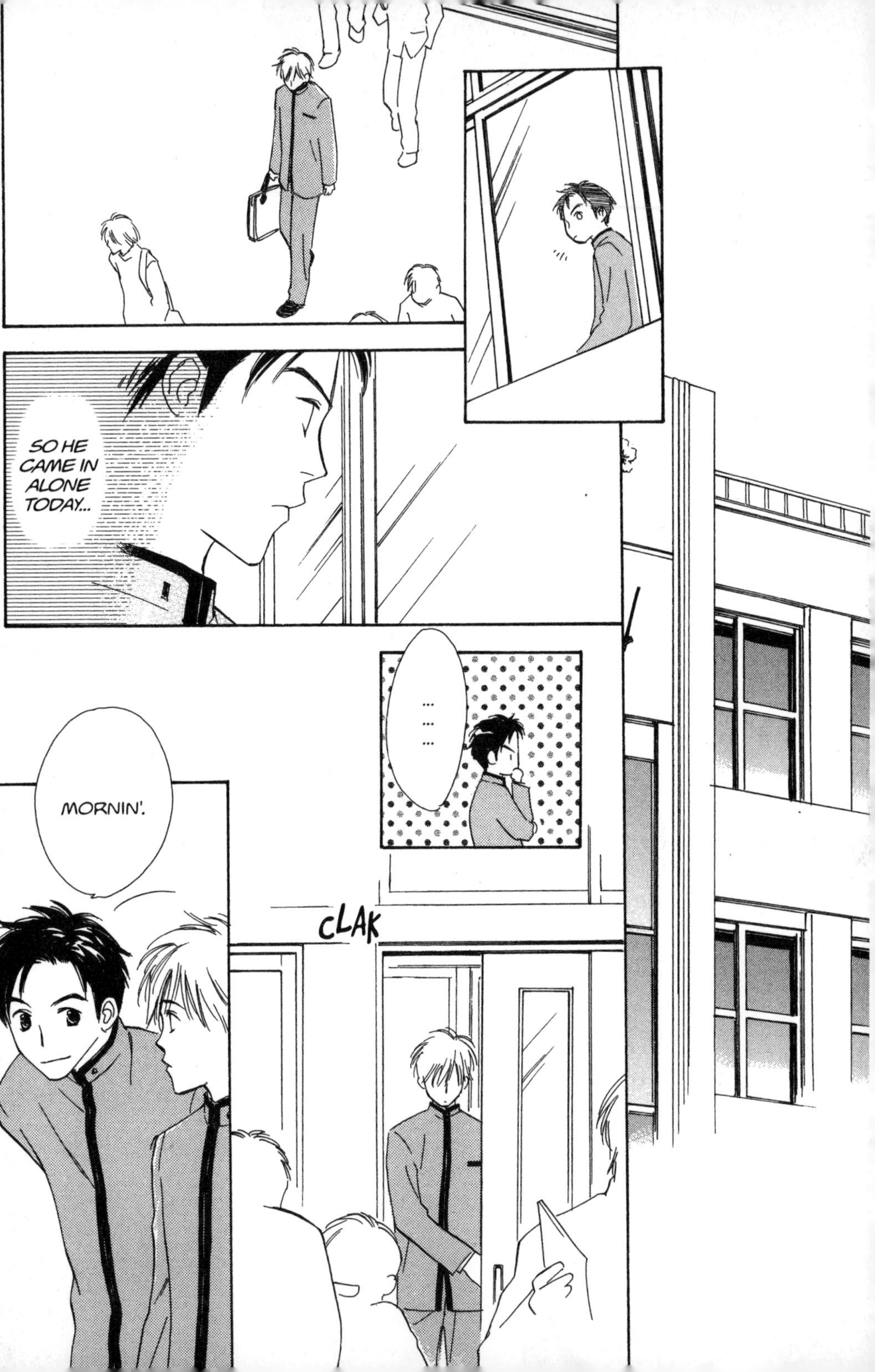
SO HE CAME IN ALONE TODAY...
... ...
CLAK
MORNIN'.

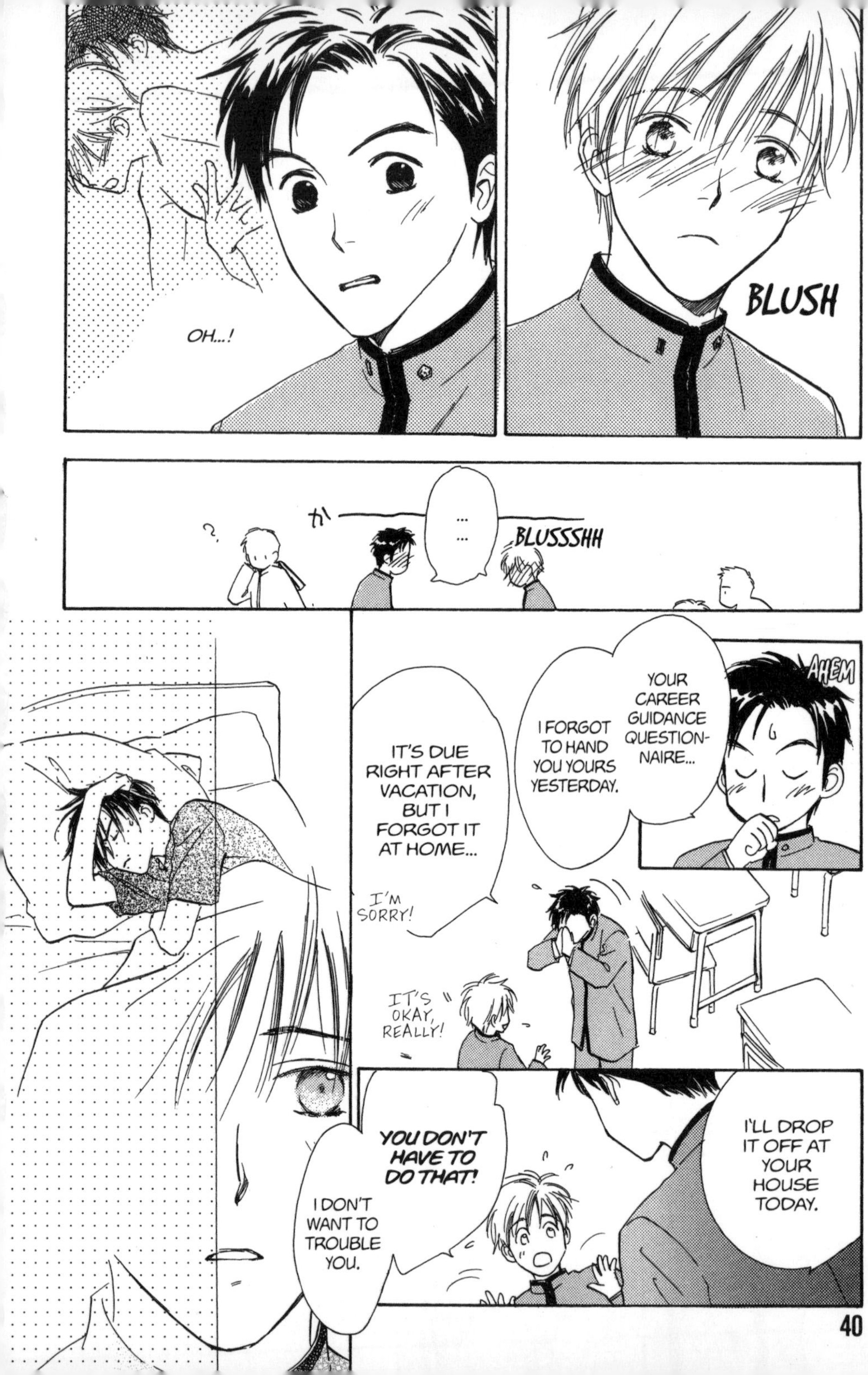
BLUSH
OH...!
BLUSSSHH
... ...
か
?
AHEM
YOUR CAREER GUIDANCE QUESTION-NAIRE...
I FORGOT TO HAND YOU YOURS YESTERDAY.
IT'S DUE RIGHT AFTER VACATION, BUT I FORGOT IT AT HOME...
I'M SORRY!
IT'S OKAY, REALLY!
I'LL DROP IT OFF AT YOUR HOUSE TODAY.
YOU DON'T HAVE TO DO THAT!
I DON'T WANT TO TROUBLE YOU.

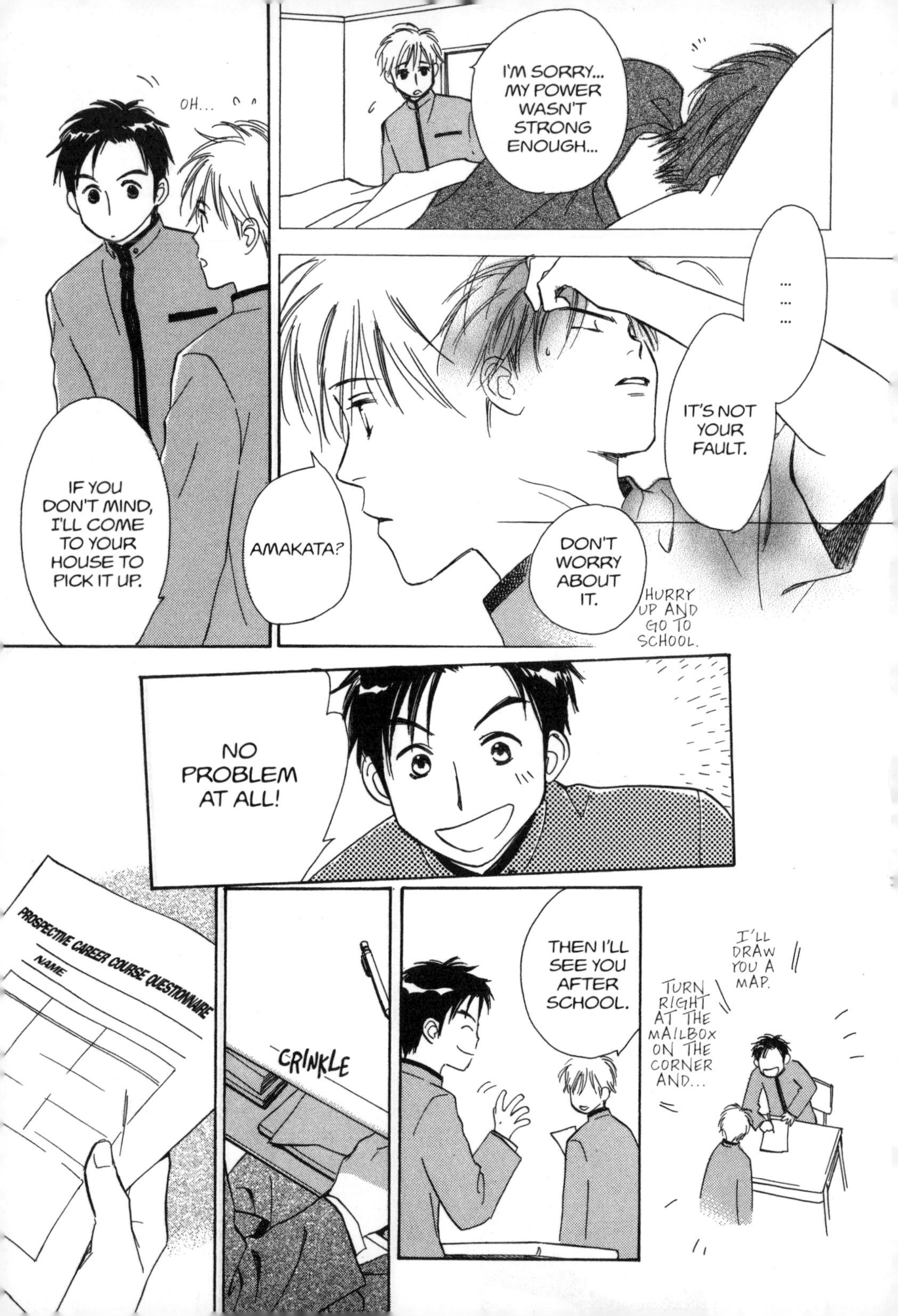
I'M SORRY... MY POWER WASN'T STRONG ENOUGH...
... ...
IT'S NOT YOUR FAULT.
DON'T WORRY ABOUT IT.
HURRY UP AND GO TO SCHOOL.
AMAKATA?
OH...
IF YOU DON'T MIND, I'LL COME TO YOUR HOUSE TO PICK IT UP.
NO PROBLEM AT ALL!
I'LL DRAW YOU A MAP.
TURN RIGHT AT THE MAILBOX ON THE CORNER AND...
THEN I'LL SEE YOU AFTER SCHOOL.
CRINKLE
PROSPECTIVE CAREER COURSE QUESTIONNAIRE
NAME

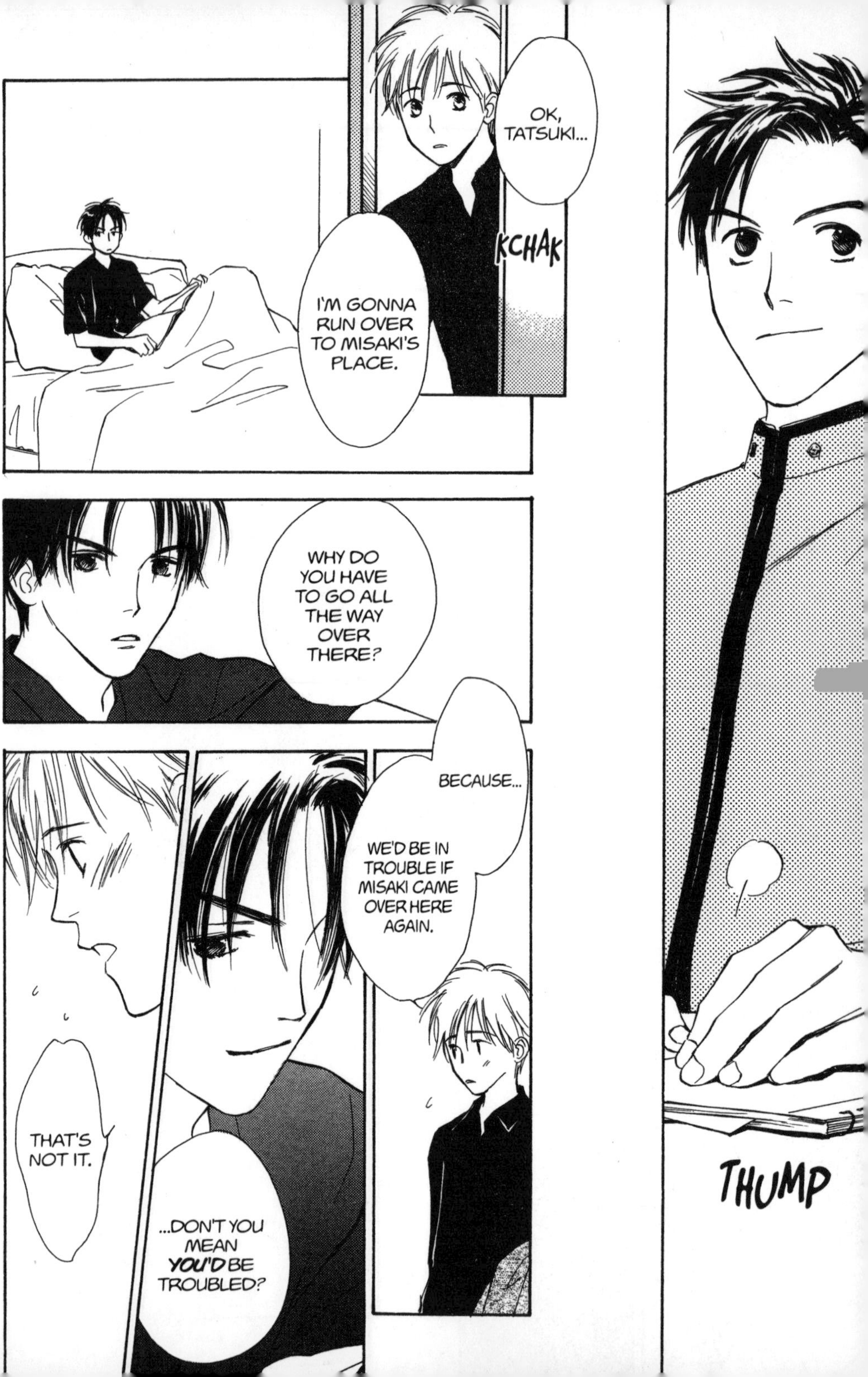
THUMP
OK, TATSUKI...
KCHAK
I'M GONNA RUN OVER TO MISAKI'S PLACE.
WHY DO YOU HAVE TO GO ALL THE WAY OVER THERE?
BECAUSE...
WE'D BE IN TROUBLE IF MISAKI CAME OVER HERE AGAIN.
...DON'T YOU MEAN YOU'D BE TROUBLED?
THAT'S NOT IT.

BESIDES, YOU HAVEN'T RECOVERED YET...

TUG

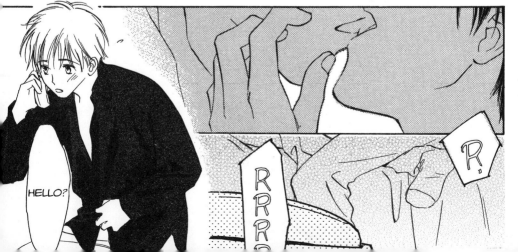

HELLO?

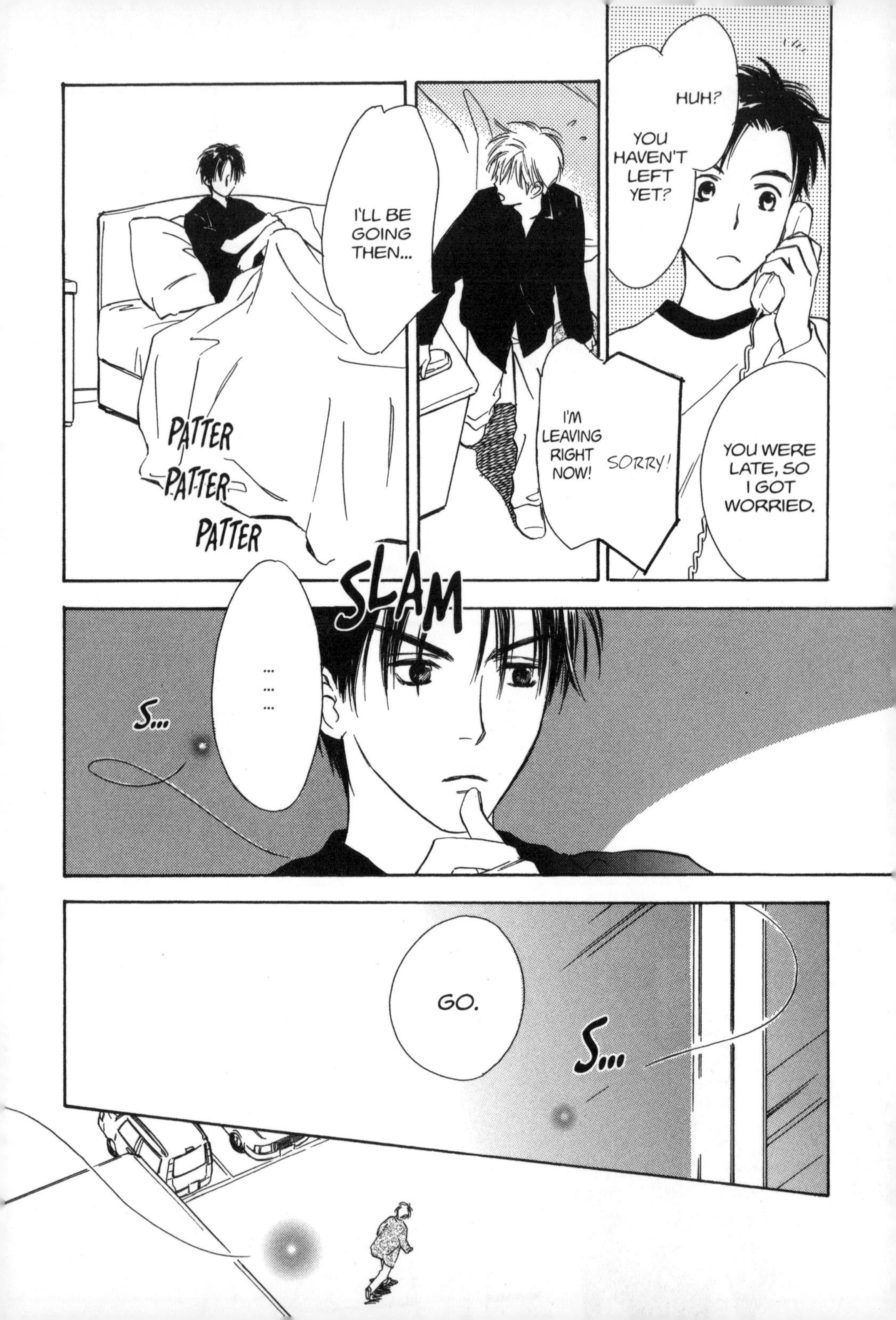
HUH?
YOU HAVEN'T LEFT YET?
YOU WERE LATE, SO I GOT WORRIED.
I'M LEAVING RIGHT NOW!
SORRY!
I'LL BE GOING THEN...
PATTER
PATTER
PATTER
SLAM
...
...
...
S...
GO.
S...

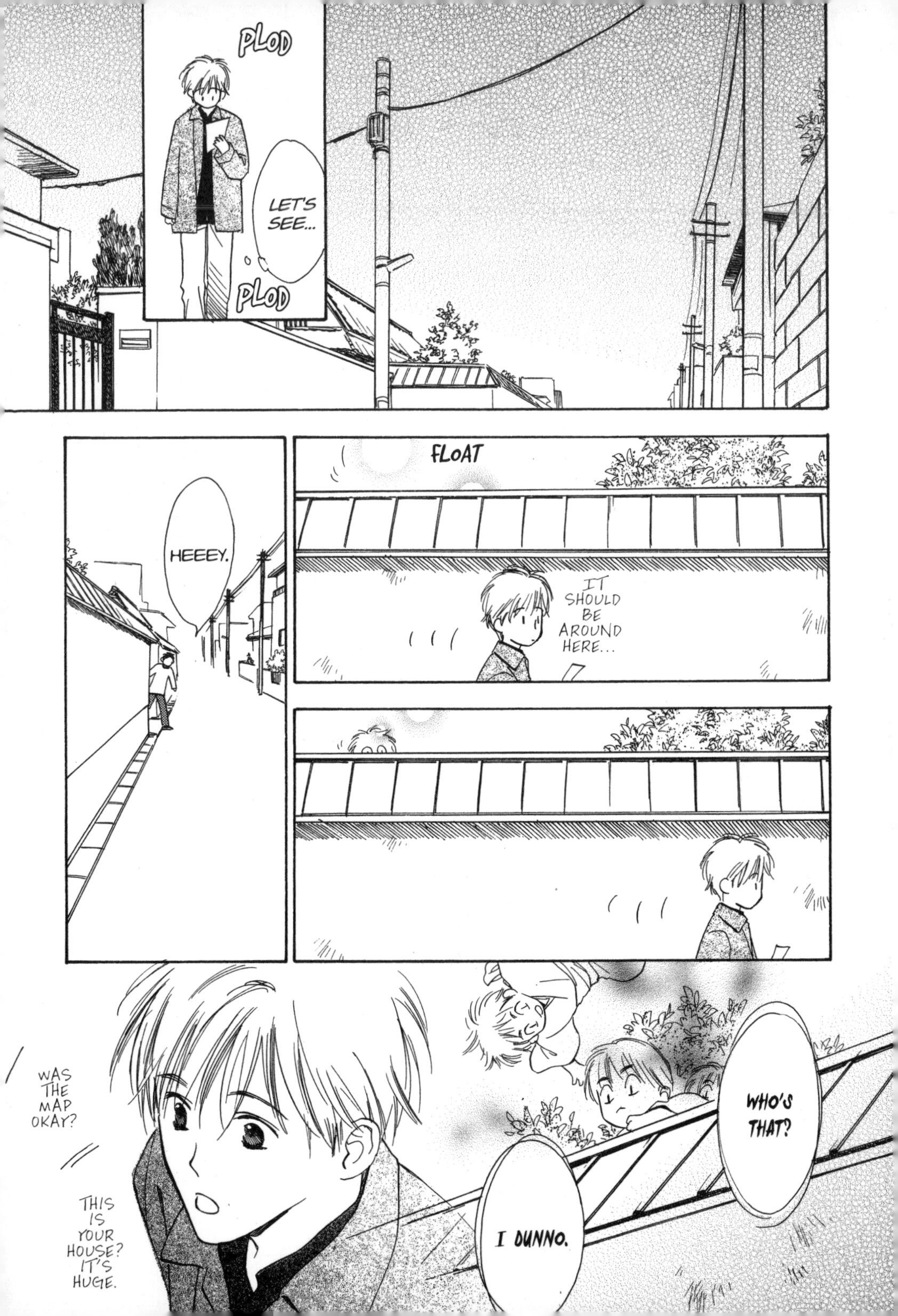
PLOD
LET'S SEE...
PLOD
FLOAT
IT SHOULD BE AROUND HERE...
HEEEY.
WHO'S THAT?
I DUNNO.
WAS THE MAP OKAY?
THIS IS YOUR HOUSE? IT'S HUGE.

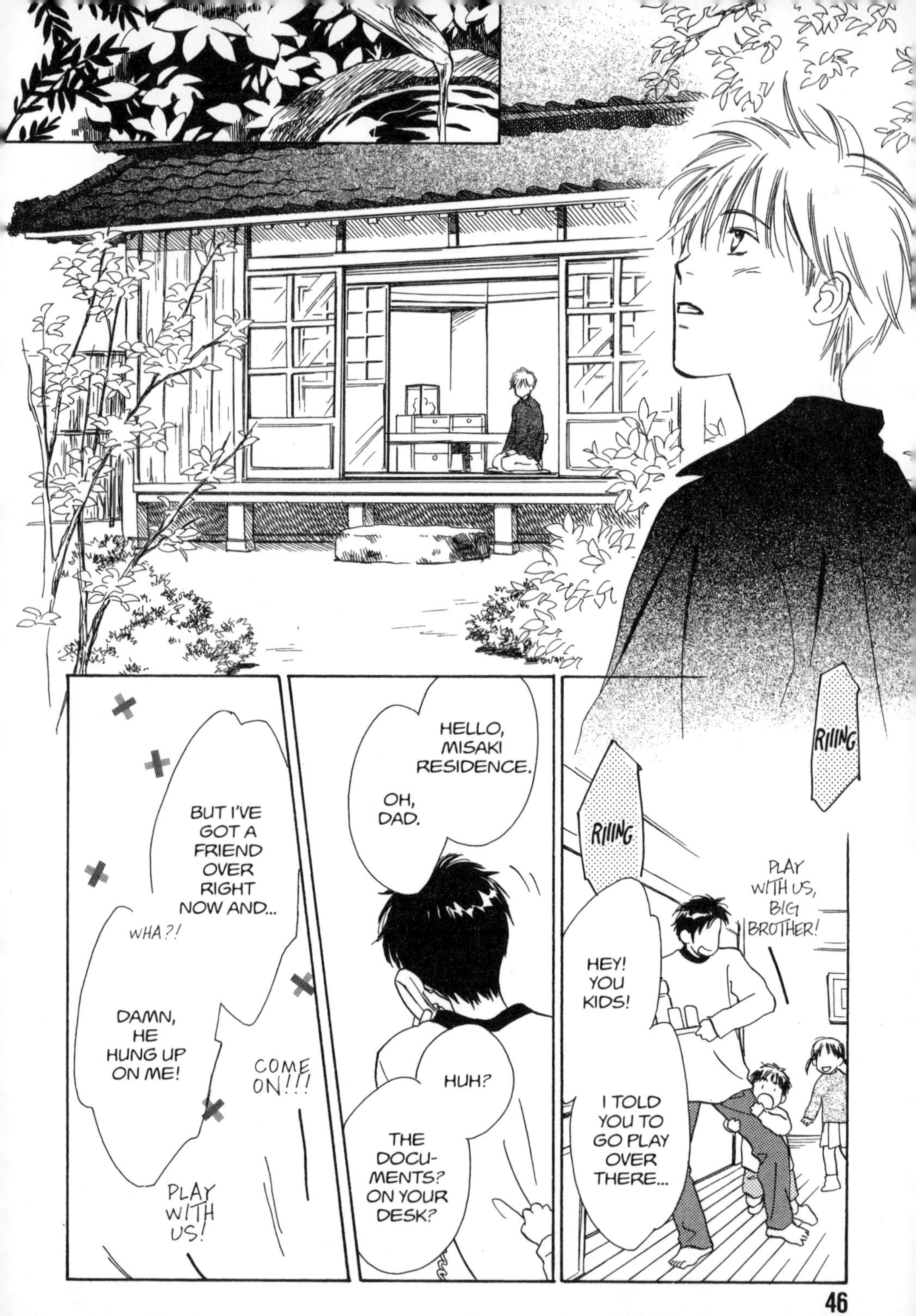
RIIING
RIIING
PLAY WITH US, BIG BROTHER!
HEY! YOU KIDS!
I TOLD YOU TO GO PLAY OVER THERE...
HELLO, MISAKI RESIDENCE.
OH, DAD.
HUH?
THE DOCU-MENTS? ON YOUR DESK?
BUT I'VE GOT A FRIEND OVER RIGHT NOW AND...
WHA?!
DAMN, HE HUNG UP ON ME!
COME ON!!!
PLAY WITH US!

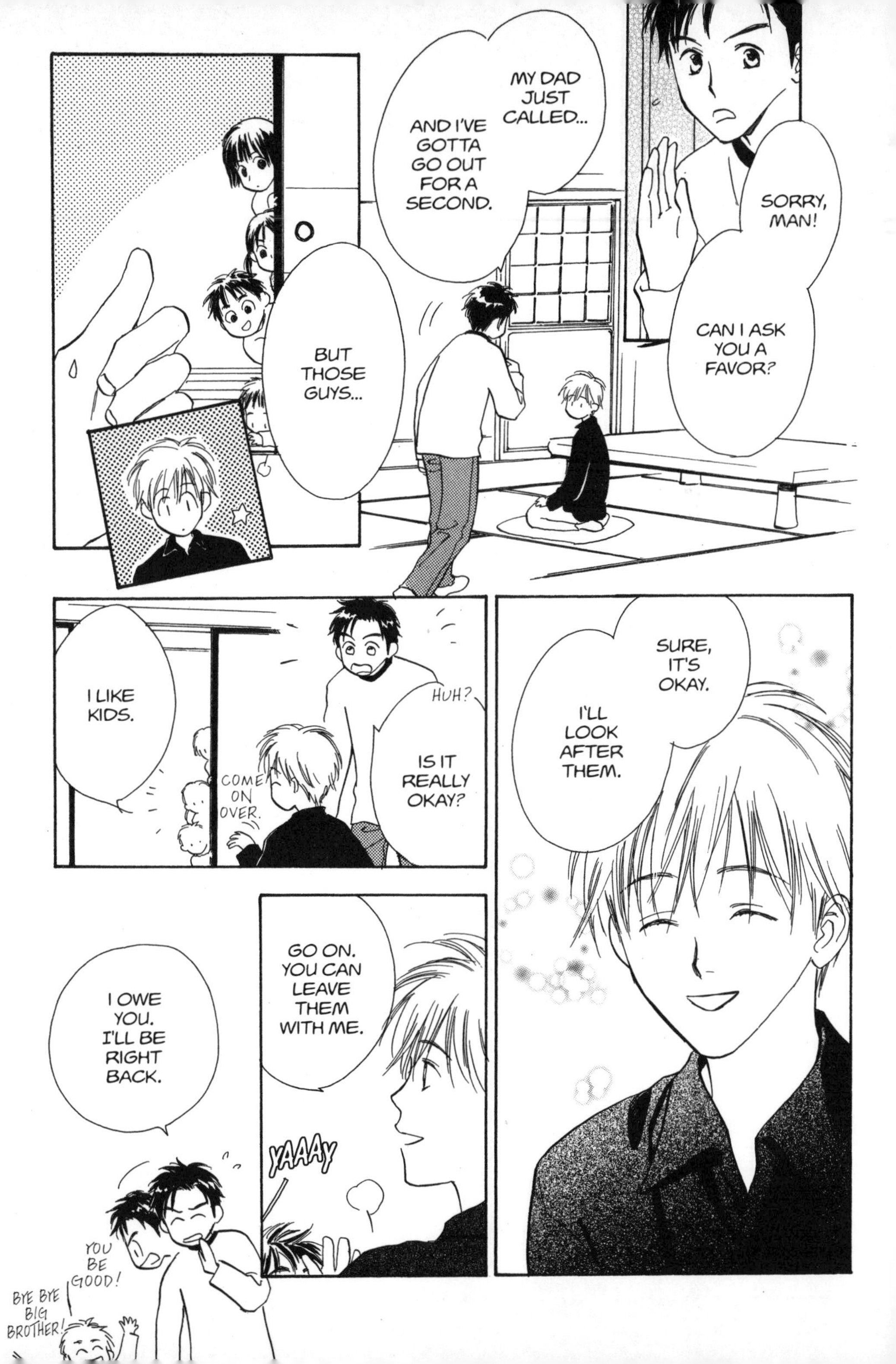
SORRY, MAN!
CAN I ASK YOU A FAVOR?
MY DAD JUST CALLED...
AND I'VE GOTTA GO OUT FOR A SECOND.
BUT THOSE GUYS...
SURE, IT'S OKAY.
I'LL LOOK AFTER THEM.
HUH?
IS IT REALLY OKAY?
I LIKE KIDS.
COME ON OVER.
GO ON. YOU CAN LEAVE THEM WITH ME.
YAAAY
I OWE YOU. I'LL BE RIGHT BACK.
YOU BE GOOD!
BYE BYE BIG BROTHER!

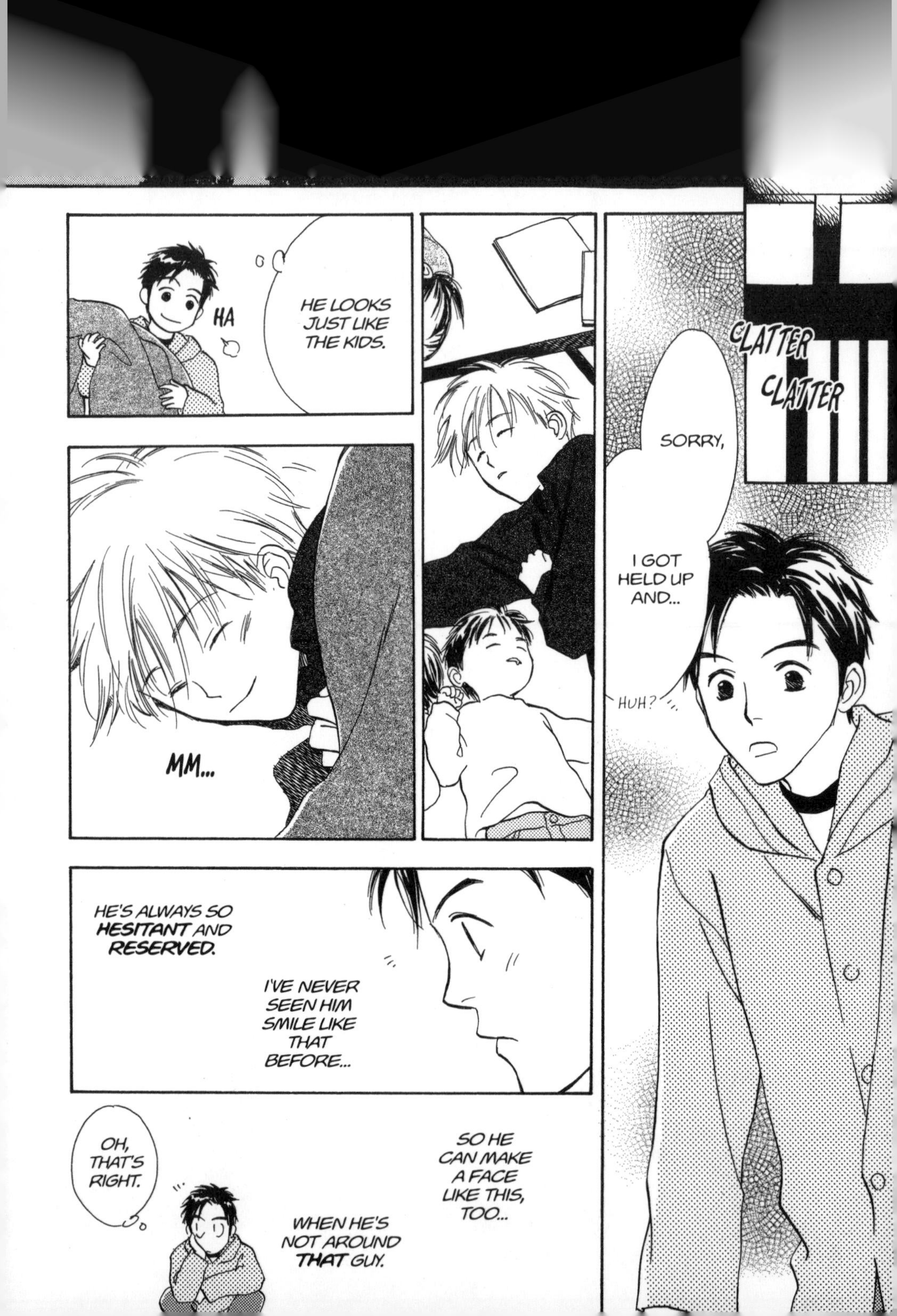
CLATTER
CLATTER
SORRY,
I GOT HELD UP AND...
HUH?
HE LOOKS JUST LIKE THE KIDS.
HA
MM...
HE'S ALWAYS SO **HESITANT** AND **RESERVED**.
I'VE NEVER SEEN HIM SMILE LIKE THAT BEFORE...
SO HE CAN MAKE A FACE LIKE THIS, TOO...
WHEN HE'S NOT AROUND **THAT** GUY.
OH, THAT'S RIGHT.

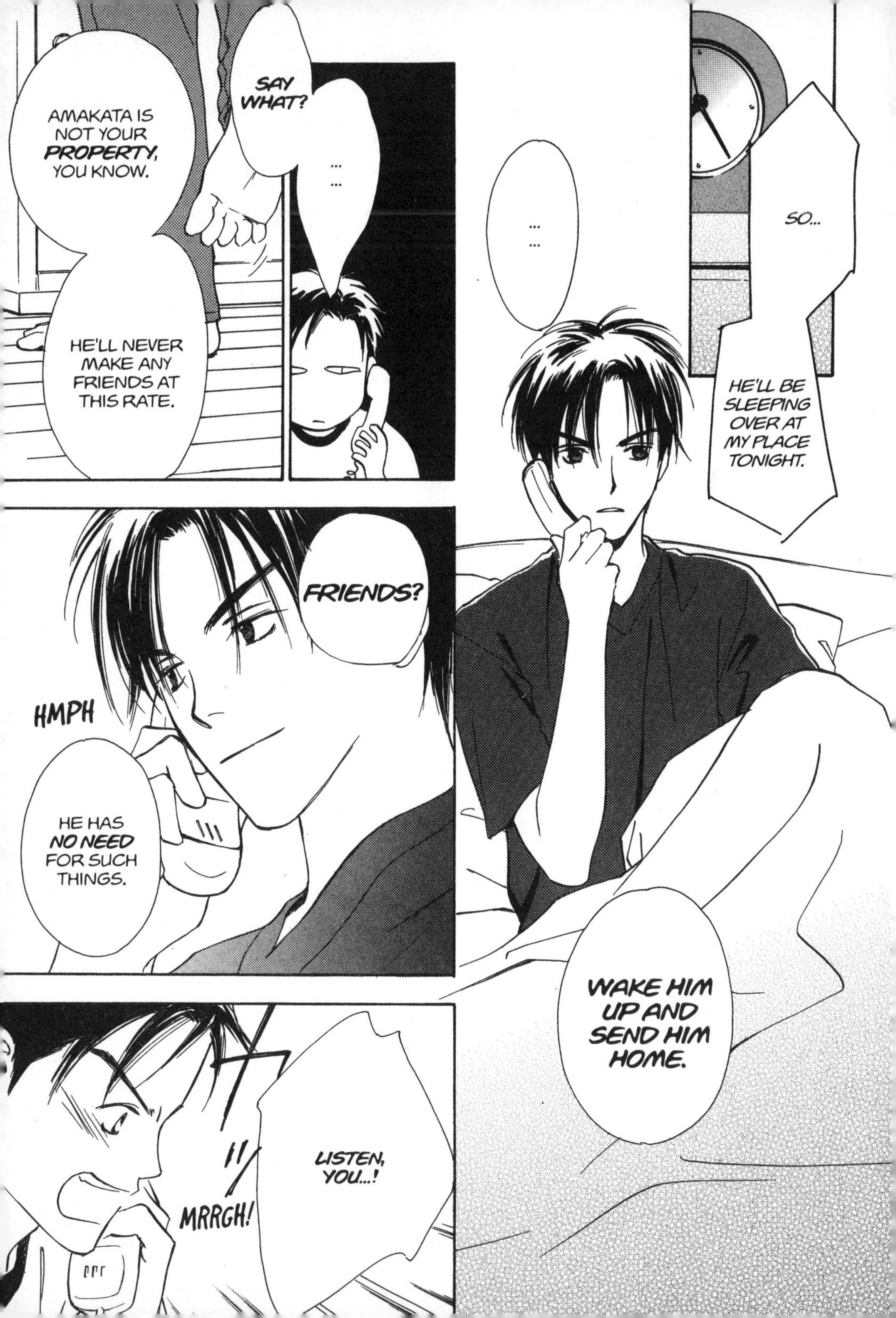

SO...
HE'LL BE SLEEPING OVER AT MY PLACE TONIGHT.
...
...
WAKE HIM UP AND SEND HIM HOME.
SAY WHAT?
...
...
AMAKATA IS NOT YOUR PROPERTY, YOU KNOW.
HE'LL NEVER MAKE ANY FRIENDS AT THIS RATE.
FRIENDS?
HMPH
HE HAS NO NEED FOR SUCH THINGS.
LISTEN, YOU...!
MRRGH!

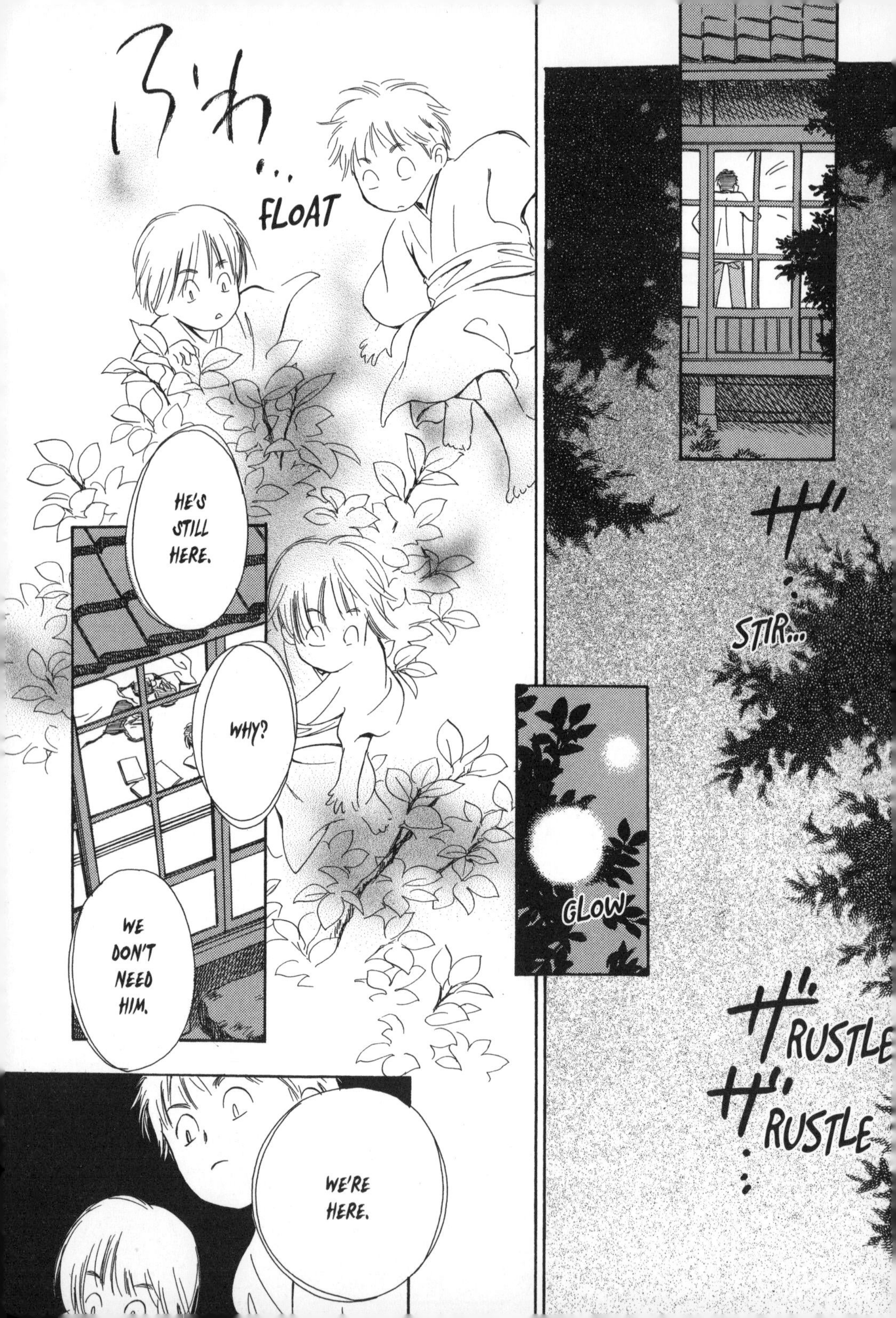

ザ
STIR...
GLOW
ザ RUSTLE
ザ RUSTLE
ふわ...
FLOAT
HE'S STILL HERE.
WHY?
WE DON'T NEED HIM.
WE'RE HERE.

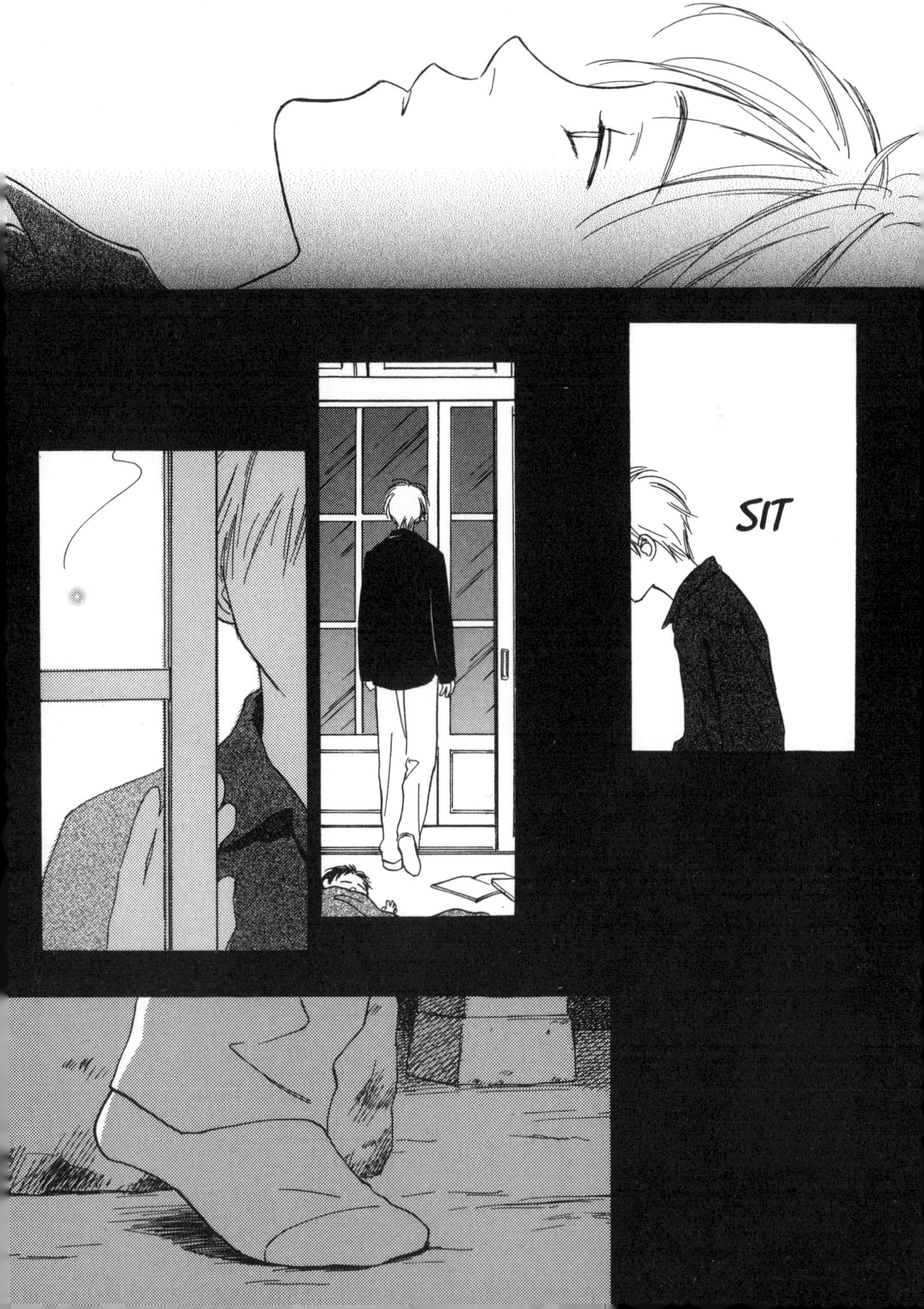
SIT

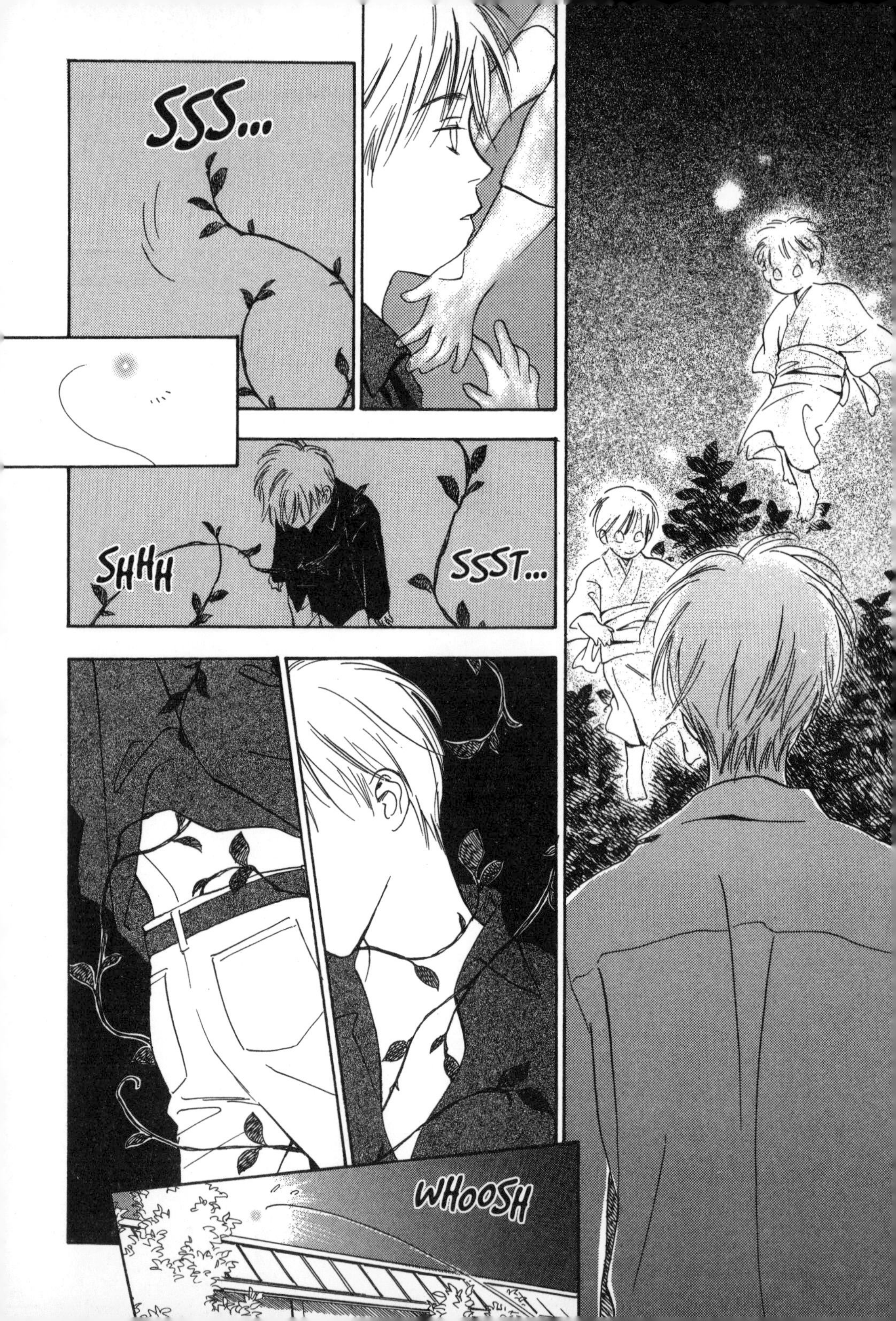
SSS...
SSST...
SHHH
WHOOSH

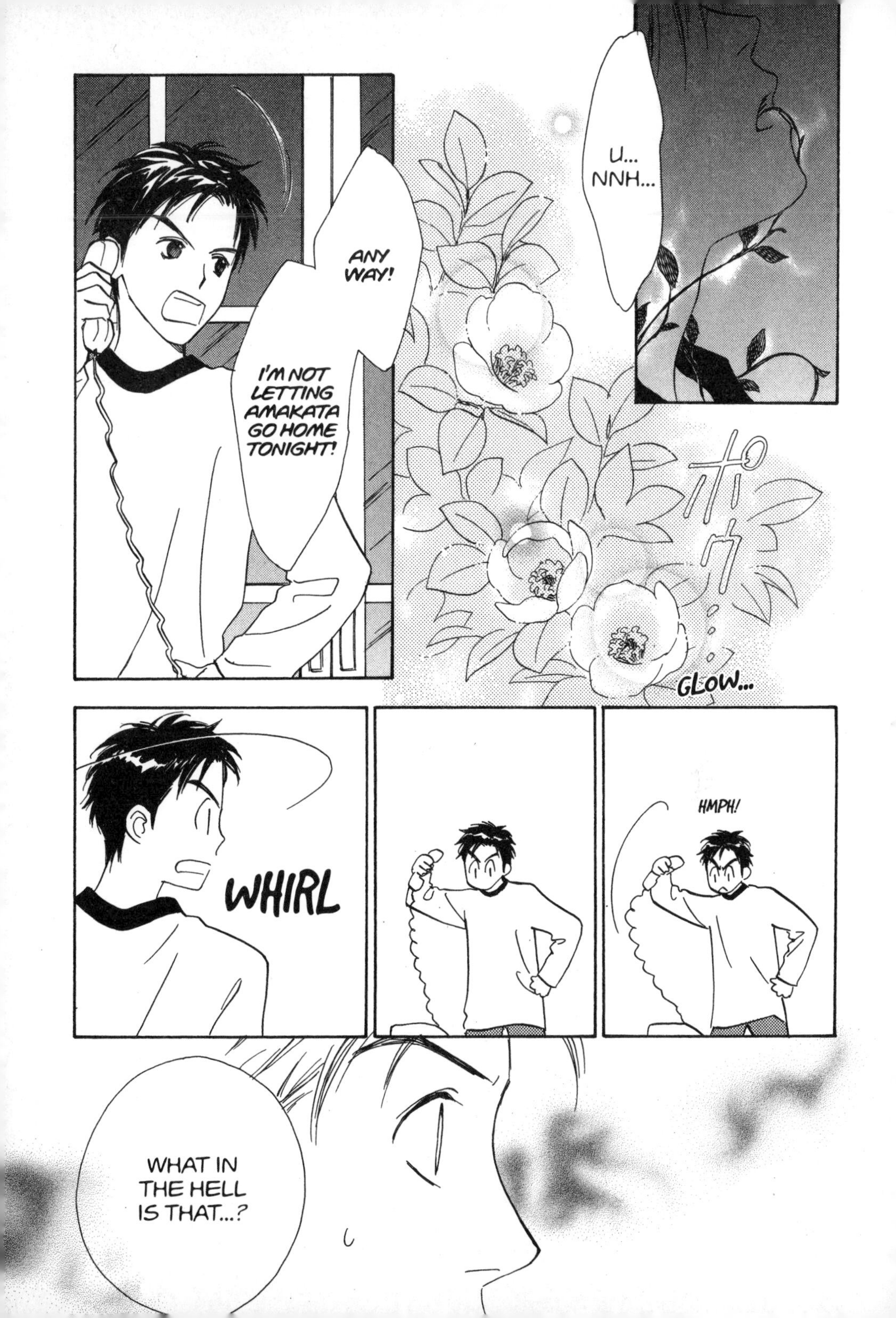
U... NNH...
ポウ...
GLOW...
ANY WAY!
I'M NOT LETTING AMAKATA GO HOME TONIGHT!
HMPH!
WHIRL
WHAT IN THE HELL IS THAT...?

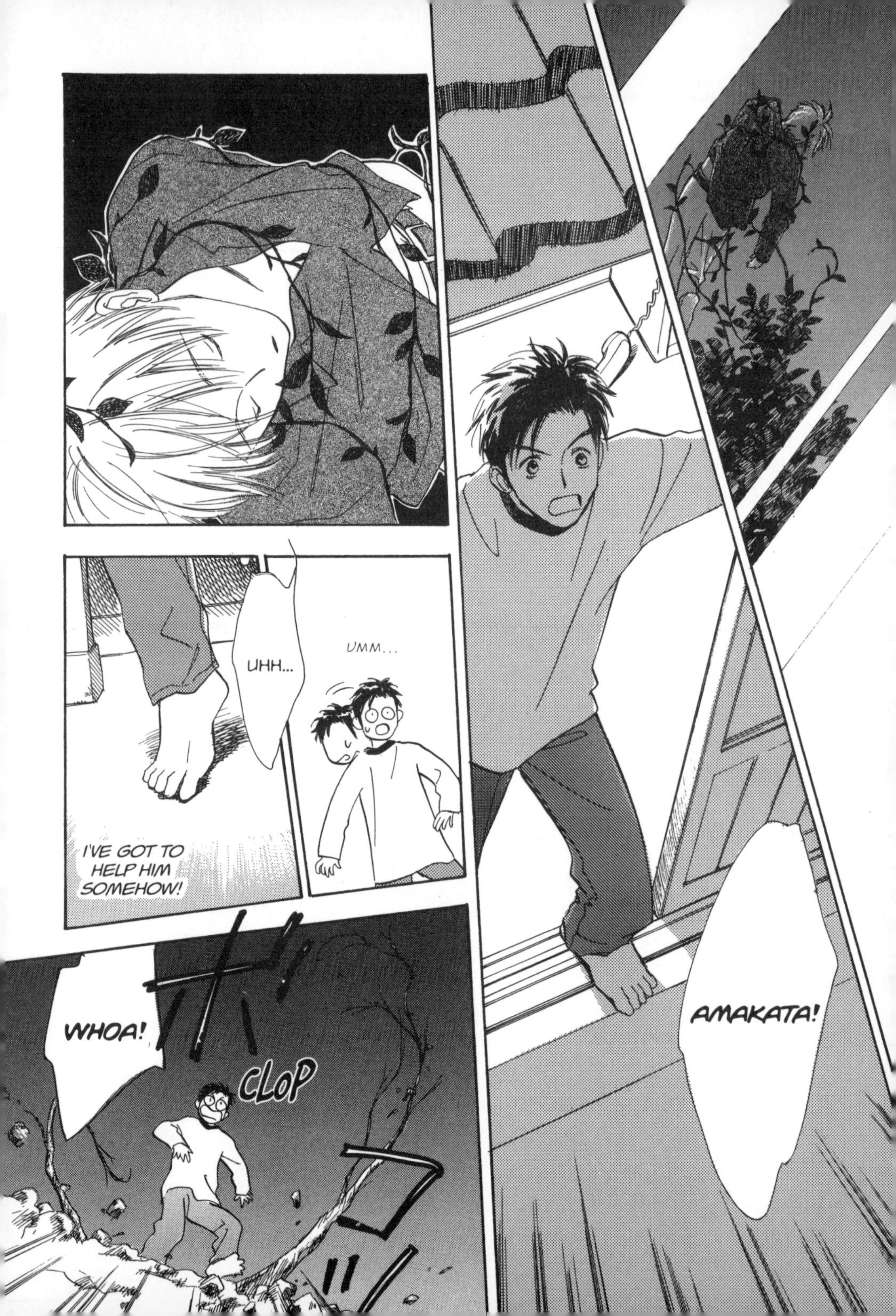
AMAKATA!
UMM...
UHH...
I'VE GOT TO HELP HIM SOMEHOW!
WHOA!
CLOP

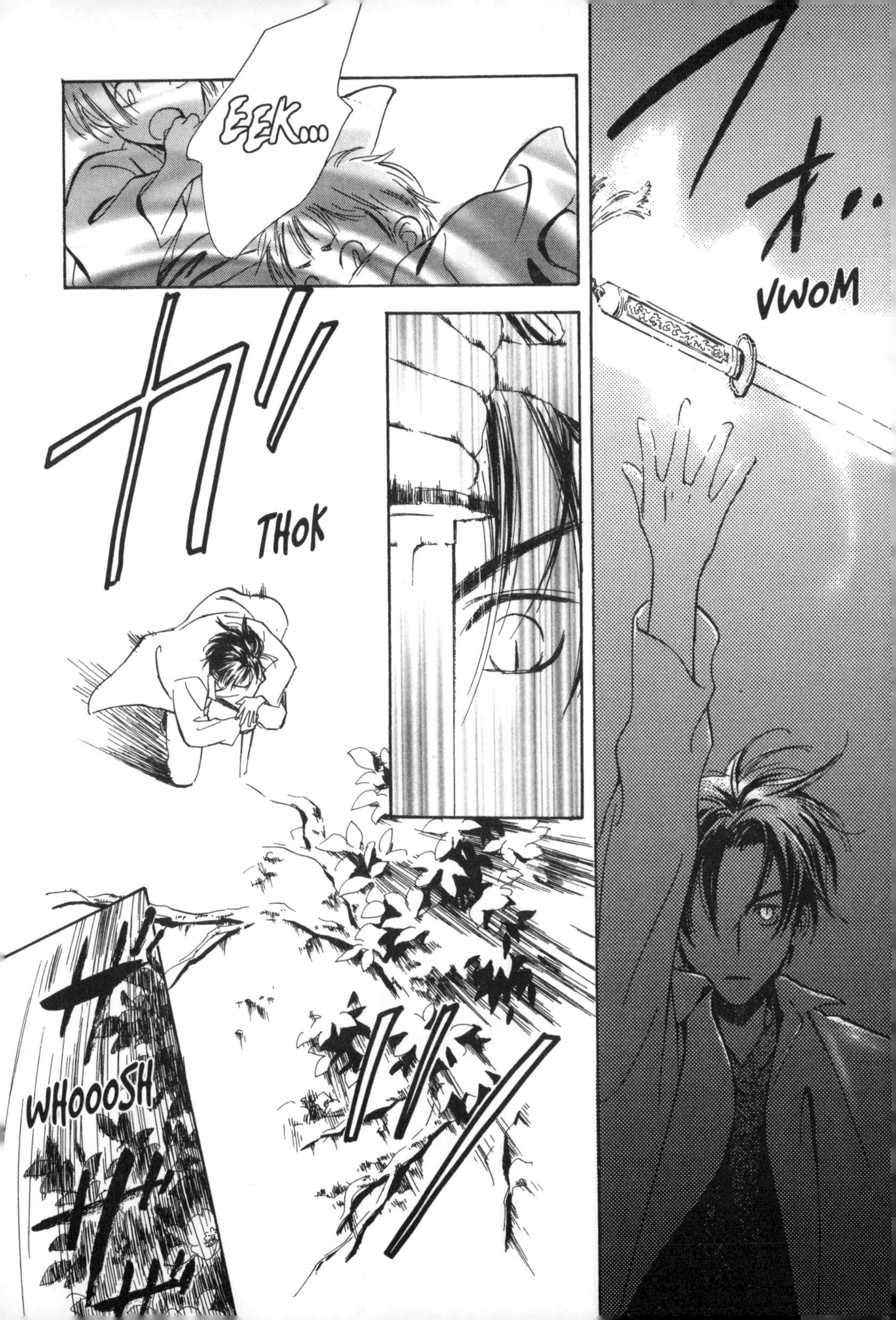
VWOM
EEK...
THOK
WHOOOSH

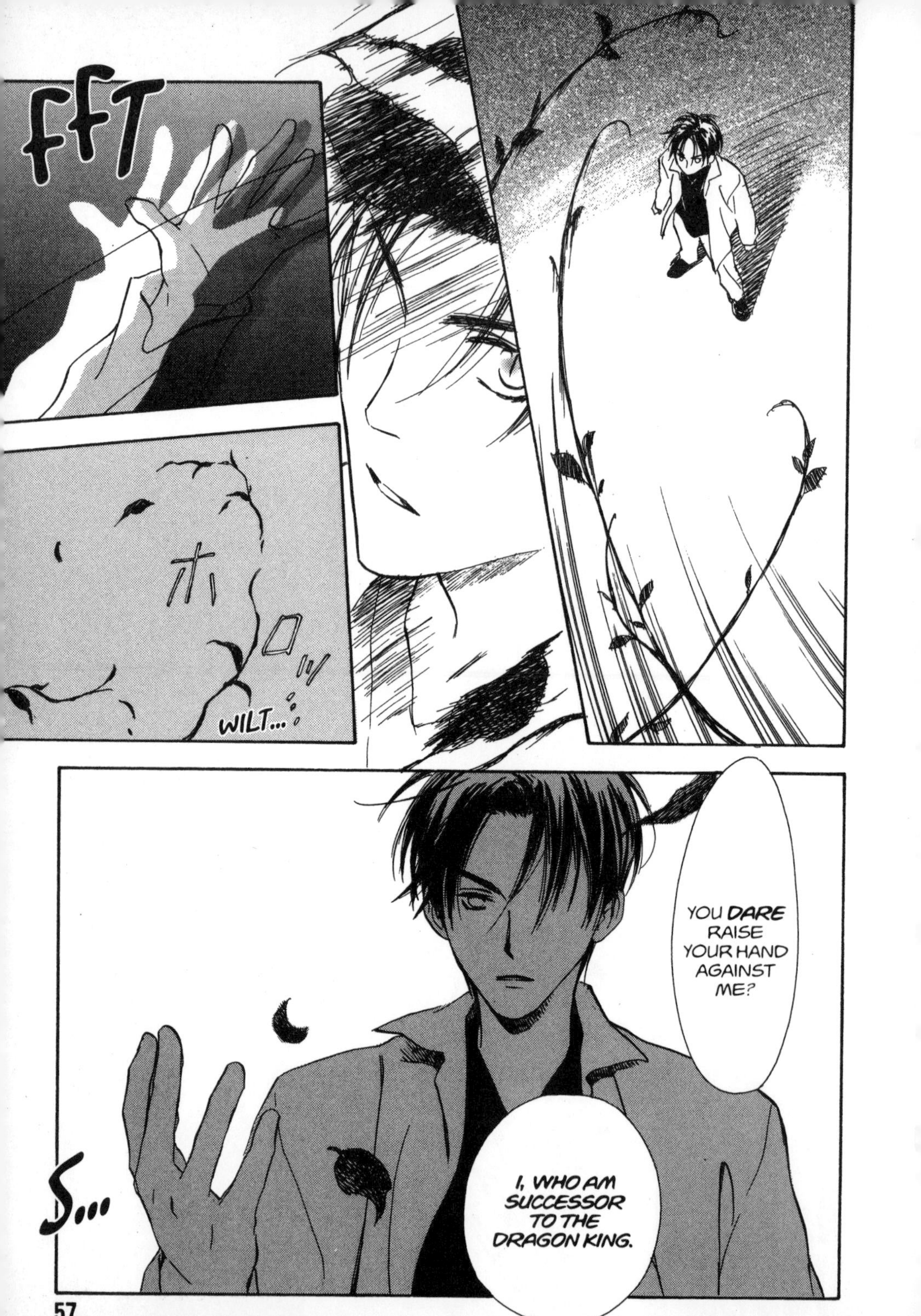
FFT
ホロッ
WILT...
YOU DARE RAISE YOUR HAND AGAINST ME?
I, WHO AM SUCCESSOR TO THE DRAGON KING.
S...

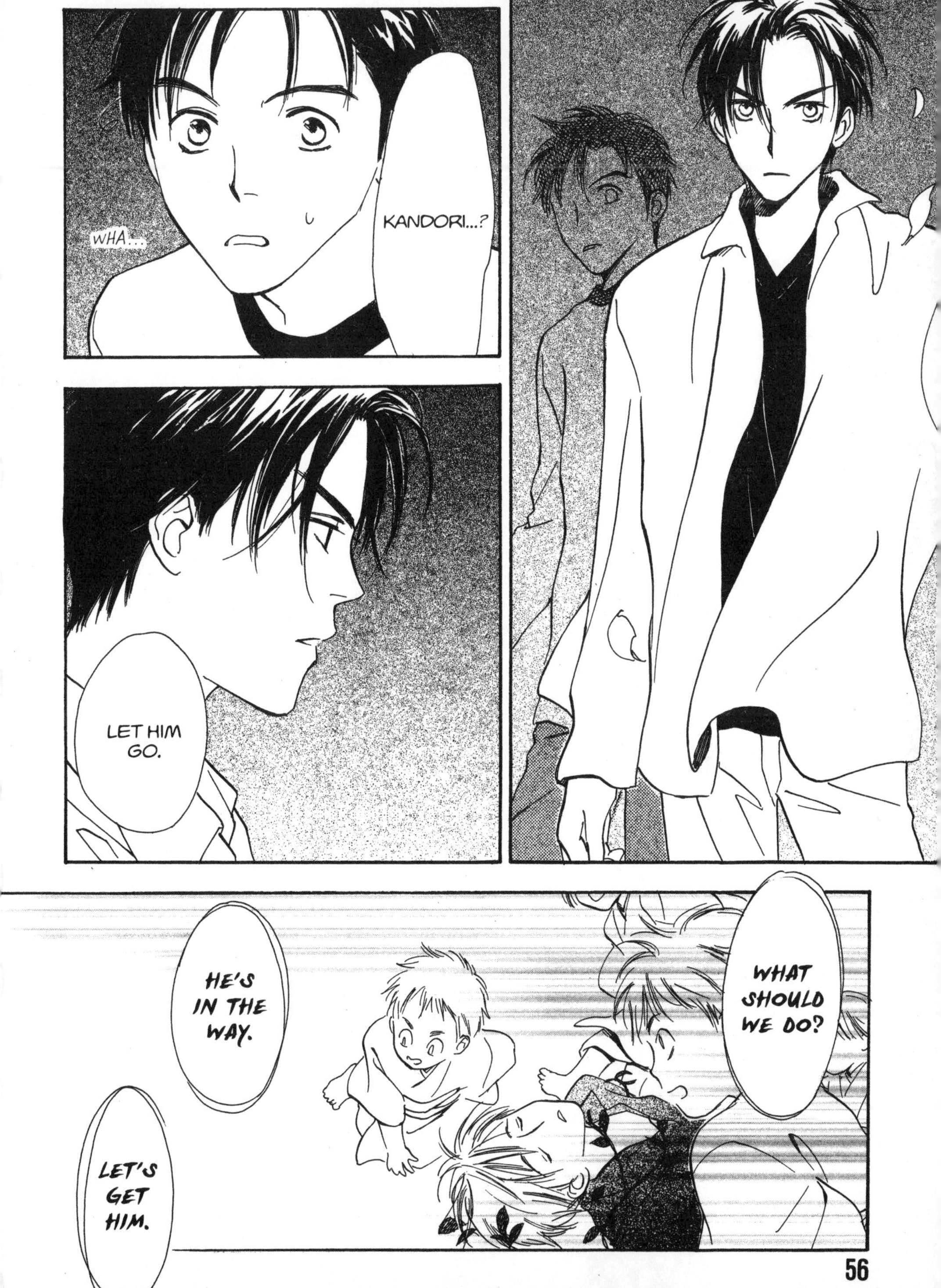
KANDORI...?
WHA...
LET HIM GO.
WHAT SHOULD WE DO?
HE'S IN THE WAY.
LET'S GET HIM.

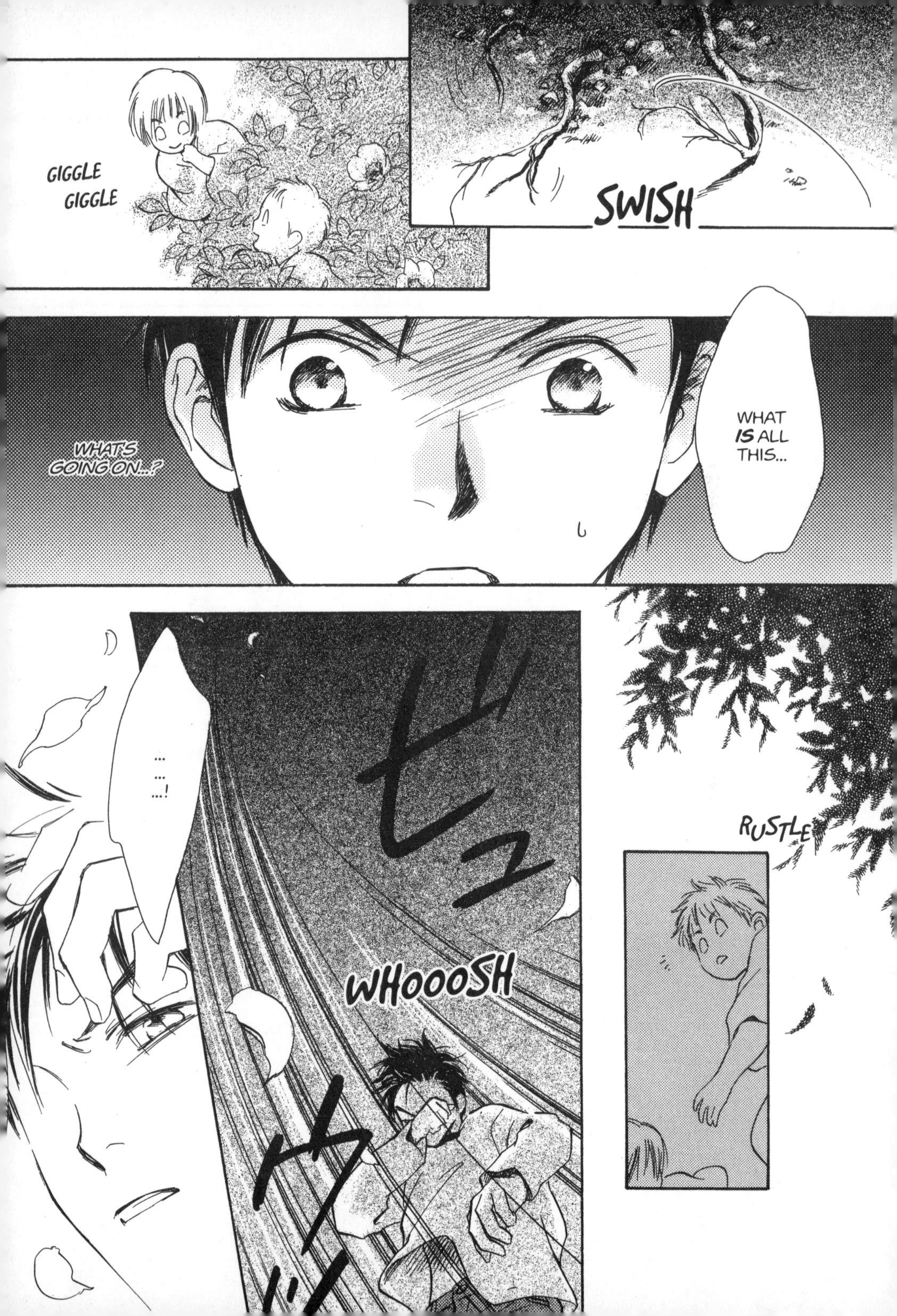
SWISH
GIGGLE GIGGLE
WHAT IS ALL THIS...
WHAT'S GOING ON...?
RUSTLE
... ...!
WHOOOSH

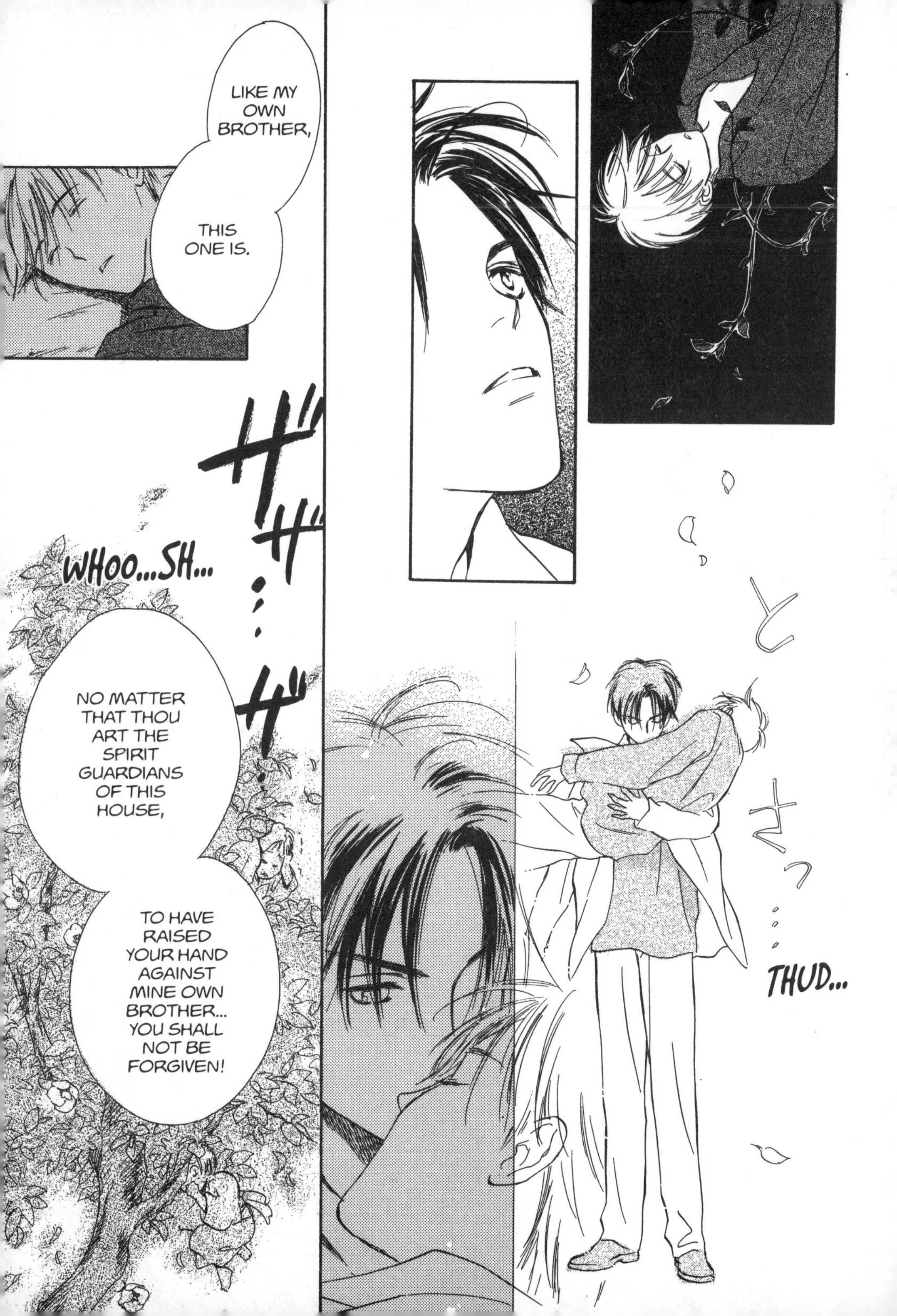
LIKE MY OWN BROTHER,
THIS ONE IS.
とさっ…
THUD...
WHOO...SH...
ザザ…ザ
NO MATTER THAT THOU ART THE SPIRIT GUARDIANS OF THIS HOUSE,
TO HAVE RAISED YOUR HAND AGAINST MINE OWN BROTHER... YOU SHALL NOT BE FORGIVEN!

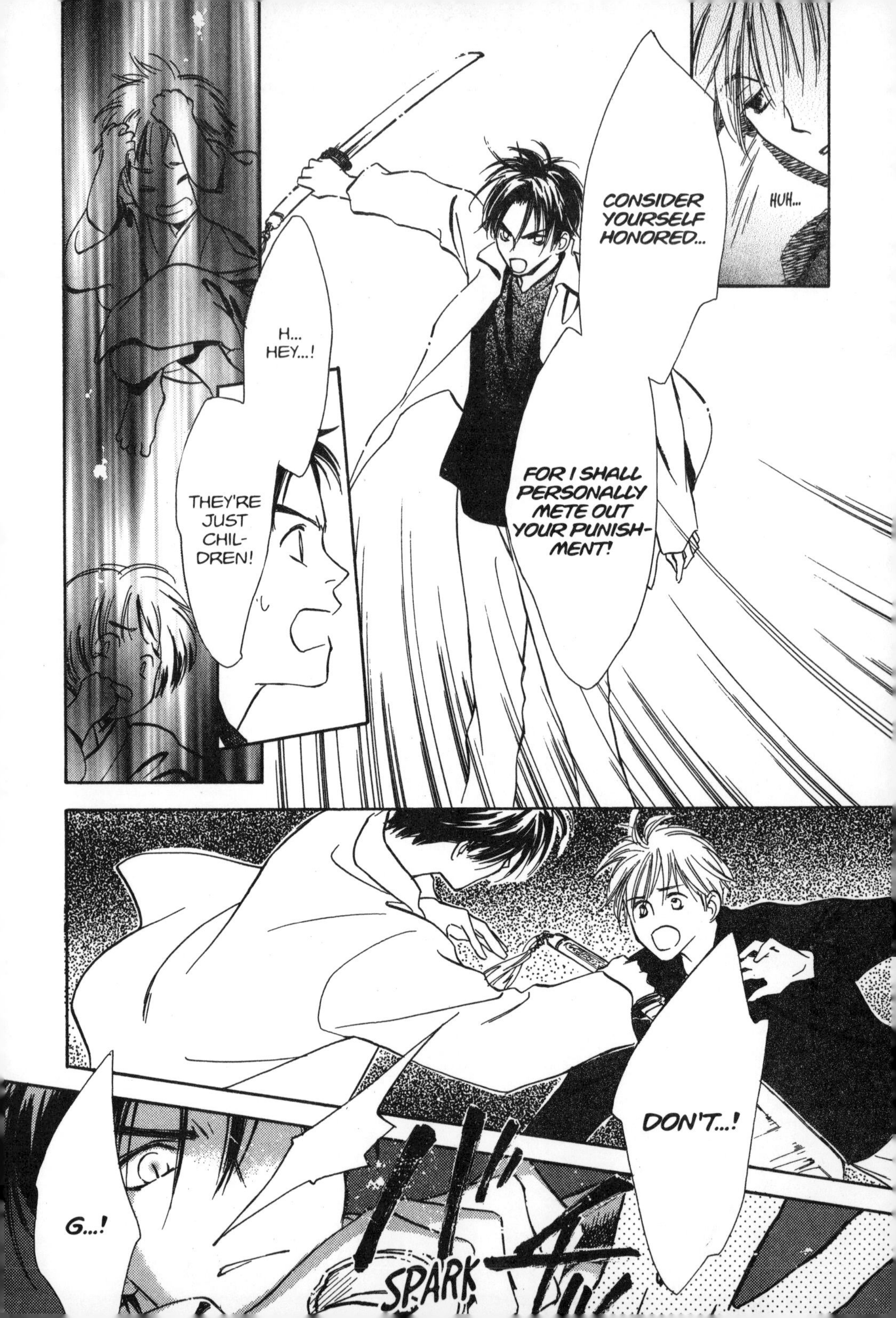
HUH...
CONSIDER YOURSELF HONORED...
FOR I SHALL PERSONALLY METE OUT YOUR PUNISH-MENT!
H... HEY...!
THEY'RE JUST CHIL-DREN!
DON'T...!
SPARK
G...!

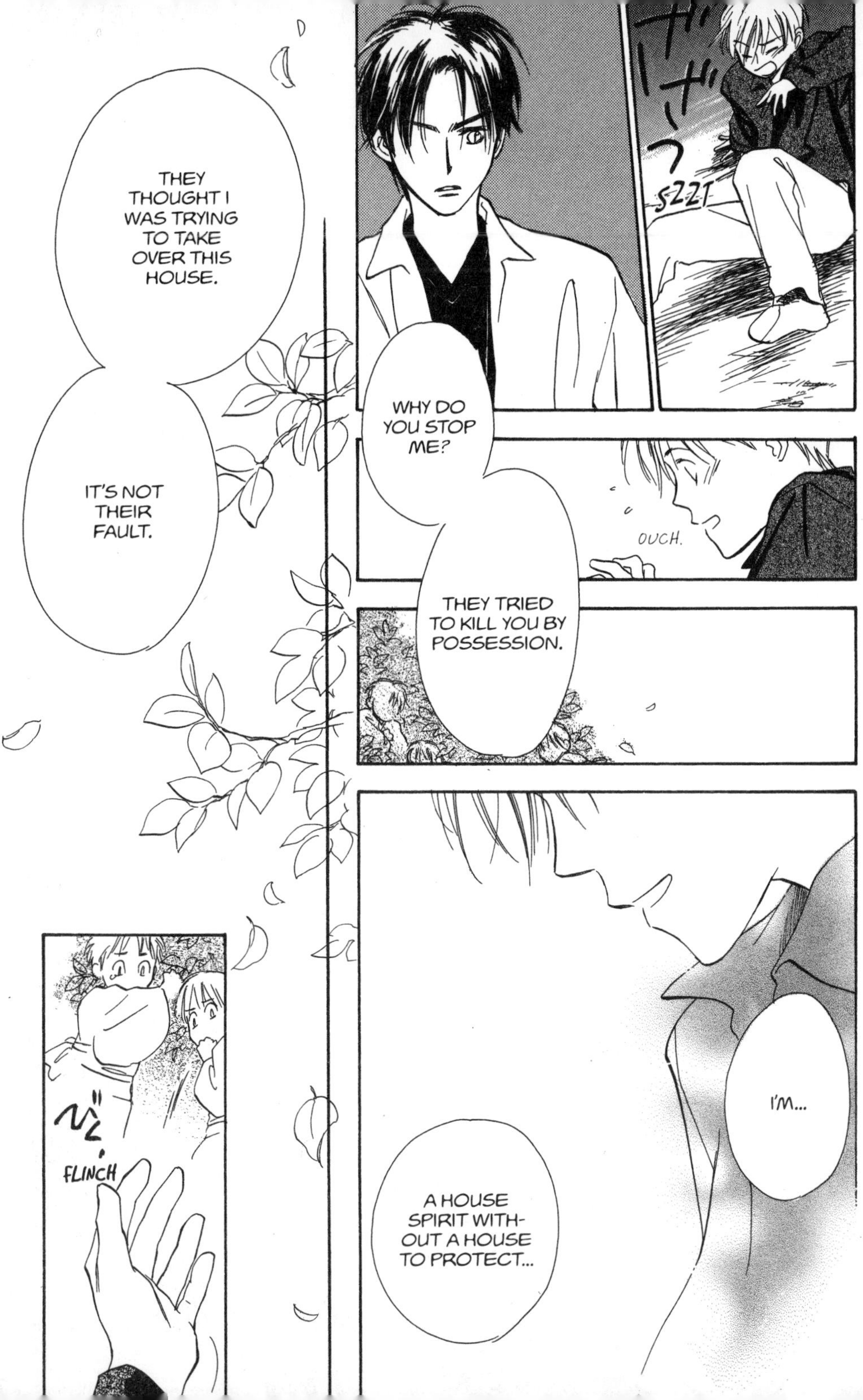
SZZT
WHY DO YOU STOP ME?
OUCH.
THEY TRIED TO KILL YOU BY POSSESSION.
I'M...
A HOUSE SPIRIT WITH-OUT A HOUSE TO PROTECT...
THEY THOUGHT I WAS TRYING TO TAKE OVER THIS HOUSE.
IT'S NOT THEIR FAULT.
FLINCH

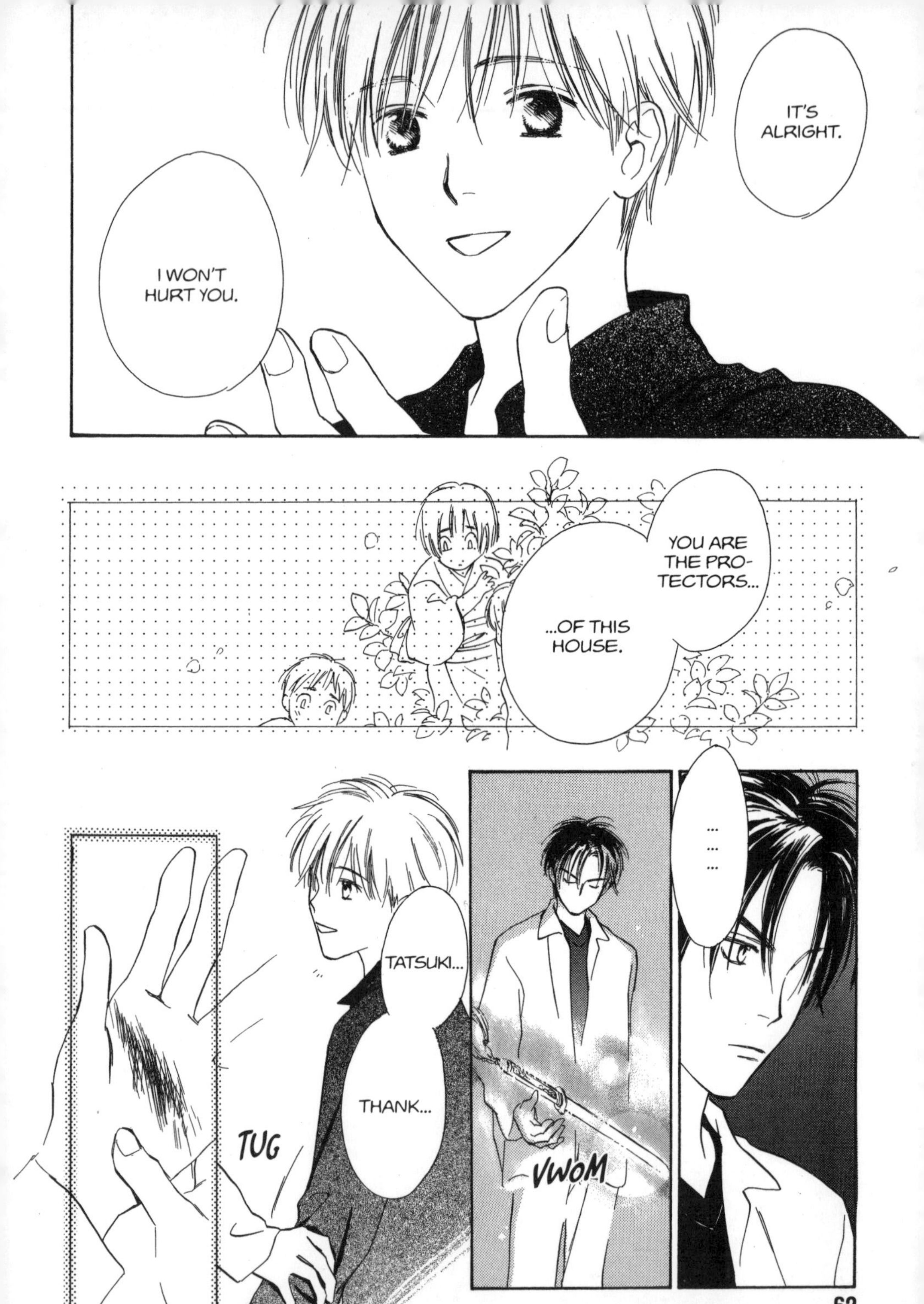
IT'S ALRIGHT.
I WON'T HURT YOU.
YOU ARE THE PRO-TECTORS...
...OF THIS HOUSE.
... ...
VWOM
TATSUKI...
THANK...
TUG

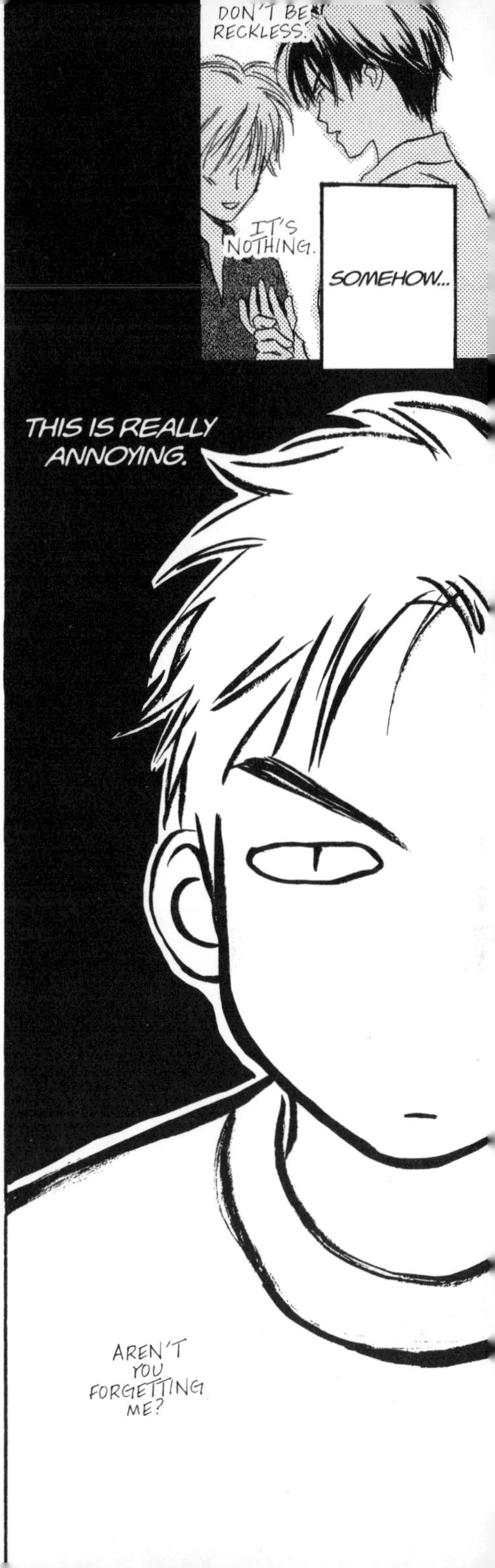
DON'T BE RECKLESS.
IT'S NOTHING.
SOMEHOW...
THIS IS REALLY ANNOYING.
AREN'T YOU FORGETTING ME?
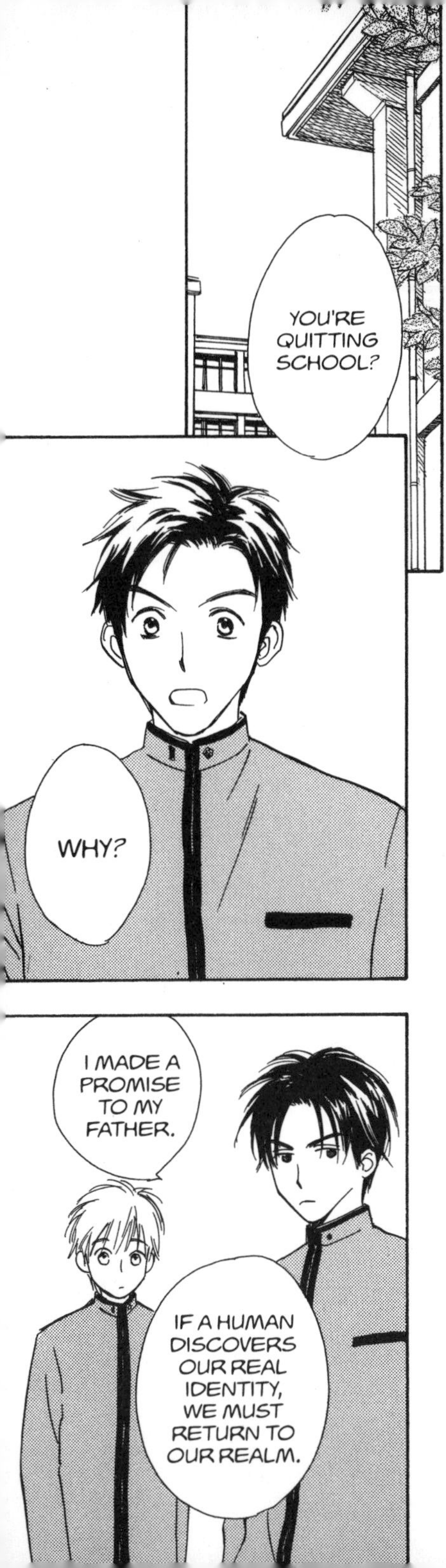
YOU'RE QUITTING SCHOOL?
WHY?
I MADE A PROMISE TO MY FATHER.
IF A HUMAN DISCOVERS OUR REAL IDENTITY, WE MUST RETURN TO OUR REALM.

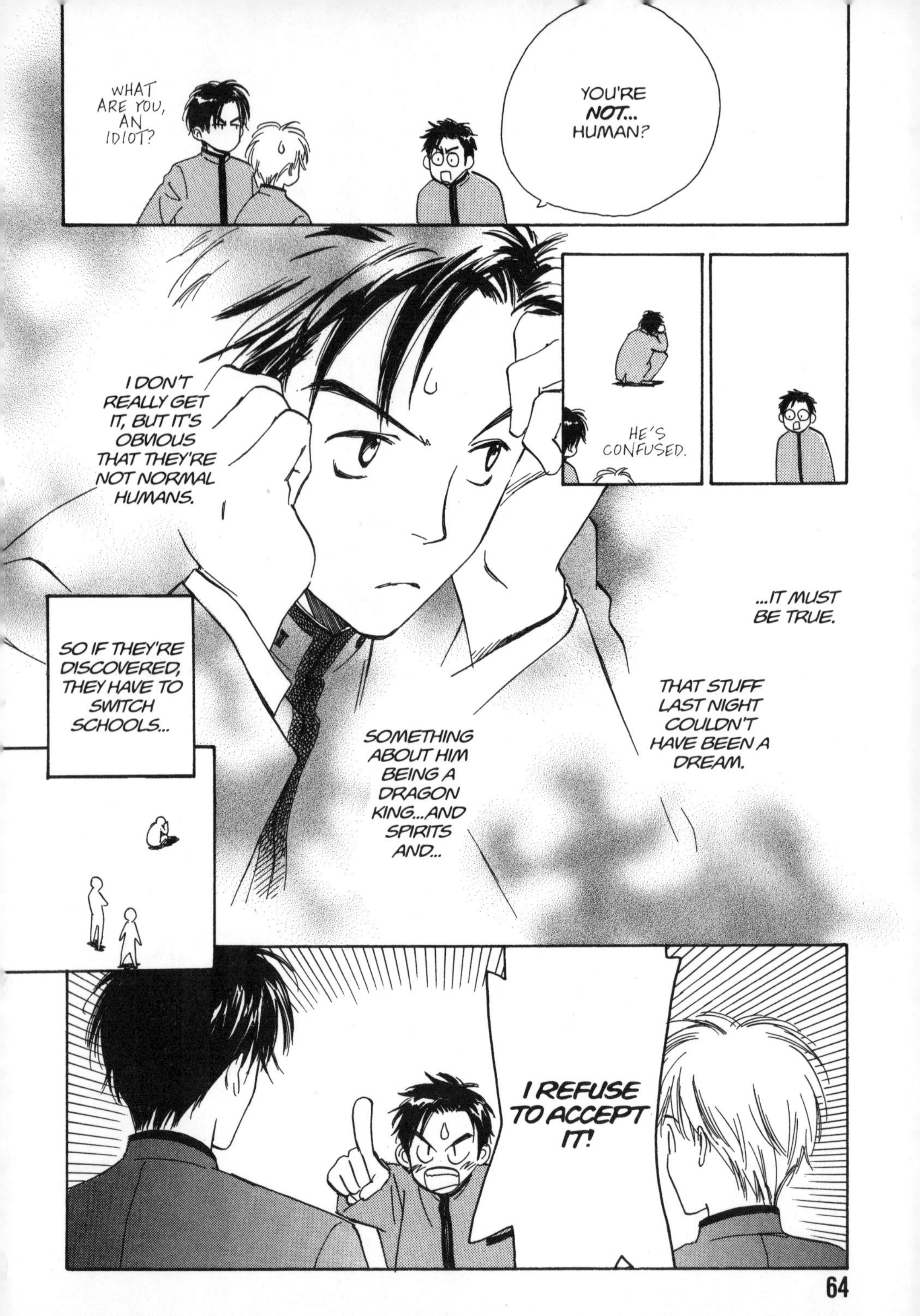
YOU'RE **NOT...** HUMAN?
WHAT ARE YOU, AN IDIOT?
HE'S CONFUSED.
...IT MUST BE TRUE.
THAT STUFF LAST NIGHT COULDN'T HAVE BEEN A DREAM.
SOMETHING ABOUT HIM BEING A DRAGON KING...AND SPIRITS AND...
I DON'T REALLY GET IT, BUT IT'S OBVIOUS THAT THEY'RE NOT NORMAL HUMANS.
SO IF THEY'RE DISCOVERED, THEY HAVE TO SWITCH SCHOOLS...
I REFUSE TO ACCEPT IT!

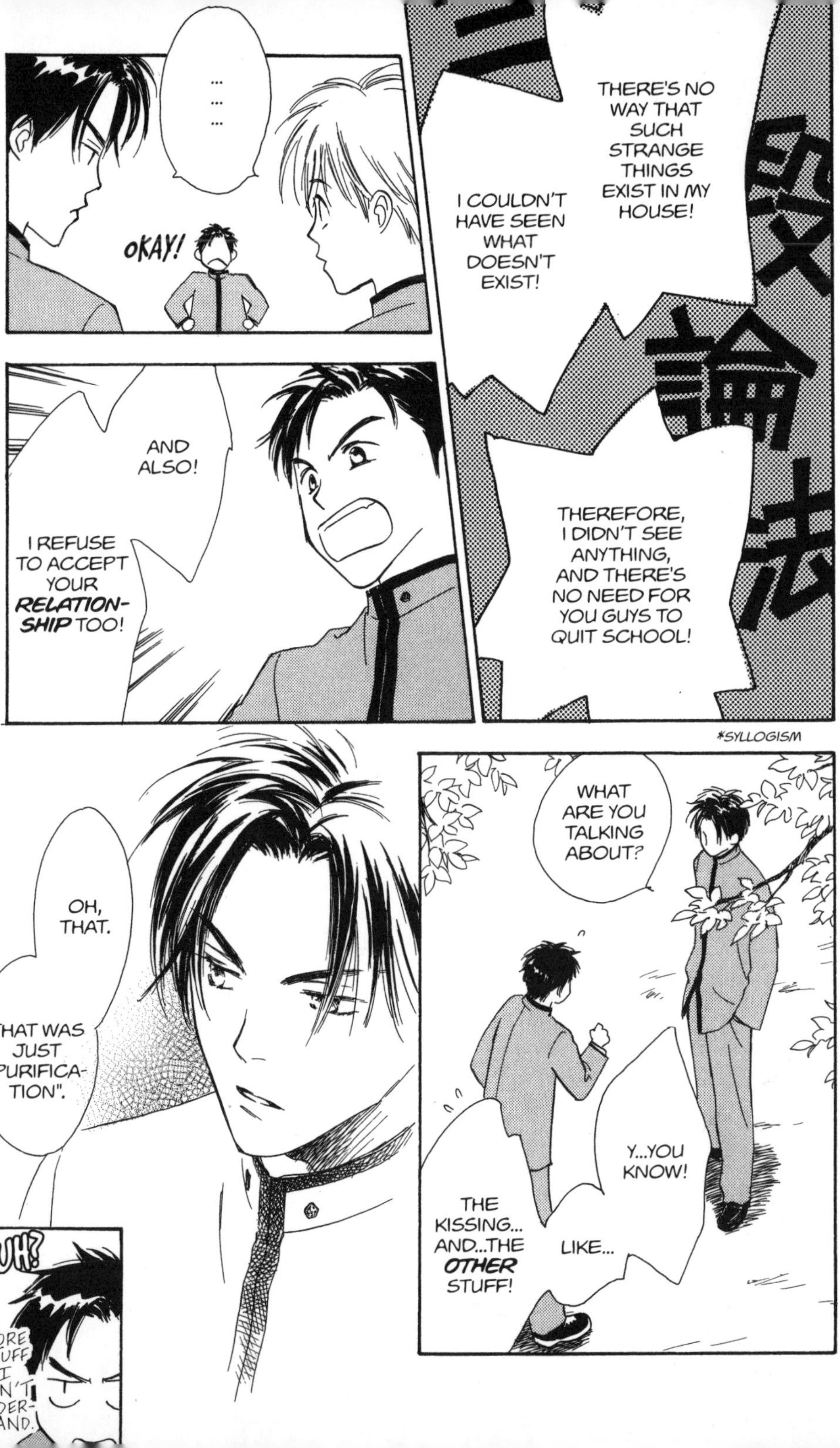
段論法
THERE'S NO WAY THAT SUCH STRANGE THINGS EXIST IN MY HOUSE!
I COULDN'T HAVE SEEN WHAT DOESN'T EXIST!
THEREFORE, I DIDN'T SEE ANYTHING, AND THERE'S NO NEED FOR YOU GUYS TO QUIT SCHOOL!
...
...
...
OKAY!
AND ALSO!
I REFUSE TO ACCEPT YOUR **RELATION-SHIP** TOO!
*SYLLOGISM
WHAT ARE YOU TALKING ABOUT?
Y...YOU KNOW!
LIKE...
THE KISSING... AND...THE **OTHER** STUFF!
OH, THAT.
THAT WAS JUST "PURIFICA-TION".
HUH?
MORE STUFF I DON'T UNDER-STAND.

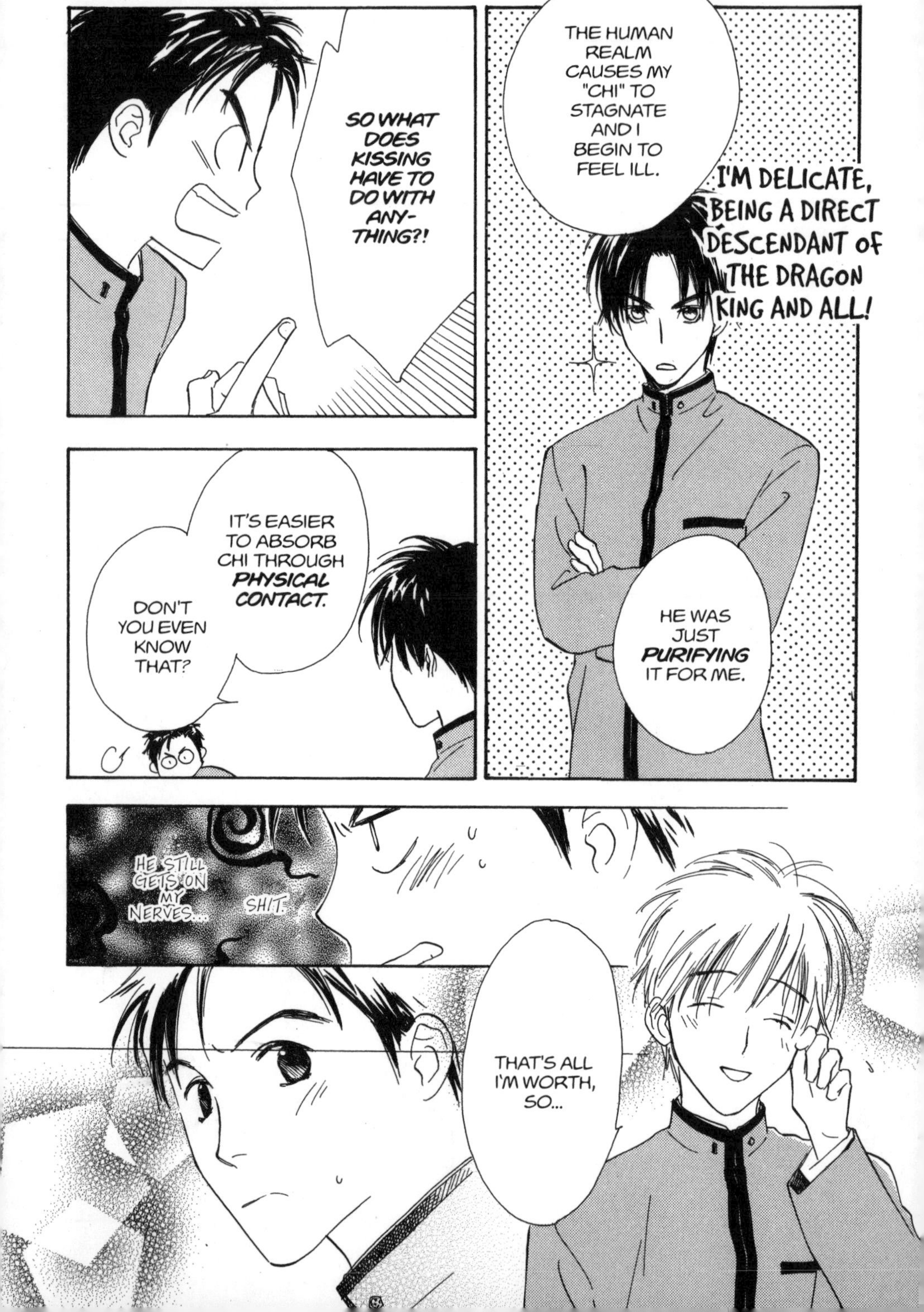
THE HUMAN REALM CAUSES MY "CHI" TO STAGNATE AND I BEGIN TO FEEL ILL.
I'M DELICATE, BEING A DIRECT DESCENDANT OF THE DRAGON KING AND ALL!
HE WAS JUST PURIFYING IT FOR ME.
SO WHAT DOES KISSING HAVE TO DO WITH ANY-THING?!
IT'S EASIER TO ABSORB CHI THROUGH PHYSICAL CONTACT.
DON'T YOU EVEN KNOW THAT?
HE STILL GETS ON MY NERVES...
SHIT.
THAT'S ALL I'M WORTH, SO...

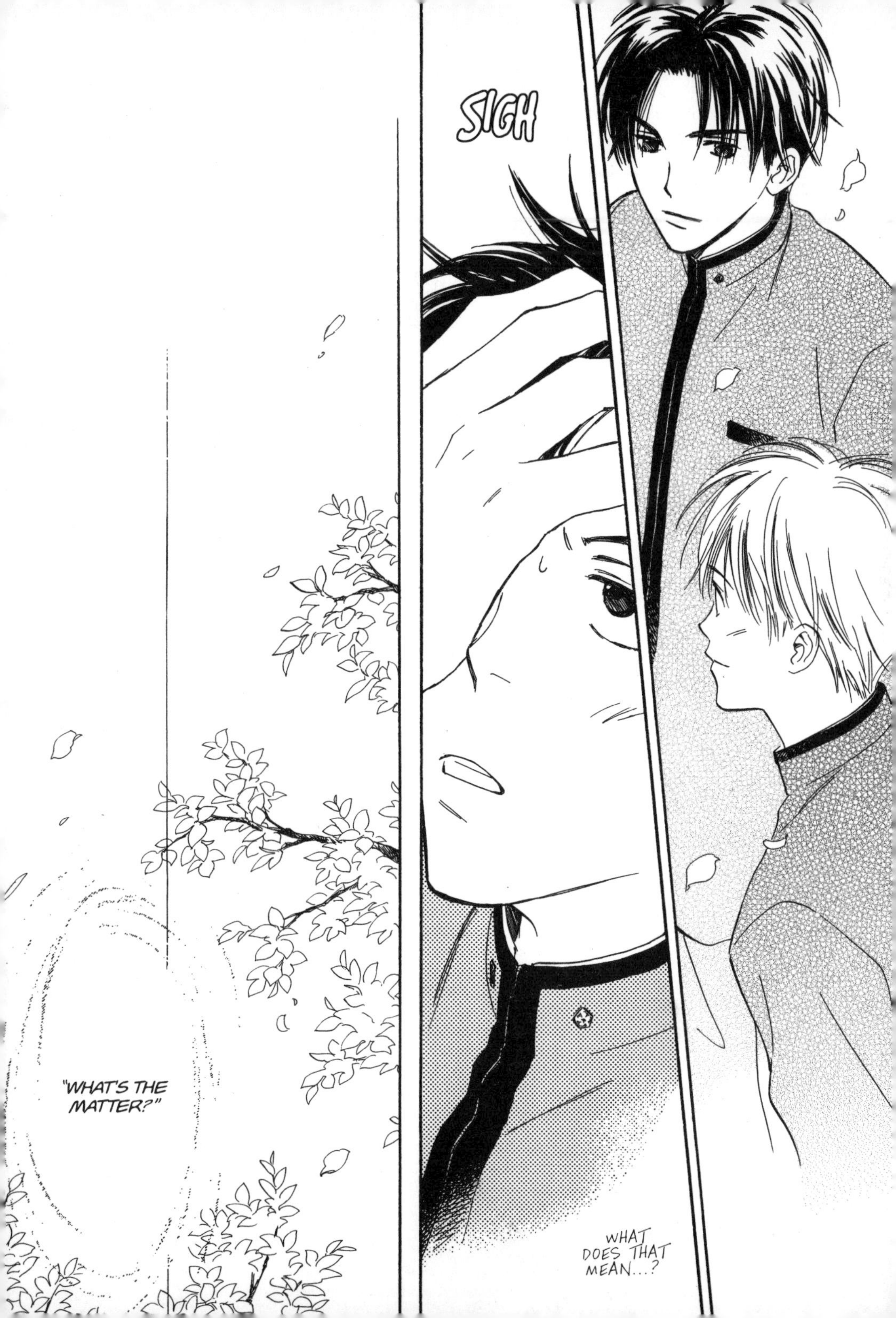
SIGH
WHAT DOES THAT MEAN...?
"WHAT'S THE MATTER?"

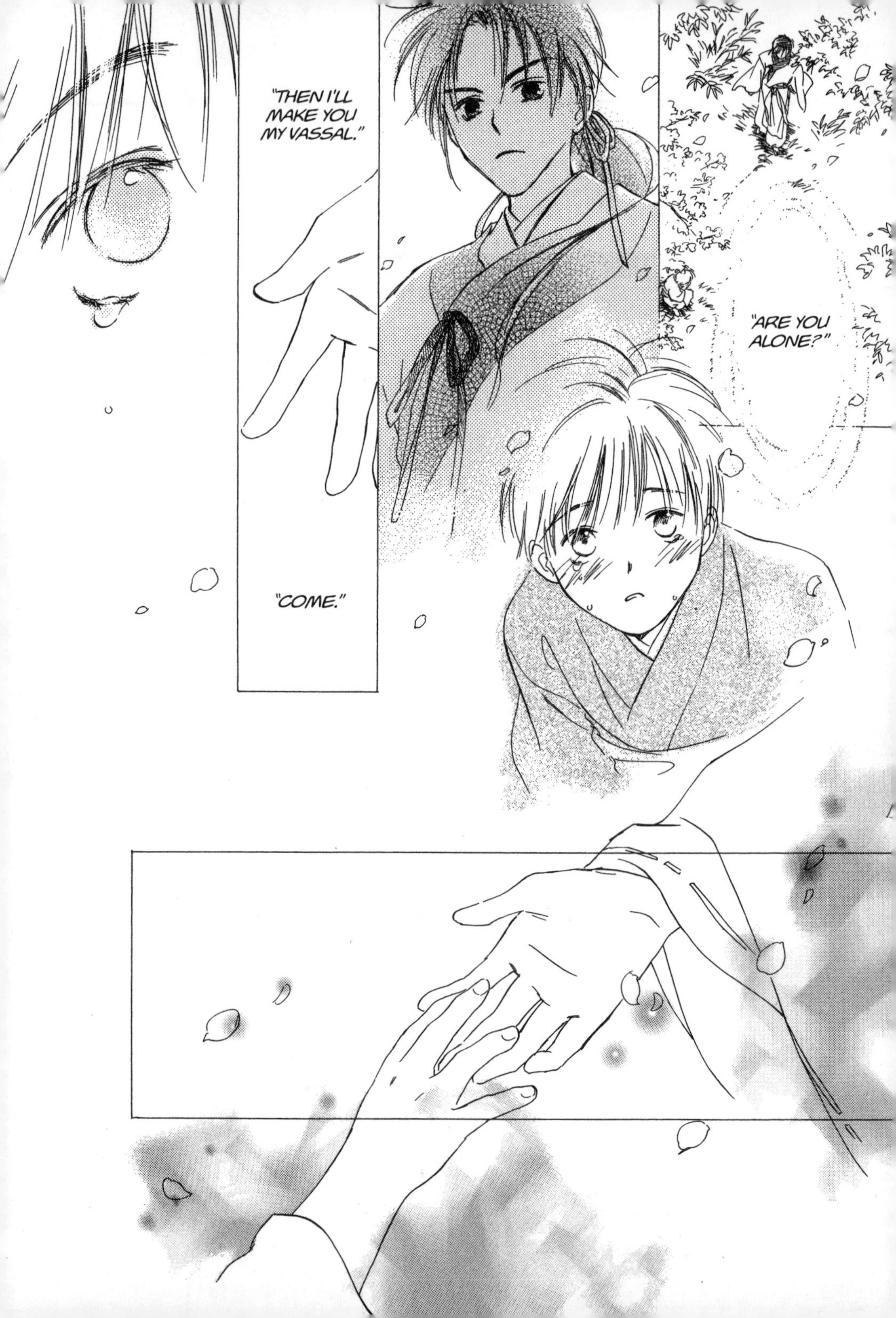
"ARE YOU ALONE?"
"THEN I'LL MAKE YOU MY VASSAL."
"COME."

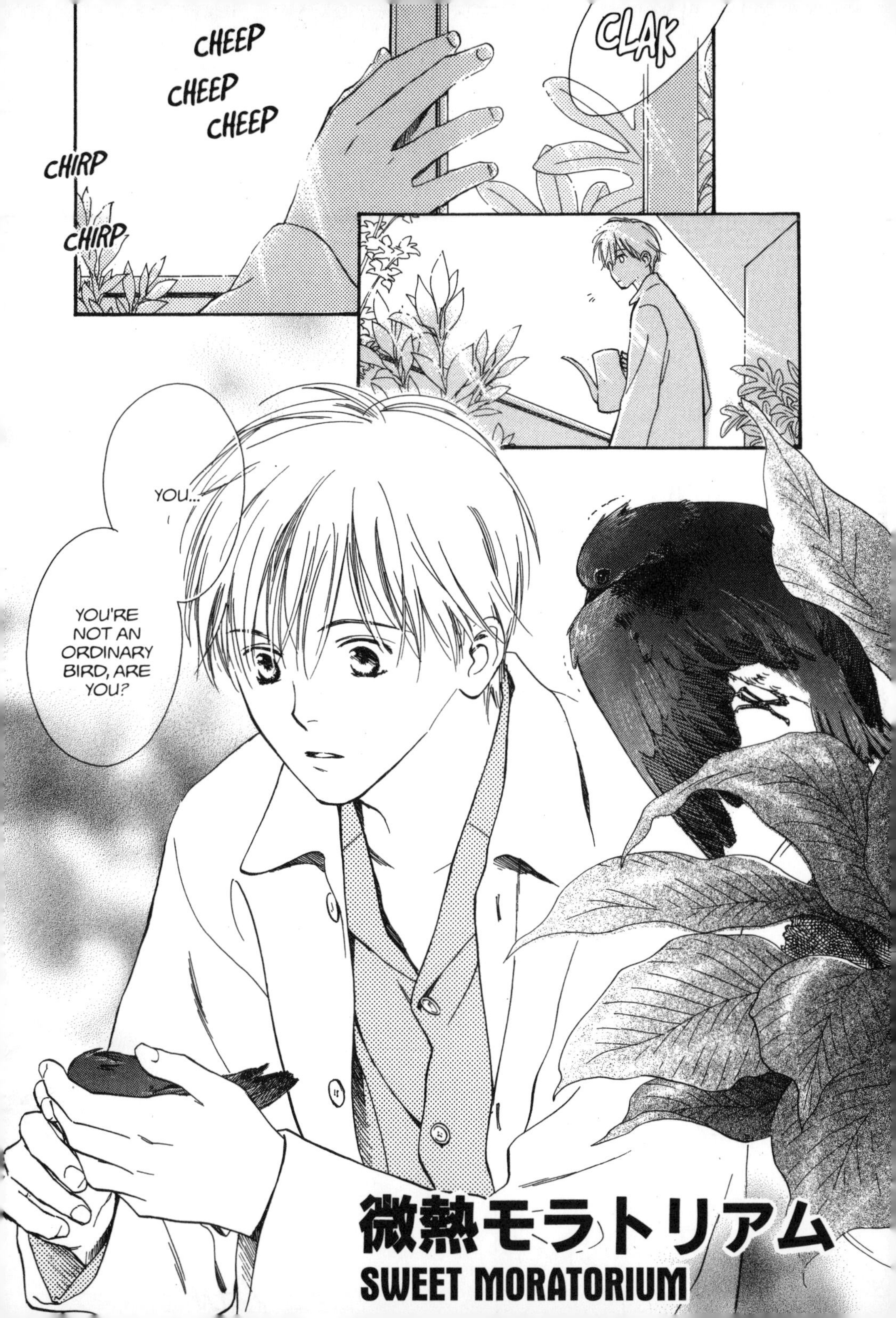
CLAK
CHEEP
CHEEP
CHEEP
CHIRP
CHIRP
YOU...
YOU'RE NOT AN ORDINARY BIRD, ARE YOU?
微熱モラトリアム
SWEET MORATORIUM

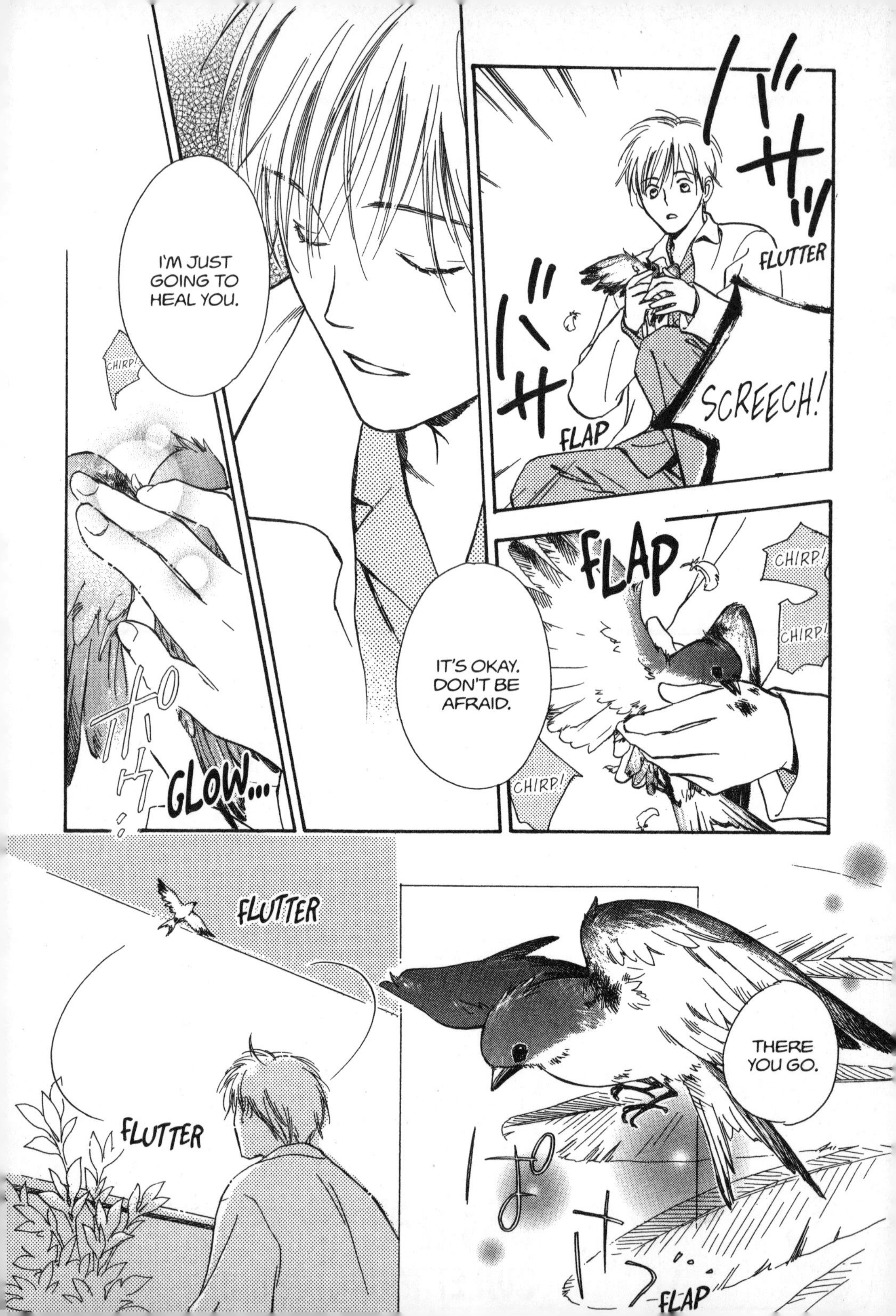
FLUTTER
SCREECH!
FLAP
FLAP
CHIRP!
CHIRP!
IT'S OKAY. DON'T BE AFRAID.
CHIRP!
I'M JUST GOING TO HEAL YOU.
CHIRP!
GLOW...
THERE YOU GO.
FLAP
FLUTTER
FLUTTER

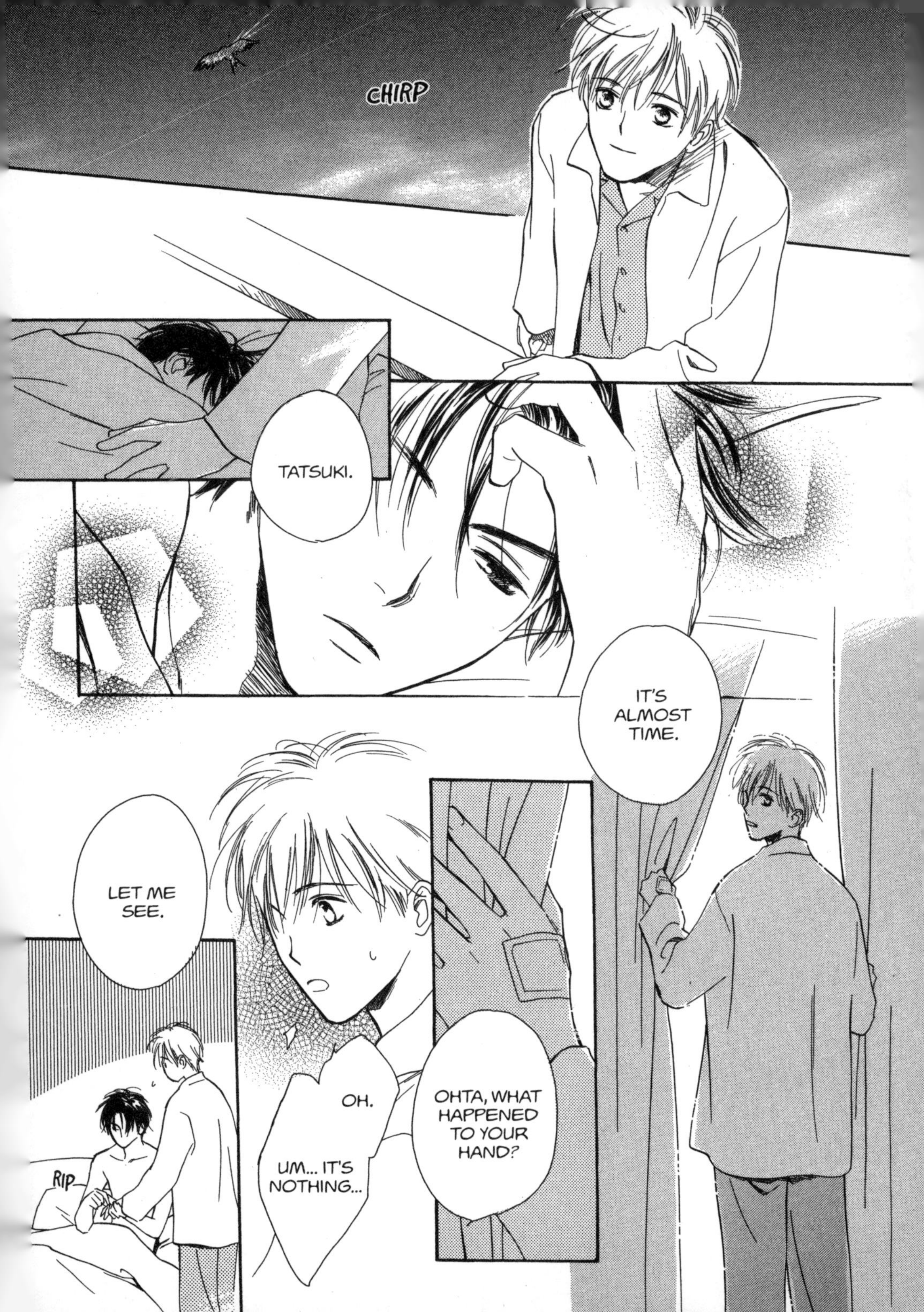
CHIRP
TATSUKI.
IT'S ALMOST TIME.
OHTA, WHAT HAPPENED TO YOUR HAND?
OH.
UM... IT'S NOTHING...
LET ME SEE.
RIP

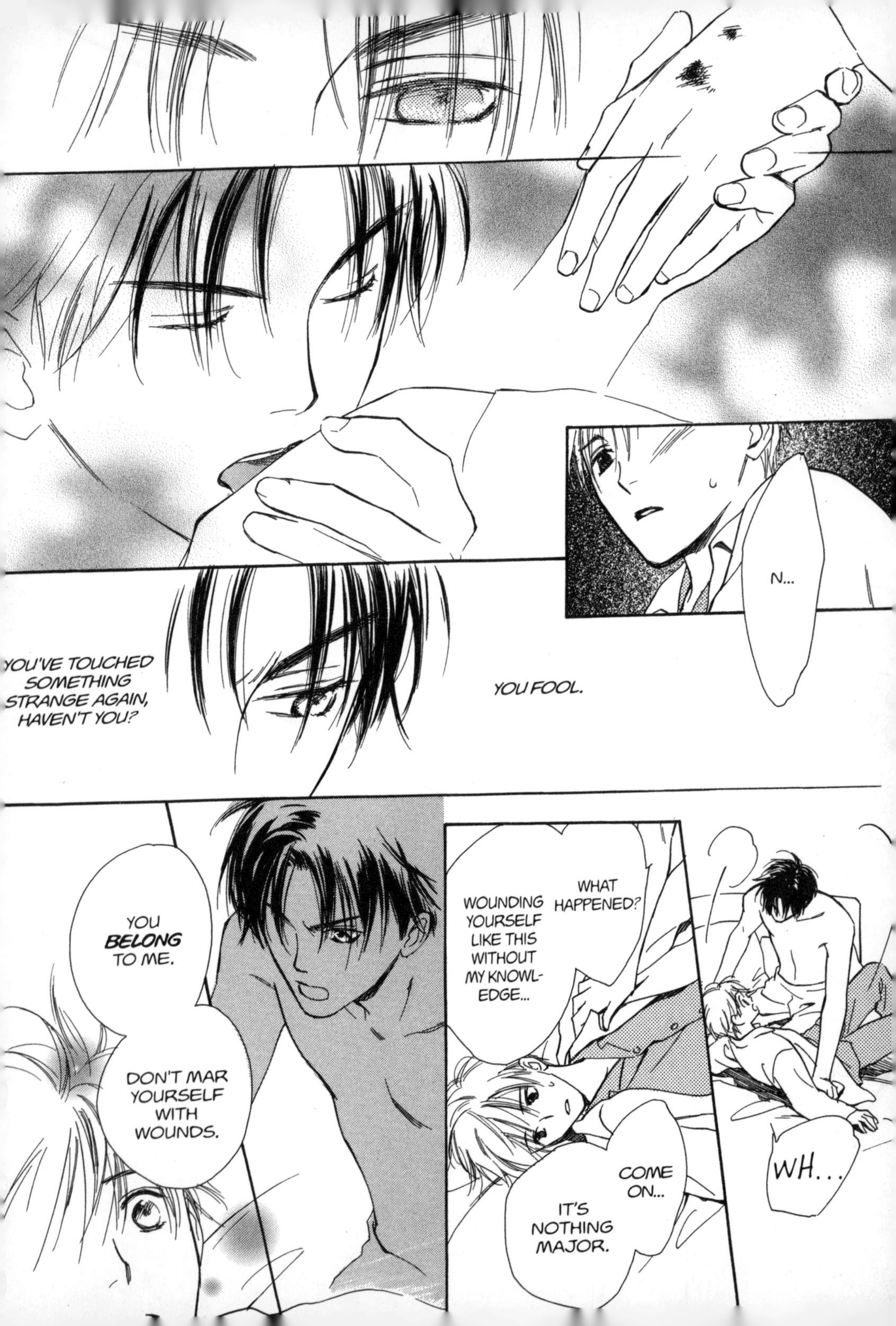
N...
YOU FOOL.
YOU'VE TOUCHED SOMETHING STRANGE AGAIN, HAVEN'T YOU?
WH...
WHAT HAPPENED?
WOUNDING YOURSELF LIKE THIS WITHOUT MY KNOWL-EDGE...
COME ON...
IT'S NOTHING MAJOR.
YOU **BELONG** TO ME.
DON'T MAR YOURSELF WITH WOUNDS.

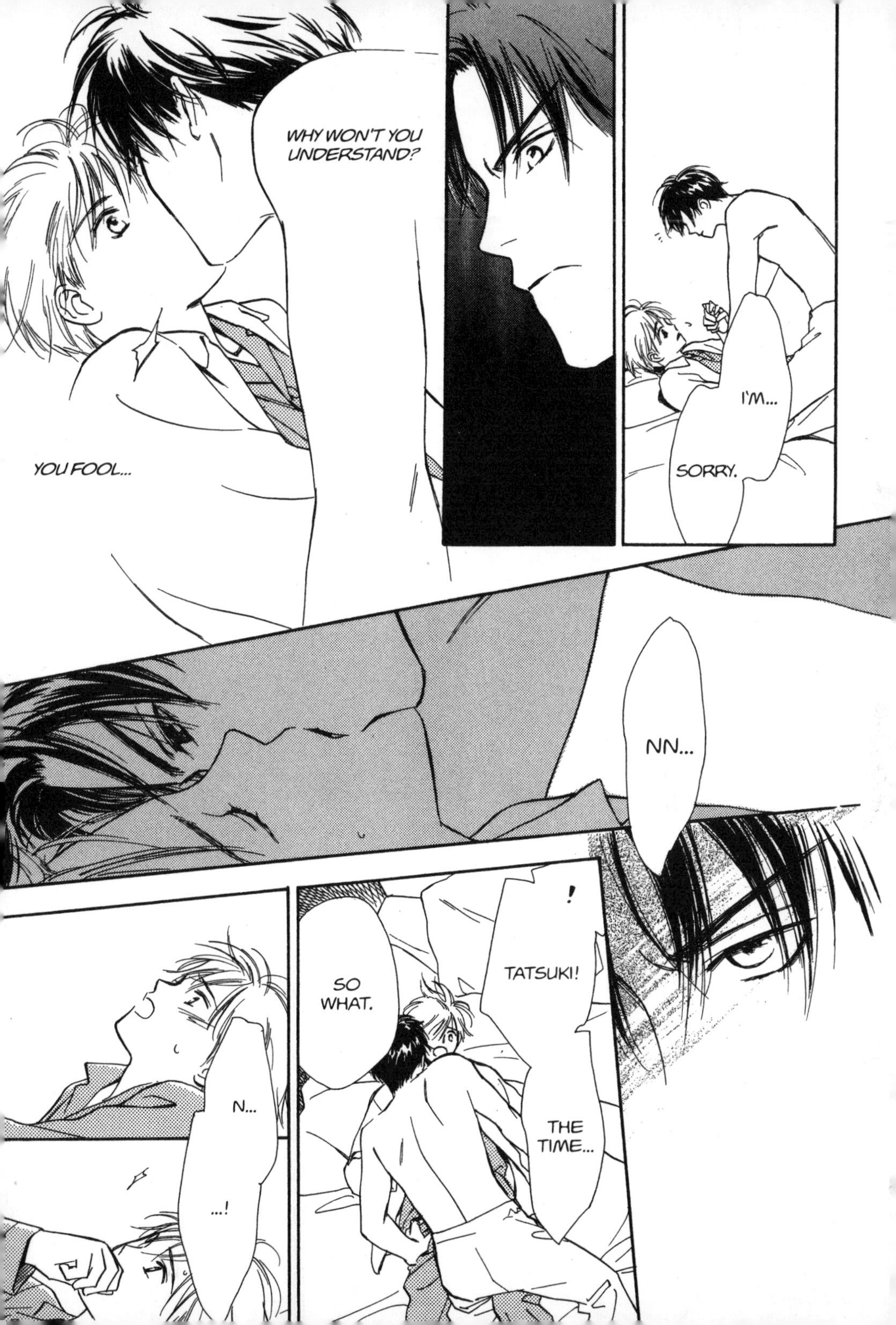
I'M...
SORRY.
WHY WON'T YOU UNDERSTAND?
YOU FOOL...
NN...
!
TATSUKI!
THE TIME...
SO WHAT.
N...
...!

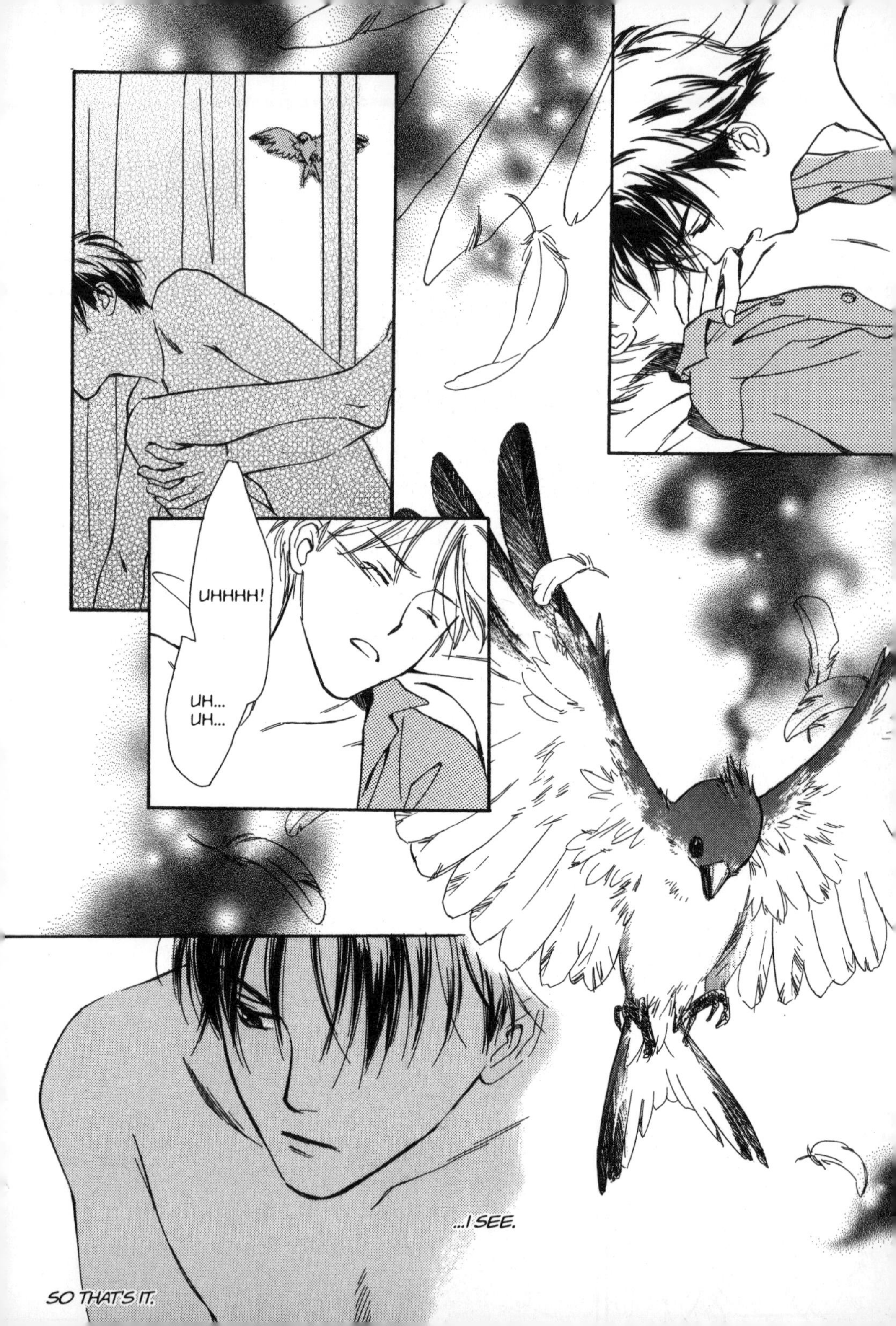
UHHHH!
UH... UH...
...I SEE.
SO THAT'S IT.

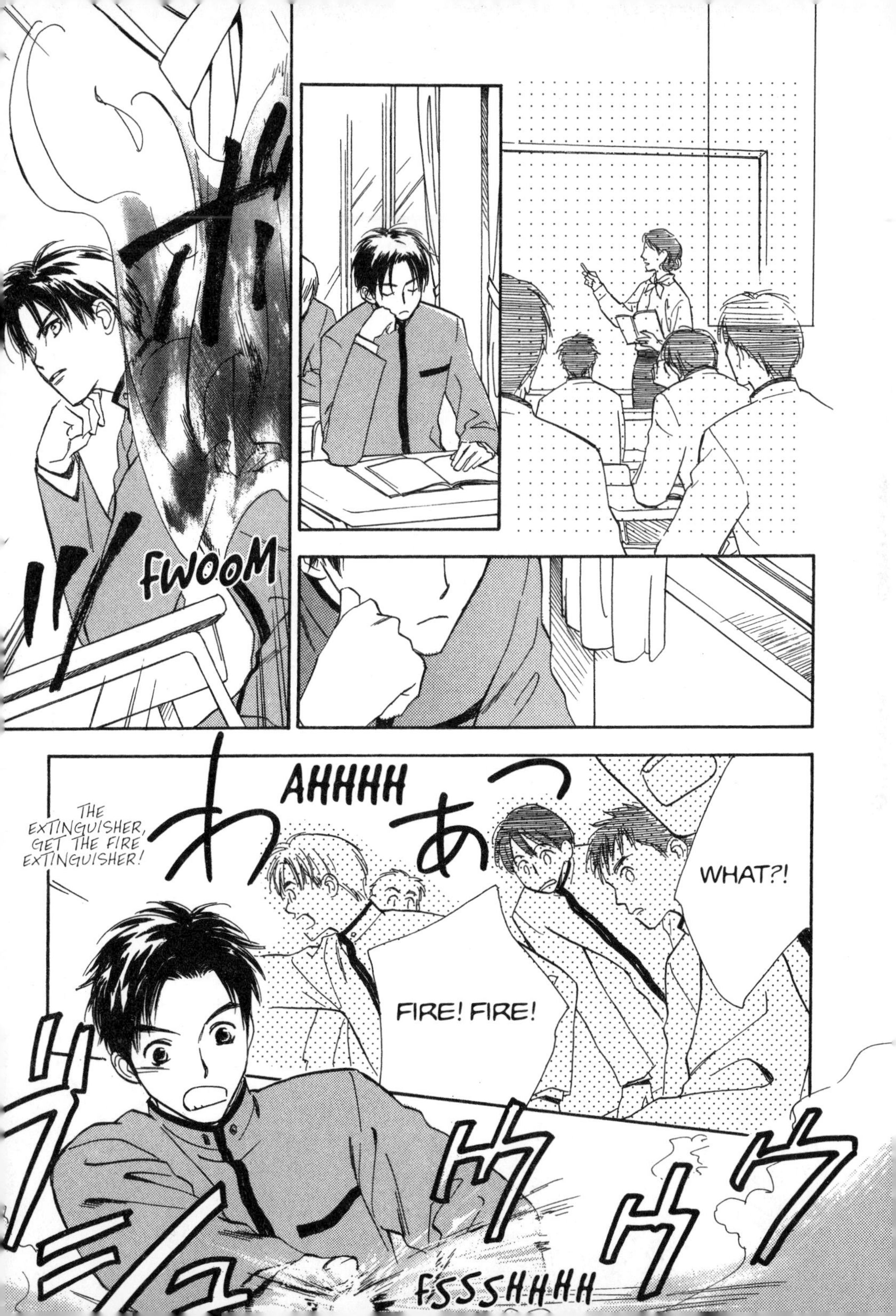
FWOOM
WHAT?!
FIRE! FIRE!
わあっ
AHHHH
THE EXTINGUISHER, GET THE FIRE EXTINGUISHER!
FSSSHHHH

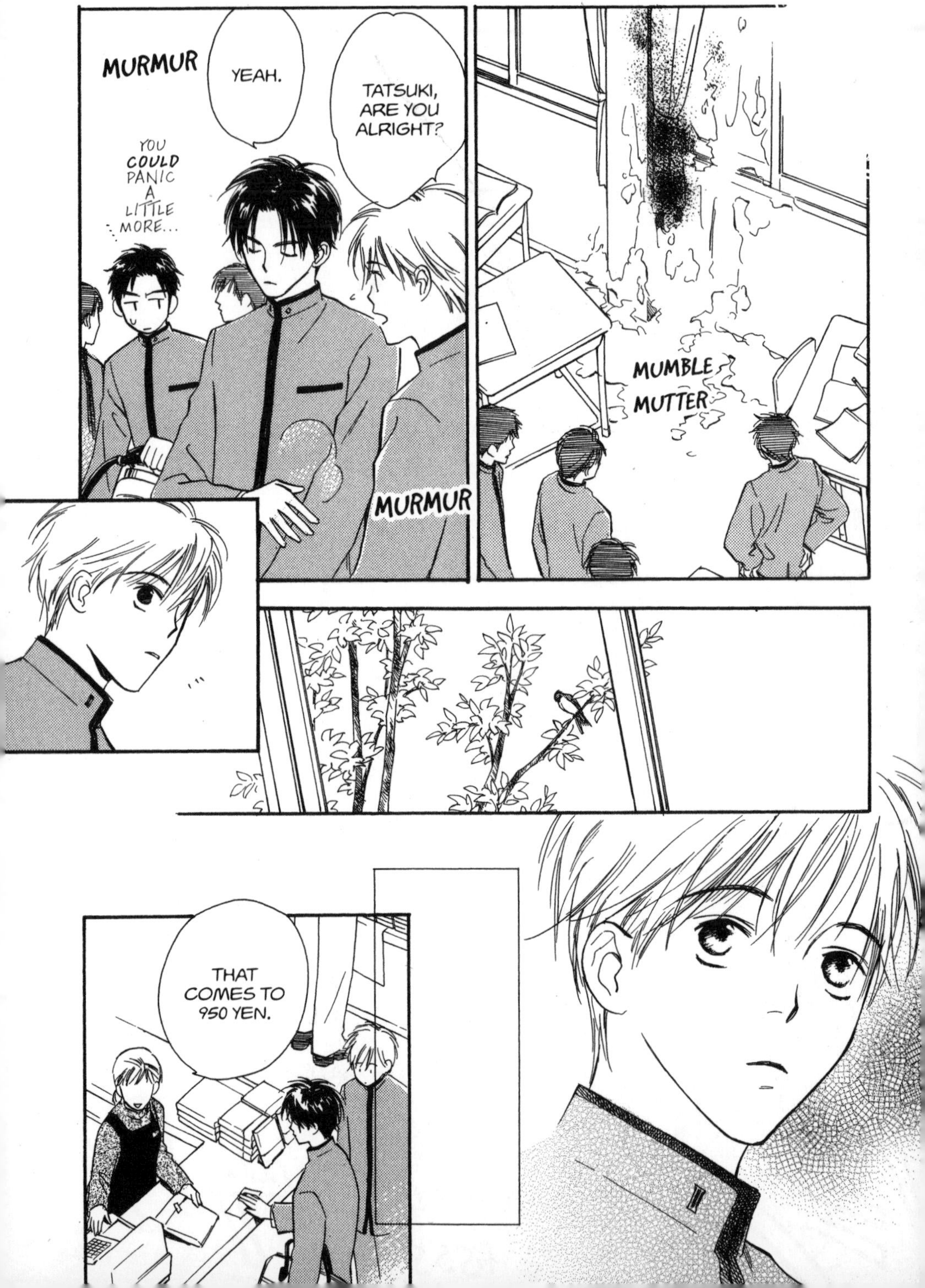
MUMBLE
MUTTER
TATSUKI, ARE YOU ALRIGHT?
YEAH.
MURMUR
YOU COULD PANIC A LITTLE MORE...
MURMUR
THAT COMES TO 950 YEN.

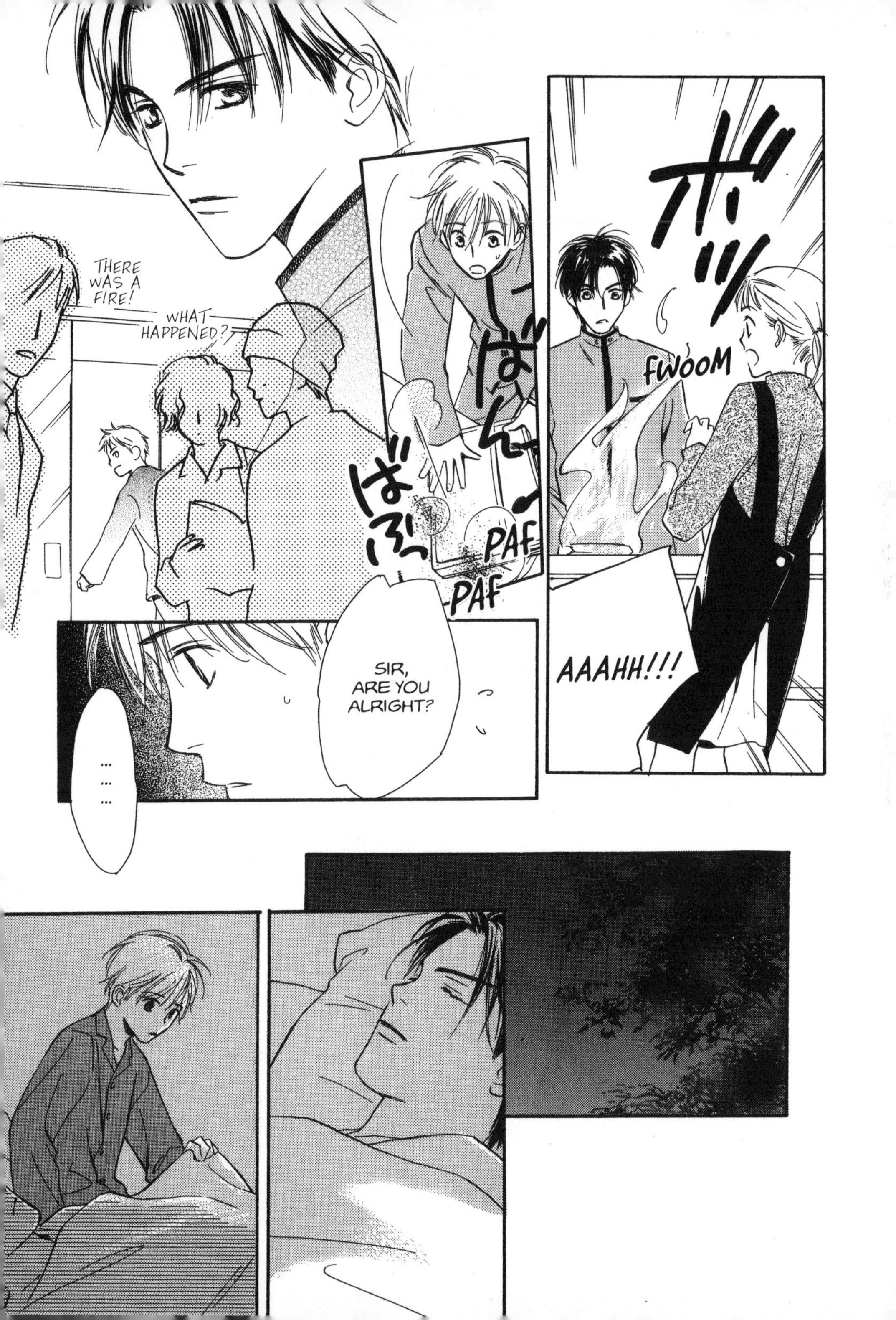
ボッ
FWOOM
AAAHH!!!
ばんっ
ばふっ
PAF
PAF
THERE WAS A FIRE!
WHAT HAPPENED?
SIR, ARE YOU ALRIGHT?
....

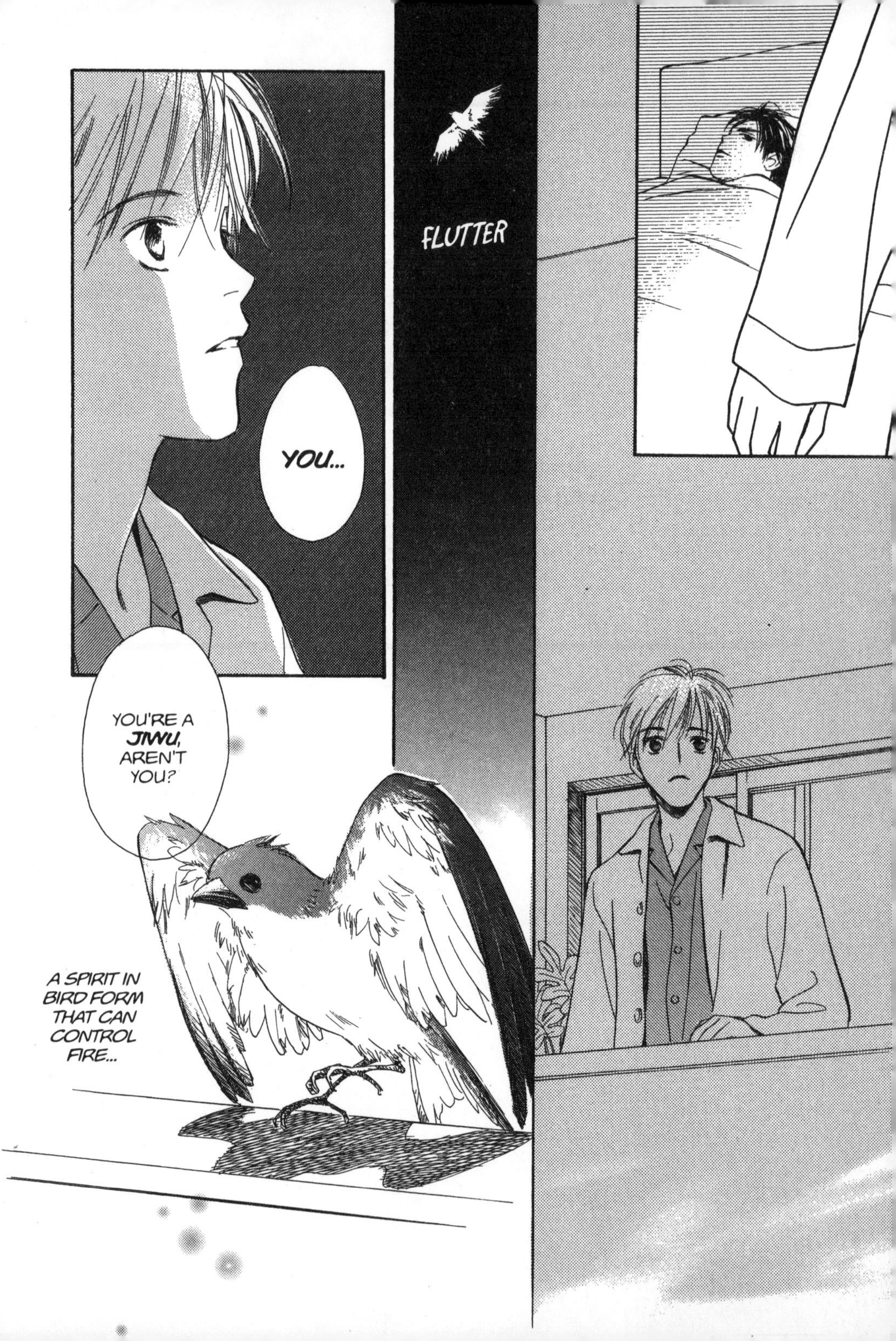
FLUTTER
YOU...
YOU'RE A JINWU, AREN'T YOU?
A SPIRIT IN BIRD FORM THAT CAN CONTROL FIRE...

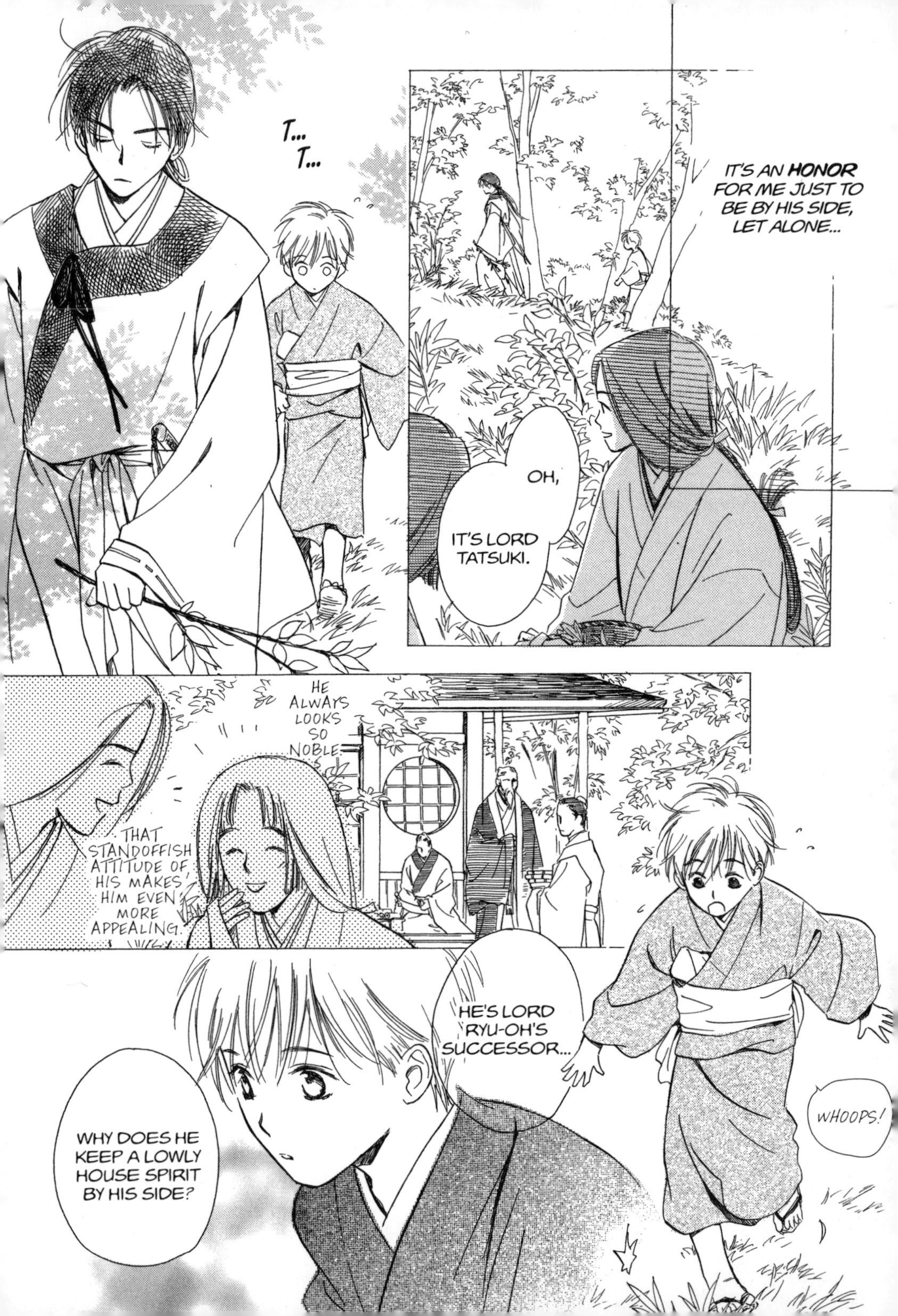
IT'S AN **HONOR** FOR ME JUST TO BE BY HIS SIDE, LET ALONE...
OH,
IT'S LORD TATSUKI.
T... T...
HE ALWAYS LOOKS SO NOBLE.
THAT STANDOFFISH ATTITUDE OF HIS MAKES HIM EVEN MORE APPEALING.
WHOOPS!
HE'S LORD RYU-OH'S SUCCESSOR...
WHY DOES HE KEEP A LOWLY HOUSE SPIRIT BY HIS SIDE?

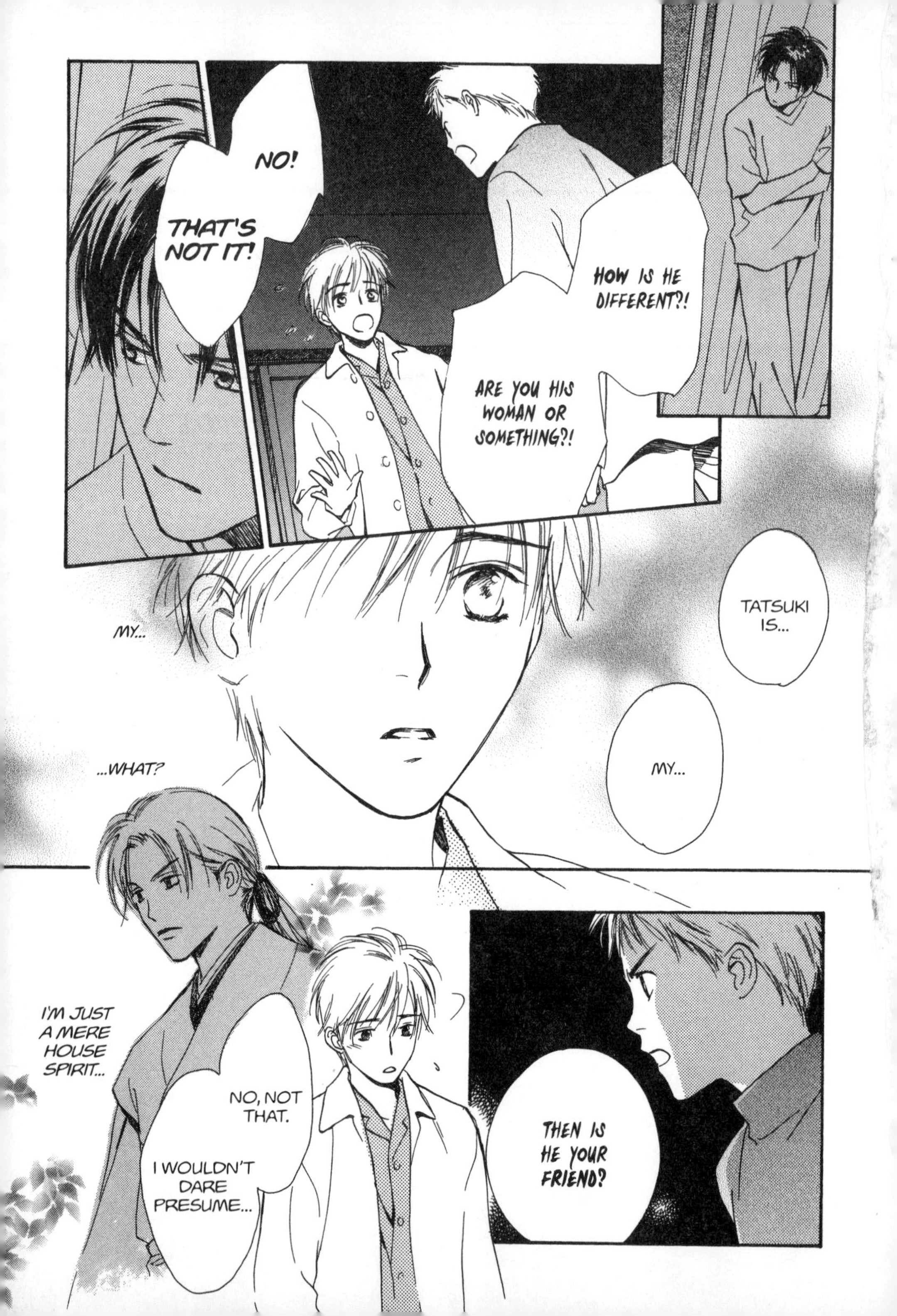
HOW IS HE DIFFERENT?!
ARE YOU HIS WOMAN OR SOMETHING?!
NO!
THAT'S NOT IT!
TATSUKI IS...
MY...
MY...
...WHAT?
THEN IS HE YOUR FRIEND?
NO, NOT THAT.
I WOULDN'T DARE PRESUME...
I'M JUST A MERE HOUSE SPIRIT...

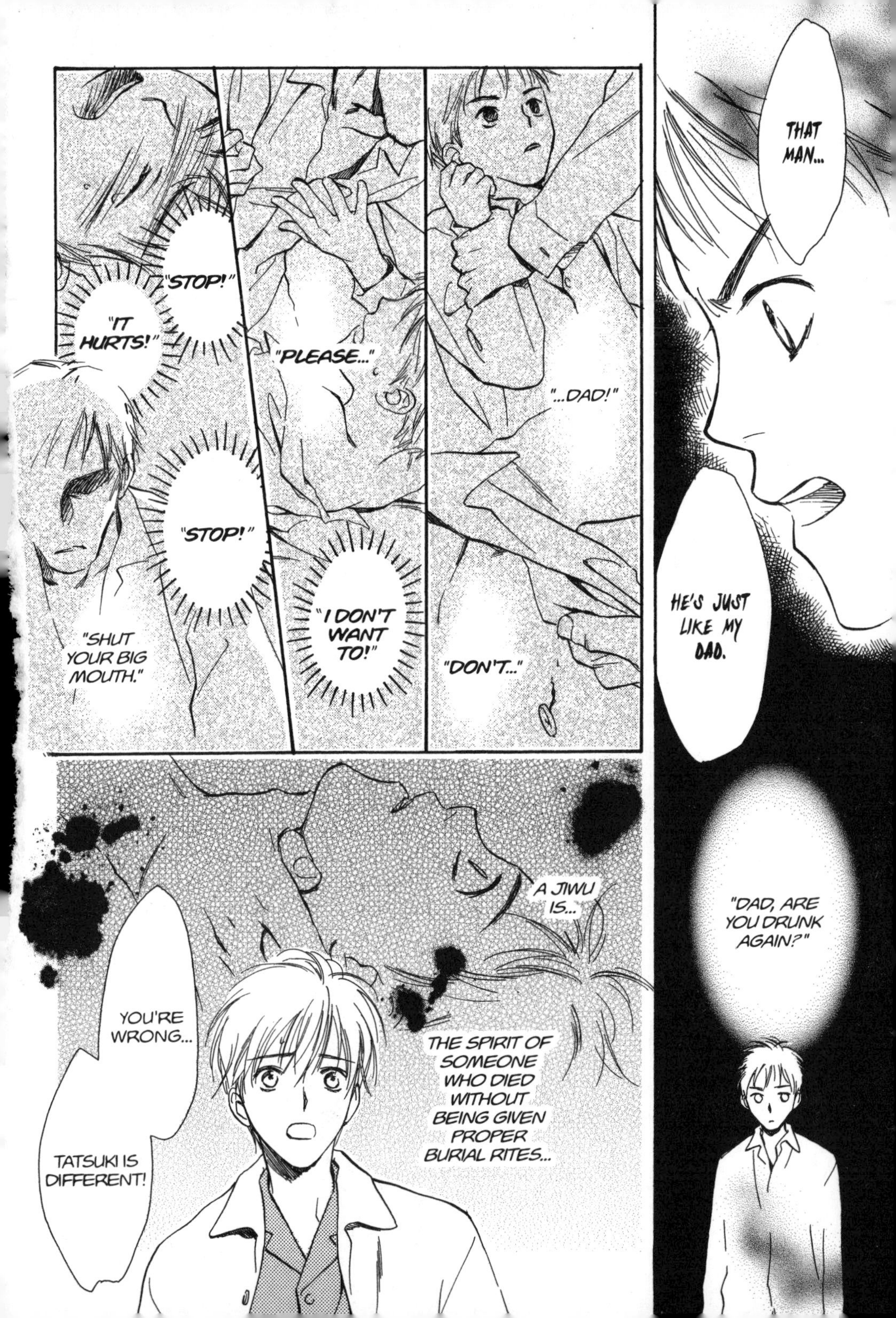
THAT MAN...
HE'S JUST LIKE MY DAD.
"DAD, ARE YOU DRUNK AGAIN?"
"...DAD!"
"DON'T..."
"PLEASE..."
"I DON'T WANT TO!"
"STOP!"
"IT HURTS!"
"STOP!"
"SHUT YOUR BIG MOUTH."
A JIWU IS...
THE SPIRIT OF SOMEONE WHO DIED WITHOUT BEING GIVEN PROPER BURIAL RITES...
YOU'RE WRONG...
TATSUKI IS DIFFERENT!

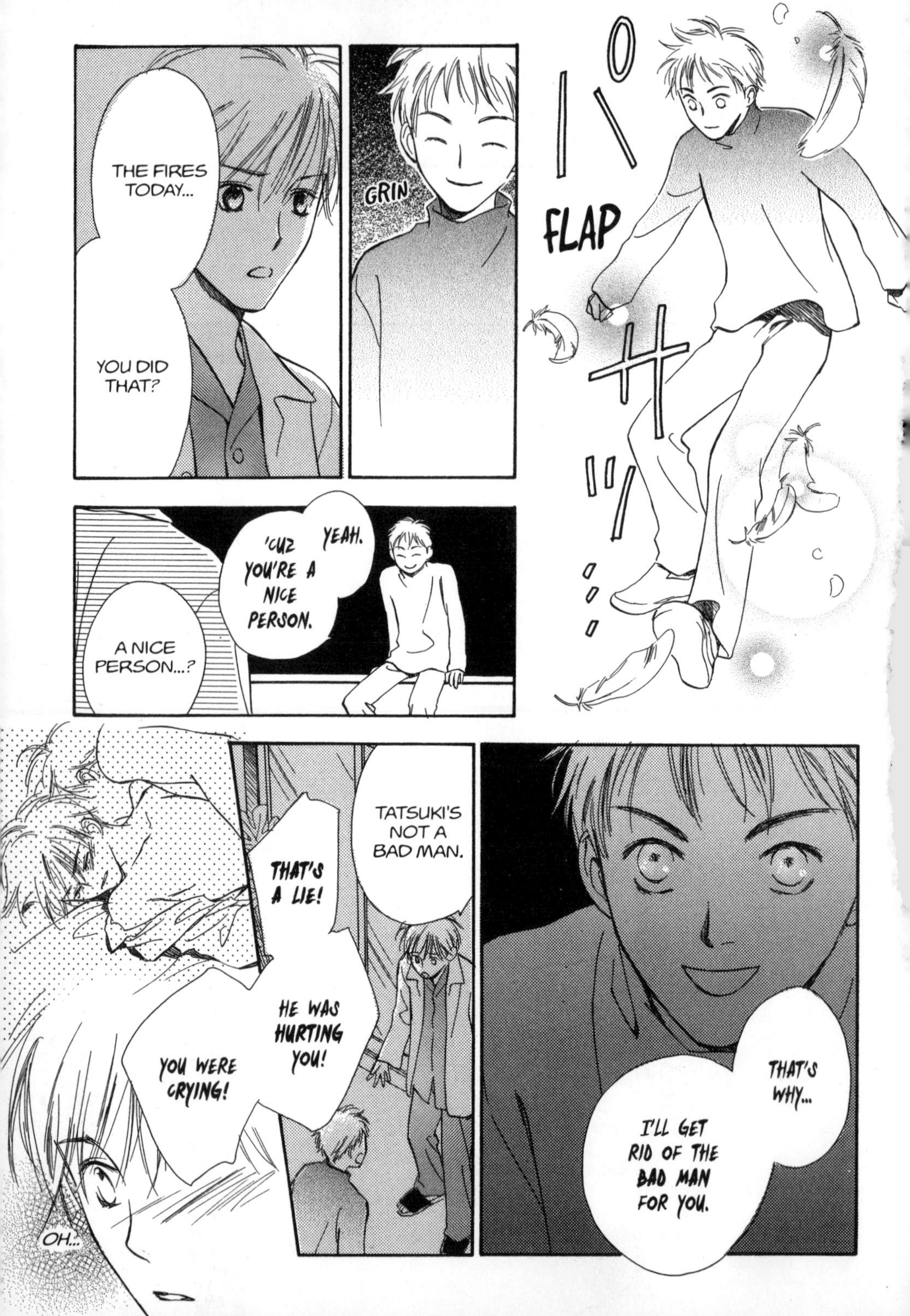
FLAP
GRIN
THE FIRES TODAY...
YOU DID THAT?
YEAH.
'CUZ YOU'RE A NICE PERSON.
A NICE PERSON...?
THAT'S WHY...
I'LL GET RID OF THE BAD MAN FOR YOU.
TATSUKI'S NOT A BAD MAN.
THAT'S A LIE!
HE WAS HURTING YOU!
YOU WERE CRYING!
OH...

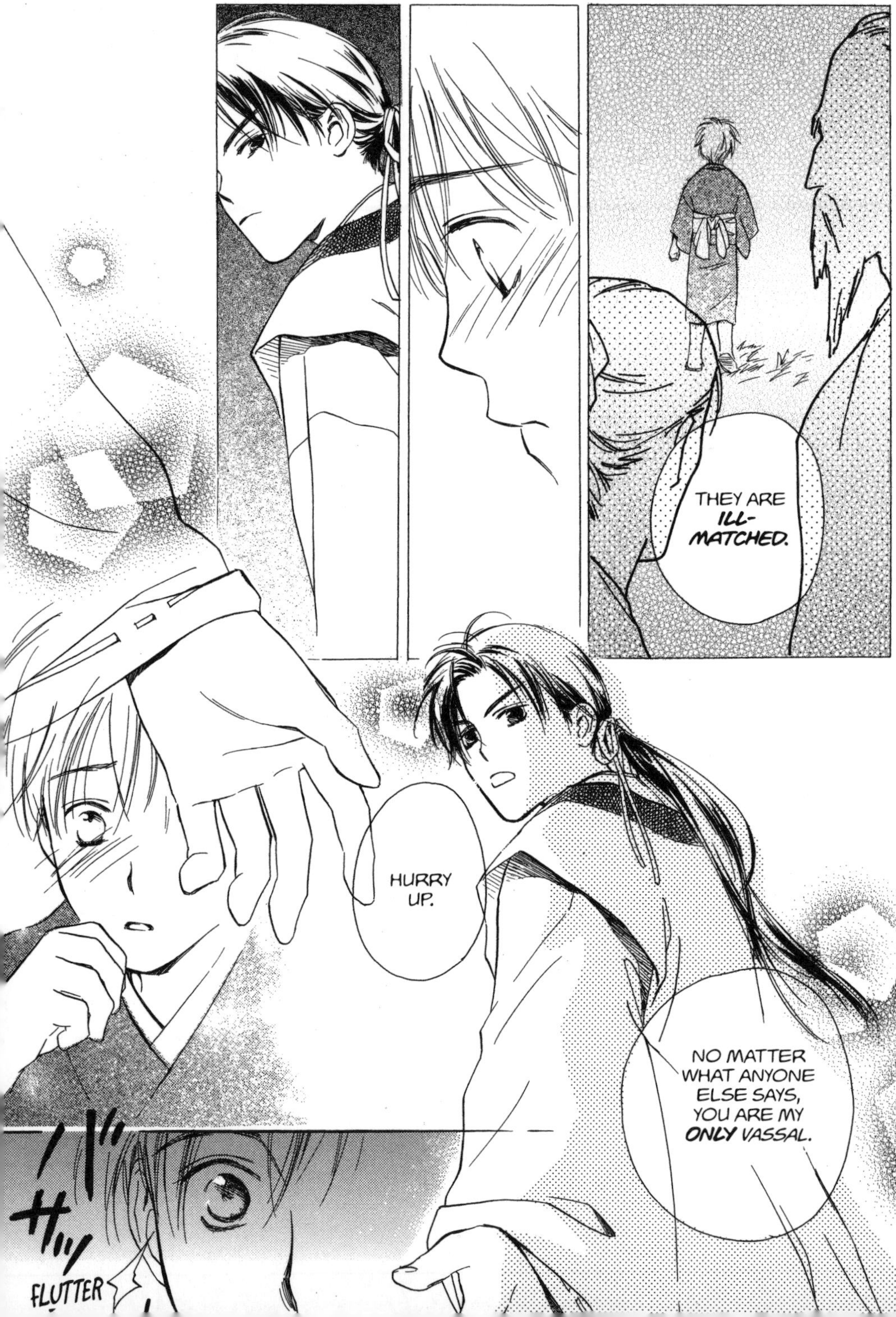
THEY ARE ILL-MATCHED.
HURRY UP.
NO MATTER WHAT ANYONE ELSE SAYS, YOU ARE MY ONLY VASSAL.
FLUTTER

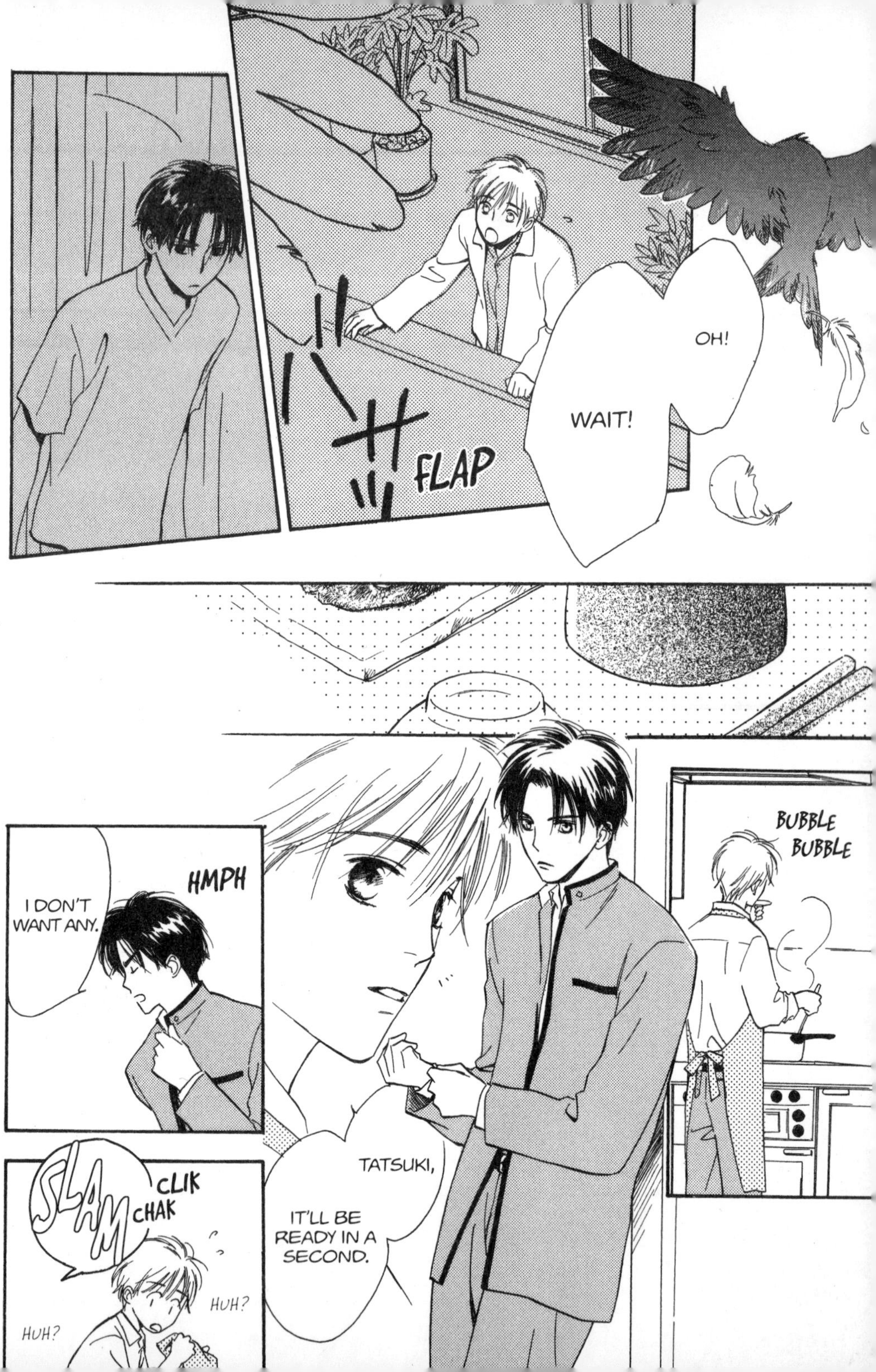

OH!
WAIT!
FLAP
BUBBLE BUBBLE
TATSUKI,
IT'LL BE READY IN A SECOND.
I DON'T WANT ANY.
HMPH
SLAM
CLIK CHAK
HUH?
HUH?

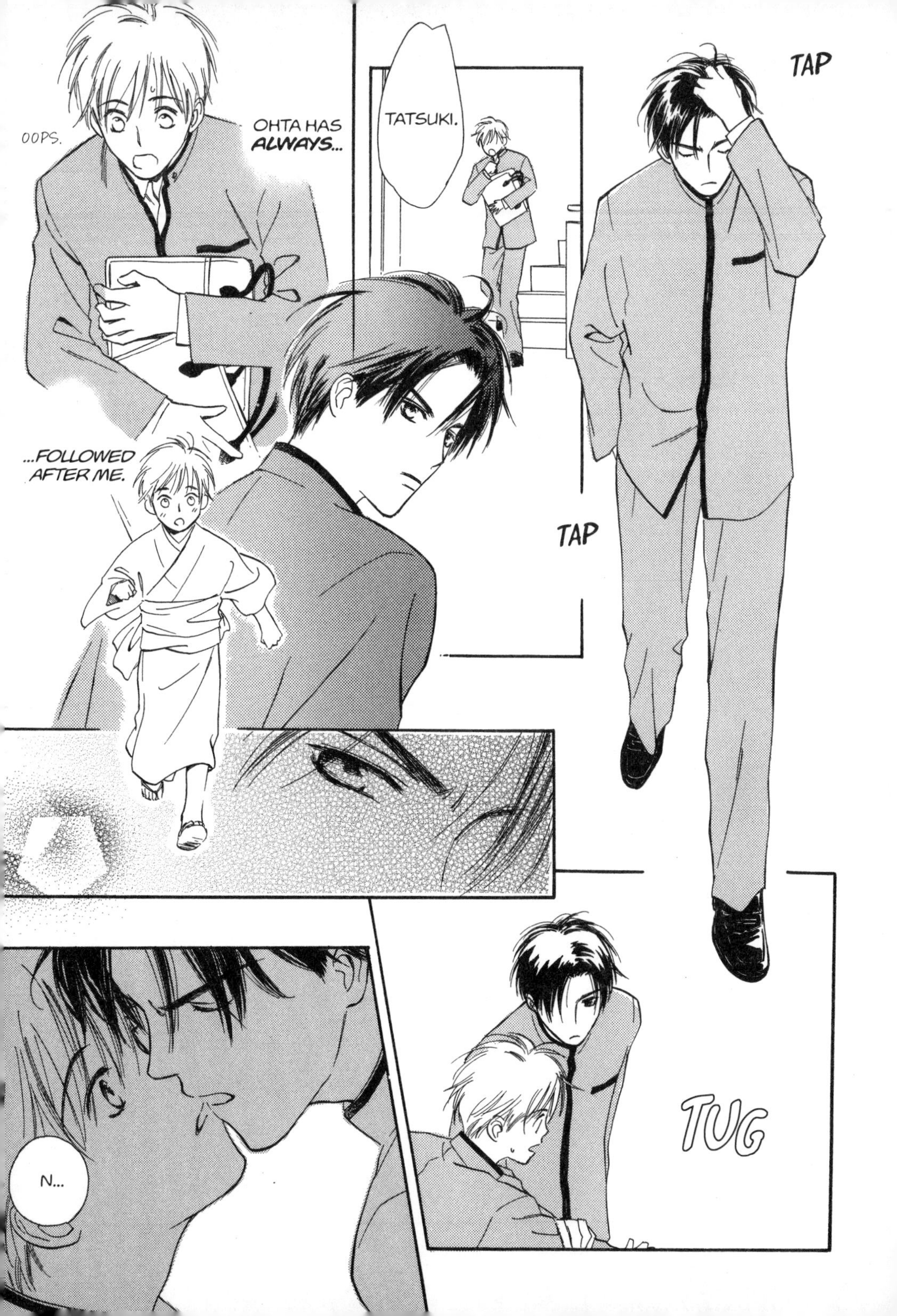
TAP
TAP
TATSUKI.
OHTA HAS ALWAYS...
OOPS.
...FOLLOWED AFTER ME.
TUG
N...

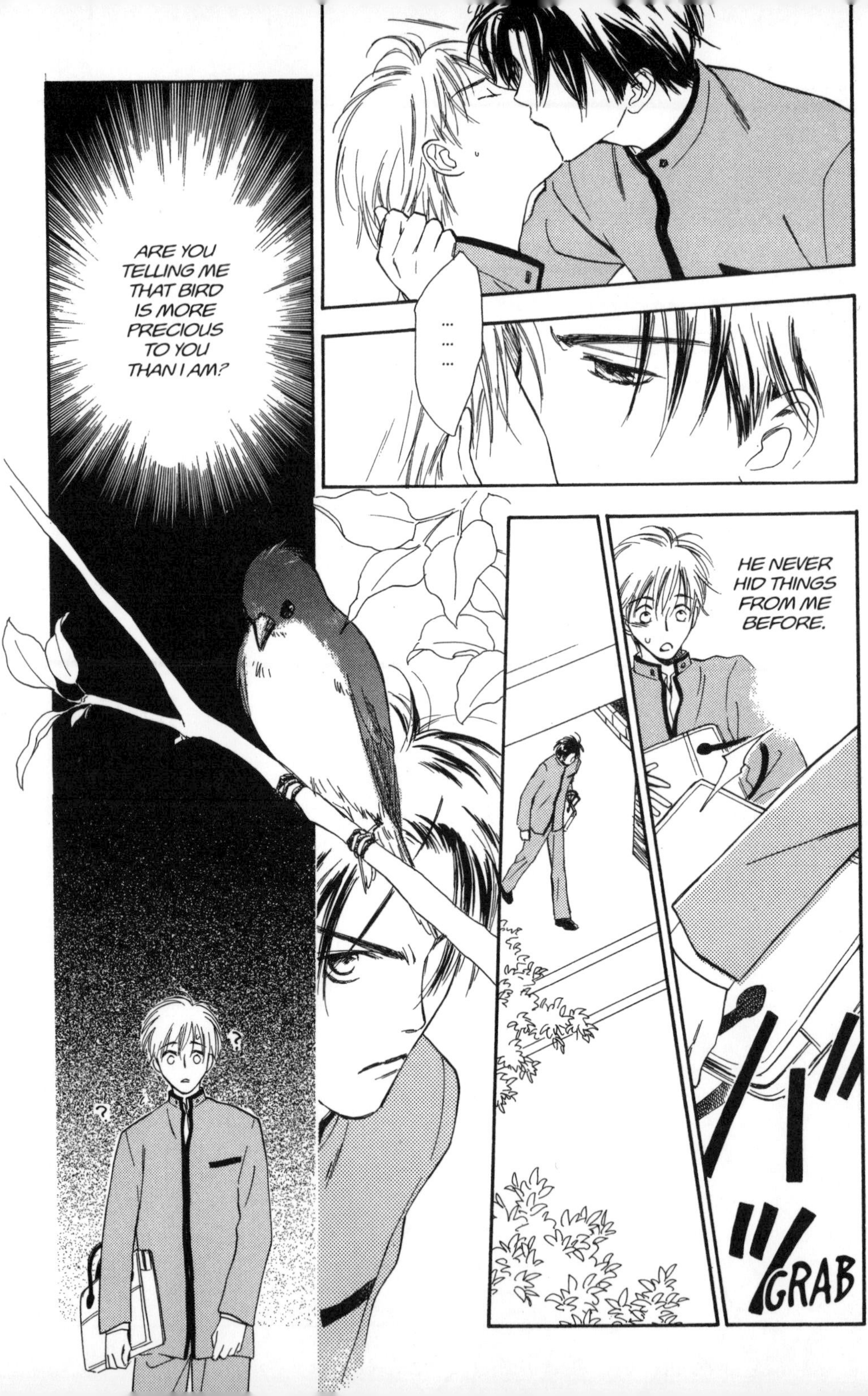
...
...
...
HE NEVER HID THINGS FROM ME BEFORE.
GRAB
ARE YOU TELLING ME THAT BIRD IS MORE PRECIOUS TO YOU THAN I AM?

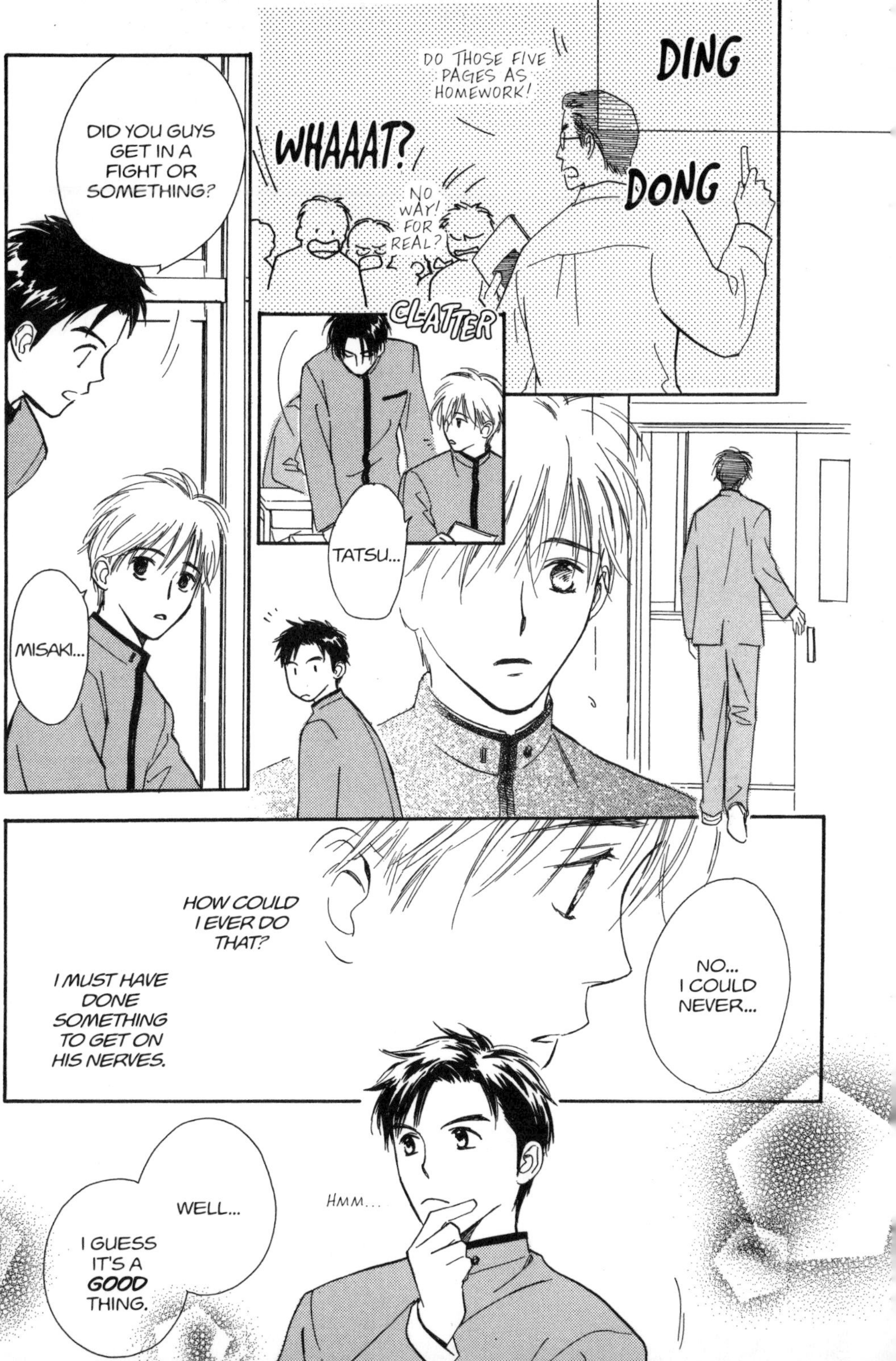
DING
DONG
DO THOSE FIVE PAGES AS HOMEWORK!
WHAAAT?
NO WAY! FOR REAL?
CLATTER
TATSU...
DID YOU GUYS GET IN A FIGHT OR SOMETHING?
MISAKI...
NO... I COULD NEVER...
HOW COULD I EVER DO THAT?
I MUST HAVE DONE SOMETHING TO GET ON HIS NERVES.
HMM...
WELL...
I GUESS IT'S A **GOOD** THING.

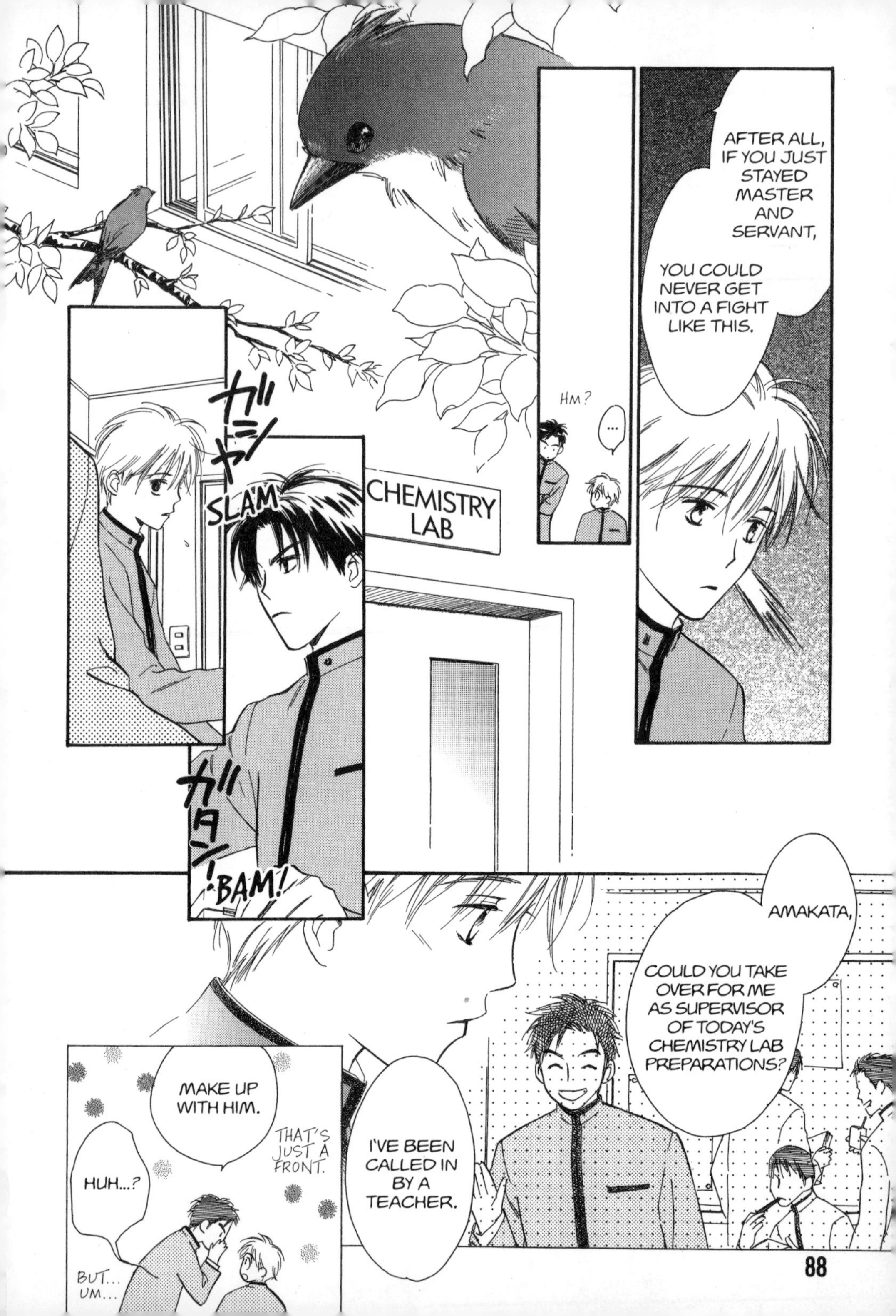

AFTER ALL, IF YOU JUST STAYED MASTER AND SERVANT,
YOU COULD NEVER GET INTO A FIGHT LIKE THIS.
HM?
...
CHEMISTRY LAB
ガシャン
SLAM
ガタン!
BAM!
AMAKATA,
COULD YOU TAKE OVER FOR ME AS SUPERVISOR OF TODAY'S CHEMISTRY LAB PREPARATIONS?
I'VE BEEN CALLED IN BY A TEACHER.
MAKE UP WITH HIM.
THAT'S JUST A FRONT.
HUH...?
BUT... UM...

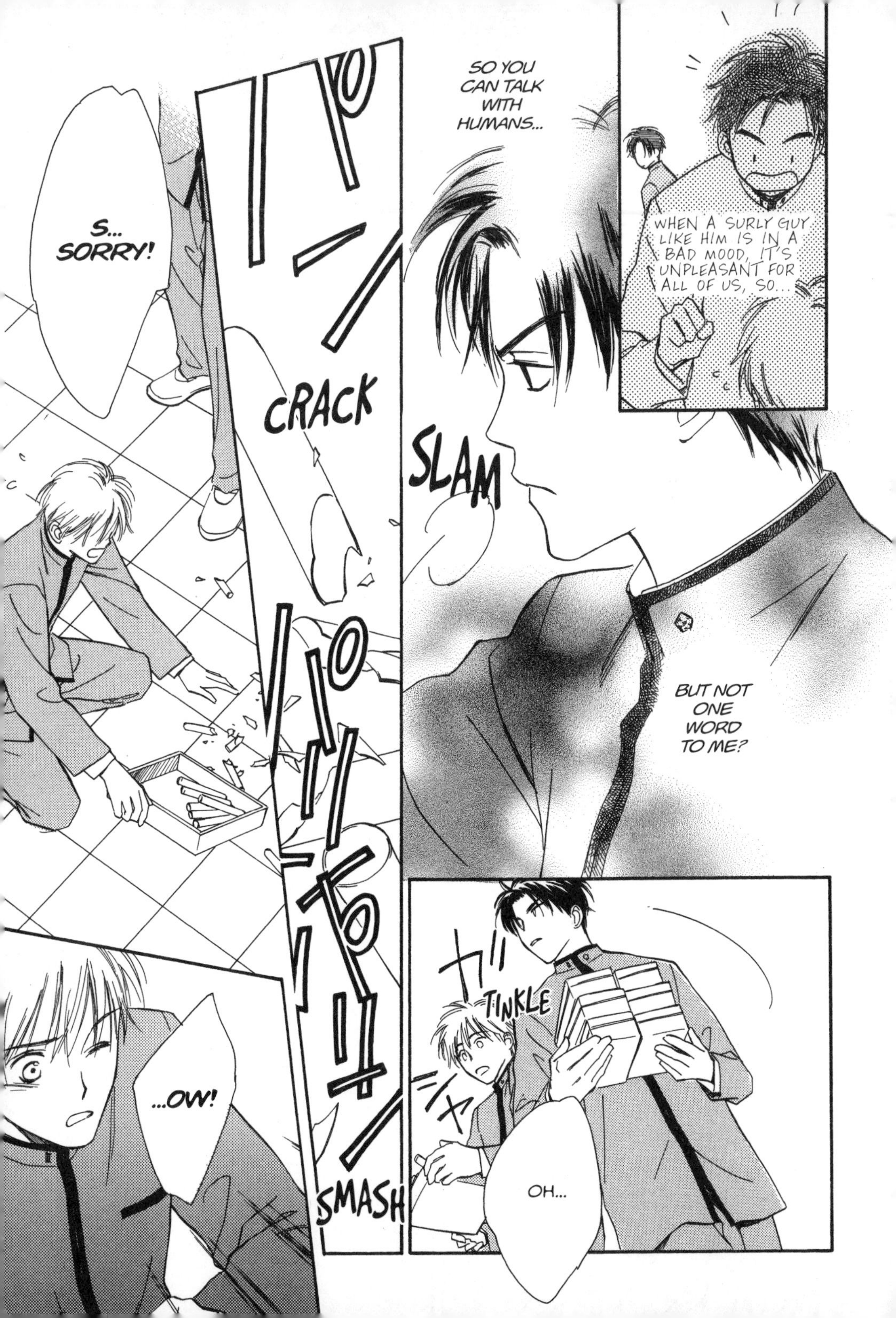
WHEN A SURLY GUY LIKE HIM IS IN A BAD MOOD, IT'S UNPLEASANT FOR ALL OF US, SO...
SO YOU CAN TALK WITH HUMANS...
BUT NOT ONE WORD TO ME?
SLAM
CRACK
SMASH
TINKLE
OH...
S... SORRY!
...OW!

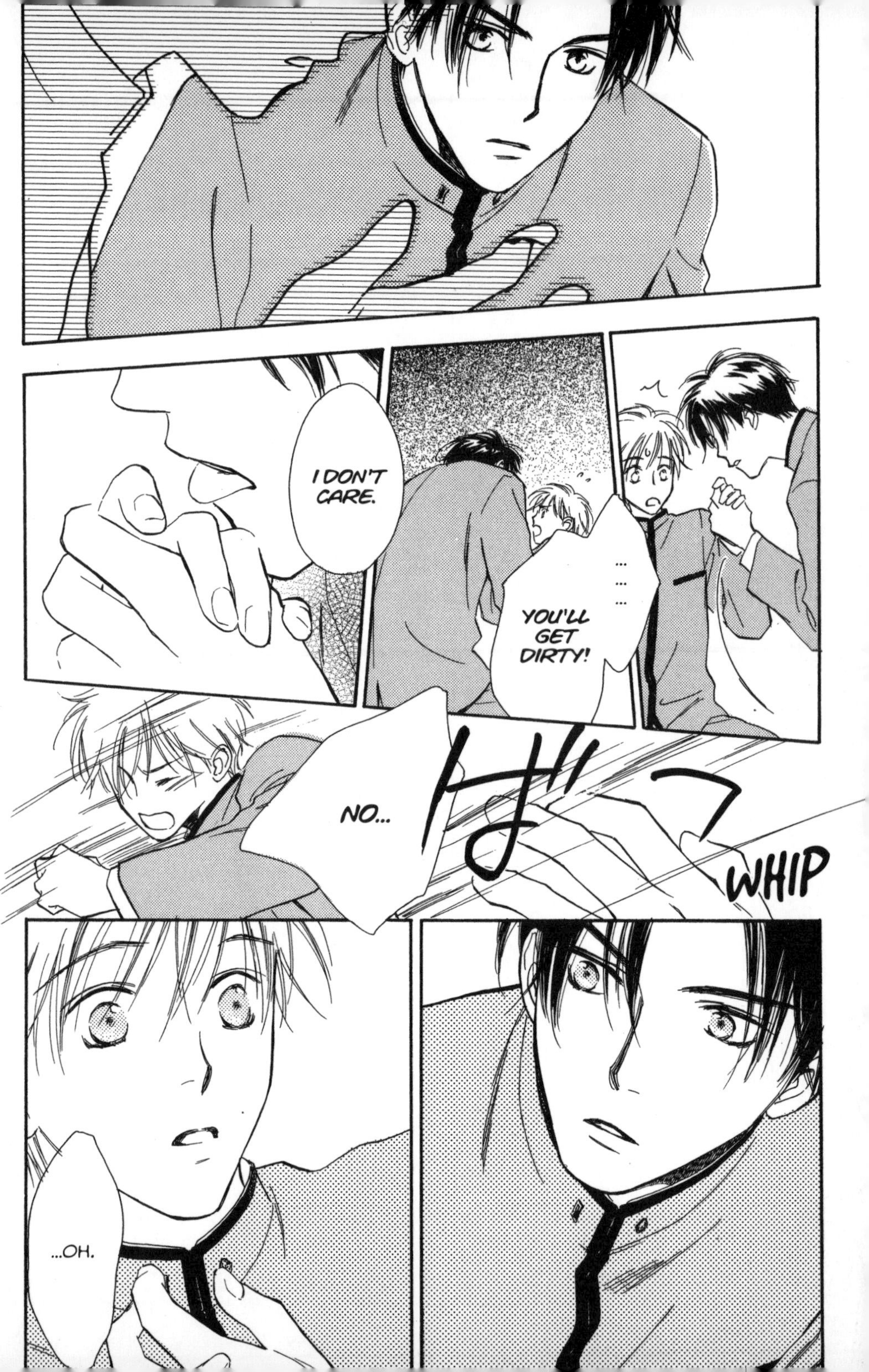

...
...
...
YOU'LL GET DIRTY!
I DON'T CARE.
NO...
ばっ
WHIP
...OH.

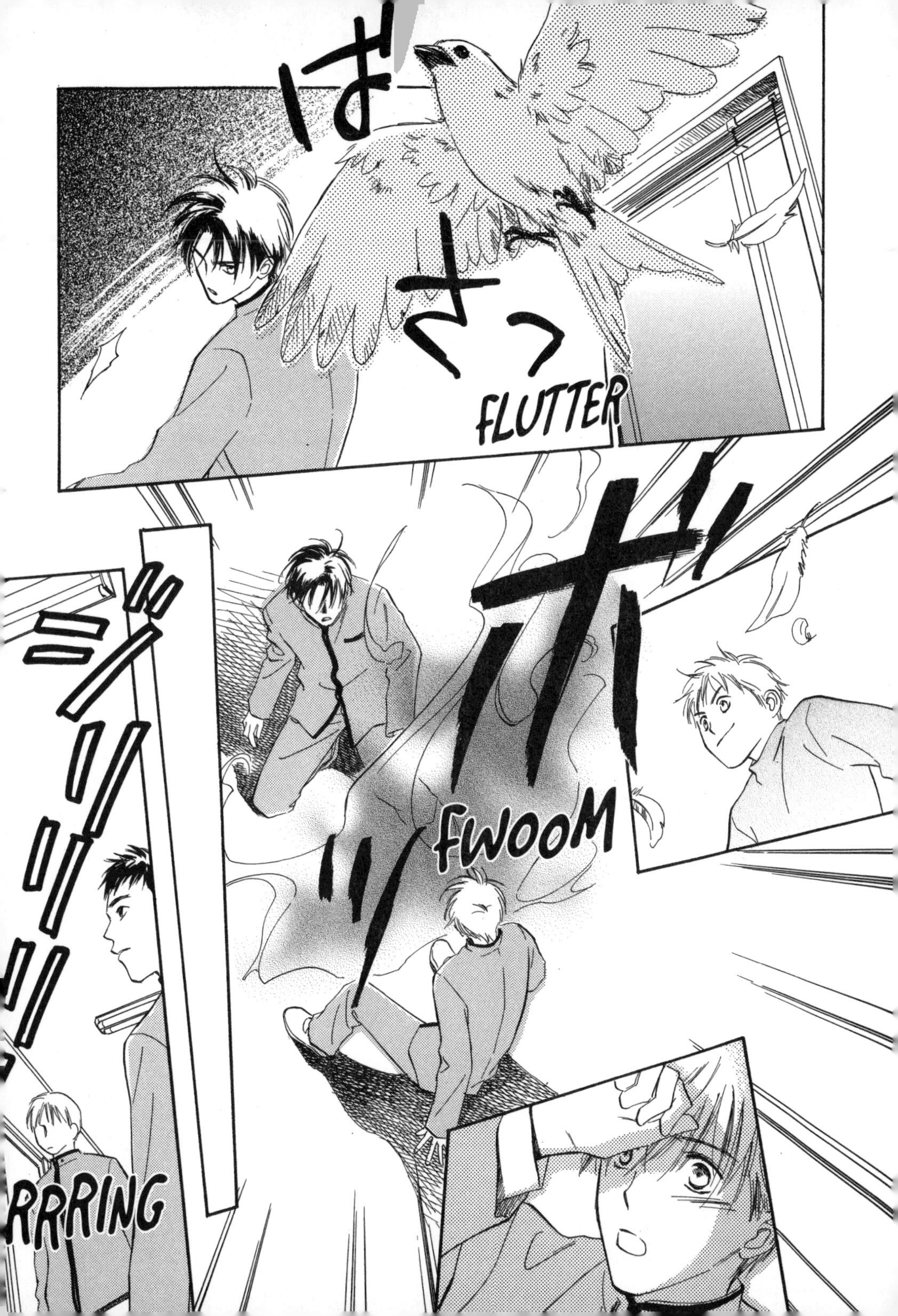
ばさっ
FLUTTER
ガッ
FWOOM
ジリリリリ
RRRING

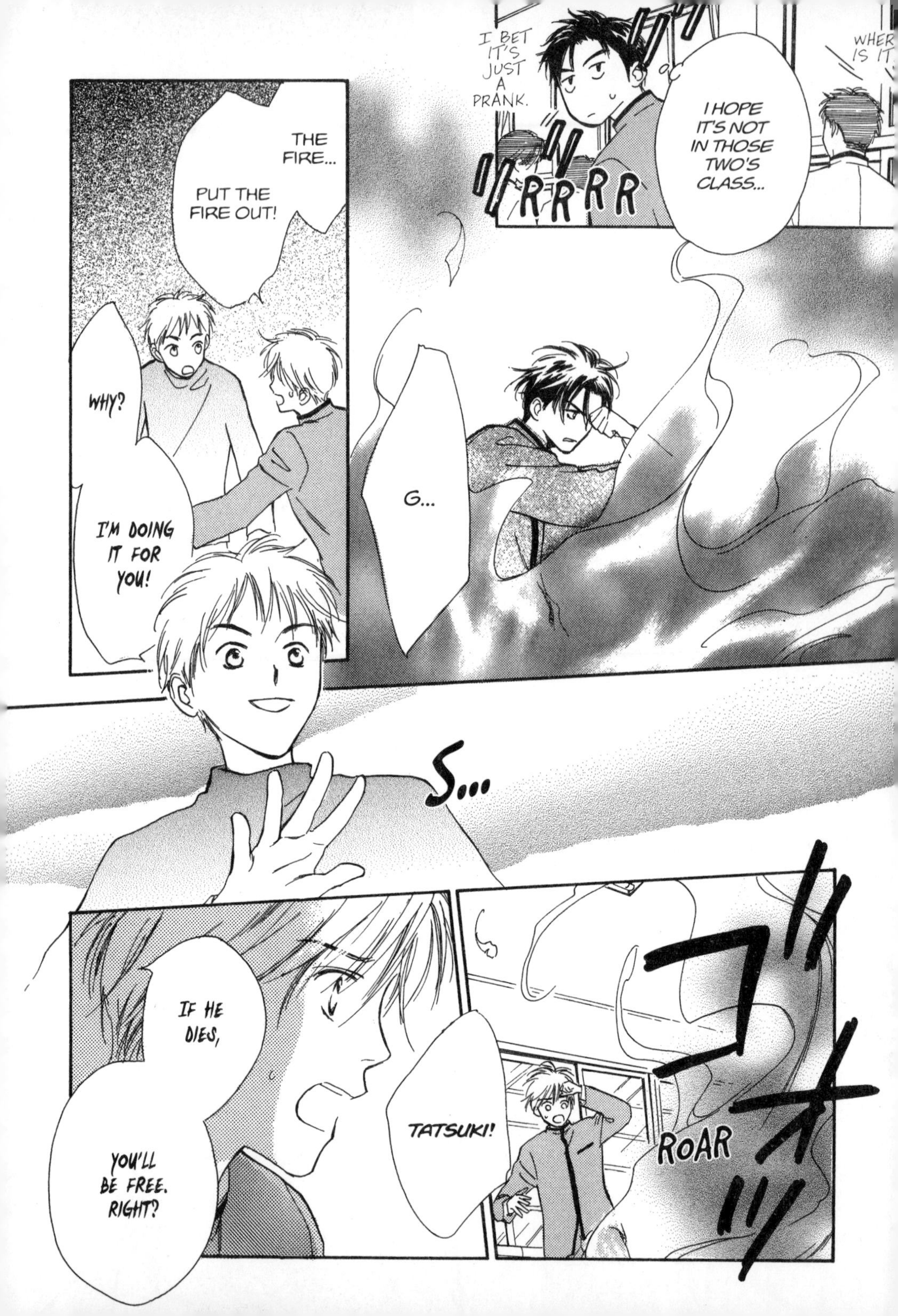

WHER IS IT
I HOPE IT'S NOT IN THOSE TWO'S CLASS...
I BET IT'S JUST A PRANK.
RRRRR
G...
THE FIRE...
PUT THE FIRE OUT!
WHY?
I'M DOING IT FOR YOU!
S...
TATSUKI!
ROAR
IF HE DIES,
YOU'LL BE FREE. RIGHT?

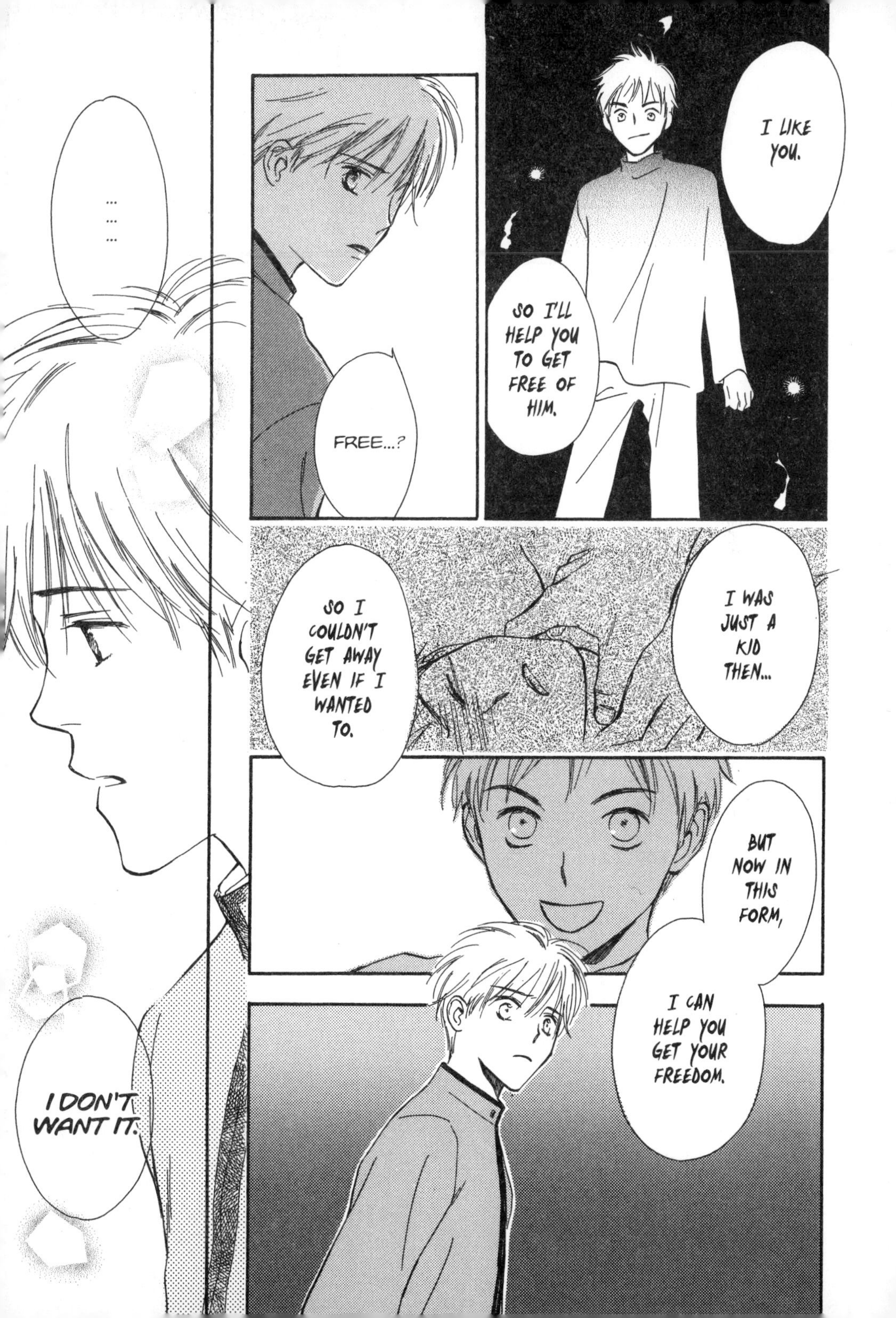
I LIKE YOU.
SO I'LL HELP YOU TO GET FREE OF HIM.
FREE...?
I WAS JUST A KID THEN...
SO I COULDN'T GET AWAY EVEN IF I WANTED TO.
BUT NOW IN THIS FORM,
I CAN HELP YOU GET YOUR FREEDOM.
....
I DON'T WANT IT.

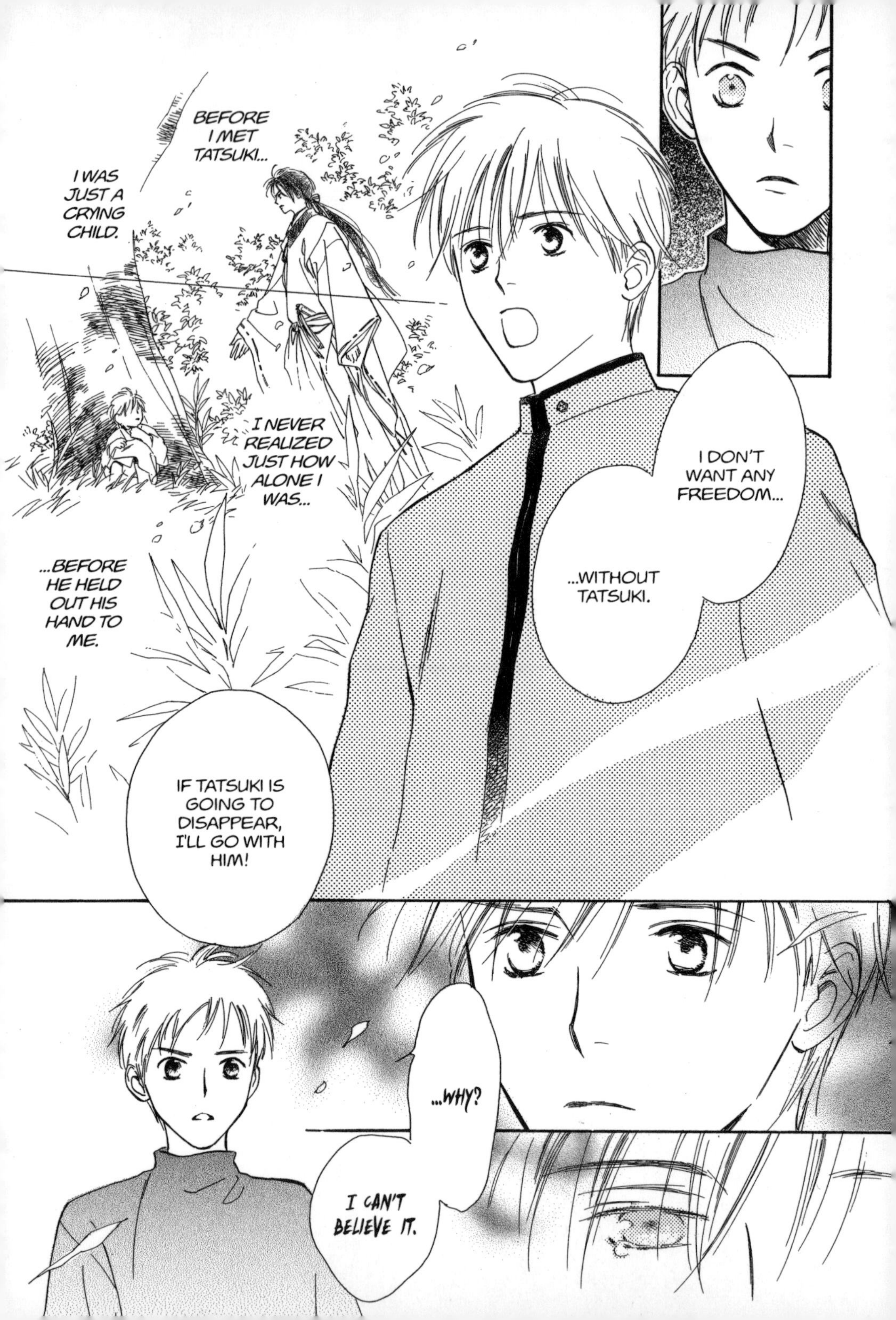
BEFORE I MET TATSUKI...
I WAS JUST A CRYING CHILD.
I NEVER REALIZED JUST HOW ALONE I WAS...
...BEFORE HE HELD OUT HIS HAND TO ME.
I DON'T WANT ANY FREEDOM...
...WITHOUT TATSUKI.
IF TATSUKI IS GOING TO DISAPPEAR, I'LL GO WITH HIM!
...WHY?
I CAN'T BELIEVE IT.

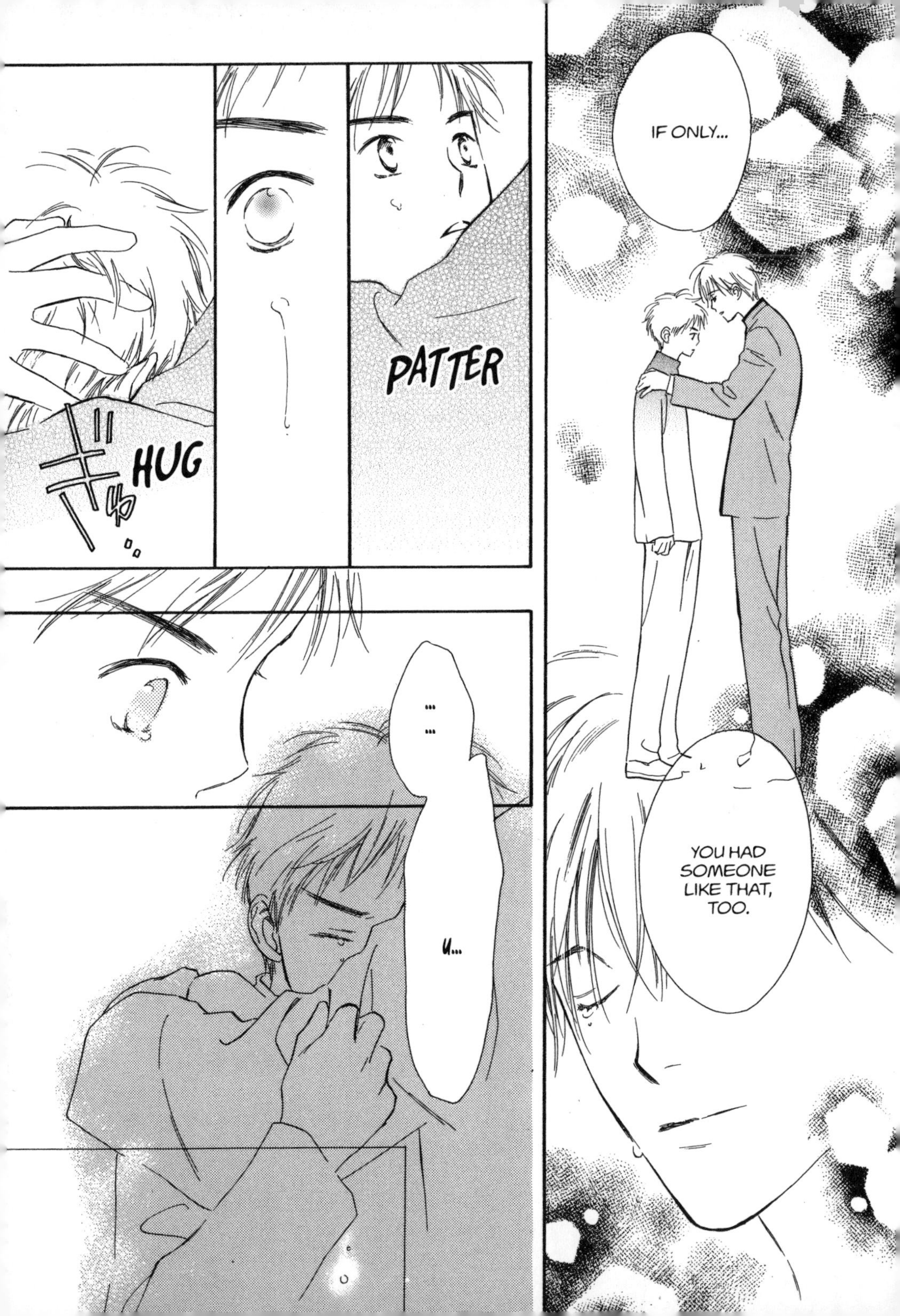
IF ONLY...
YOU HAD SOMEONE LIKE THAT, TOO.
PATTER
HUG
...
...
U...

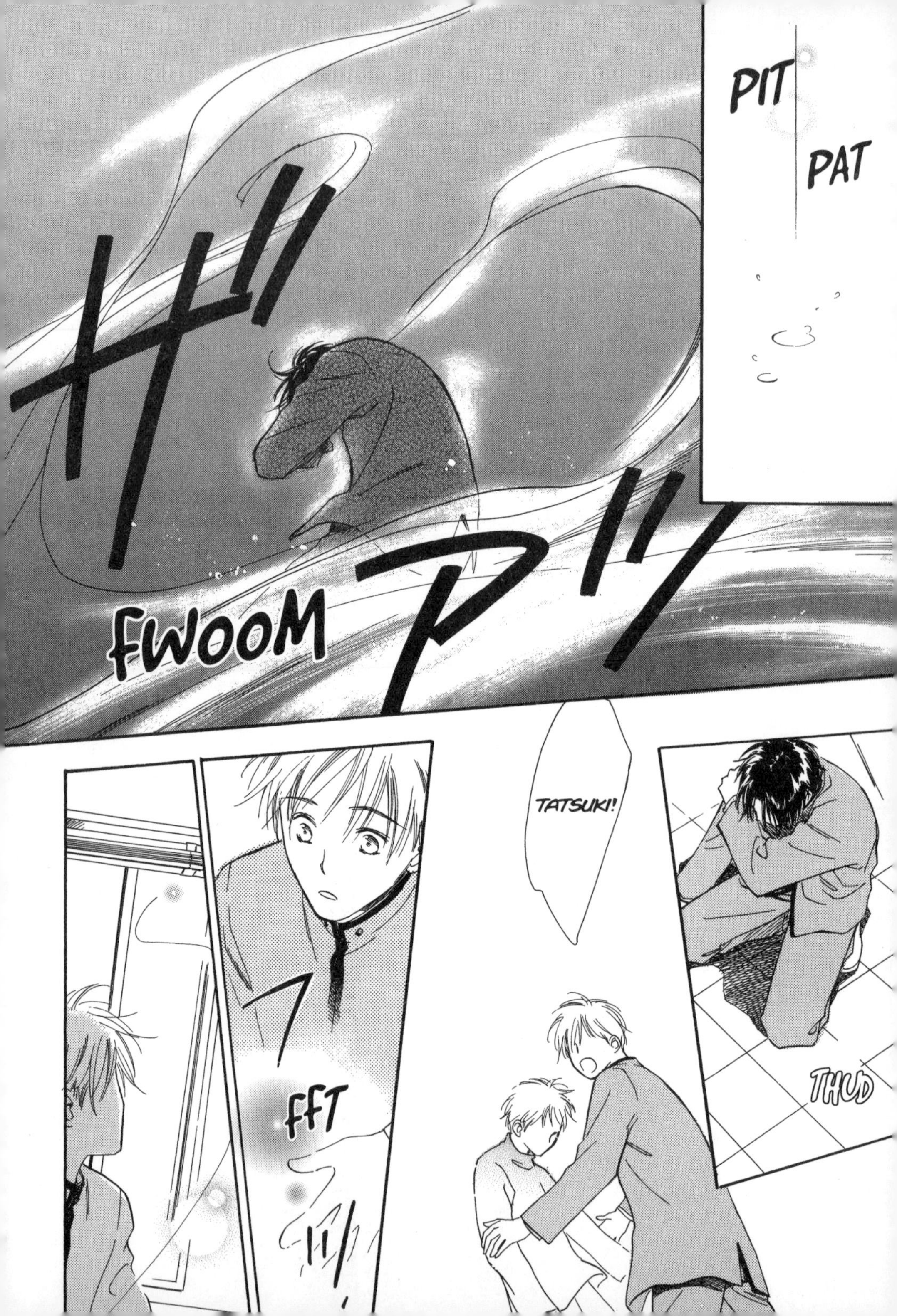
PIT
PAT
FWOOM
TATSUKI!
THUD
FFT

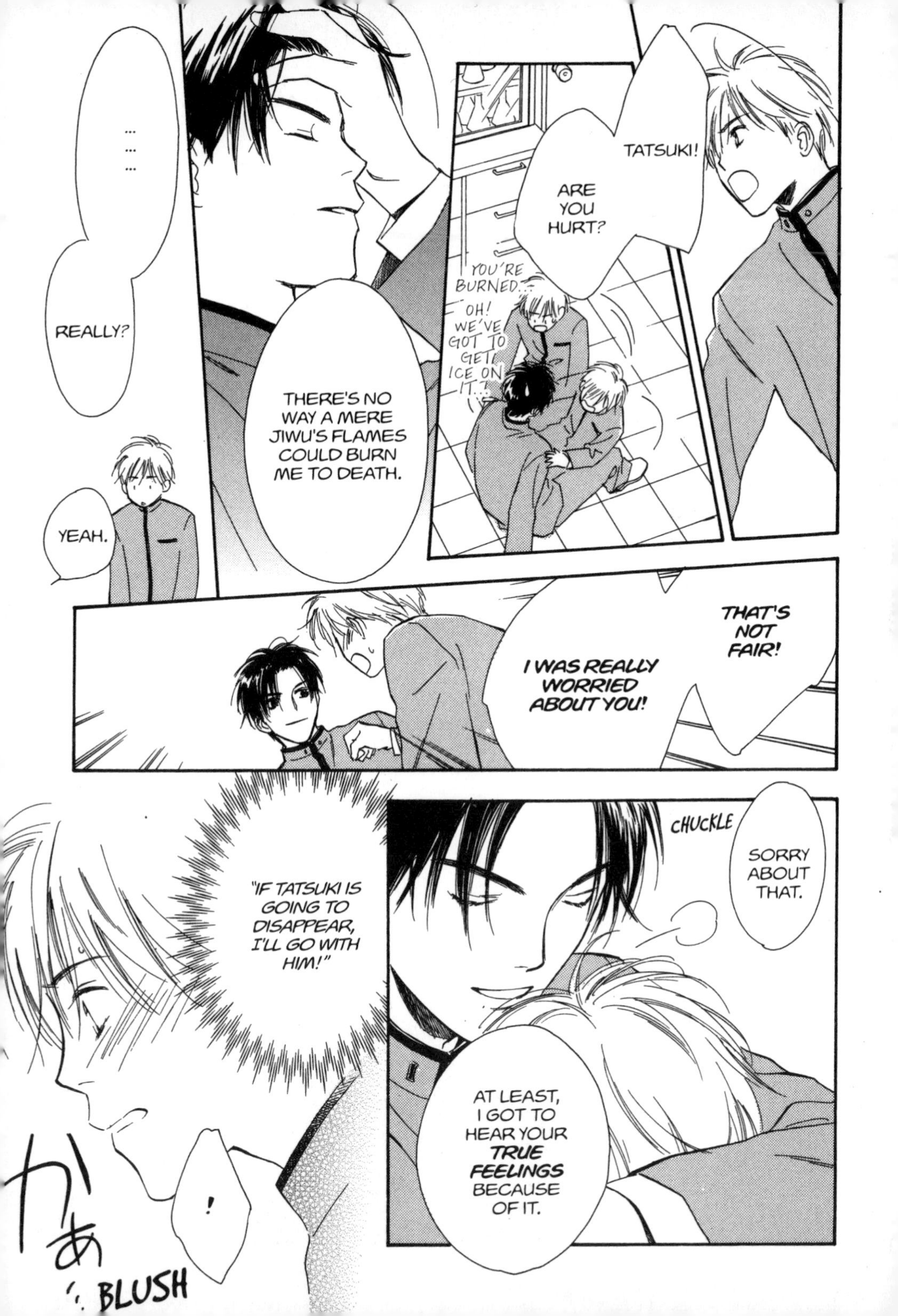
TATSUKI!
ARE YOU HURT?
YOU'RE BURNED...
OH! WE'VE GOT TO GET ICE ON IT...
THERE'S NO WAY A MERE JIWU'S FLAMES COULD BURN ME TO DEATH.
.... REALLY?
YEAH.
THAT'S NOT FAIR!
I WAS REALLY WORRIED ABOUT YOU!
CHUCKLE
SORRY ABOUT THAT.
AT LEAST, I GOT TO HEAR YOUR TRUE FEELINGS BECAUSE OF IT.
"IF TATSUKI IS GOING TO DISAPPEAR, I'LL GO WITH HIM!"
!
かあ
BLUSH

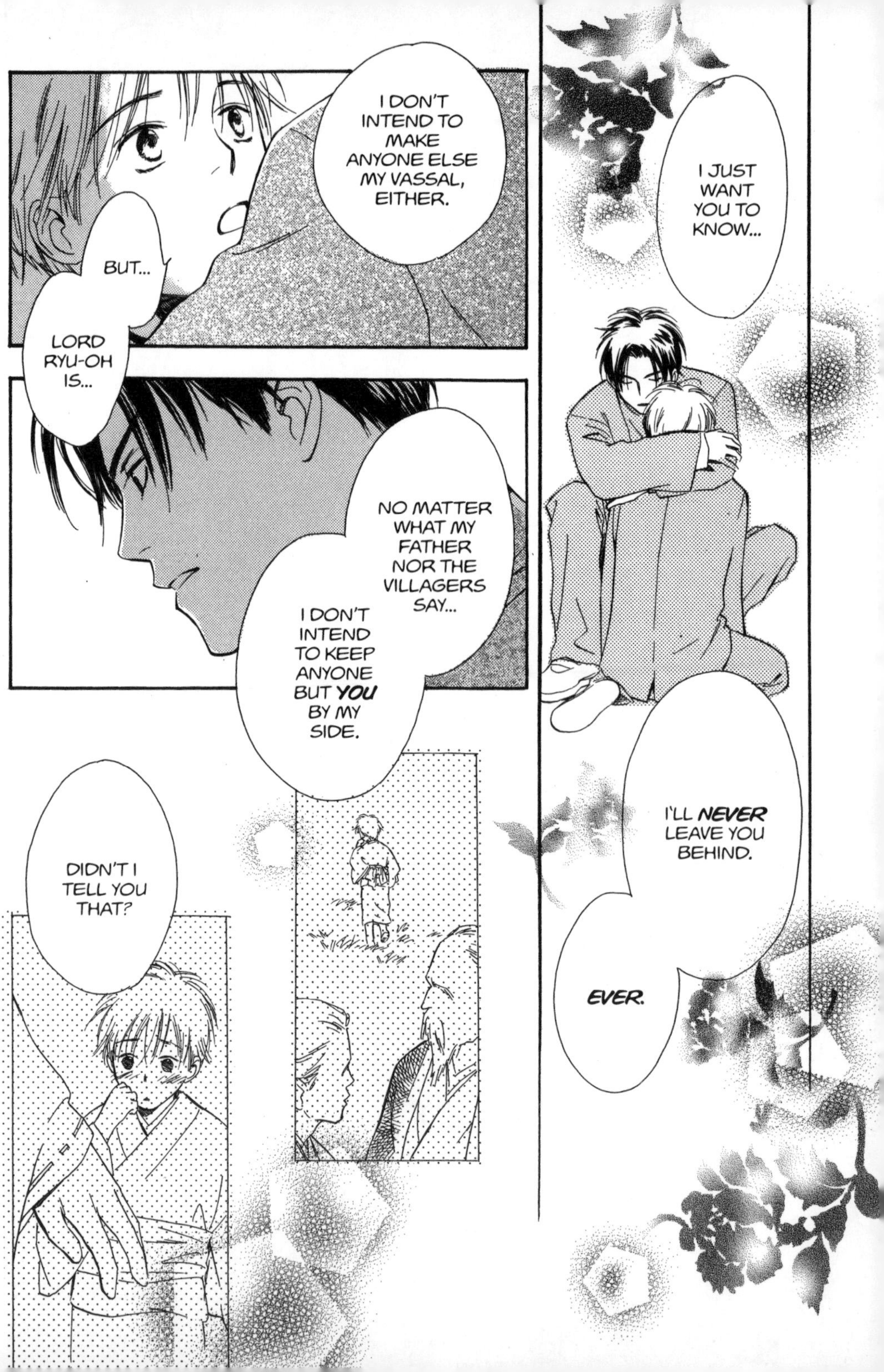
I JUST WANT YOU TO KNOW...
I'LL NEVER LEAVE YOU BEHIND.
EVER.
I DON'T INTEND TO MAKE ANYONE ELSE MY VASSAL, EITHER.
BUT...
LORD RYU-OH IS...
NO MATTER WHAT MY FATHER NOR THE VILLAGERS SAY...
I DON'T INTEND TO KEEP ANYONE BUT YOU BY MY SIDE.
DIDN'T I TELL YOU THAT?

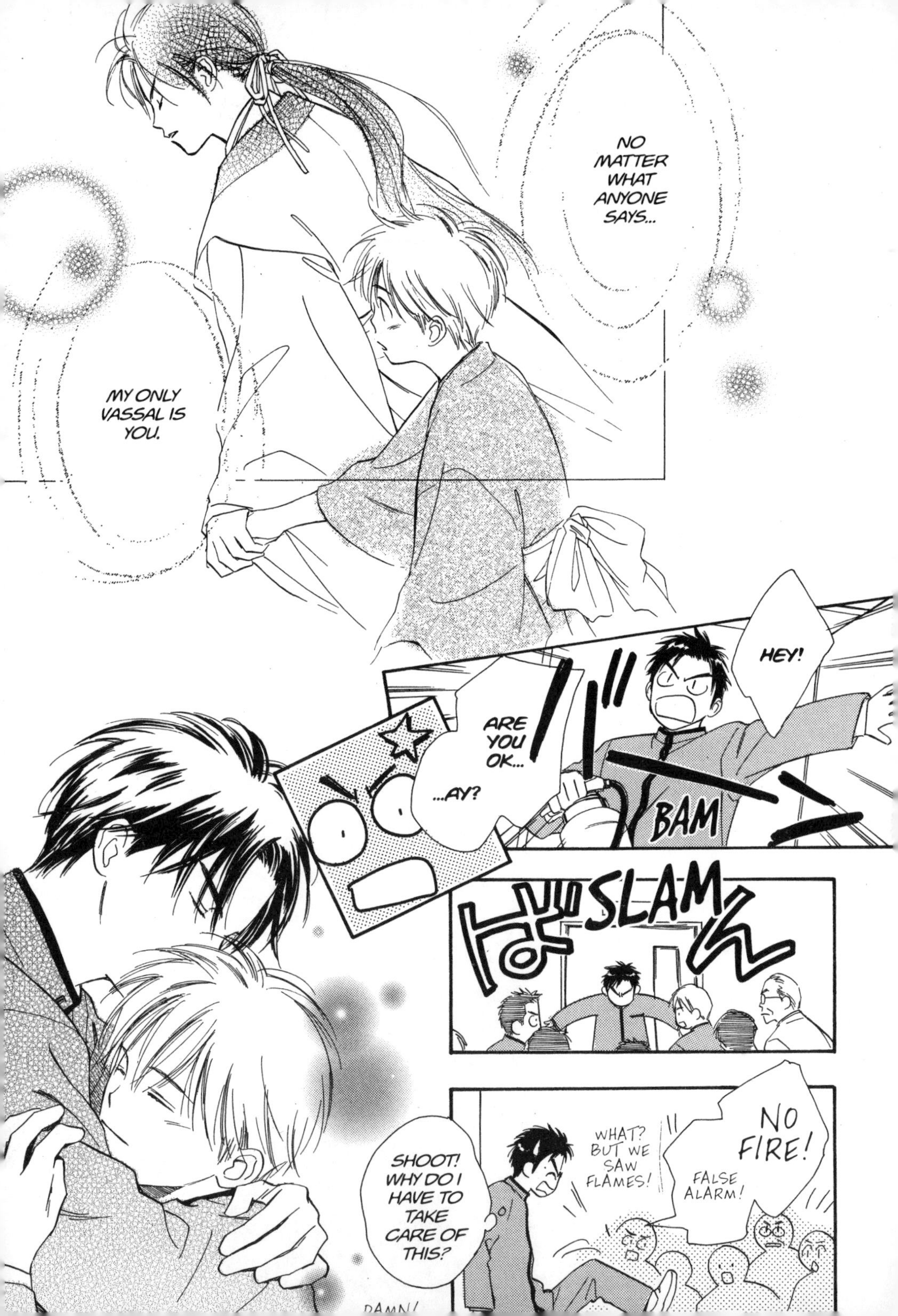
NO MATTER WHAT ANYONE SAYS...
MY ONLY VASSAL IS YOU.
HEY!
ARE YOU OK...
...AY?
BAM
ば SLAM ん
NO FIRE!
WHAT? BUT WE SAW FLAMES!
FALSE ALARM!
SHOOT! WHY DO I HAVE TO TAKE CARE OF THIS?
DAMN!

NO, I DIDN'T
CUT MY HAIR
BECAUSE I
GOT DUMPED
OR ANYTHING.

IT'S 'CUZ
I'M SO
FASHIONABLE,
Y'KNOW?

I'M TRYING
TO CHANGE
MY IMAGE.

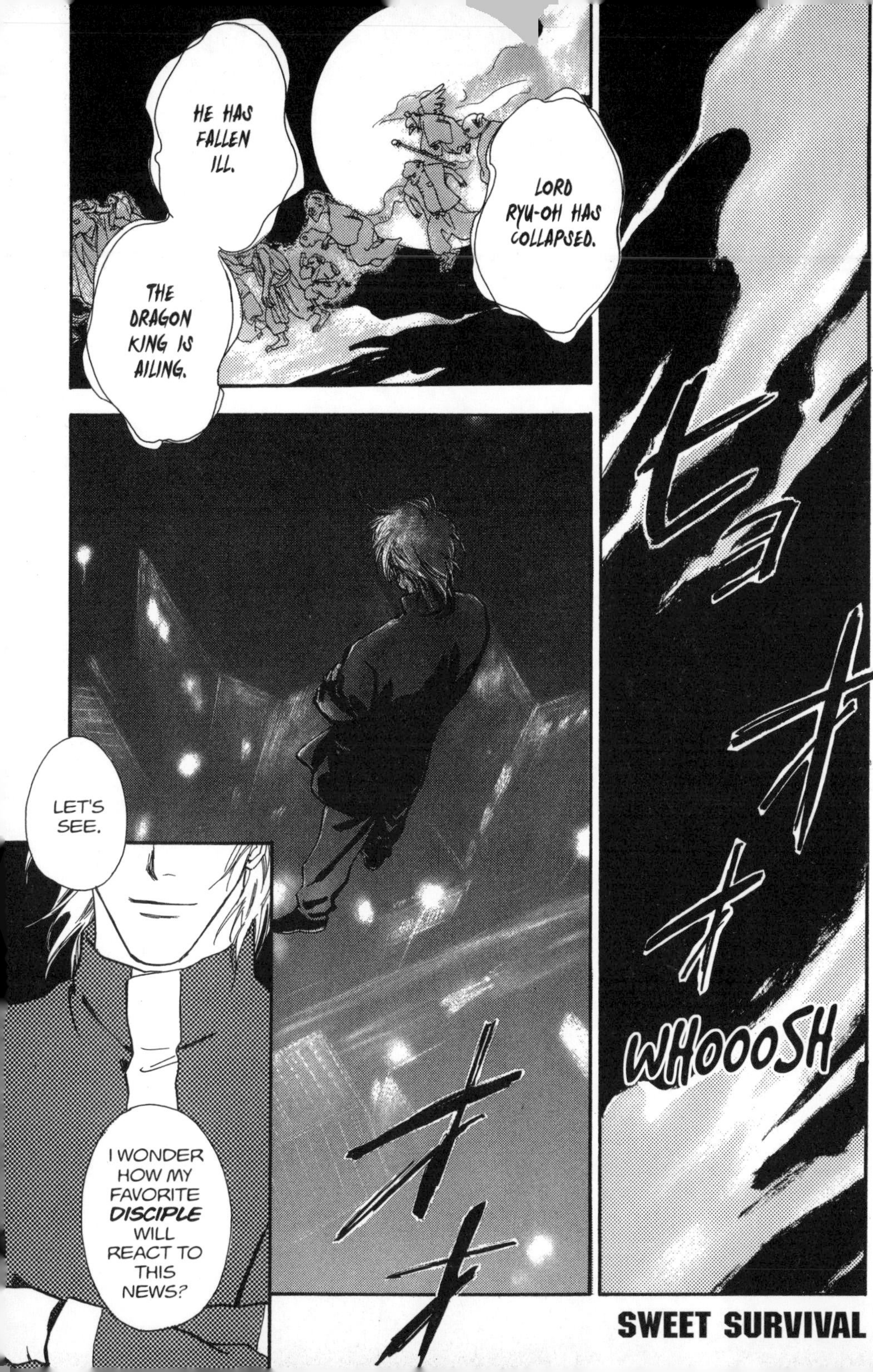

ヒョオオ
WHOOOSH
LORD RYU-OH HAS COLLAPSED.
HE HAS FALLEN ILL.
THE DRAGON KING IS AILING.
LET'S SEE.
I WONDER HOW MY FAVORITE **DISCIPLE** WILL REACT TO THIS NEWS?

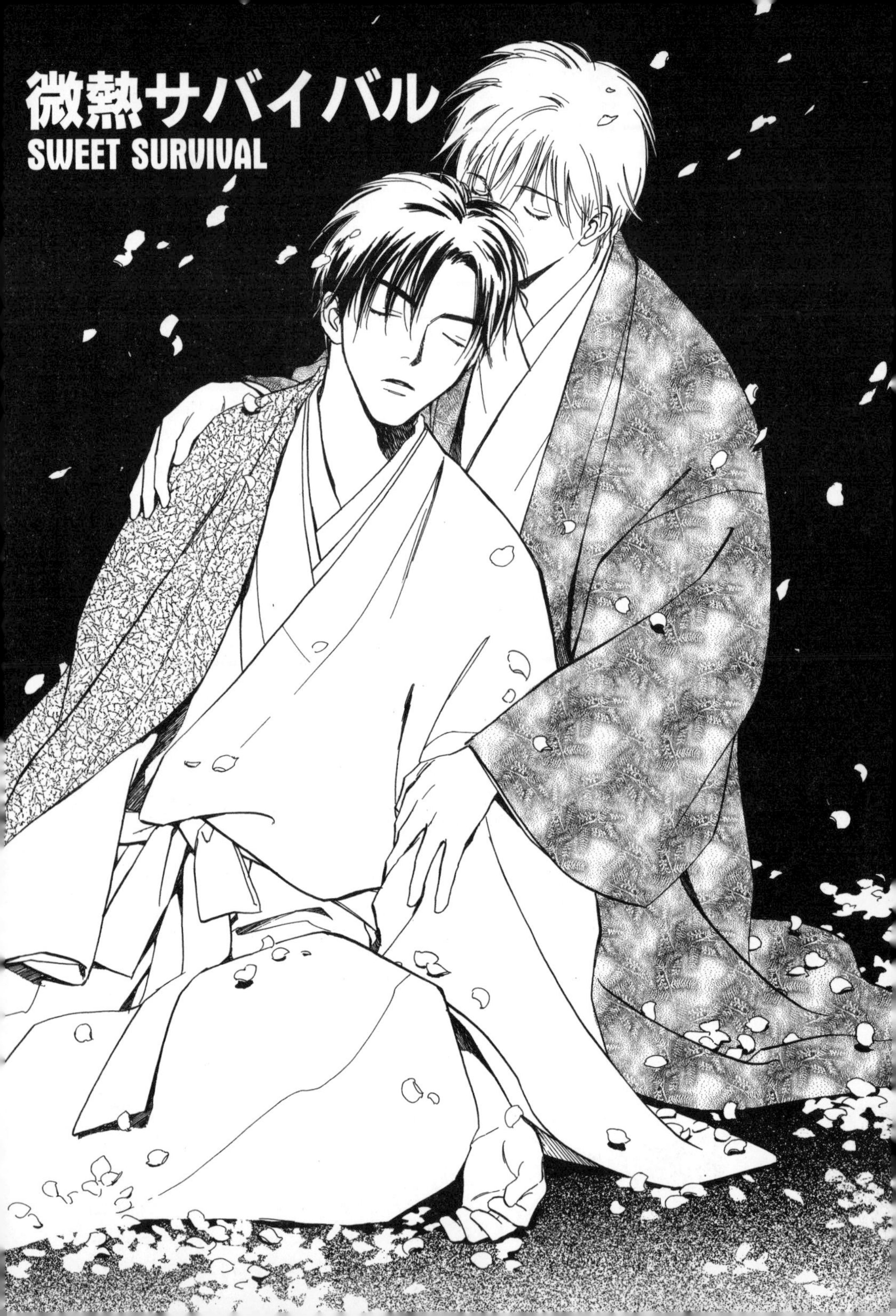
微熱サバイバル
SWEET SURVIVAL

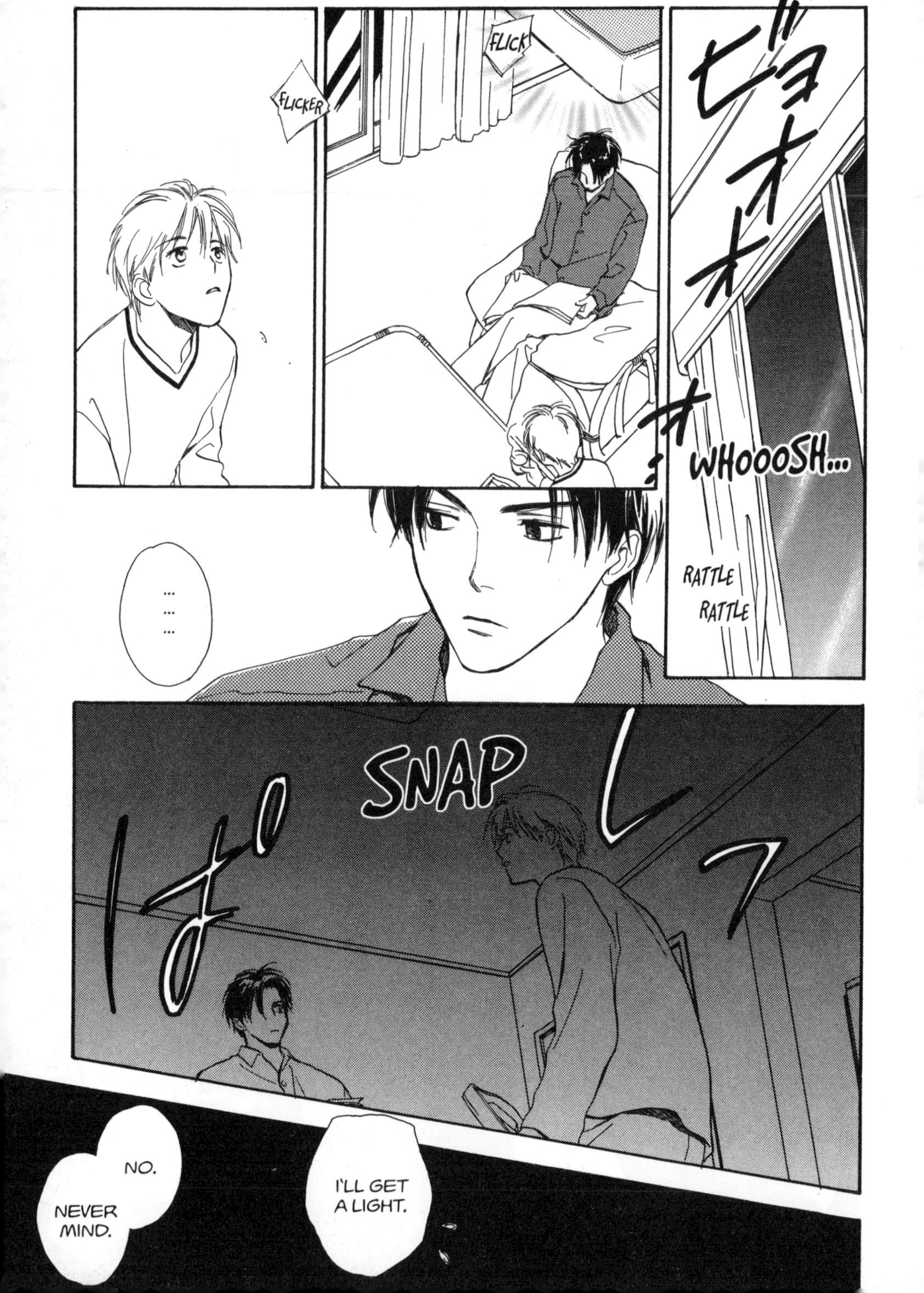
ビョオオオ
WHOOOSH...
RATTLE RATTLE
FLICK
FLICKER
...
...
...
SNAP
I'LL GET A LIGHT.
NO.
NEVER MIND.

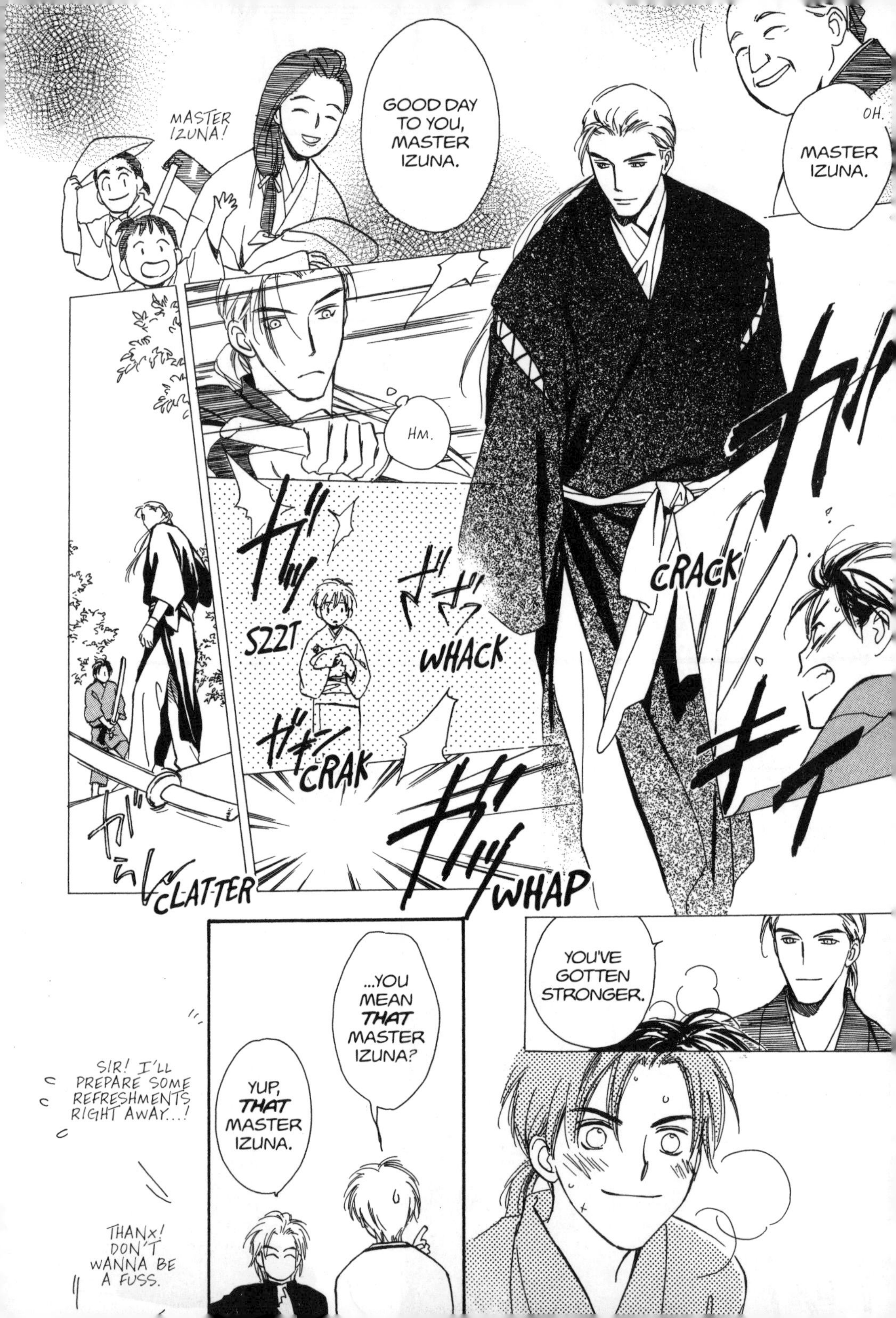
OH.
MASTER IZUNA.
GOOD DAY TO YOU, MASTER IZUNA.
MASTER IZUNA!
CRACK
HM.
SZZT
WHACK
CRAK
WHAP
CLATTER
YOU'VE GOTTEN STRONGER.
...YOU MEAN *THAT* MASTER IZUNA?
YUP, *THAT* MASTER IZUNA.
SIR! I'LL PREPARE SOME REFRESHMENTS RIGHT AWAY...!
THANX! DON'T WANNA BE A FUSS.

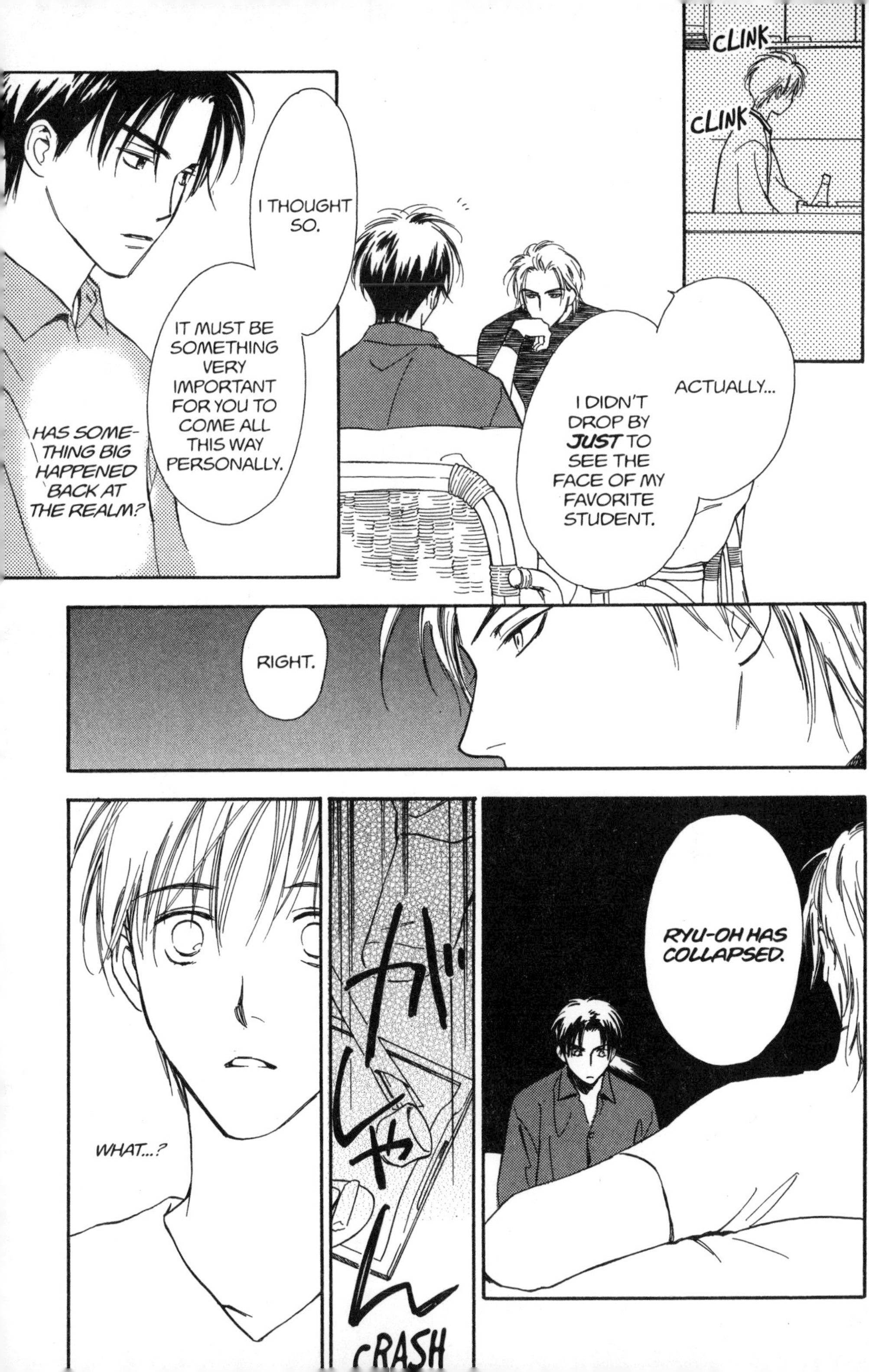
CLINK
CLINK
ACTUALLY...
I DIDN'T DROP BY **JUST** TO SEE THE FACE OF MY FAVORITE STUDENT.
I THOUGHT SO.
IT MUST BE SOMETHING VERY IMPORTANT FOR YOU TO COME ALL THIS WAY PERSONALLY.
HAS SOMETHING BIG HAPPENED BACK AT THE REALM?
RIGHT.
RYU-OH HAS COLLAPSED.
CRASH
WHAT...?

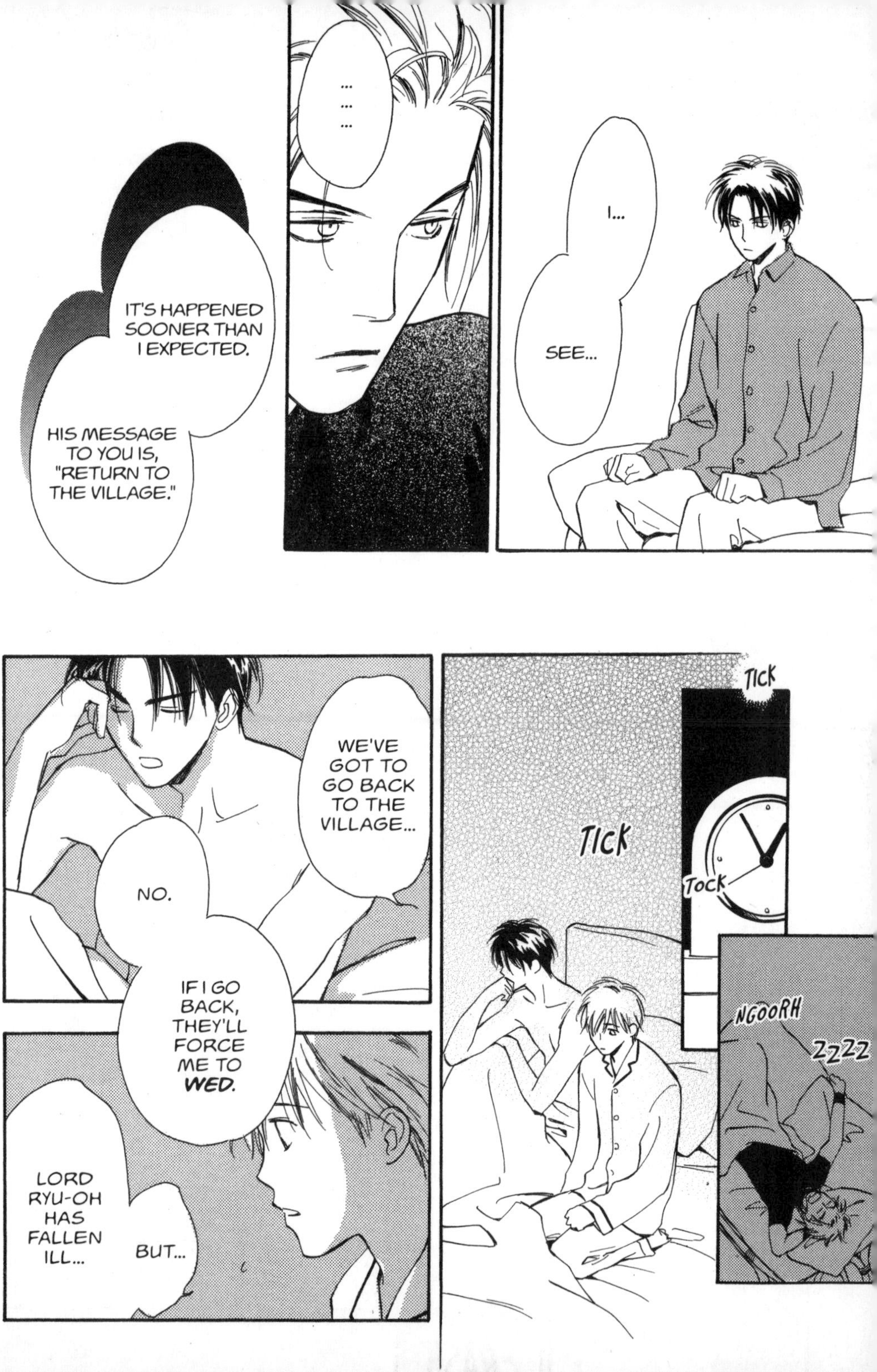
I...
SEE...
...
...
...
IT'S HAPPENED SOONER THAN I EXPECTED.
HIS MESSAGE TO YOU IS, "RETURN TO THE VILLAGE."
TICK
TICK
TOCK
NGOORH
ZZZZ
WE'VE GOT TO GO BACK TO THE VILLAGE...
NO.
IF I GO BACK, THEY'LL FORCE ME TO **WED**.
LORD RYU-OH HAS FALLEN ILL...
BUT...

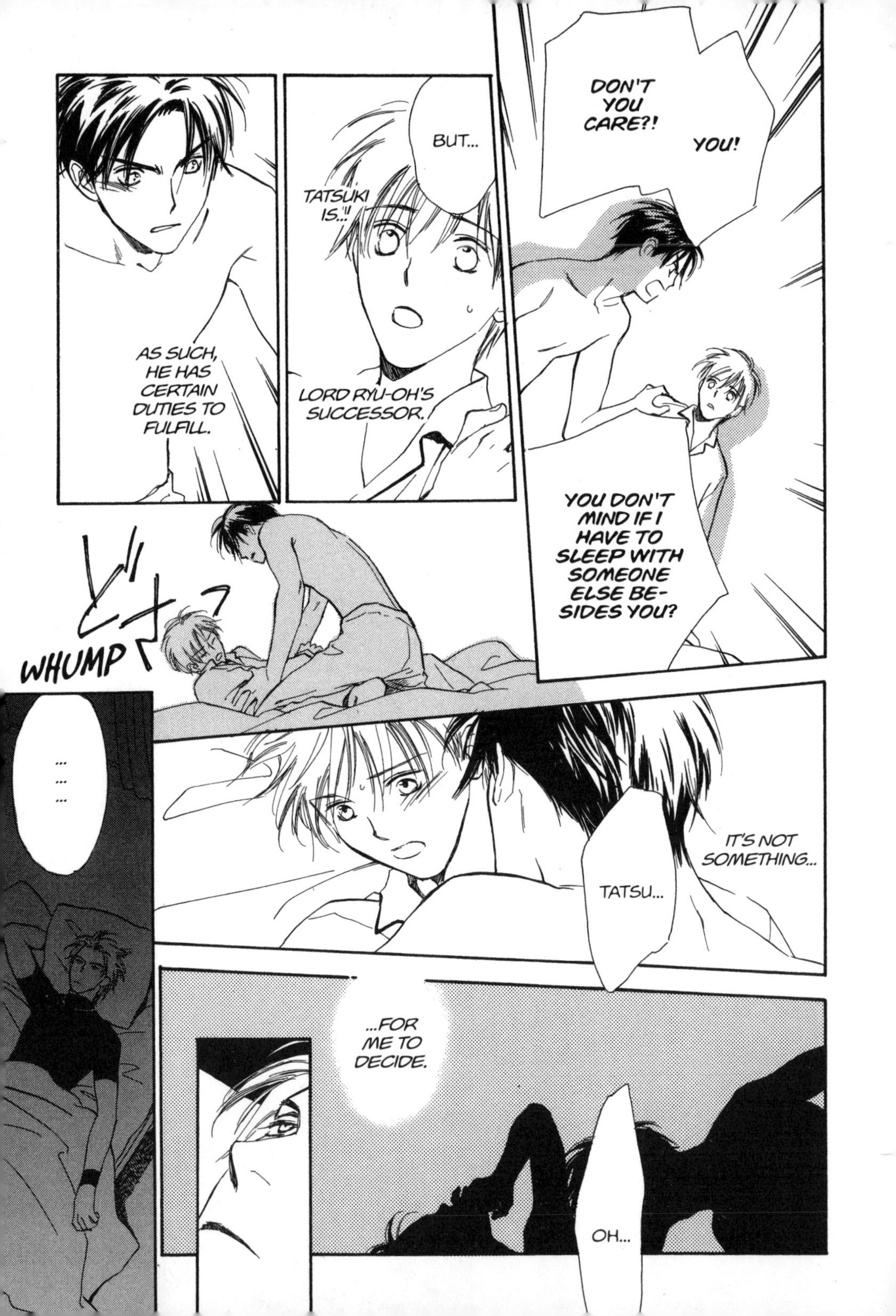
DON'T YOU CARE?!
YOU!
YOU DON'T MIND IF I HAVE TO SLEEP WITH SOMEONE ELSE BE-SIDES YOU?
BUT...
TATSUKI IS...
LORD RYU-OH'S SUCCESSOR.
AS SUCH, HE HAS CERTAIN DUTIES TO FULFILL.
WHUMP
IT'S NOT SOMETHING...
TATSU...
...FOR ME TO DECIDE.
OH...
...
...
...

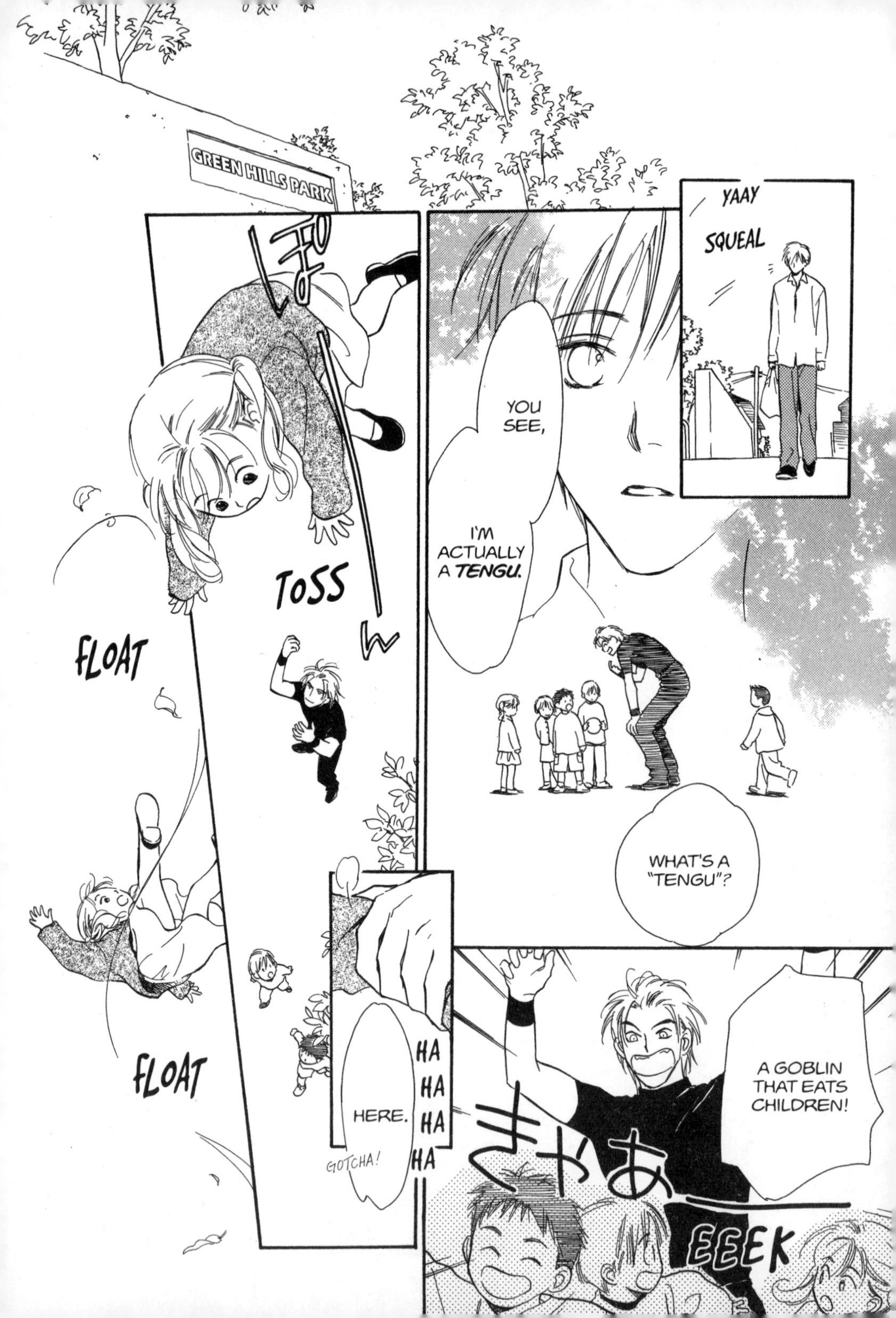
GREEN HILLS PARK
YAAY
SQUEAL
YOU SEE,
I'M ACTUALLY A *TENGU.*
WHAT'S A "TENGU"?
A GOBLIN THAT EATS CHILDREN!
きゃあー
EEEK
TOSS
FLOAT
HA HA HA HA
HERE.
GOTCHA!
FLOAT

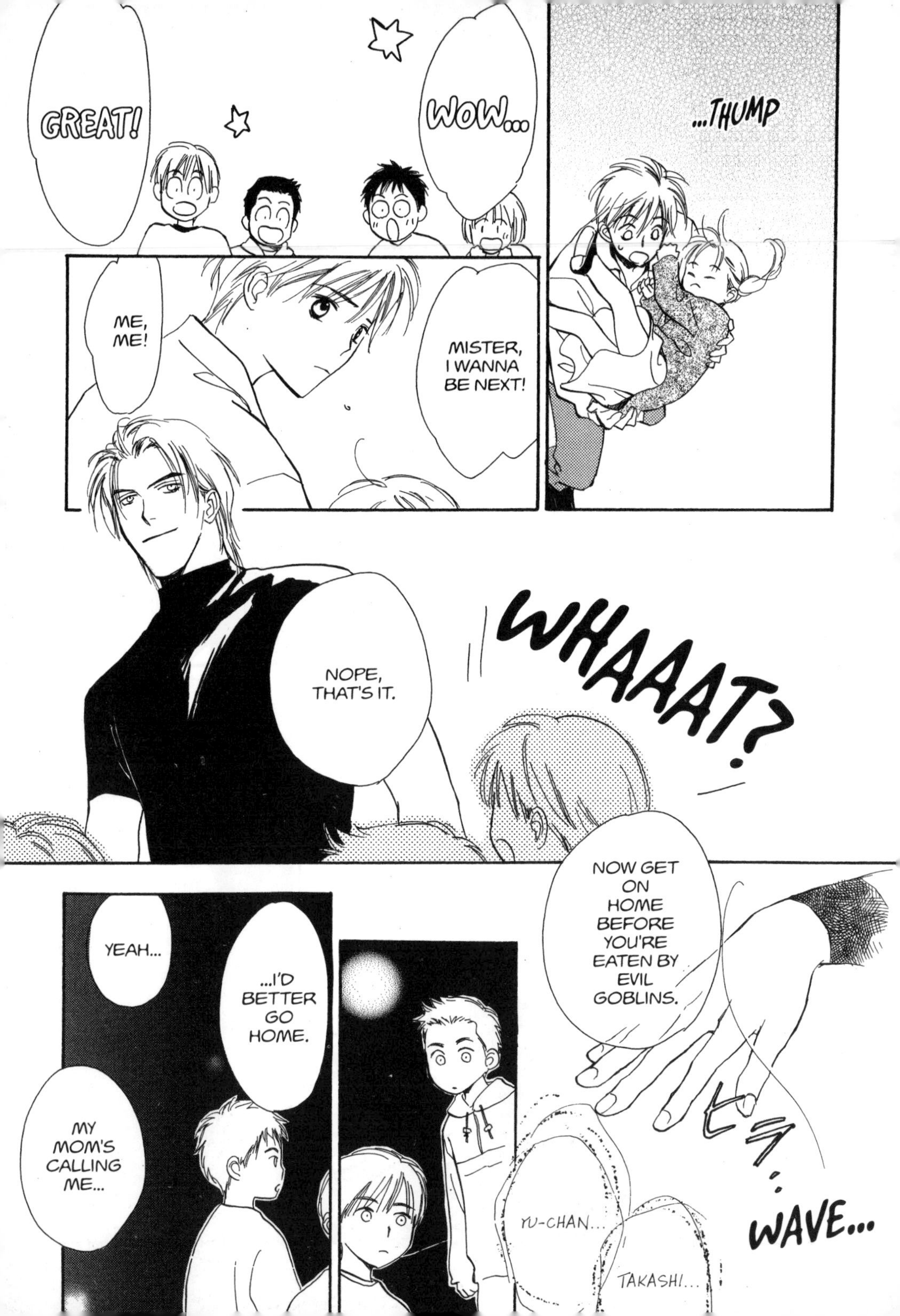
...THUMP
WOW...
GREAT!
MISTER, I WANNA BE NEXT!
ME, ME!
NOPE, THAT'S IT.
WHAAAT?
NOW GET ON HOME BEFORE YOU'RE EATEN BY EVIL GOBLINS.
ヒラ
WAVE...
YU-CHAN...
TAKASHI...
YEAH...
...I'D BETTER GO HOME.
MY MOM'S CALLING ME...

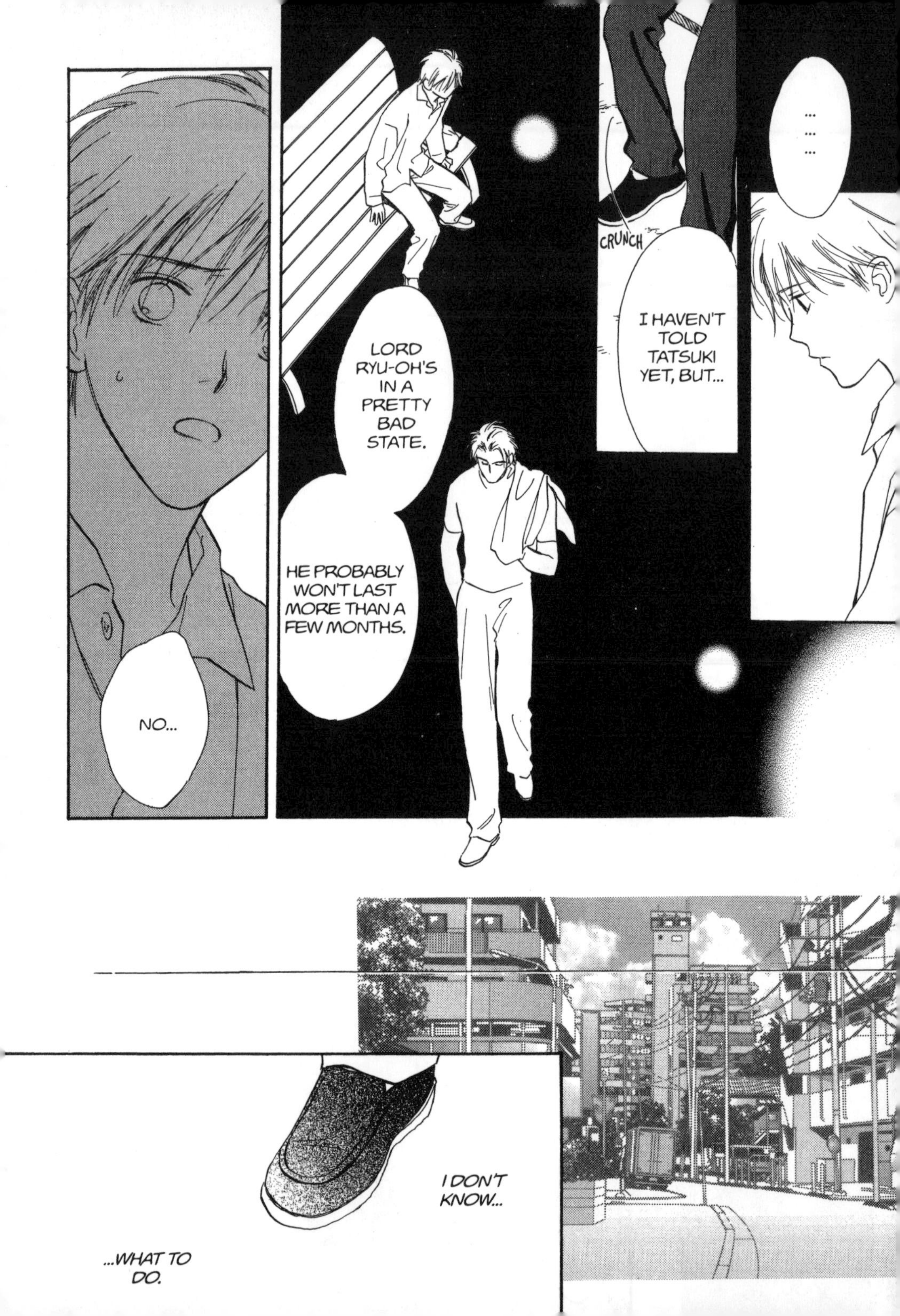

...
...
...
CRUNCH
I HAVEN'T TOLD TATSUKI YET, BUT...
LORD RYU-OH'S IN A PRETTY BAD STATE.
HE PROBABLY WON'T LAST MORE THAN A FEW MONTHS.
NO...
I DON'T KNOW...
...WHAT TO DO.

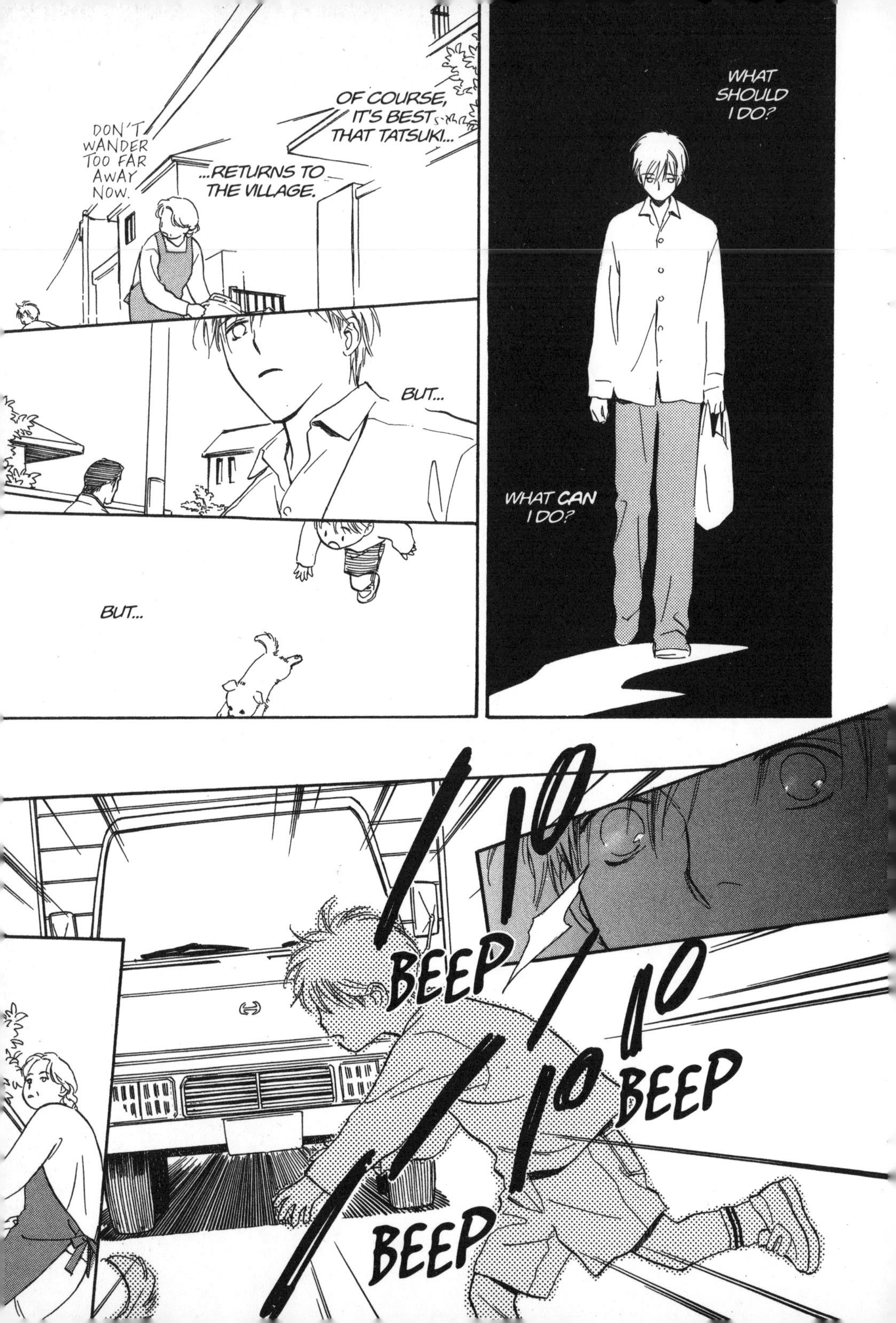
WHAT SHOULD I DO?
WHAT CAN I DO?
OF COURSE, IT'S BEST THAT TATSUKI...
DON'T WANDER TOO FAR AWAY NOW.
...RETURNS TO THE VILLAGE.
BUT...
BUT...
BEEP
BEEP
BEEP

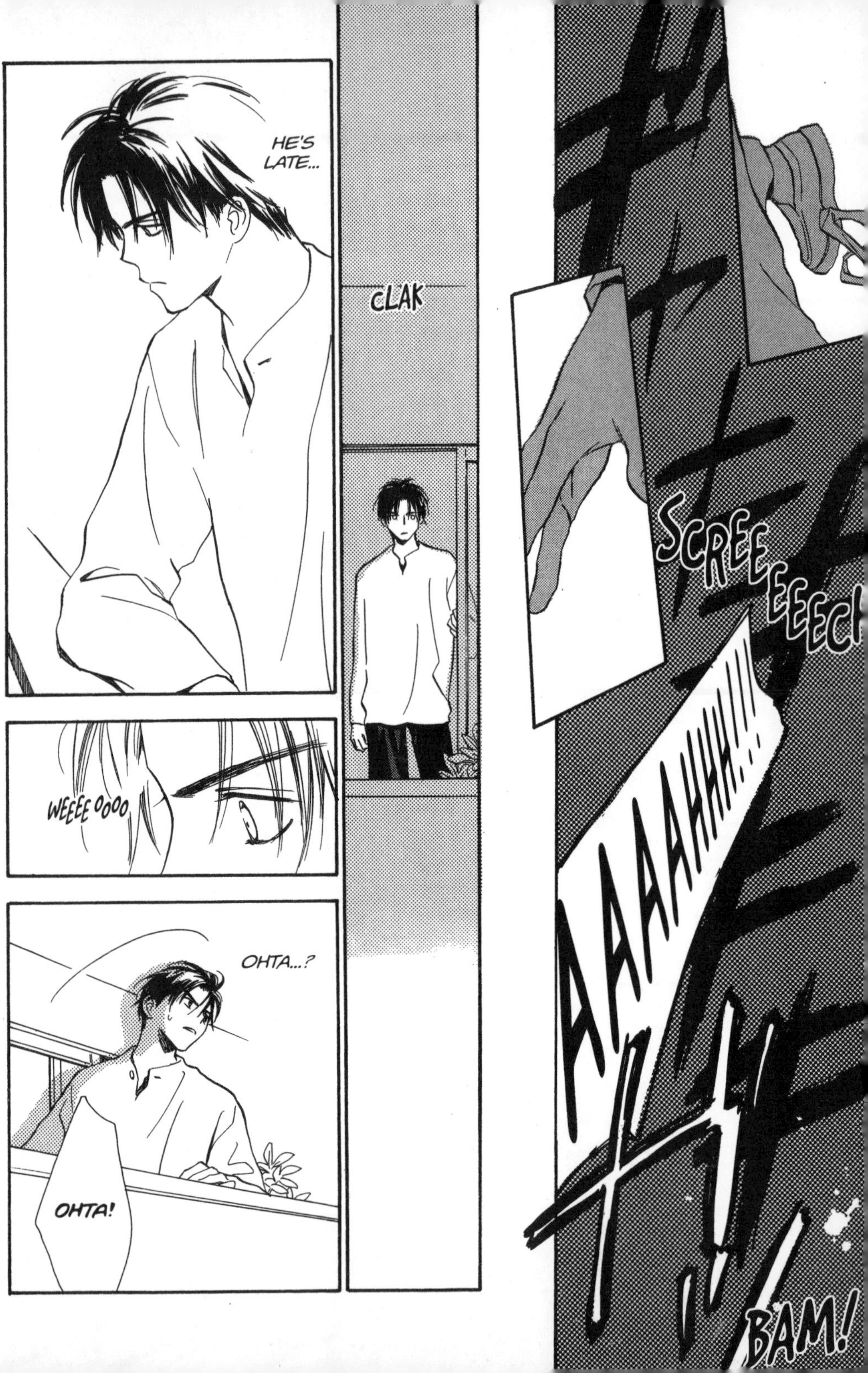
SCREEEEEECH
AAAAHHH!!
BAM!
CLAK
HE'S LATE...
WEEEE OOOO
OHTA...?
OHTA!

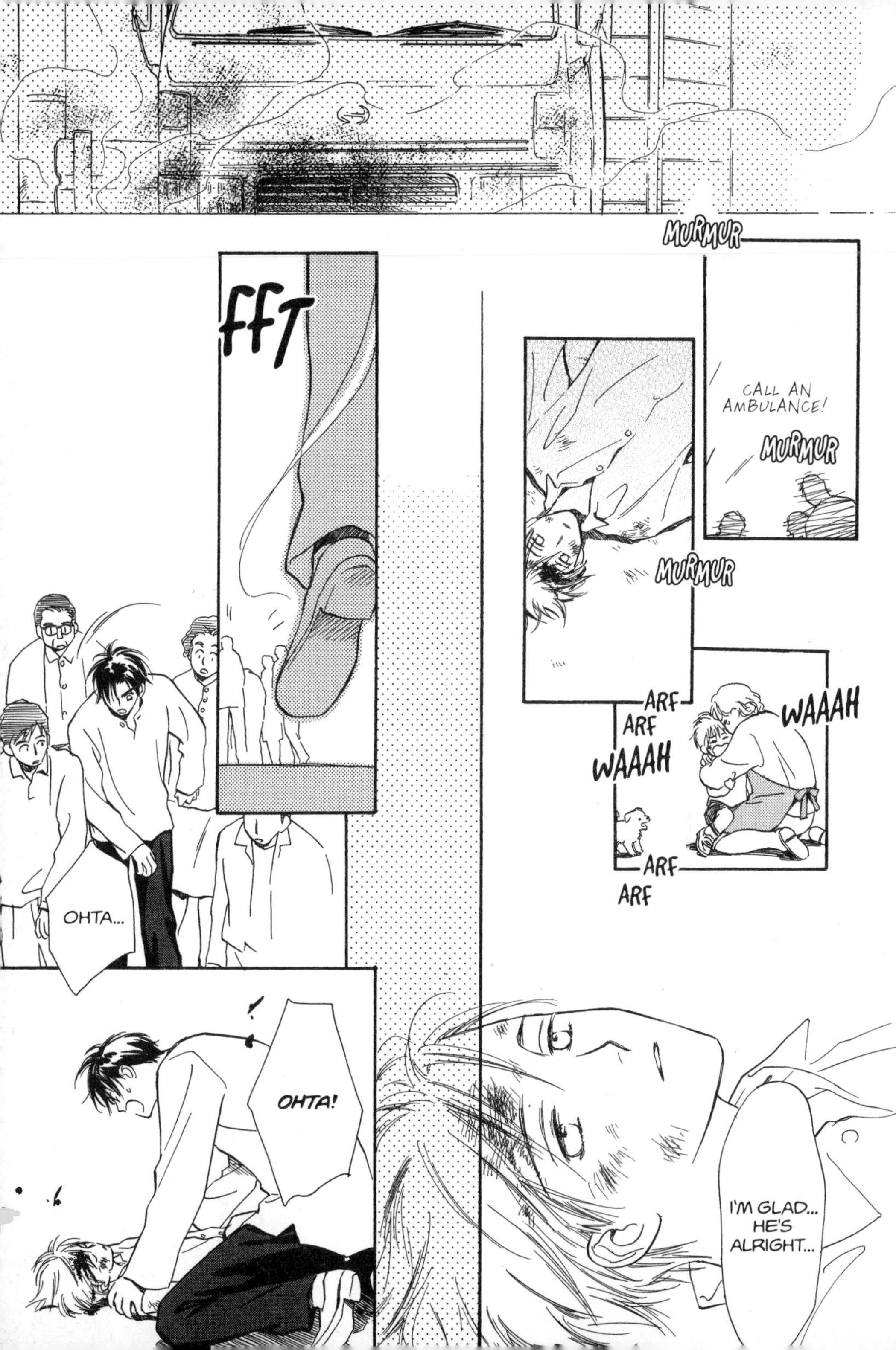
MURMUR
CALL AN AMBULANCE!
MURMUR
MURMUR
ARF ARF
WAAAH
WAAAH
ARF ARF
FFT
OHTA...
I'M GLAD... HE'S ALRIGHT...
OHTA!

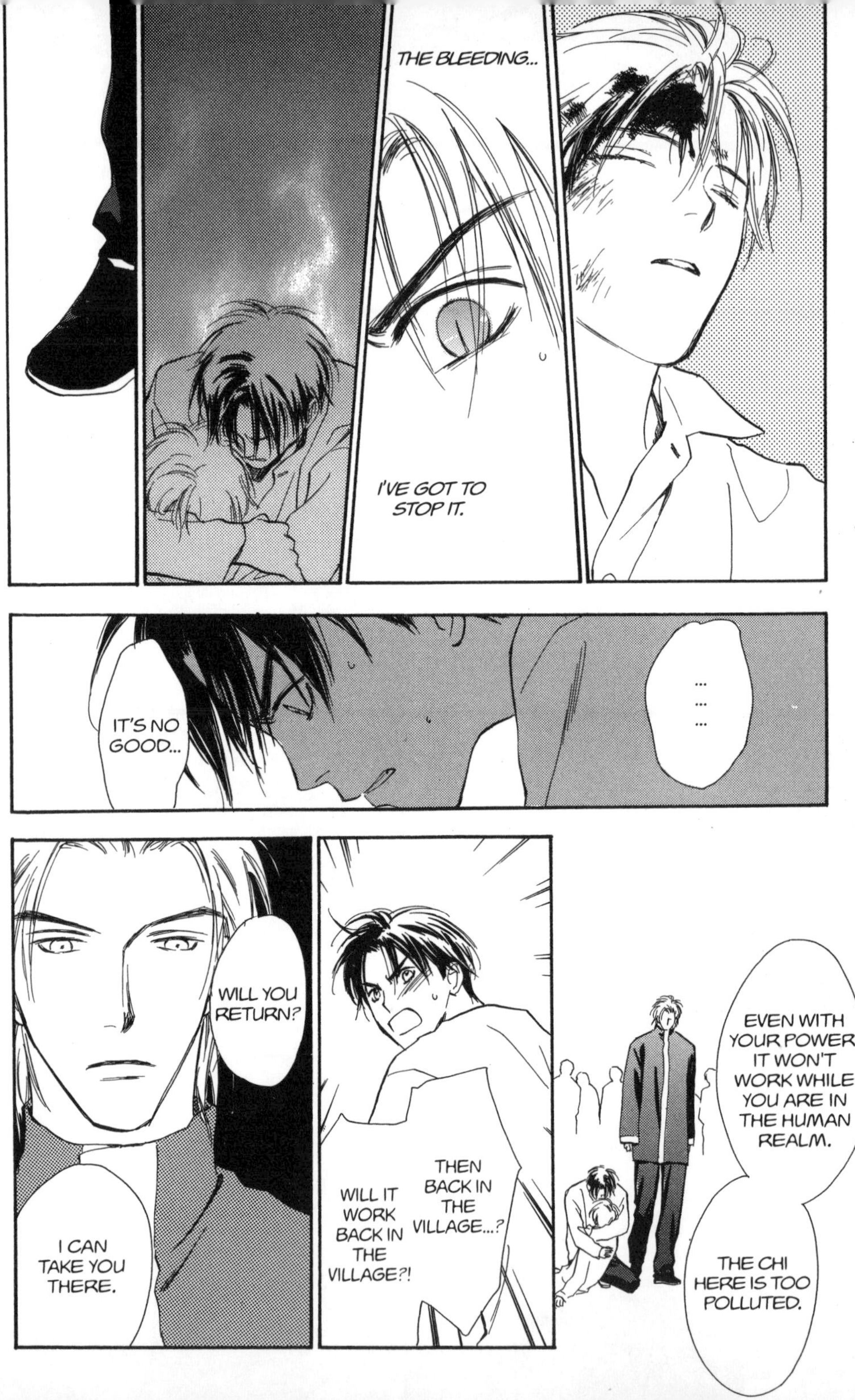
THE BLEEDING...
I'VE GOT TO STOP IT.
...
...
...
IT'S NO GOOD...
EVEN WITH YOUR POWER, IT WON'T WORK WHILE YOU ARE IN THE HUMAN REALM.
THE CHI HERE IS TOO POLLUTED.
THEN BACK IN THE VILLAGE...?
WILL IT WORK BACK IN THE VILLAGE?!
WILL YOU RETURN?
I CAN TAKE YOU THERE.

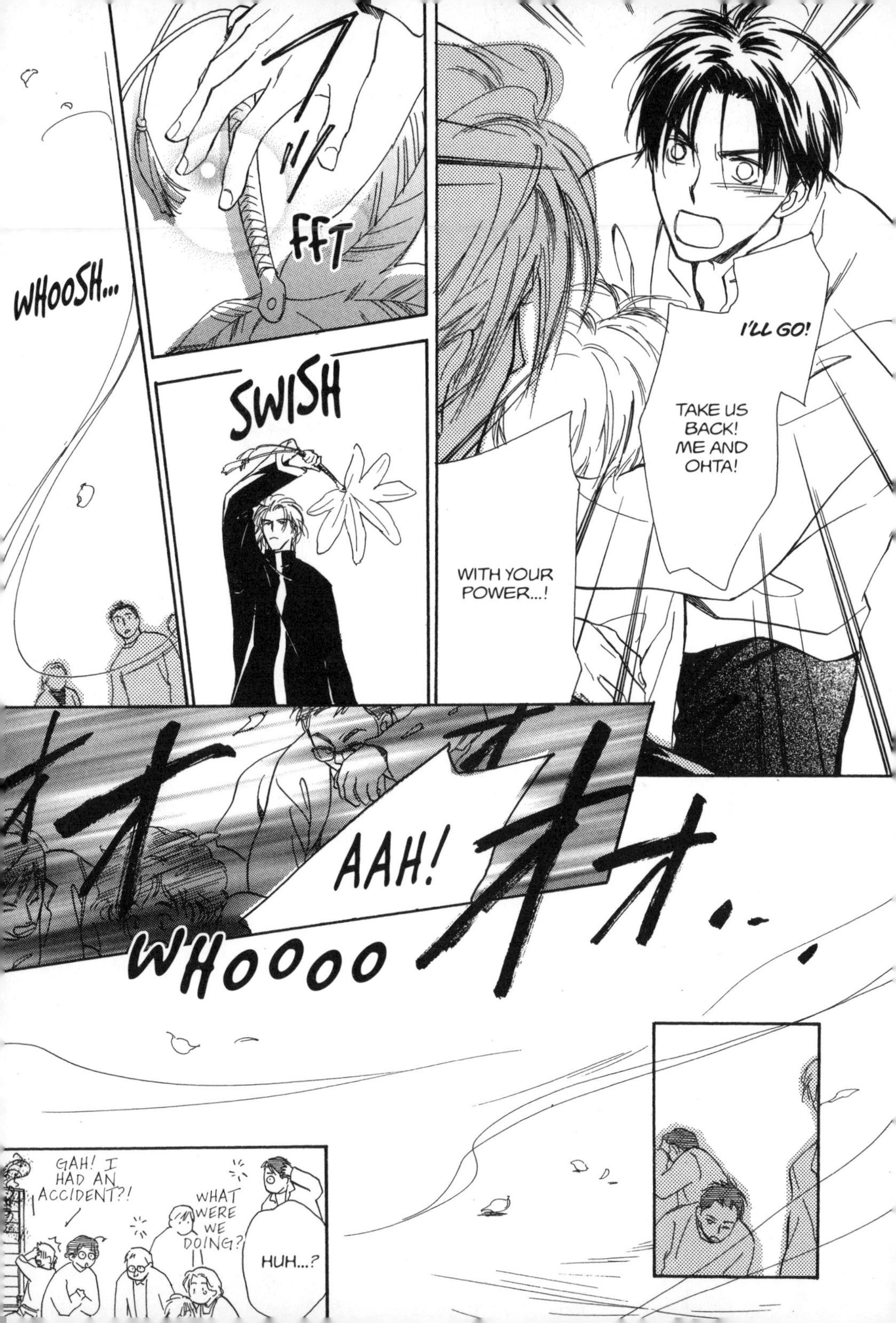
I'LL GO!
TAKE US BACK! ME AND OHTA!
WITH YOUR POWER...!
FFT
WHOOSH...
SWISH
AAH!
WHOOOO
HUH...?
WHAT WERE WE DOING?
GAH! I HAD AN ACCIDENT?!

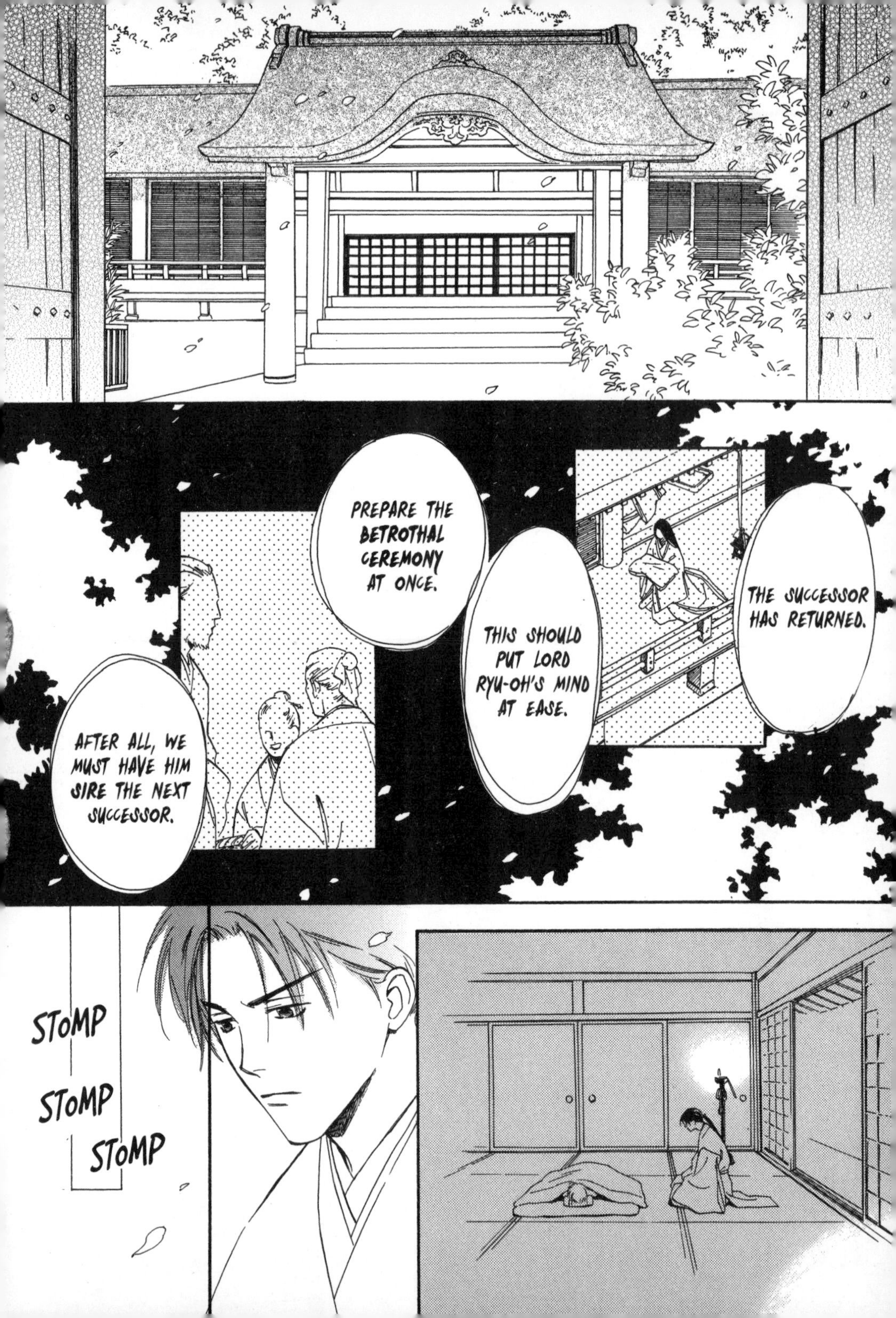
THE SUCCESSOR HAS RETURNED.
THIS SHOULD PUT LORD RYU-OH'S MIND AT EASE.
PREPARE THE BETROTHAL CEREMONY AT ONCE.
AFTER ALL, WE MUST HAVE HIM SIRE THE NEXT SUCCESSOR.
STOMP
STOMP
STOMP

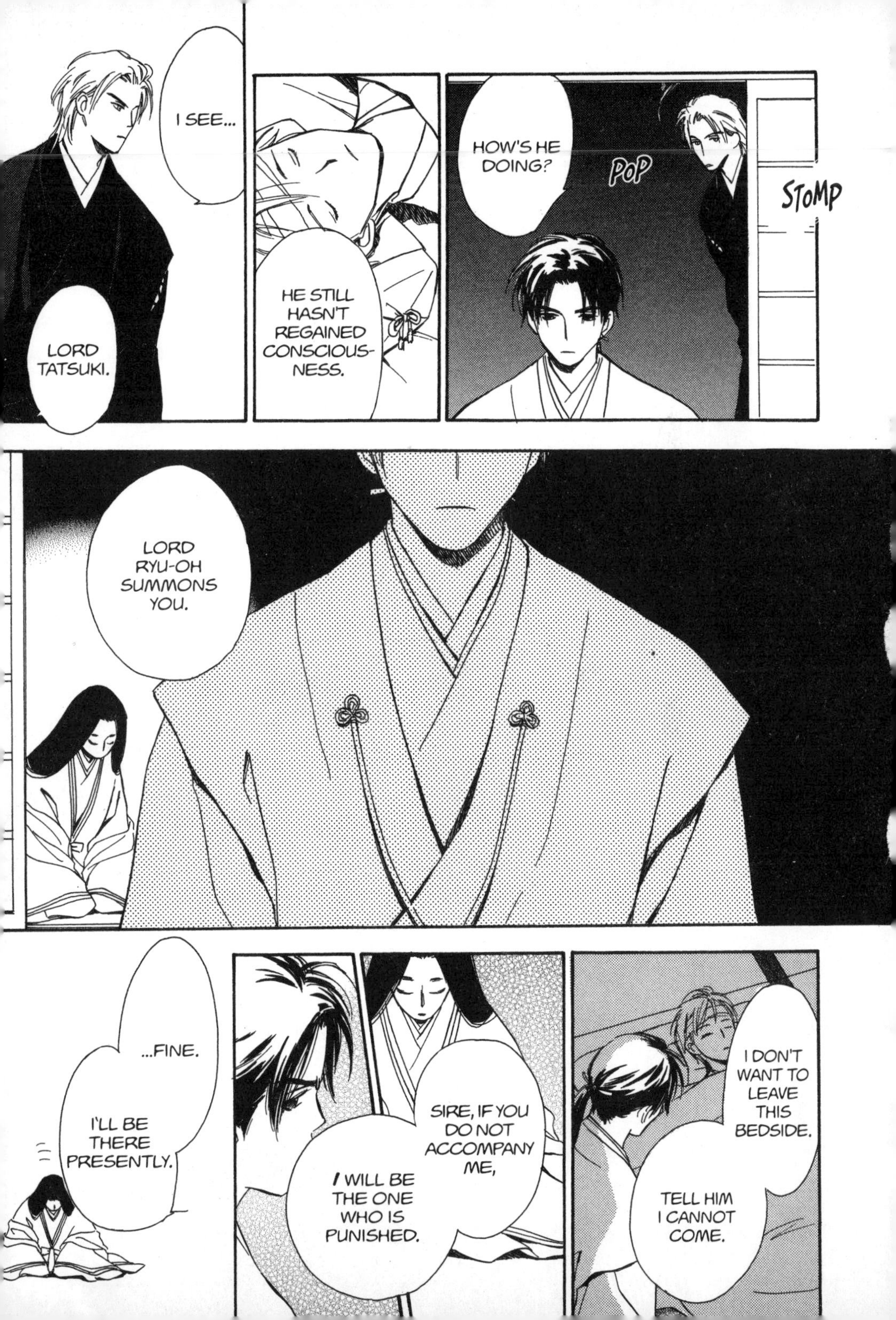
STOMP
POP
HOW'S HE DOING?
HE STILL HASN'T REGAINED CONSCIOUSNESS.
I SEE...
LORD TATSUKI.
LORD RYU-OH SUMMONS YOU.
I DON'T WANT TO LEAVE THIS BEDSIDE.
TELL HIM I CANNOT COME.
SIRE, IF YOU DO NOT ACCOMPANY ME,
I WILL BE THE ONE WHO IS PUNISHED.
...FINE.
I'LL BE THERE PRESENTLY.

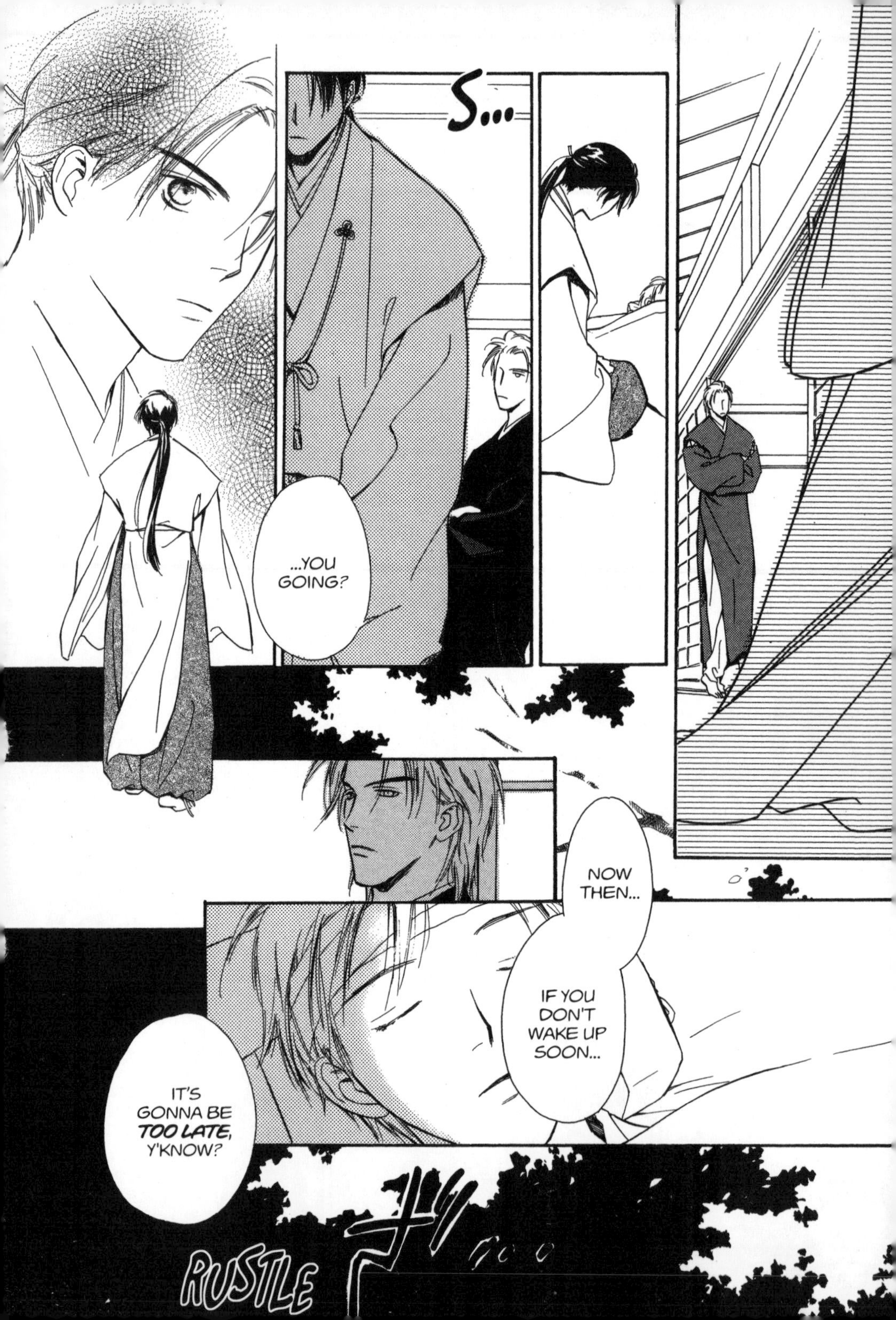
S...
...YOU GOING?
NOW THEN...
IF YOU DON'T WAKE UP SOON...
IT'S GONNA BE **TOO LATE**, Y'KNOW?
RUSTLE

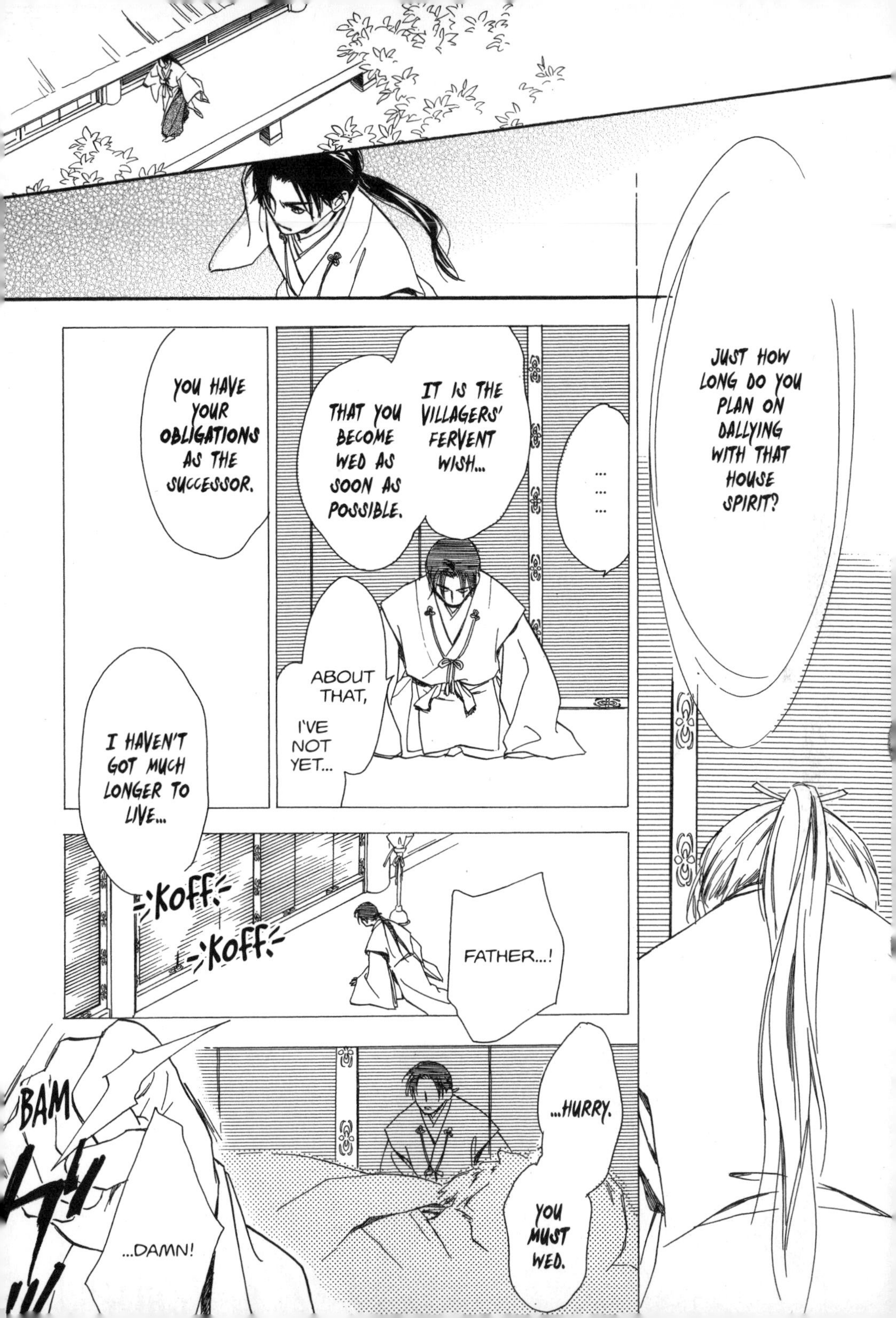
JUST HOW LONG DO YOU PLAN ON DALLYING WITH THAT HOUSE SPIRIT?
IT IS THE VILLAGERS' FERVENT WISH...
THAT YOU BECOME WED AS SOON AS POSSIBLE.
...
...
...
ABOUT THAT,
I'VE NOT YET...
YOU HAVE YOUR OBLIGATIONS AS THE SUCCESSOR.
I HAVEN'T GOT MUCH LONGER TO LIVE...
KOFF
KOFF
FATHER...!
...HURRY.
YOU MUST WED.
BAM
...DAMN!

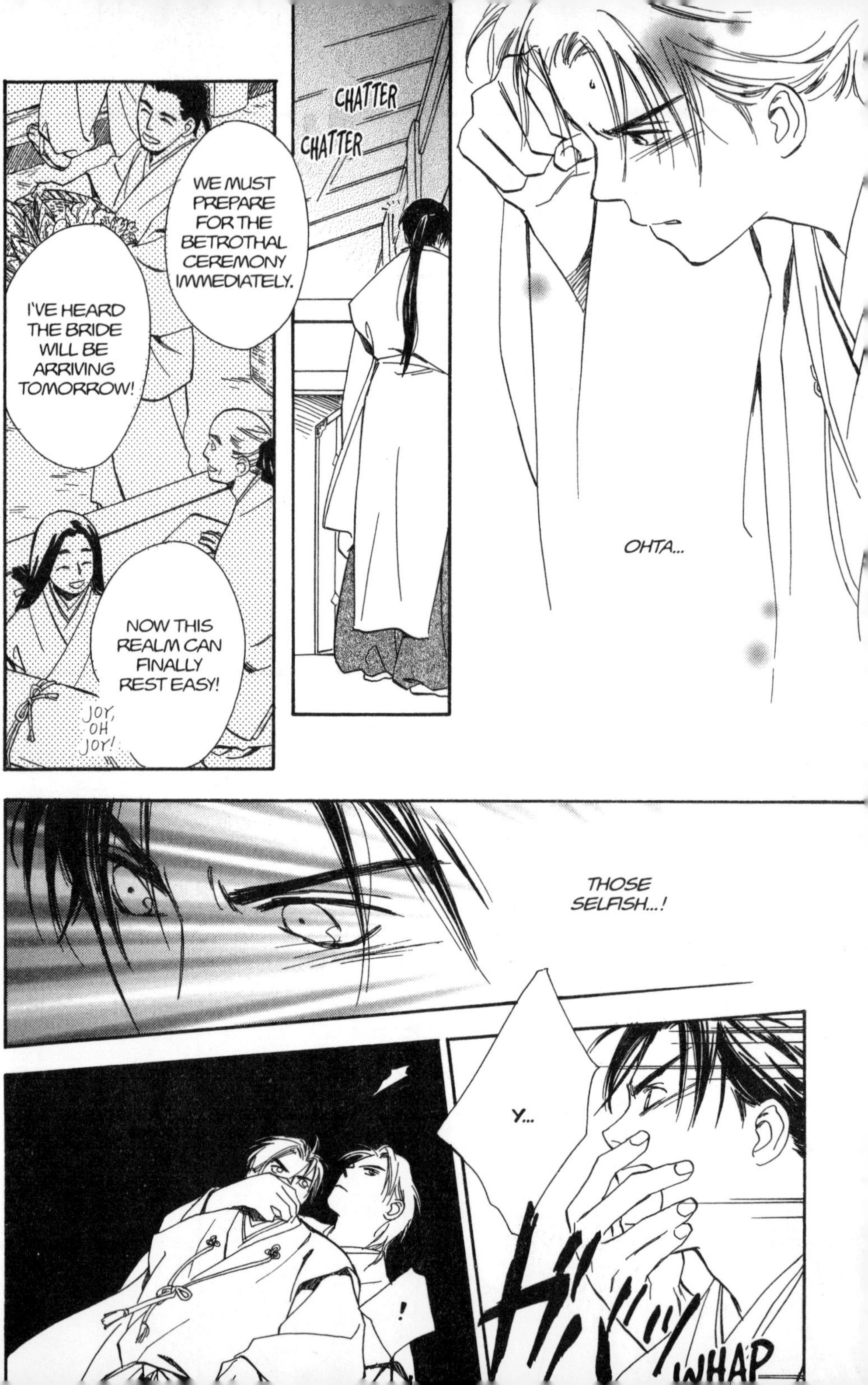
OHTA...
CHATTER
CHATTER
WE MUST PREPARE FOR THE BETROTHAL CEREMONY IMMEDIATELY.
I'VE HEARD THE BRIDE WILL BE ARRIVING TOMORROW!
NOW THIS REALM CAN FINALLY REST EASY!
JOY, OH JOY!
THOSE SELFISH...!
Y...
WHAP
!

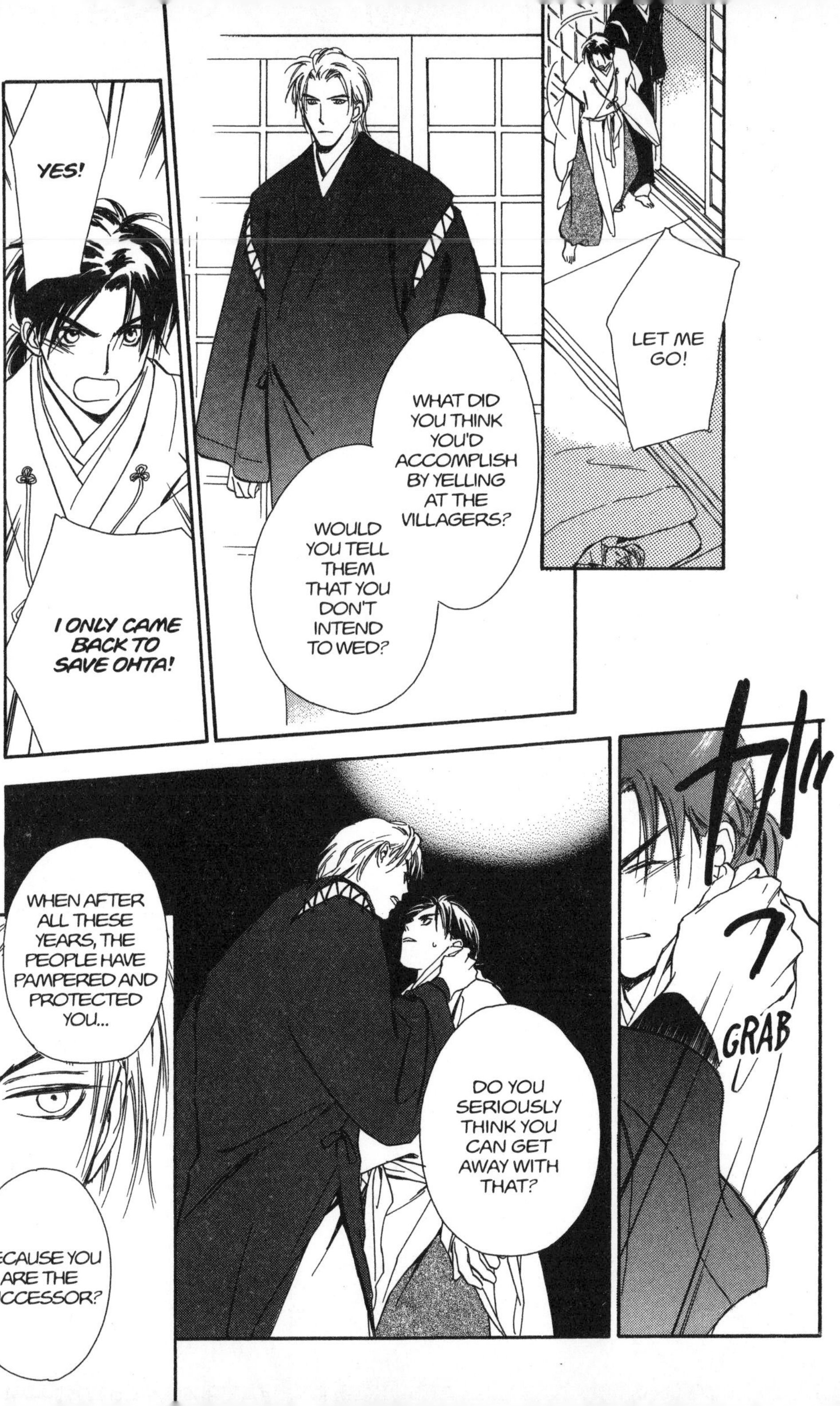
LET ME GO!
WHAT DID YOU THINK YOU'D ACCOMPLISH BY YELLING AT THE VILLAGERS?
WOULD YOU TELL THEM THAT YOU DON'T INTEND TO WED?
YES!
I ONLY CAME BACK TO SAVE OHTA!
GRAB
DO YOU SERIOUSLY THINK YOU CAN GET AWAY WITH THAT?
WHEN AFTER ALL THESE YEARS, THE PEOPLE HAVE PAMPERED AND PROTECTED YOU...
BECAUSE YOU ARE THE SUCCESSOR?

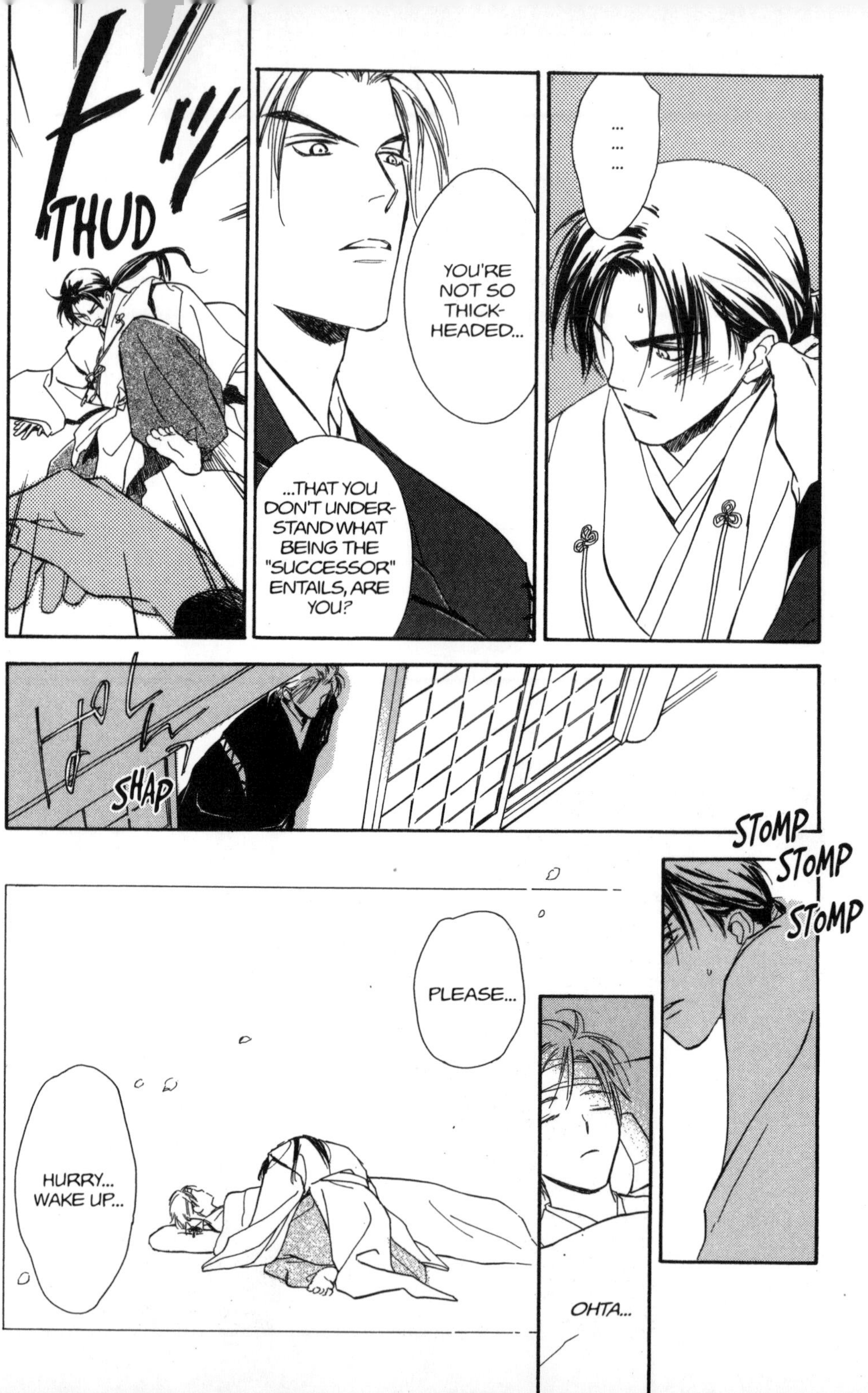
...
...
...
YOU'RE NOT SO THICK-HEADED...
...THAT YOU DON'T UNDERSTAND WHAT BEING THE "SUCCESSOR" ENTAILS, ARE YOU?
ドッ
THUD
SHAP
STOMP
STOMP
STOMP
OHTA...
PLEASE...
HURRY... WAKE UP...

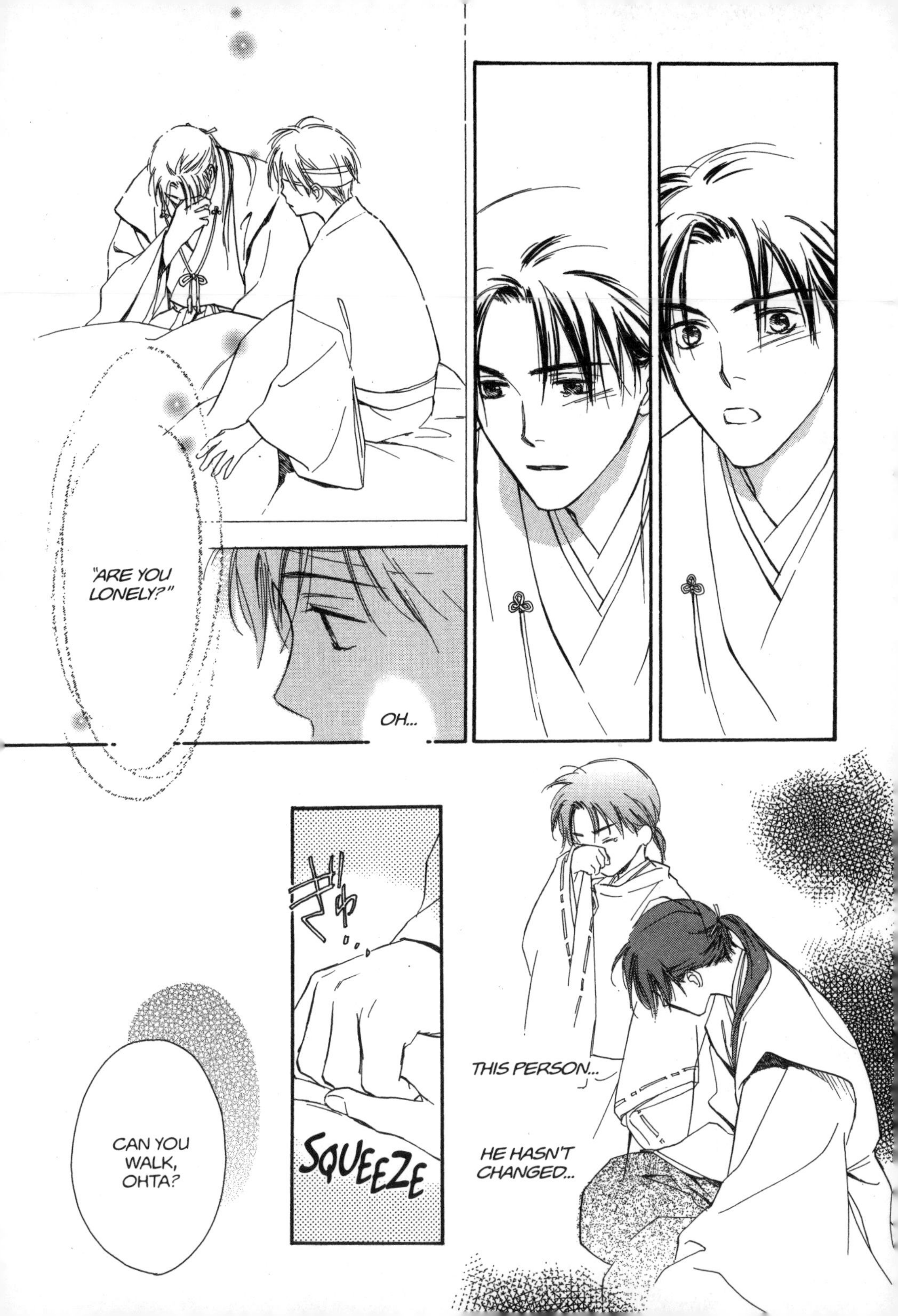
"ARE YOU LONELY?"
OH...
THIS PERSON...
HE HASN'T CHANGED...
ぎゅ...
SQUEEZE
CAN YOU WALK, OHTA?

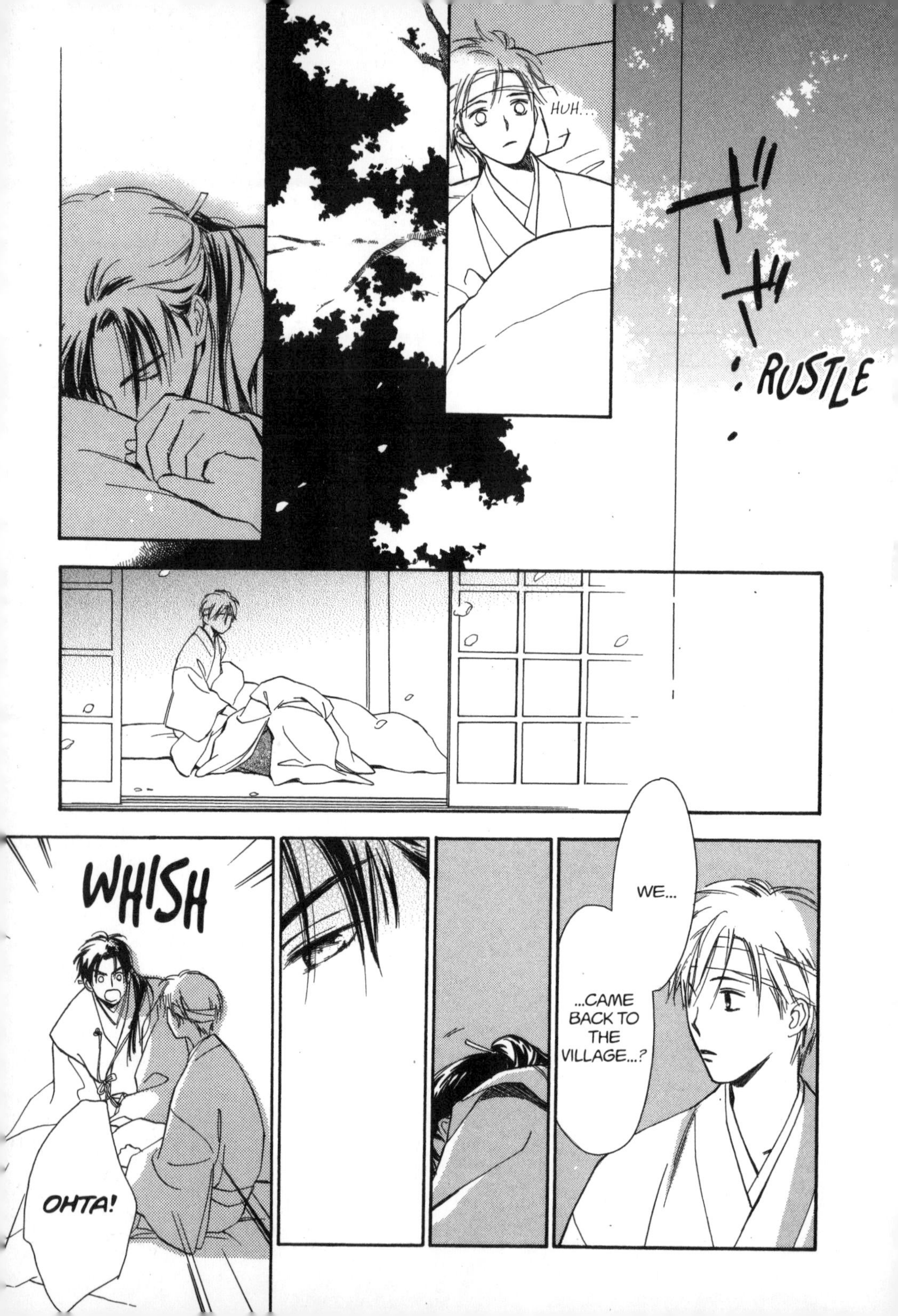
ザーザー: RUSTLE
HUH...
WE...
...CAME BACK TO THE VILLAGE...?
WHISH
OHTA!

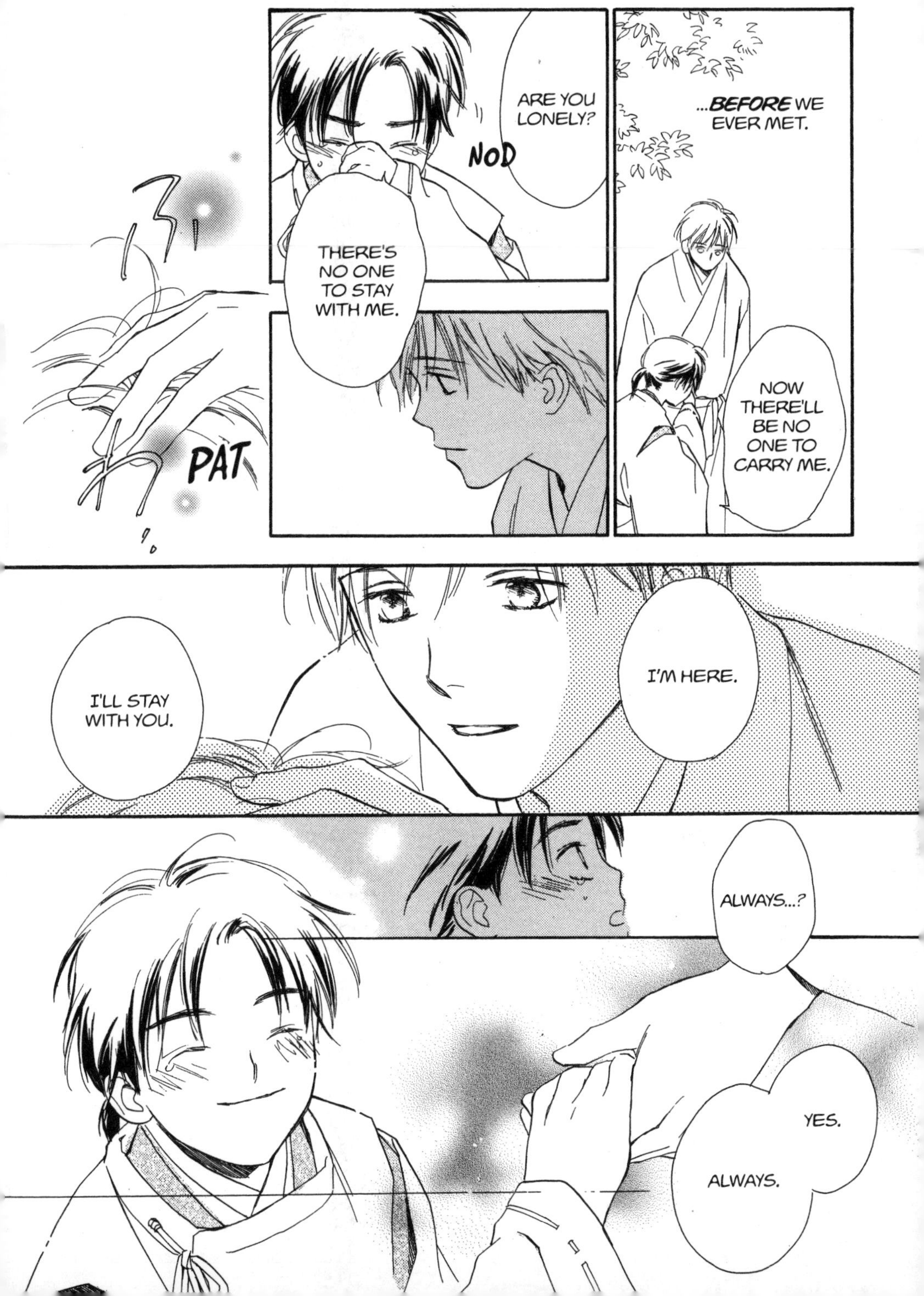
...BEFORE WE EVER MET.
NOW THERE'LL BE NO ONE TO CARRY ME.
ARE YOU LONELY?
NOD
THERE'S NO ONE TO STAY WITH ME.
PAT
I'M HERE.
I'LL STAY WITH YOU.
ALWAYS...?
YES. ALWAYS.

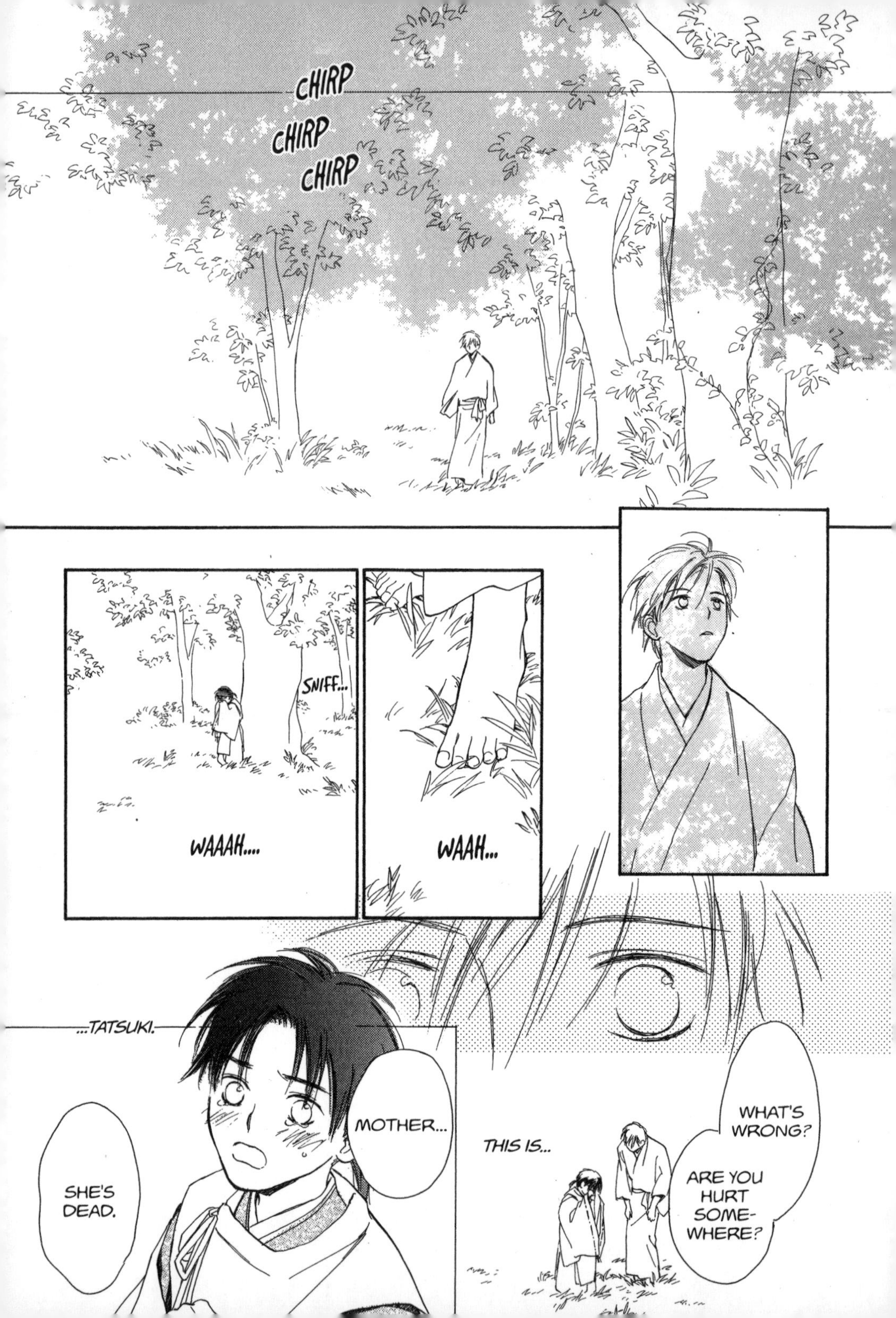
CHIRP
CHIRP
CHIRP
WAAH...
SNIFF...
WAAAH....
WHAT'S WRONG?
ARE YOU HURT SOME-WHERE?
THIS IS...
...TATSUKI.
MOTHER...
SHE'S DEAD.

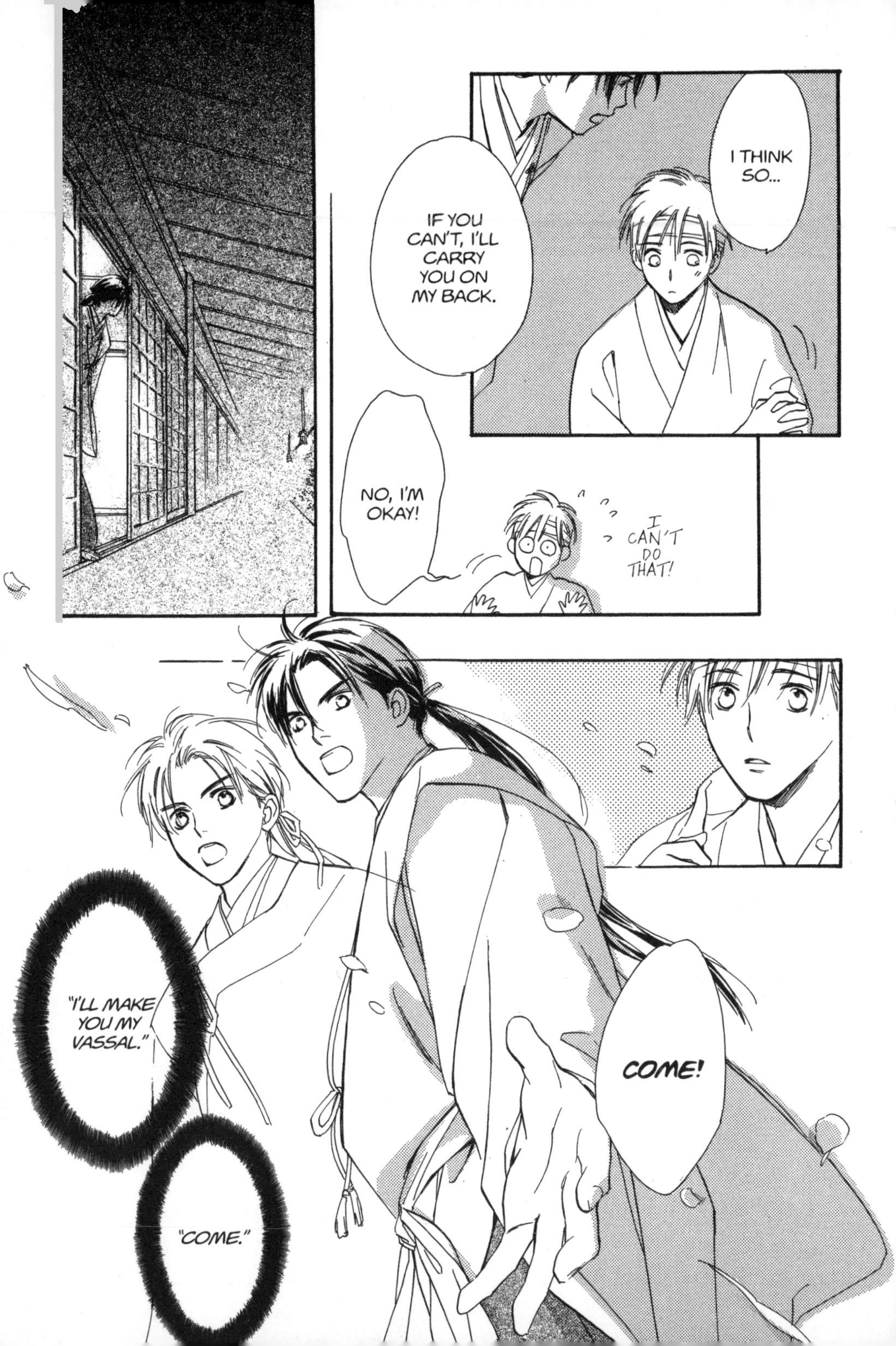
I THINK SO...
IF YOU CAN'T, I'LL CARRY YOU ON MY BACK.
NO, I'M OKAY!
I CAN'T DO THAT!
COME!
"I'LL MAKE YOU MY VASSAL."
"COME."

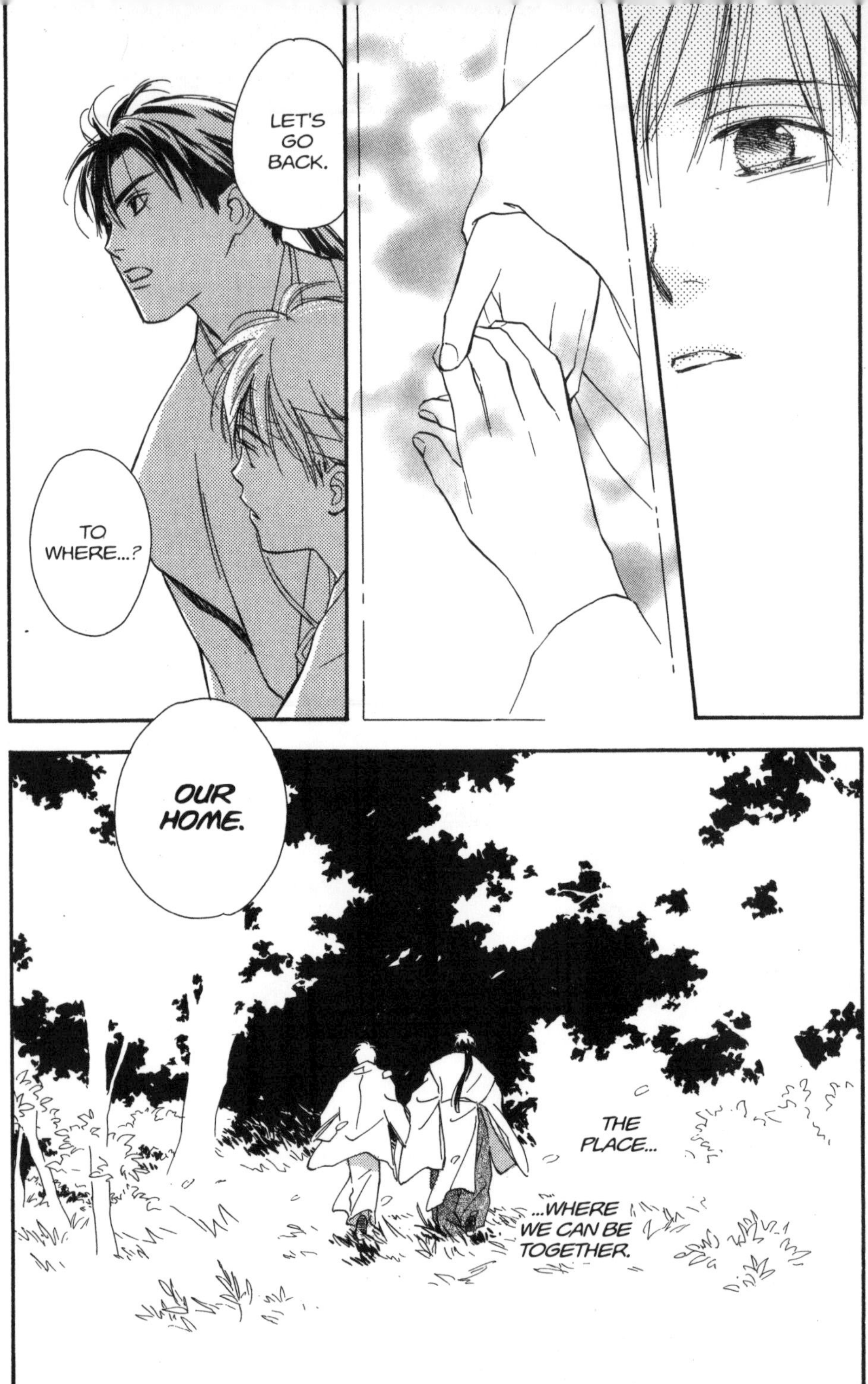
LET'S GO BACK.
TO WHERE...?
OUR HOME.
THE PLACE...
...WHERE WE CAN BE TOGETHER.

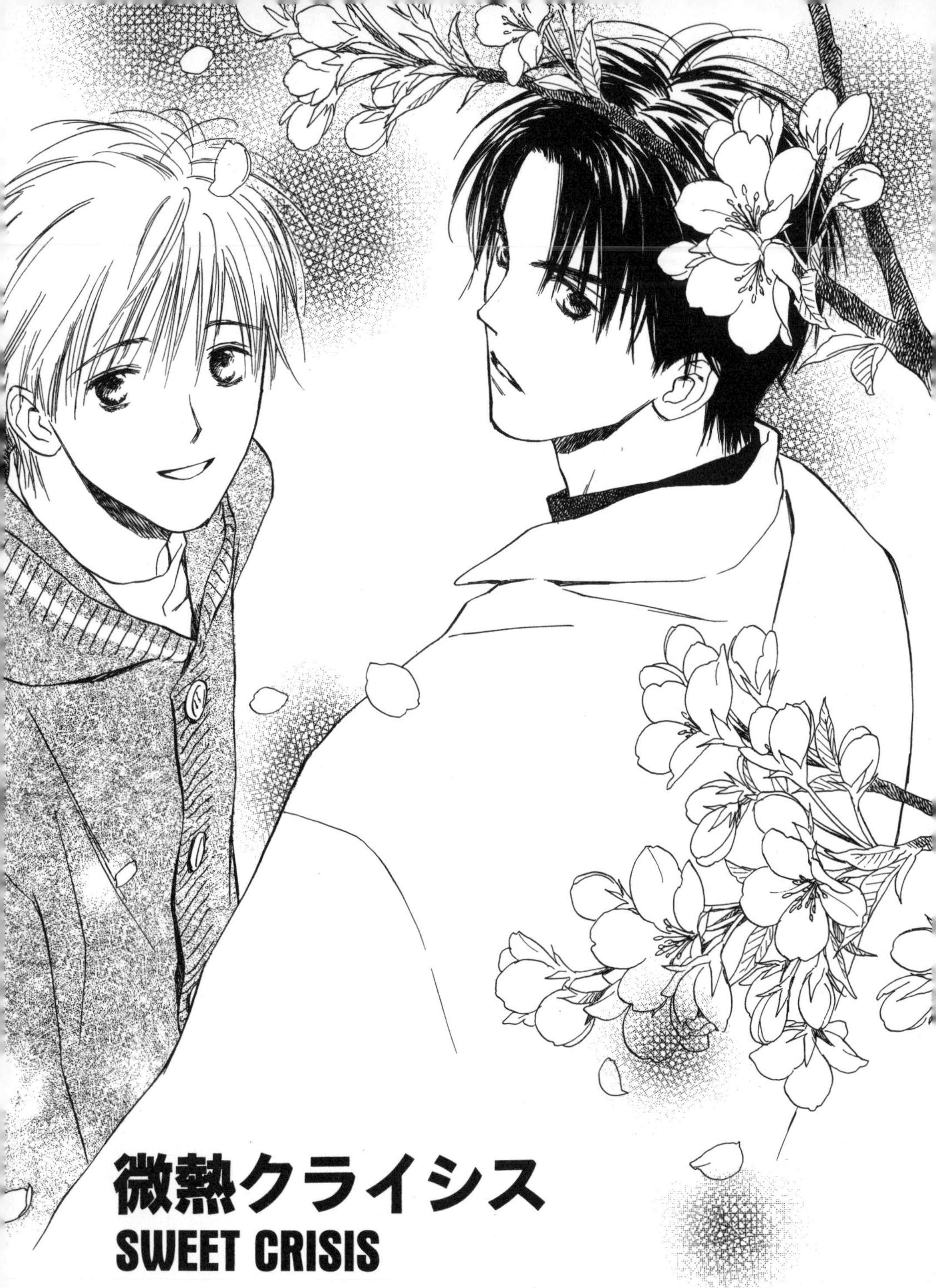

微熱クライシス
SWEET CRISIS

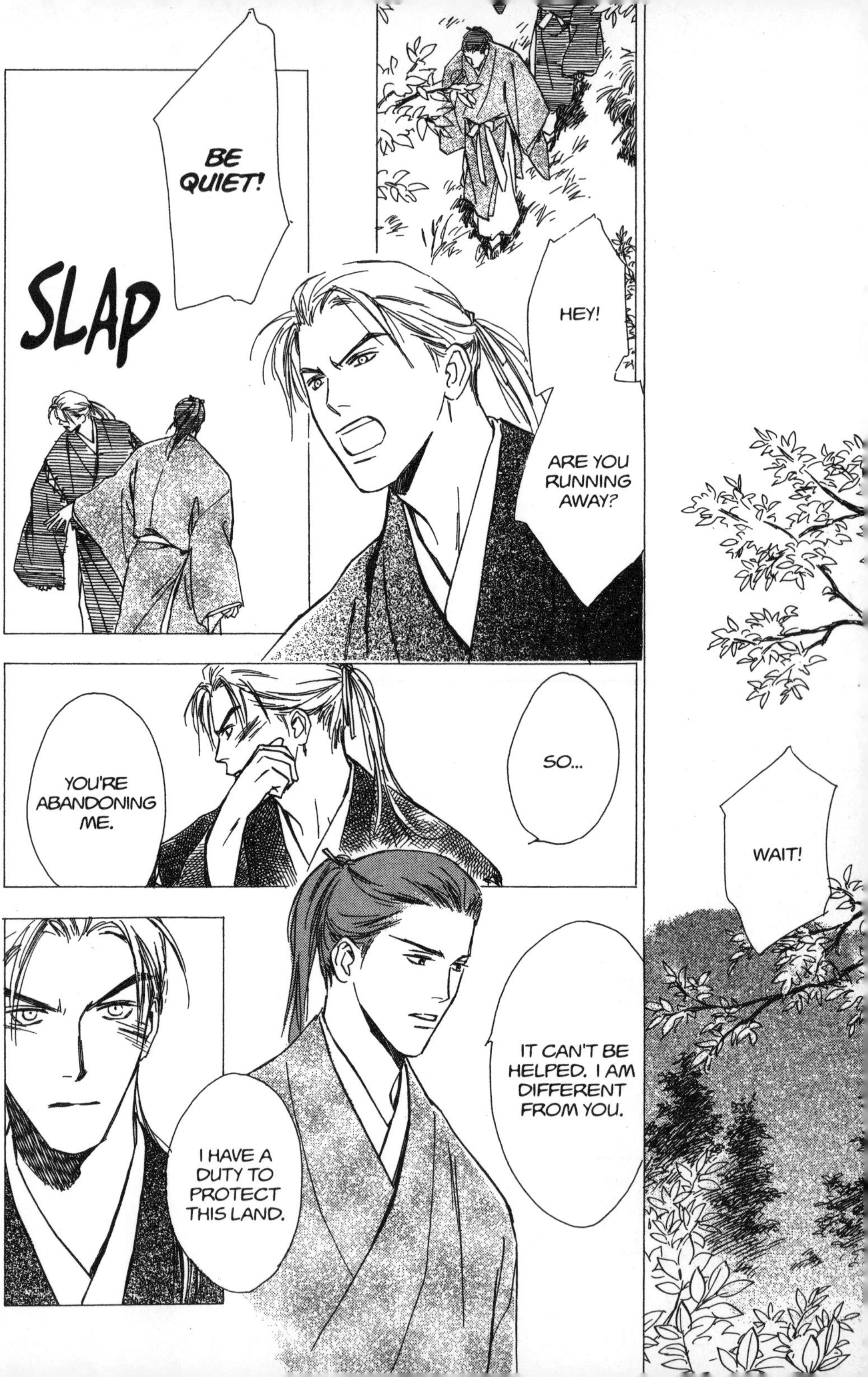
WAIT!
HEY!
ARE YOU RUNNING AWAY?
BE QUIET!
SLAP
SO...
YOU'RE ABANDONING ME.
IT CAN'T BE HELPED. I AM DIFFERENT FROM YOU.
I HAVE A DUTY TO PROTECT THIS LAND.

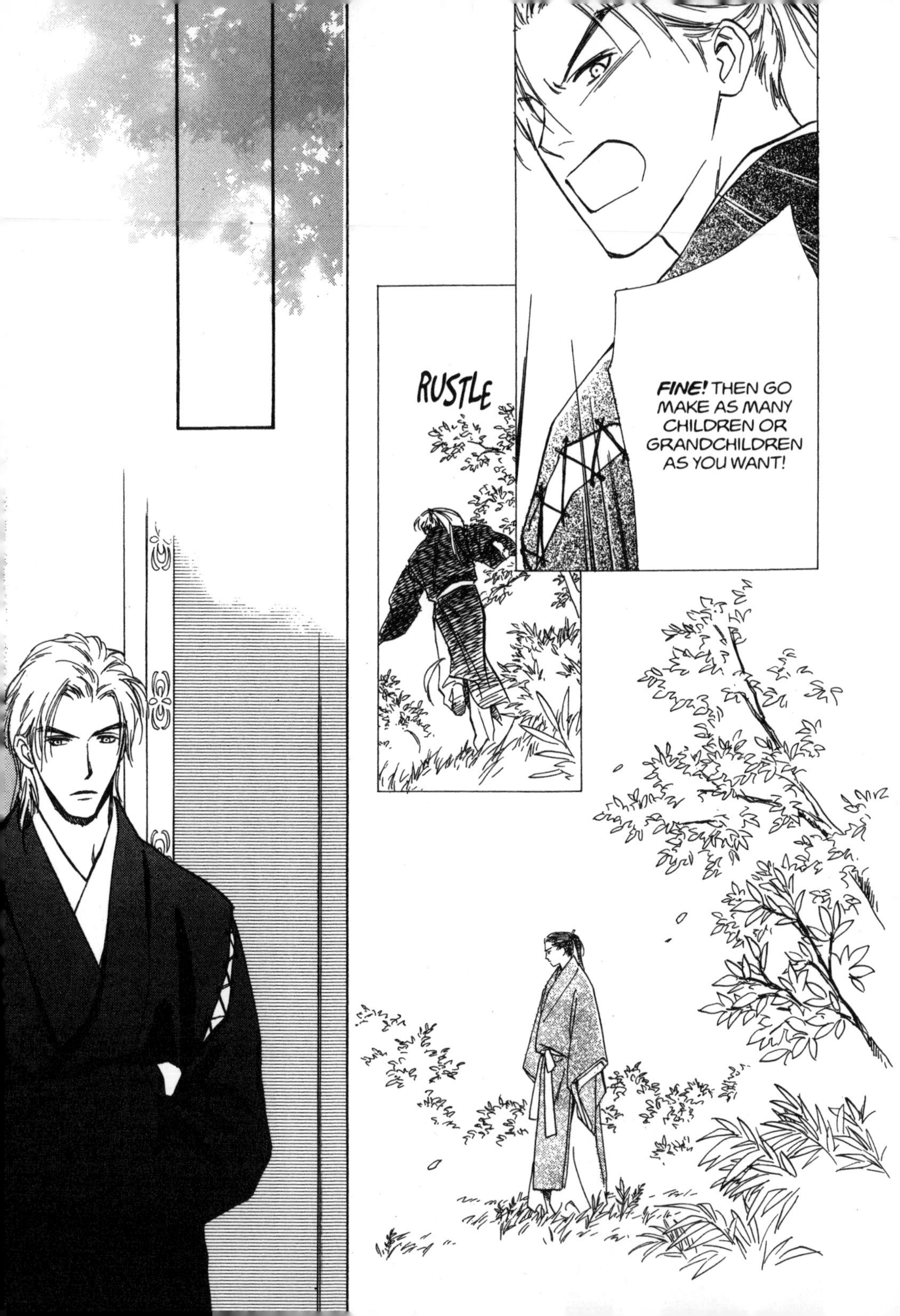
FINE! THEN GO MAKE AS MANY CHILDREN OR GRANDCHILDREN AS YOU WANT!
RUSTLE

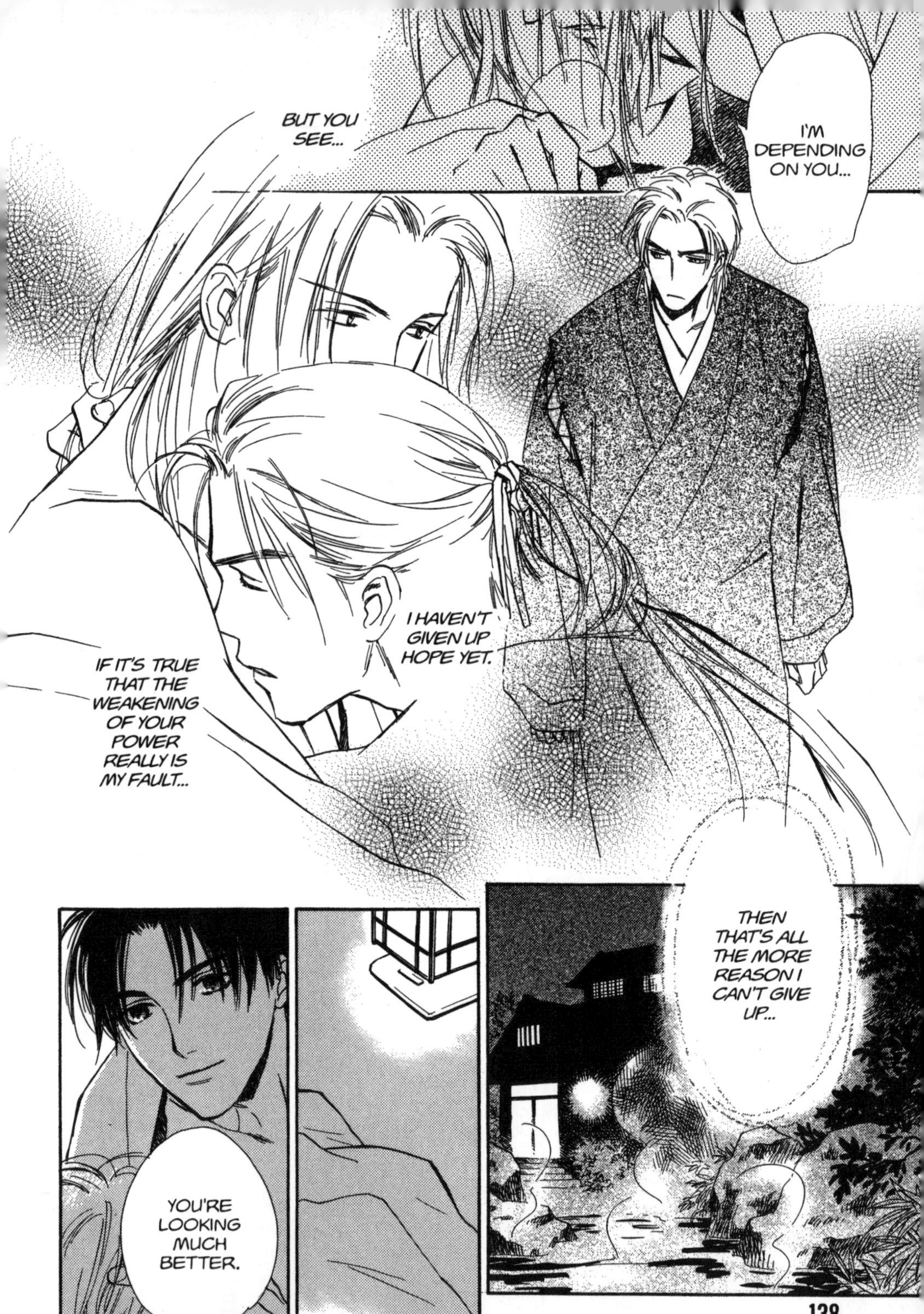
I'M DEPENDING ON YOU...
BUT YOU SEE...
I HAVEN'T GIVEN UP HOPE YET.
IF IT'S TRUE THAT THE WEAKENING OF YOUR POWER REALLY IS MY FAULT...
THEN THAT'S ALL THE MORE REASON I CAN'T GIVE UP...
YOU'RE LOOKING MUCH BETTER.

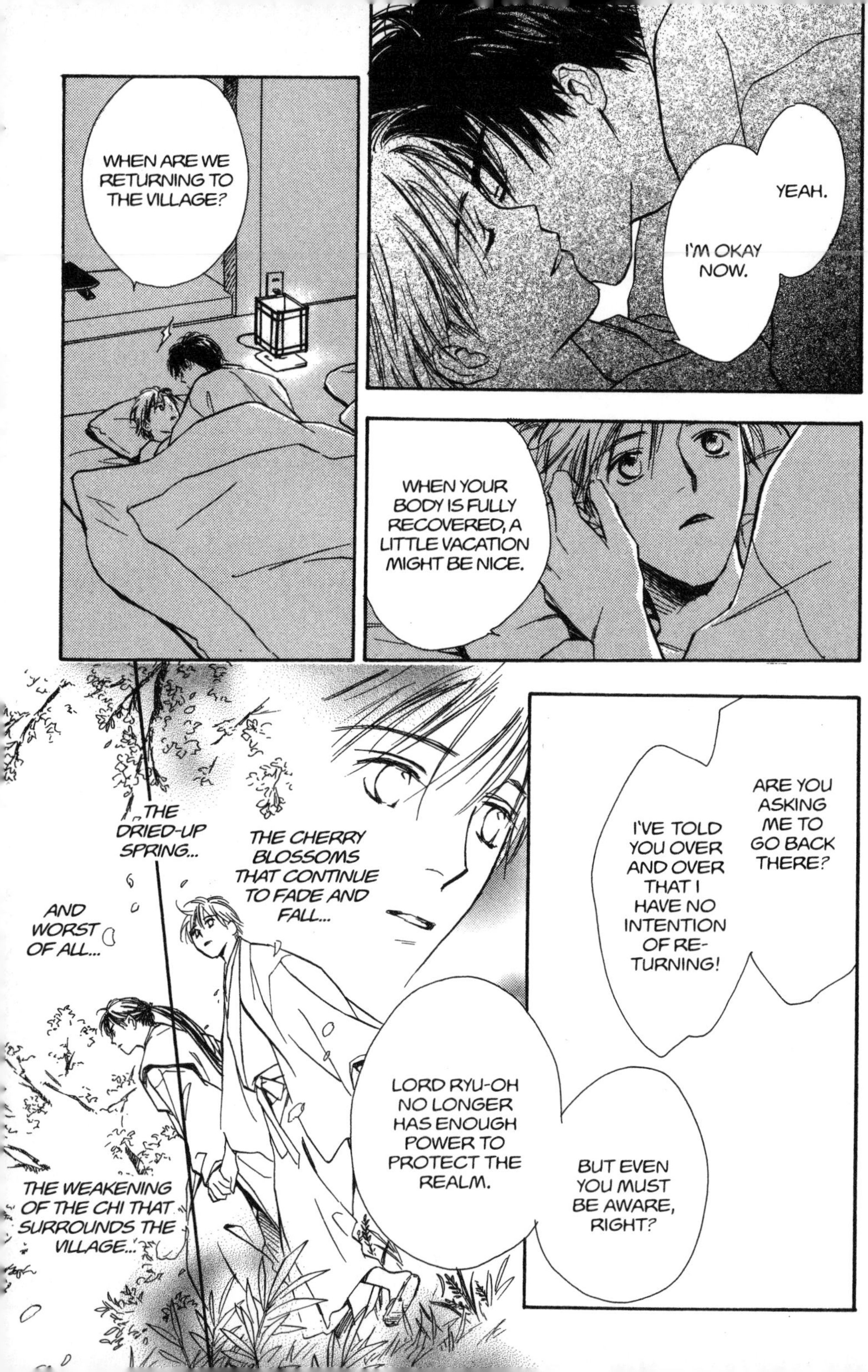
YEAH.
I'M OKAY NOW.
WHEN YOUR BODY IS FULLY RECOVERED, A LITTLE VACATION MIGHT BE NICE.
WHEN ARE WE RETURNING TO THE VILLAGE?
ARE YOU ASKING ME TO GO BACK THERE?
I'VE TOLD YOU OVER AND OVER THAT I HAVE NO INTENTION OF RE-TURNING!
LORD RYU-OH NO LONGER HAS ENOUGH POWER TO PROTECT THE REALM.
BUT EVEN YOU MUST BE AWARE, RIGHT?
...THE DRIED-UP SPRING...
THE CHERRY BLOSSOMS THAT CONTINUE TO FADE AND FALL...
AND WORST OF ALL...
THE WEAKENING OF THE CHI THAT SURROUNDS THE VILLAGE...

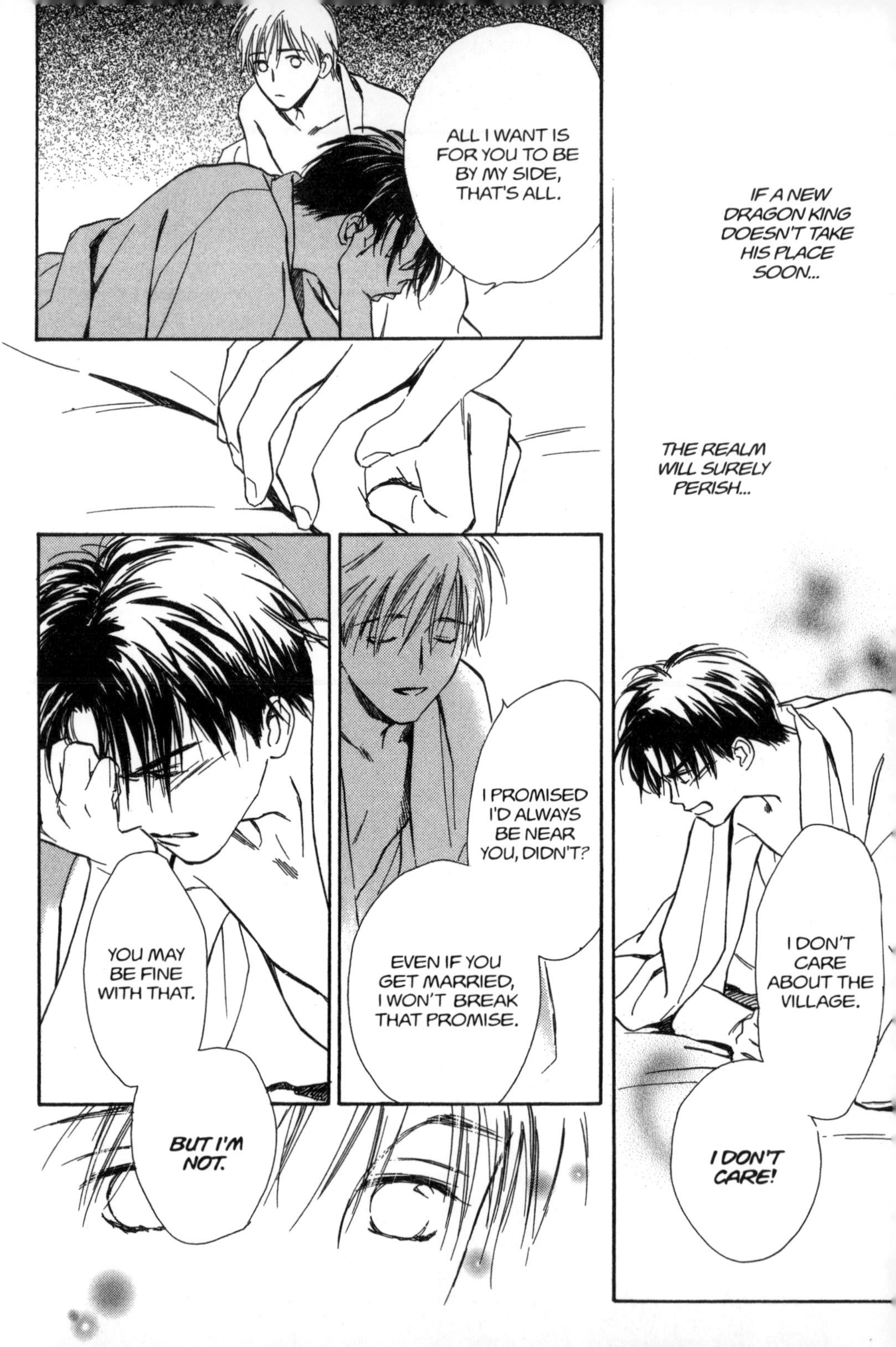
IF A NEW DRAGON KING DOESN'T TAKE HIS PLACE SOON...
THE REALM WILL SURELY PERISH...
I DON'T CARE ABOUT THE VILLAGE.
I DON'T CARE!
ALL I WANT IS FOR YOU TO BE BY MY SIDE, THAT'S ALL.
I PROMISED I'D ALWAYS BE NEAR YOU, DIDN'T?
EVEN IF YOU GET MARRIED, I WON'T BREAK THAT PROMISE.
YOU MAY BE FINE WITH THAT.
BUT I'M NOT.

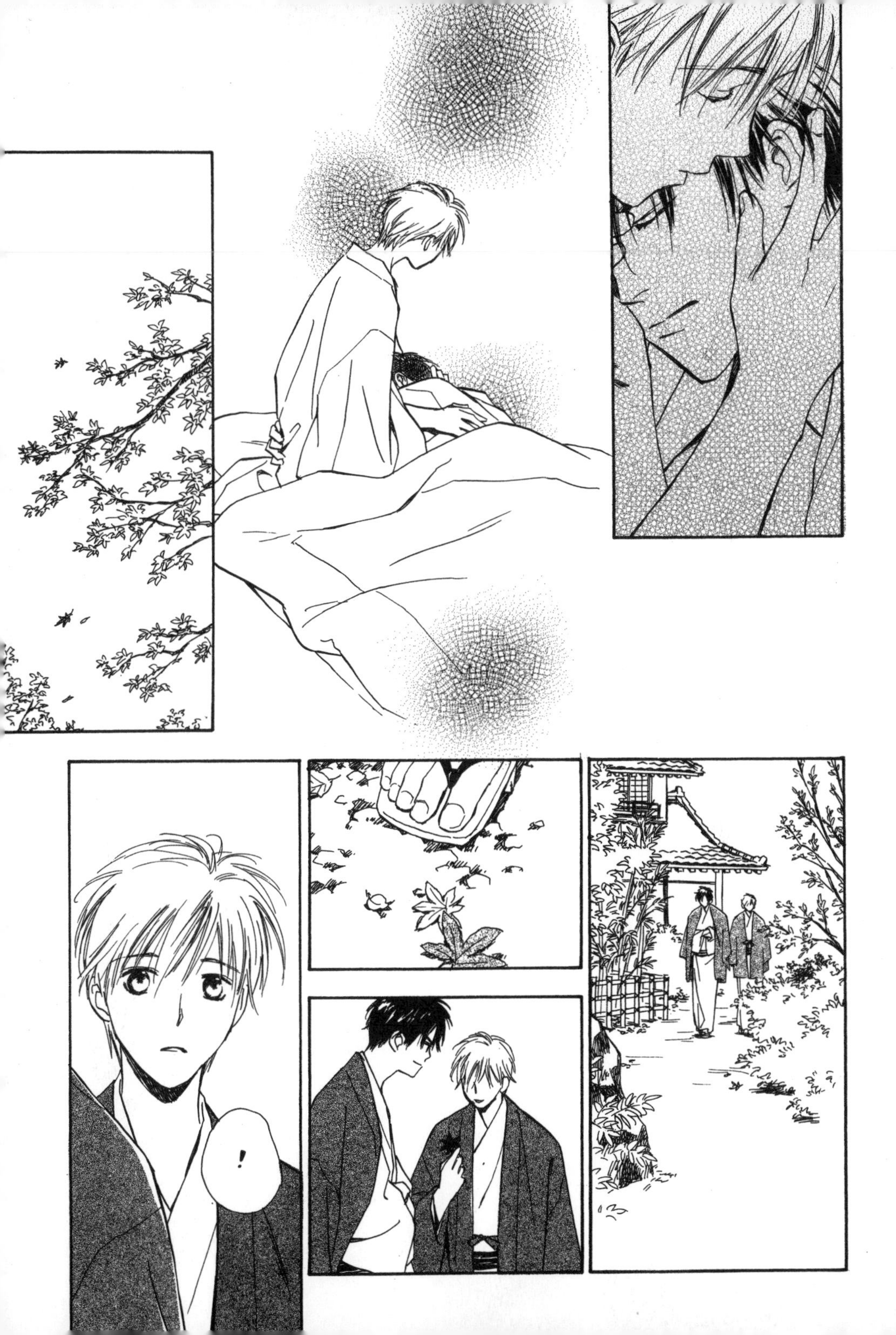
!

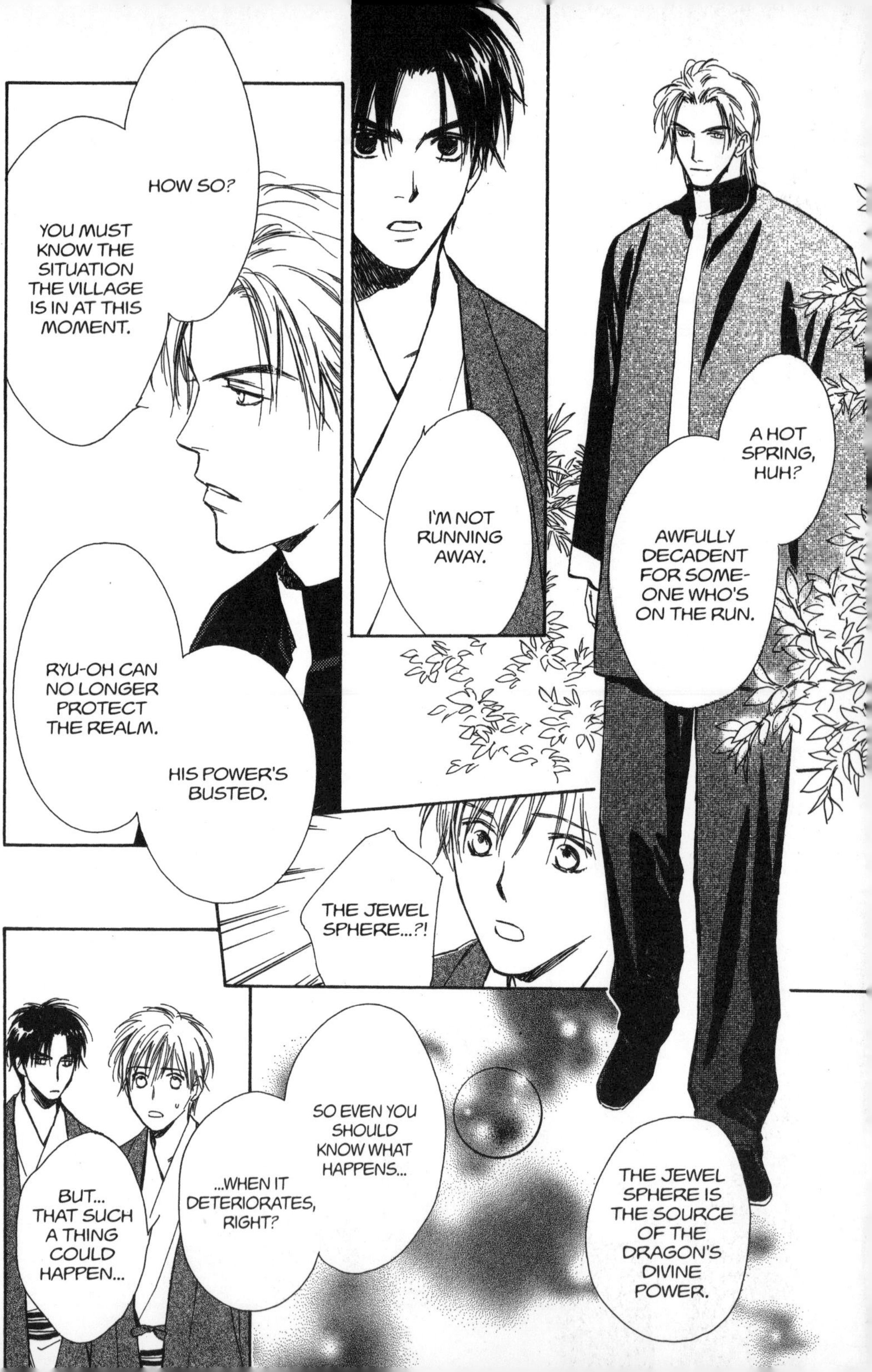
A HOT SPRING, HUH?
AWFULLY DECADENT FOR SOME-ONE WHO'S ON THE RUN.
I'M NOT RUNNING AWAY.
HOW SO?
YOU MUST KNOW THE SITUATION THE VILLAGE IS IN AT THIS MOMENT.
RYU-OH CAN NO LONGER PROTECT THE REALM.
HIS POWER'S BUSTED.
THE JEWEL SPHERE...?!
THE JEWEL SPHERE IS THE SOURCE OF THE DRAGON'S DIVINE POWER.
SO EVEN YOU SHOULD KNOW WHAT HAPPENS...
...WHEN IT DETERIORATES, RIGHT?
BUT... THAT SUCH A THING COULD HAPPEN...

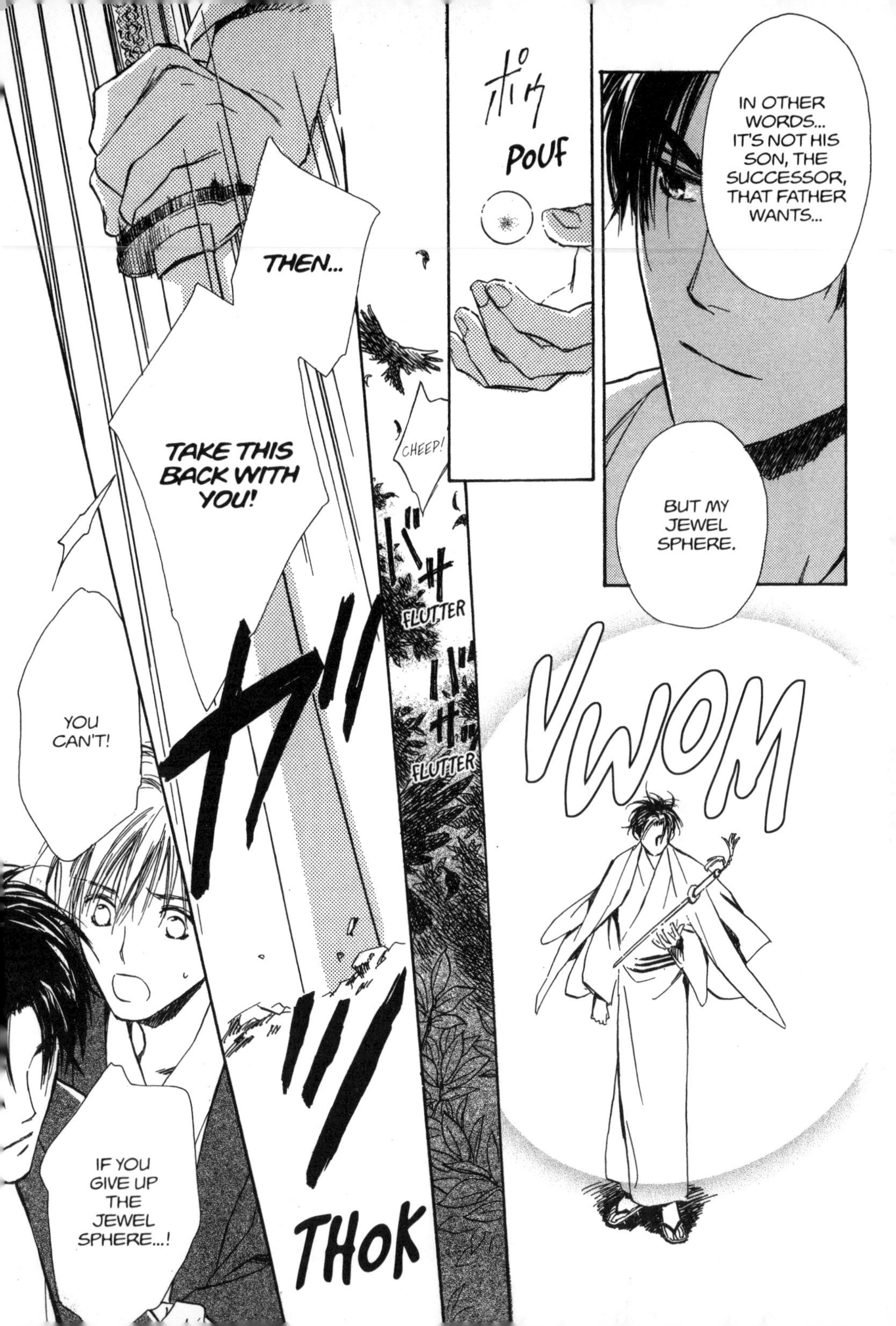
IN OTHER WORDS... IT'S NOT HIS SON, THE SUCCESSOR, THAT FATHER WANTS...
BUT MY JEWEL SPHERE.
ポフ
POUF
CHEEP!
THEN...
TAKE THIS BACK WITH YOU!
VWOM
FLUTTER
FLUTTER
THOK
YOU CAN'T!
IF YOU GIVE UP THE JEWEL SPHERE...!

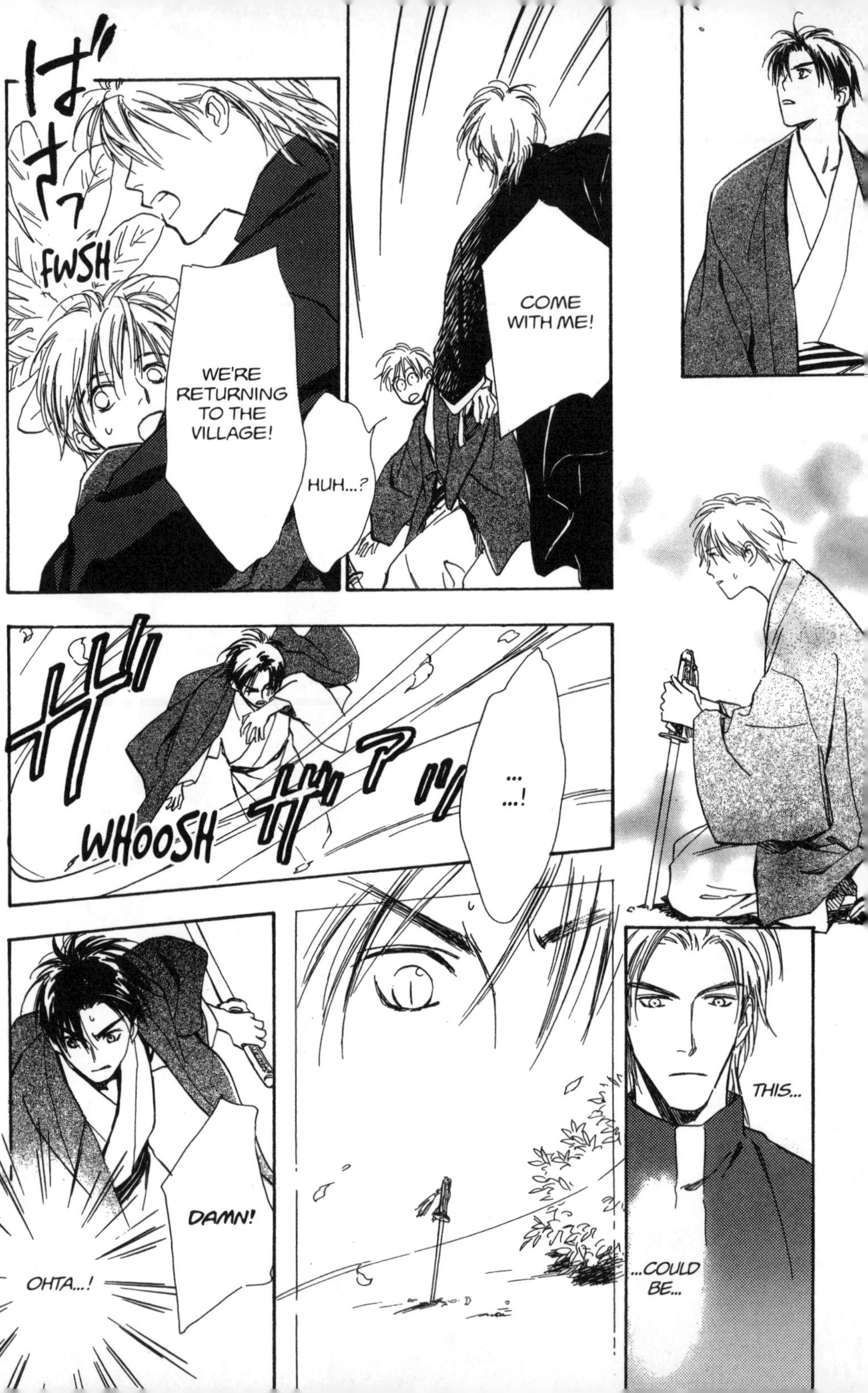
COME WITH ME!
HUH...?
ばさっ
FWSH
WE'RE RETURNING TO THE VILLAGE!
...
...!
ザザァッ
WHOOSH
THIS...
...COULD BE...
DAMN!
OHTA...!

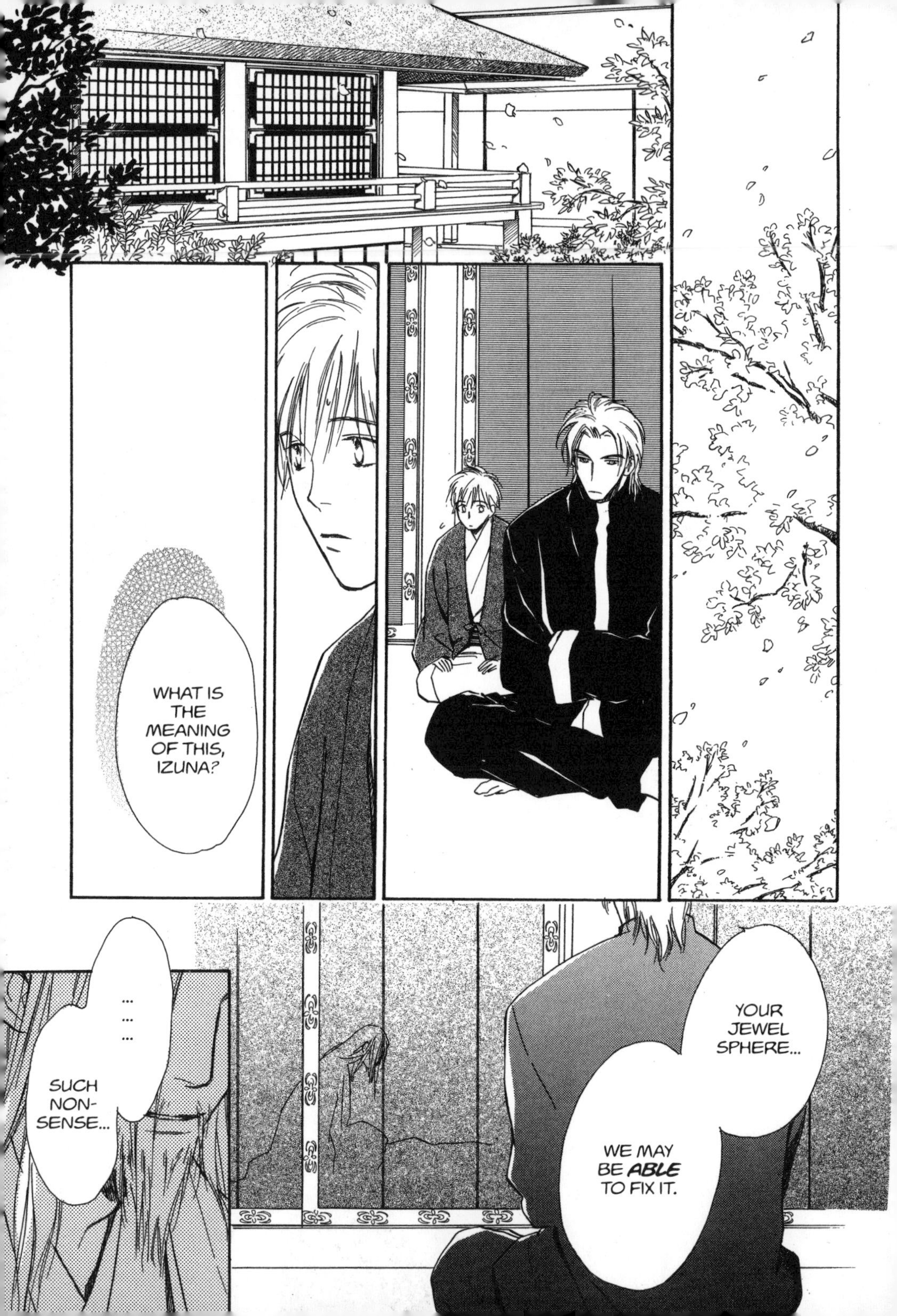
WHAT IS THE MEANING OF THIS, IZUNA?
YOUR JEWEL SPHERE...
WE MAY BE **ABLE** TO FIX IT.
...
...
...
SUCH NON-SENSE...

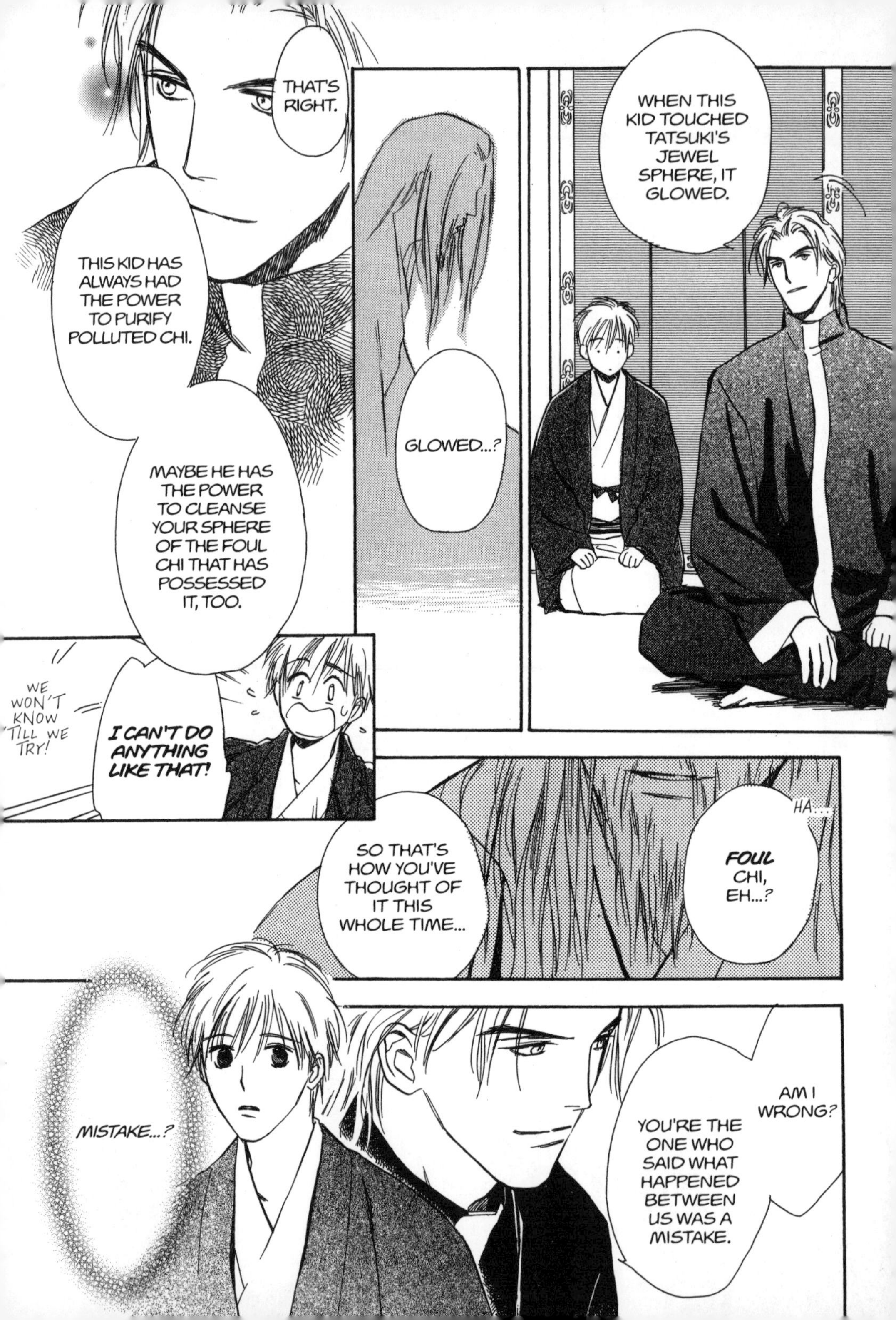
WHEN THIS KID TOUCHED TATSUKI'S JEWEL SPHERE, IT GLOWED.
GLOWED...?
THAT'S RIGHT.
THIS KID HAS ALWAYS HAD THE POWER TO PURIFY POLLUTED CHI.
MAYBE HE HAS THE POWER TO CLEANSE YOUR SPHERE OF THE FOUL CHI THAT HAS POSSESSED IT, TOO.
I CAN'T DO ANYTHING LIKE THAT!
WE WON'T KNOW TILL WE TRY!
HA...
FOUL CHI, EH...?
SO THAT'S HOW YOU'VE THOUGHT OF IT THIS WHOLE TIME...
AM I WRONG?
YOU'RE THE ONE WHO SAID WHAT HAPPENED BETWEEN US WAS A MISTAKE.
MISTAKE...?

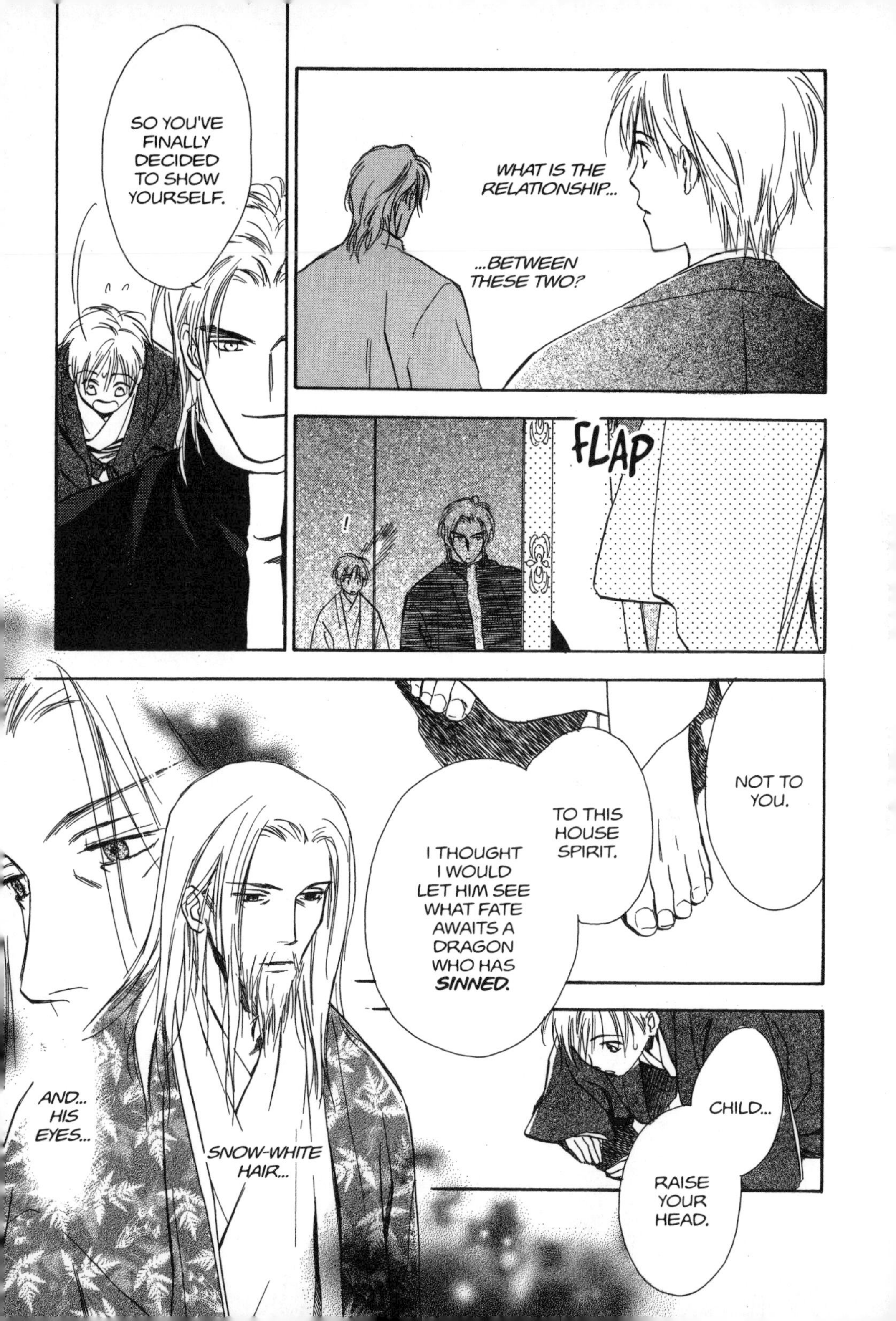
WHAT IS THE RELATIONSHIP...
...BETWEEN THESE TWO?
FLAP
!
SO YOU'VE FINALLY DECIDED TO SHOW YOURSELF.
NOT TO YOU.
TO THIS HOUSE SPIRIT.
I THOUGHT I WOULD LET HIM SEE WHAT FATE AWAITS A DRAGON WHO HAS **SINNED**.
CHILD...
RAISE YOUR HEAD.
SNOW-WHITE HAIR...
AND... HIS EYES...

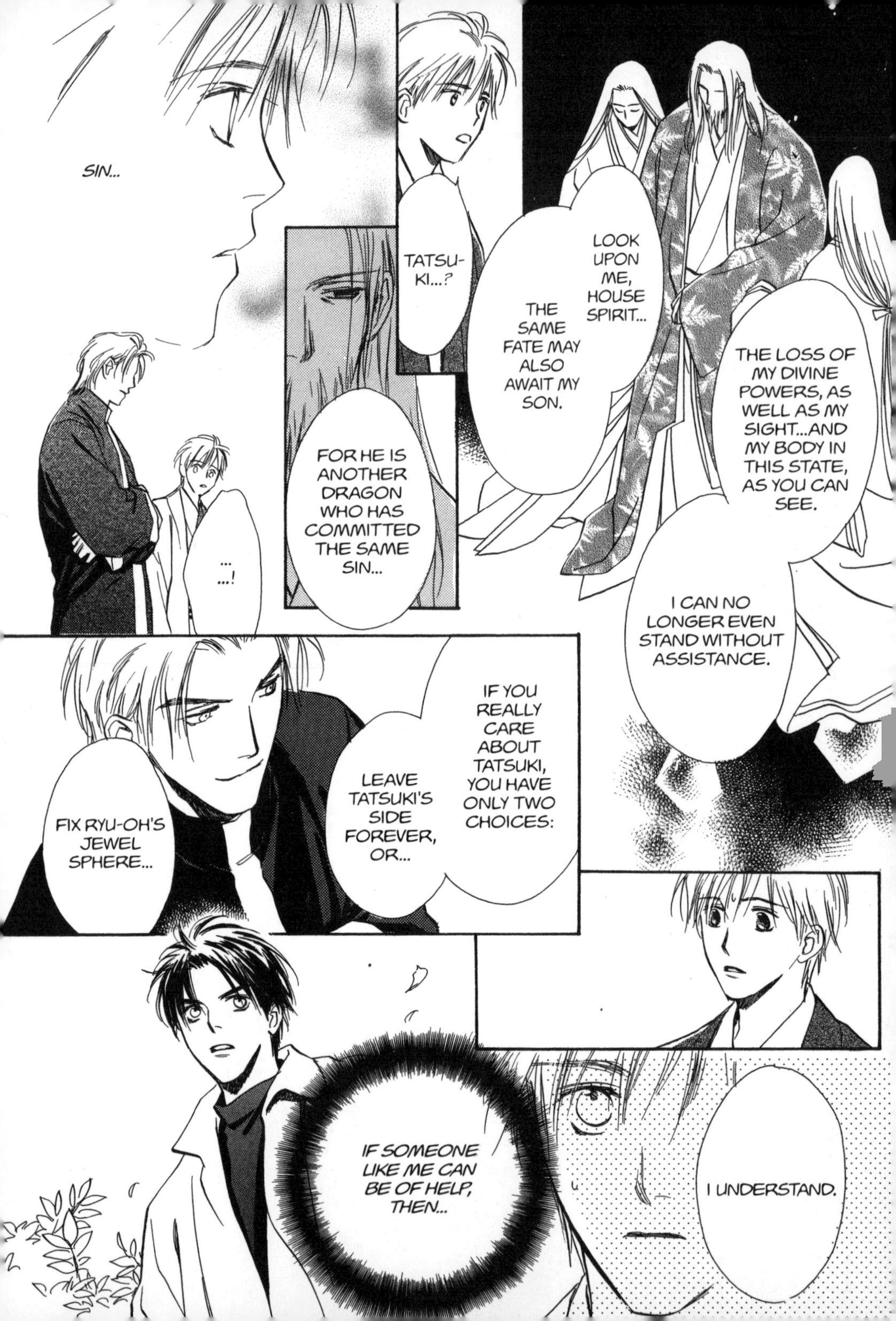
LOOK UPON ME, HOUSE SPIRIT...
THE LOSS OF MY DIVINE POWERS, AS WELL AS MY SIGHT...AND MY BODY IN THIS STATE, AS YOU CAN SEE.
I CAN NO LONGER EVEN STAND WITHOUT ASSISTANCE.
THE SAME FATE MAY ALSO AWAIT MY SON.
TATSU-KI...?
FOR HE IS ANOTHER DRAGON WHO HAS COMMITTED THE SAME SIN...
SIN...
... ...!
IF YOU REALLY CARE ABOUT TATSUKI, YOU HAVE ONLY TWO CHOICES:
LEAVE TATSUKI'S SIDE FOREVER, OR...
FIX RYU-OH'S JEWEL SPHERE...
I UNDERSTAND.
IF SOMEONE LIKE ME CAN BE OF HELP, THEN...

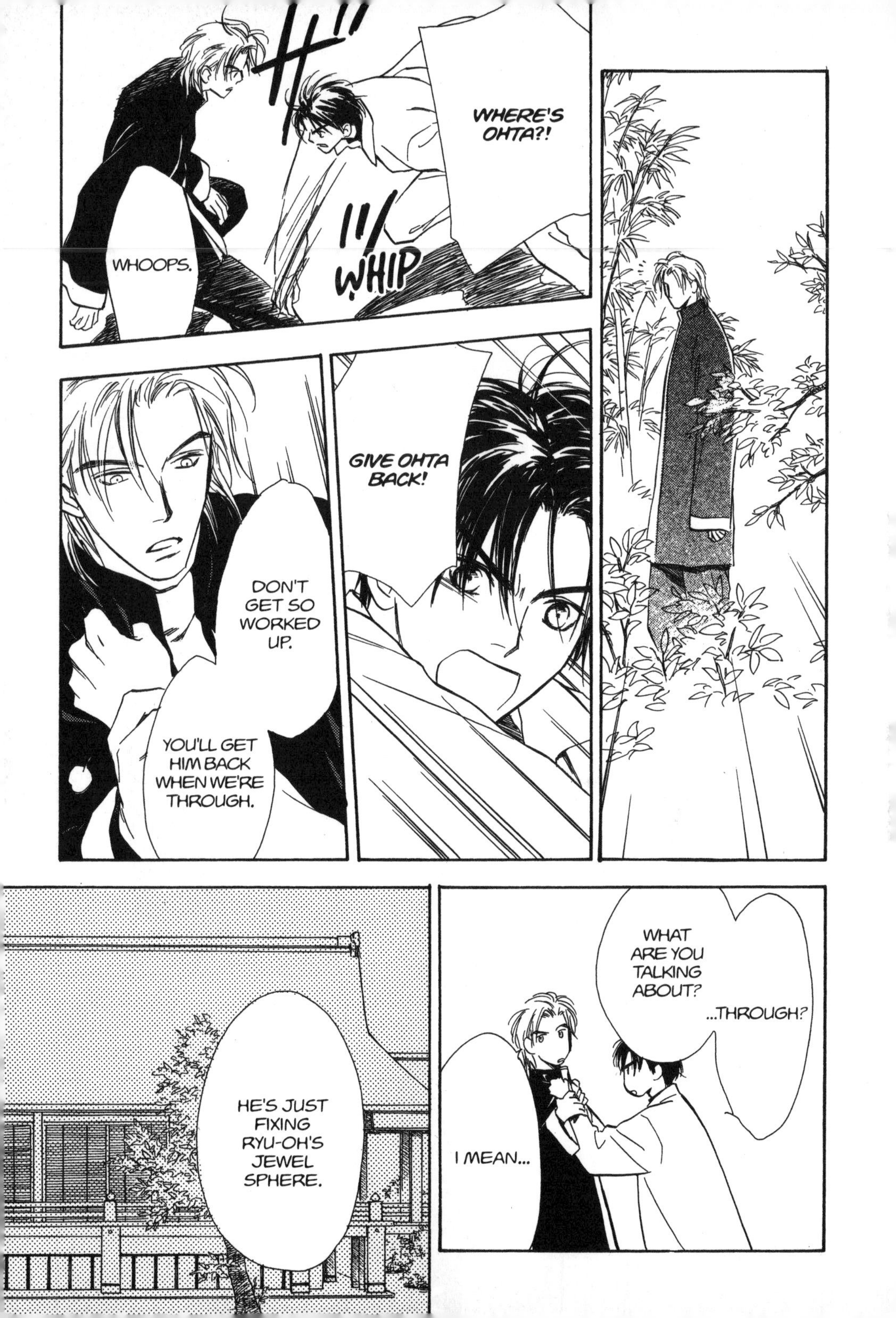
WHERE'S OHTA?!
WHIP
WHOOPS.
GIVE OHTA BACK!
DON'T GET SO WORKED UP.
YOU'LL GET HIM BACK WHEN WE'RE THROUGH.
WHAT ARE YOU TALKING ABOUT?
...THROUGH?
I MEAN...
HE'S JUST FIXING RYU-OH'S JEWEL SPHERE.

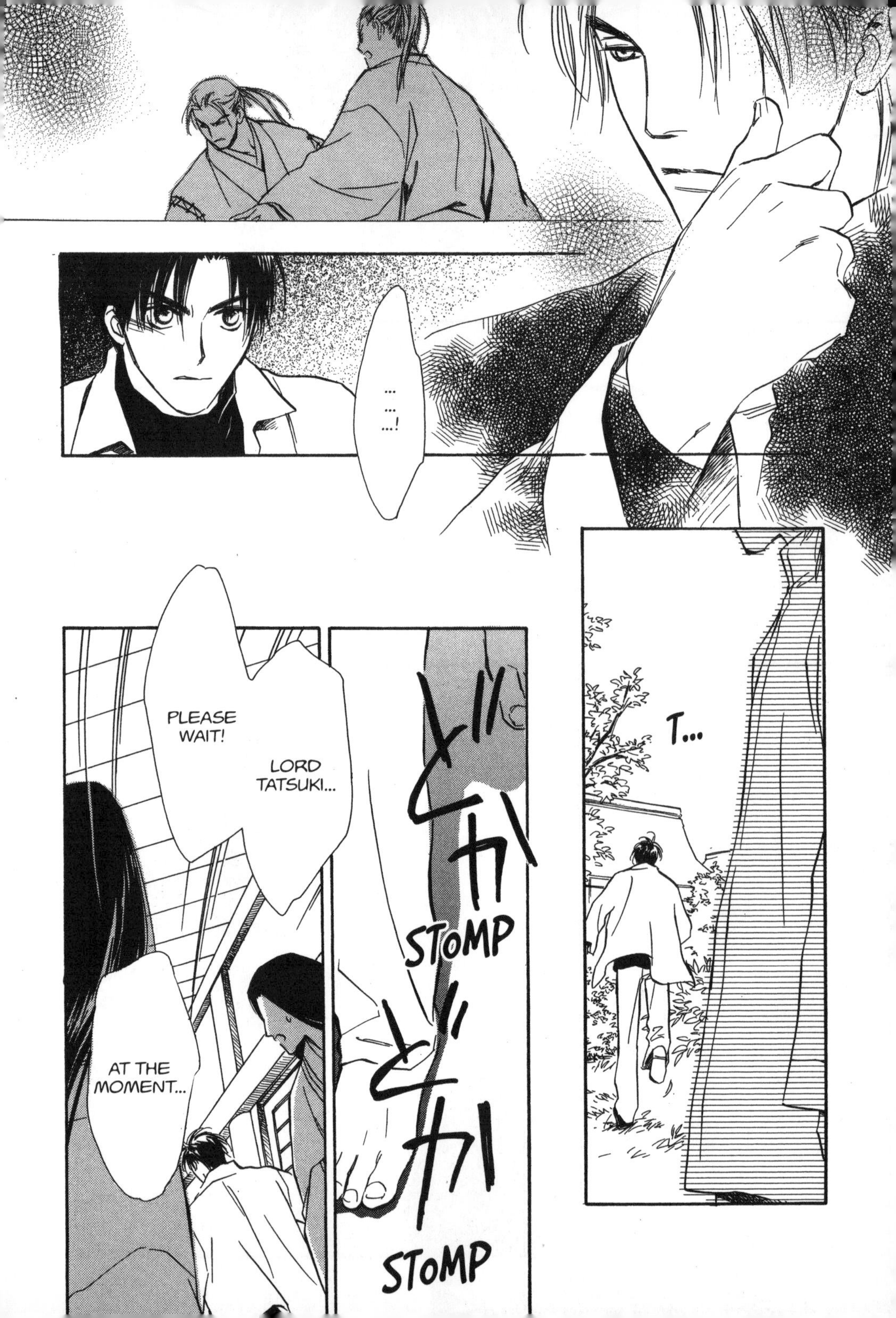
... ...!
T...
どか
STOMP
どか
STOMP
PLEASE WAIT!
LORD TATSUKI...
AT THE MOMENT...

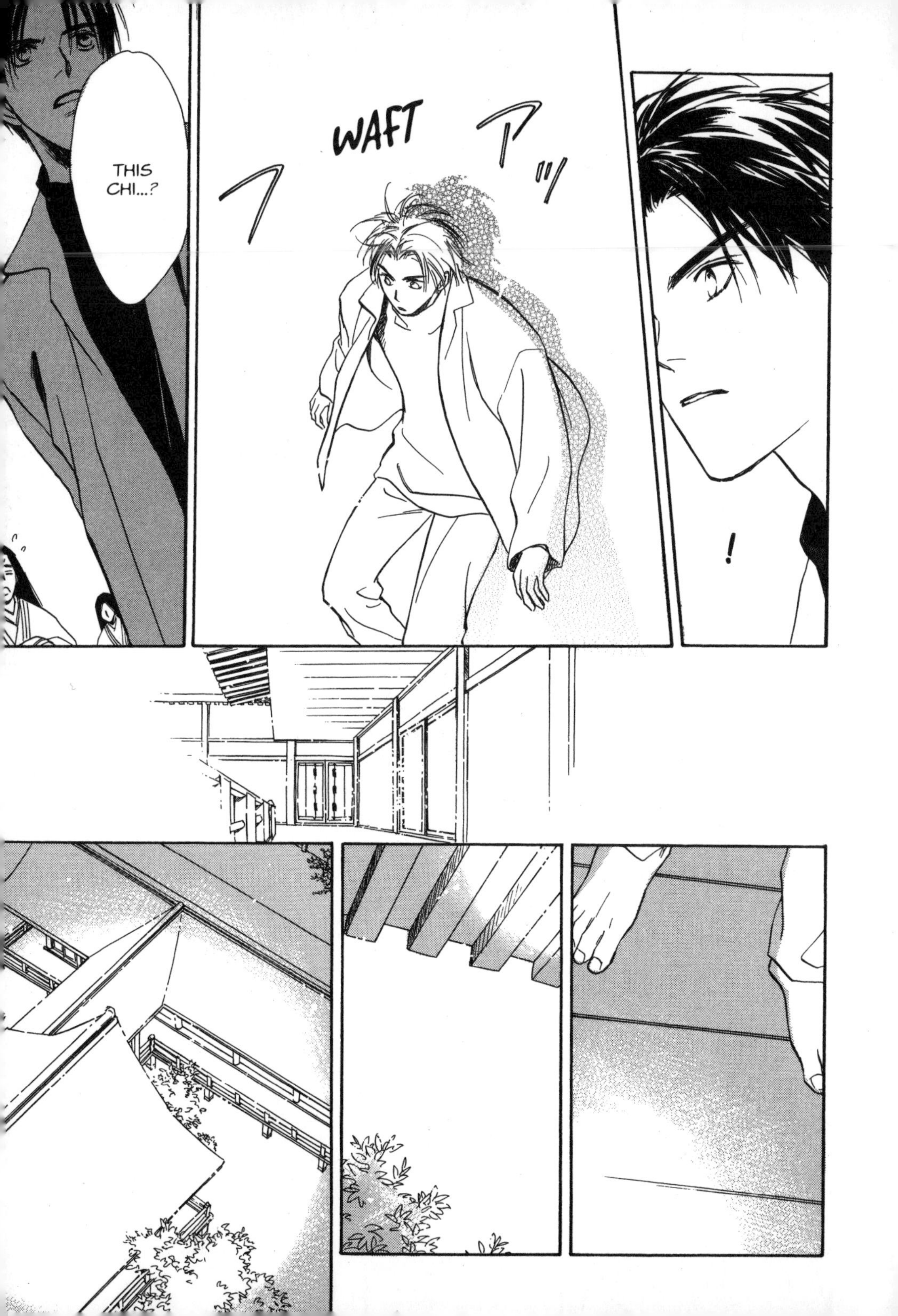
!
アッ
WAFT
フ
THIS CHI...?

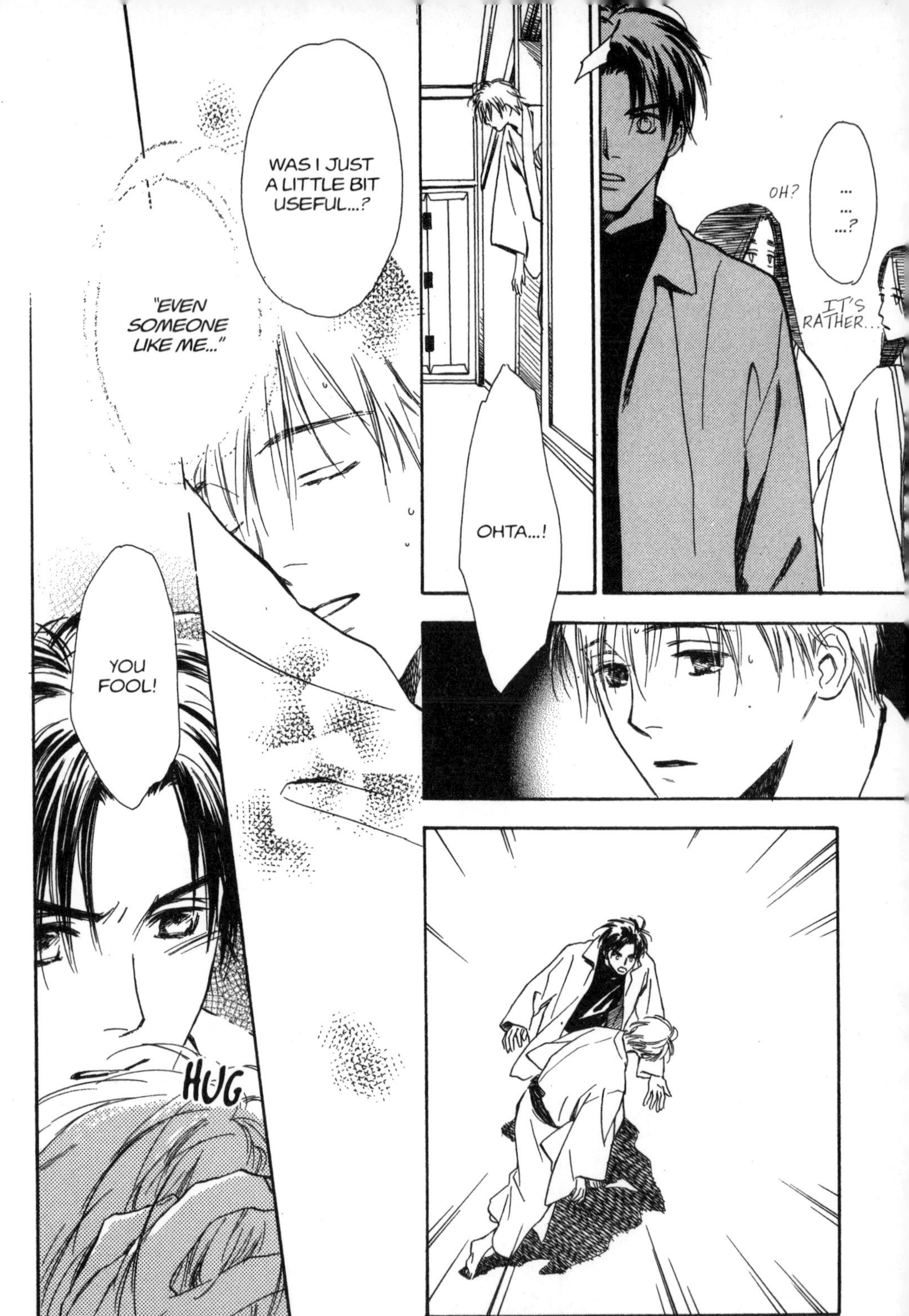

... ...?
OH?
IT'S RATHER...
OHTA...!
WAS I JUST A LITTLE BIT USEFUL...?
"EVEN SOMEONE LIKE ME..."
YOU FOOL!
HUG

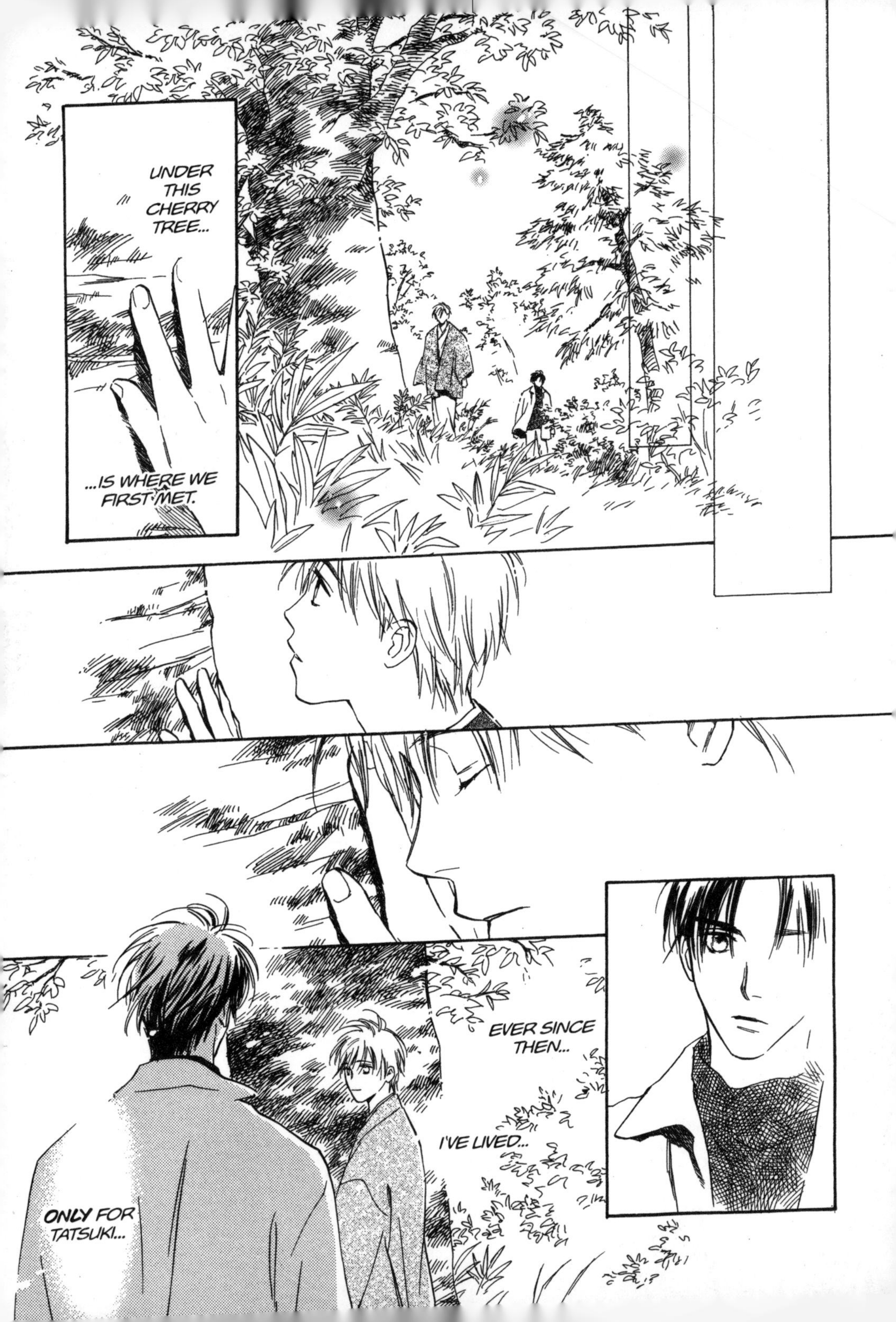
UNDER THIS CHERRY TREE...
...IS WHERE WE FIRST MET.
EVER SINCE THEN...
I'VE LIVED...
ONLY FOR TATSUKI...

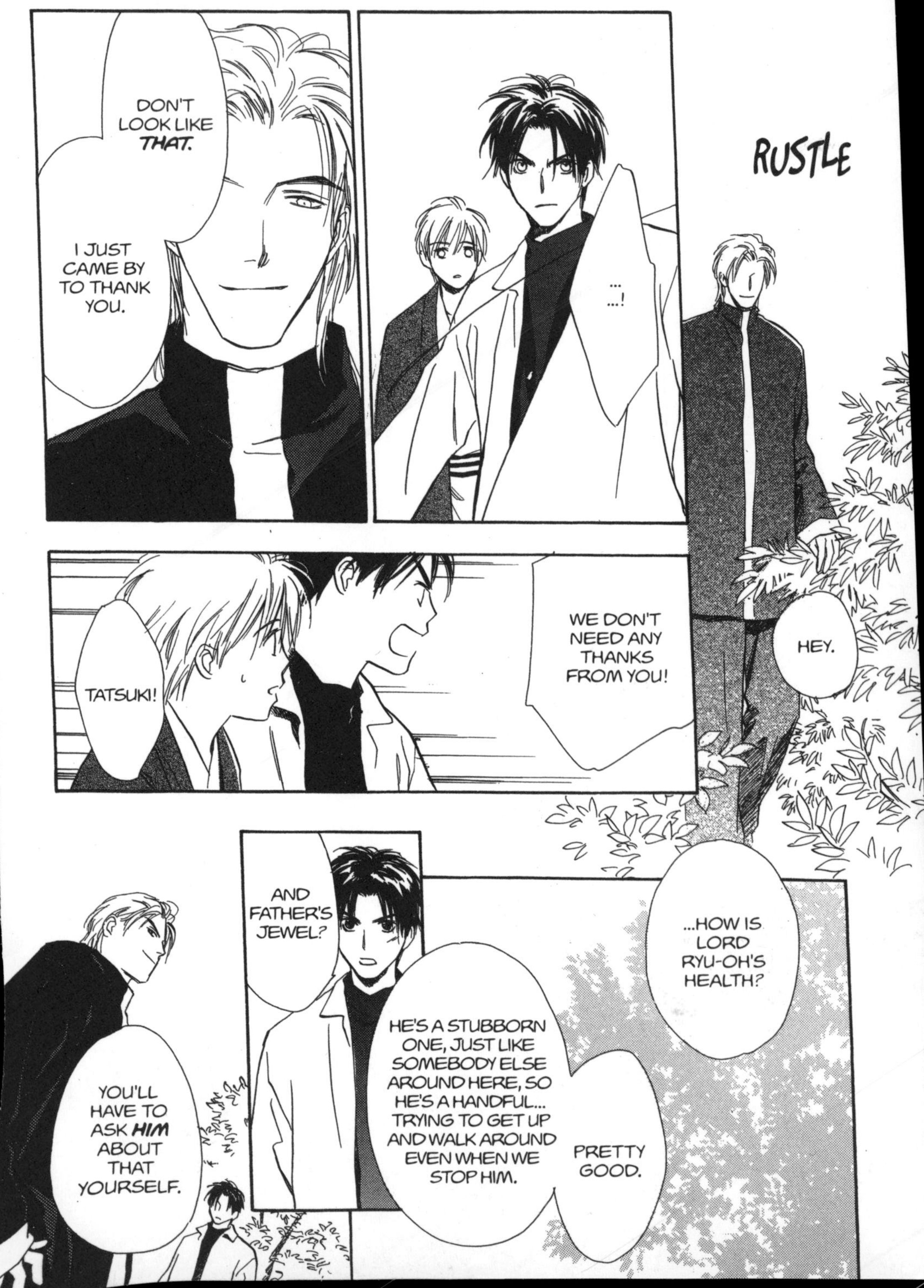
RUSTLE
HEY.
... ...!
DON'T LOOK LIKE *THAT.*
I JUST CAME BY TO THANK YOU.
WE DON'T NEED ANY THANKS FROM YOU!
TATSUKI!
...HOW IS LORD RYU-OH'S HEALTH?
PRETTY GOOD.
HE'S A STUBBORN ONE, JUST LIKE SOMEBODY ELSE AROUND HERE, SO HE'S A HANDFUL... TRYING TO GET UP AND WALK AROUND EVEN WHEN WE STOP HIM.
AND FATHER'S JEWEL?
YOU'LL HAVE TO ASK *HIM* ABOUT THAT YOURSELF.

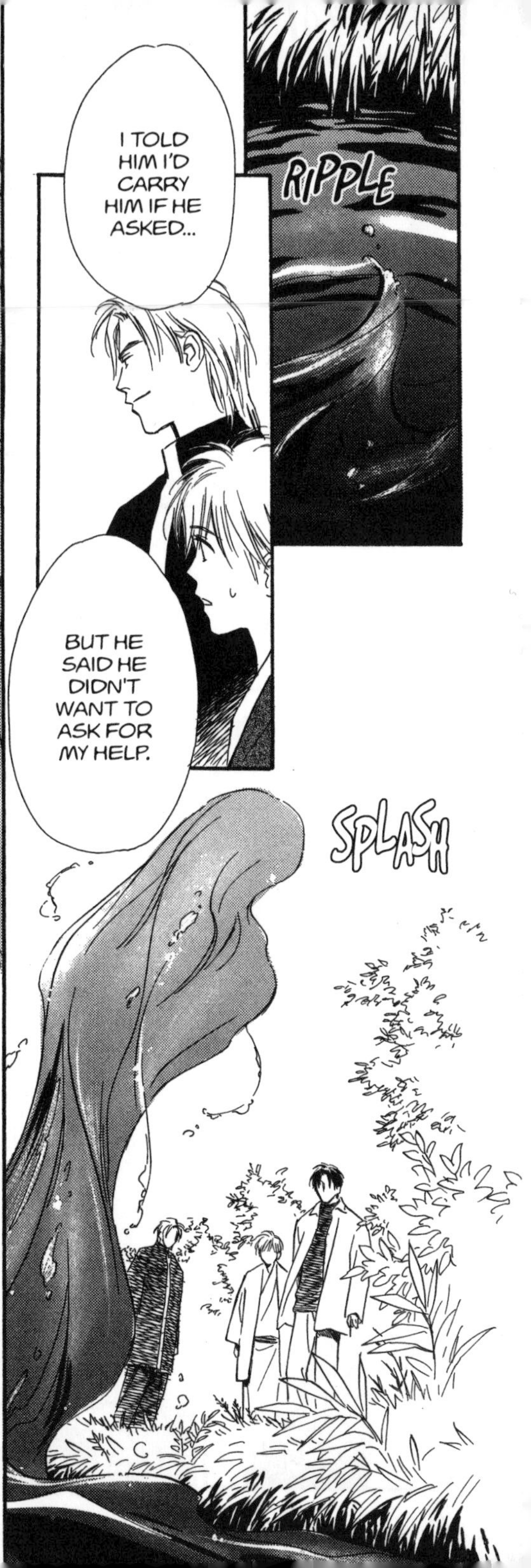
RIPPLE
I TOLD HIM I'D CARRY HIM IF HE ASKED...
BUT HE SAID HE DIDN'T WANT TO ASK FOR MY HELP.
SPLASH
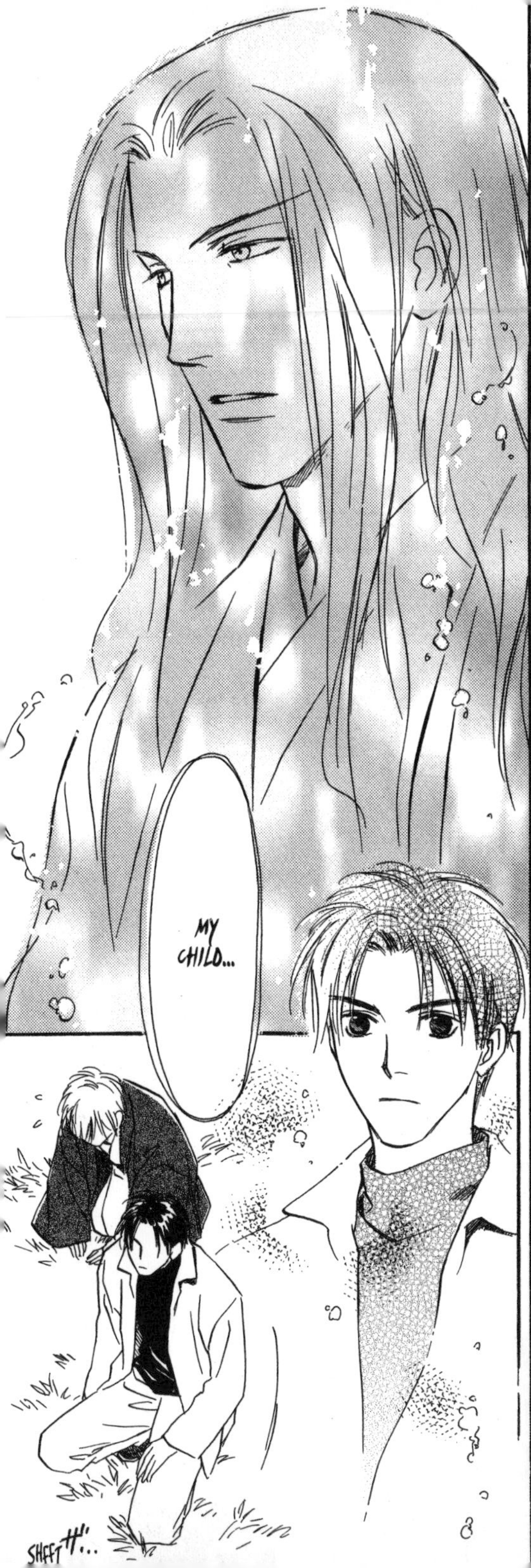
MY CHILD...
SHFFT...

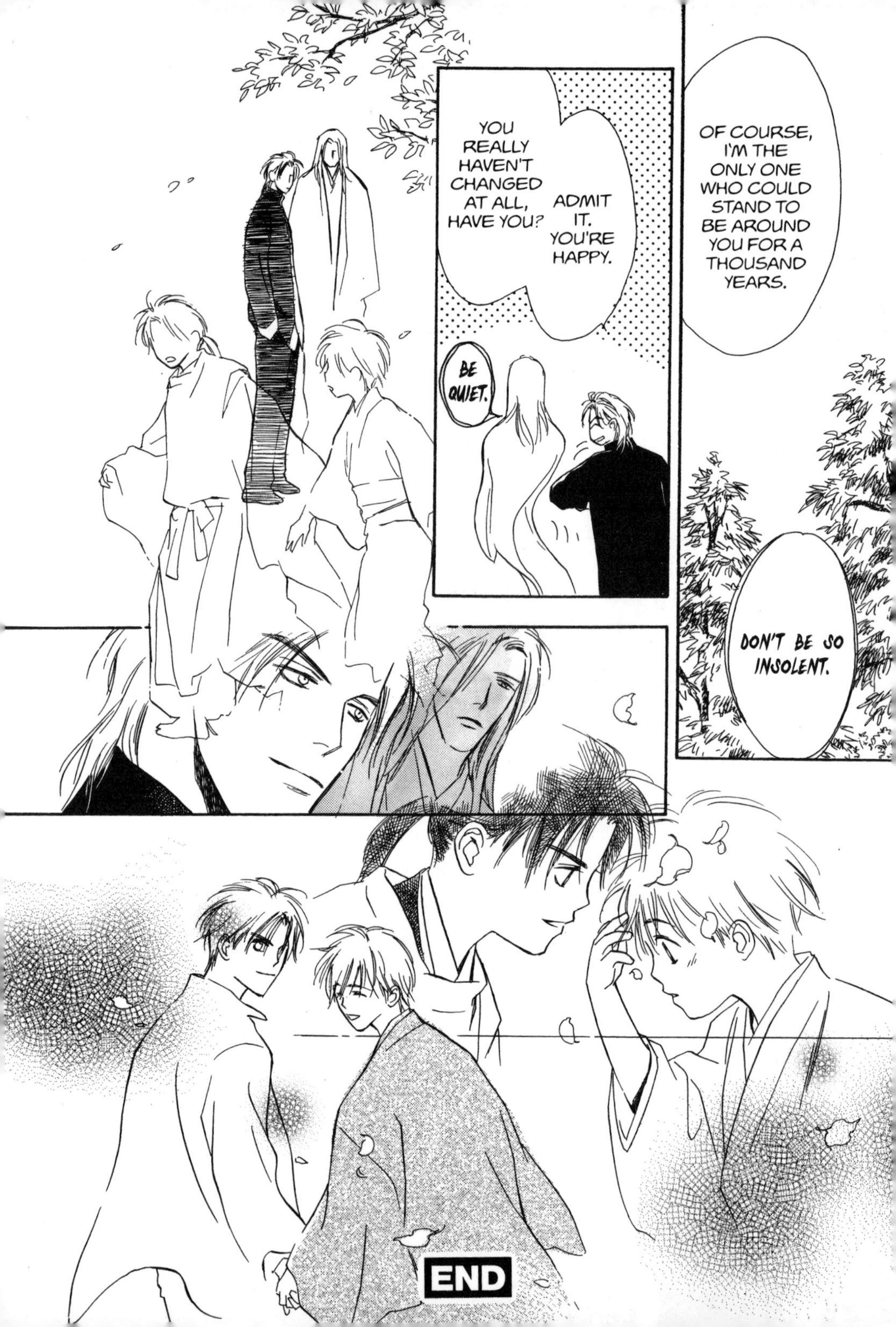
OF COURSE, I'M THE ONLY ONE WHO COULD STAND TO BE AROUND YOU FOR A THOUSAND YEARS.
DON'T BE SO INSOLENT.
YOU REALLY HAVEN'T CHANGED AT ALL, HAVE YOU?
ADMIT IT. YOU'RE HAPPY.
BE QUIET.
END

A SWEET MEALTIME

KOUHEI VERSION

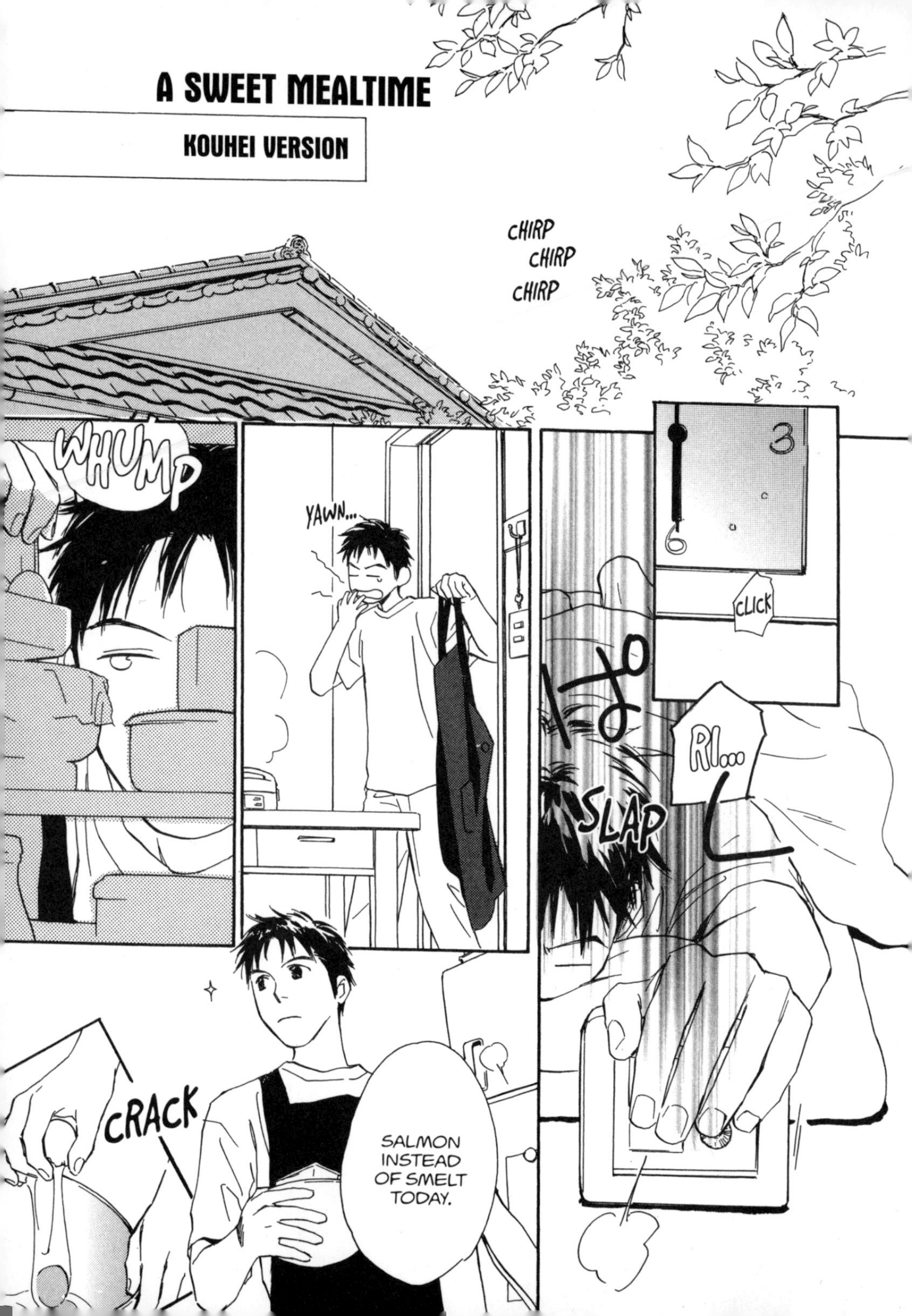

CHIRP
CHIRP
CHIRP
CLICK
RI...
SLAP
YAWN...
WHUMP
SALMON INSTEAD OF SMELT TODAY.
CRACK

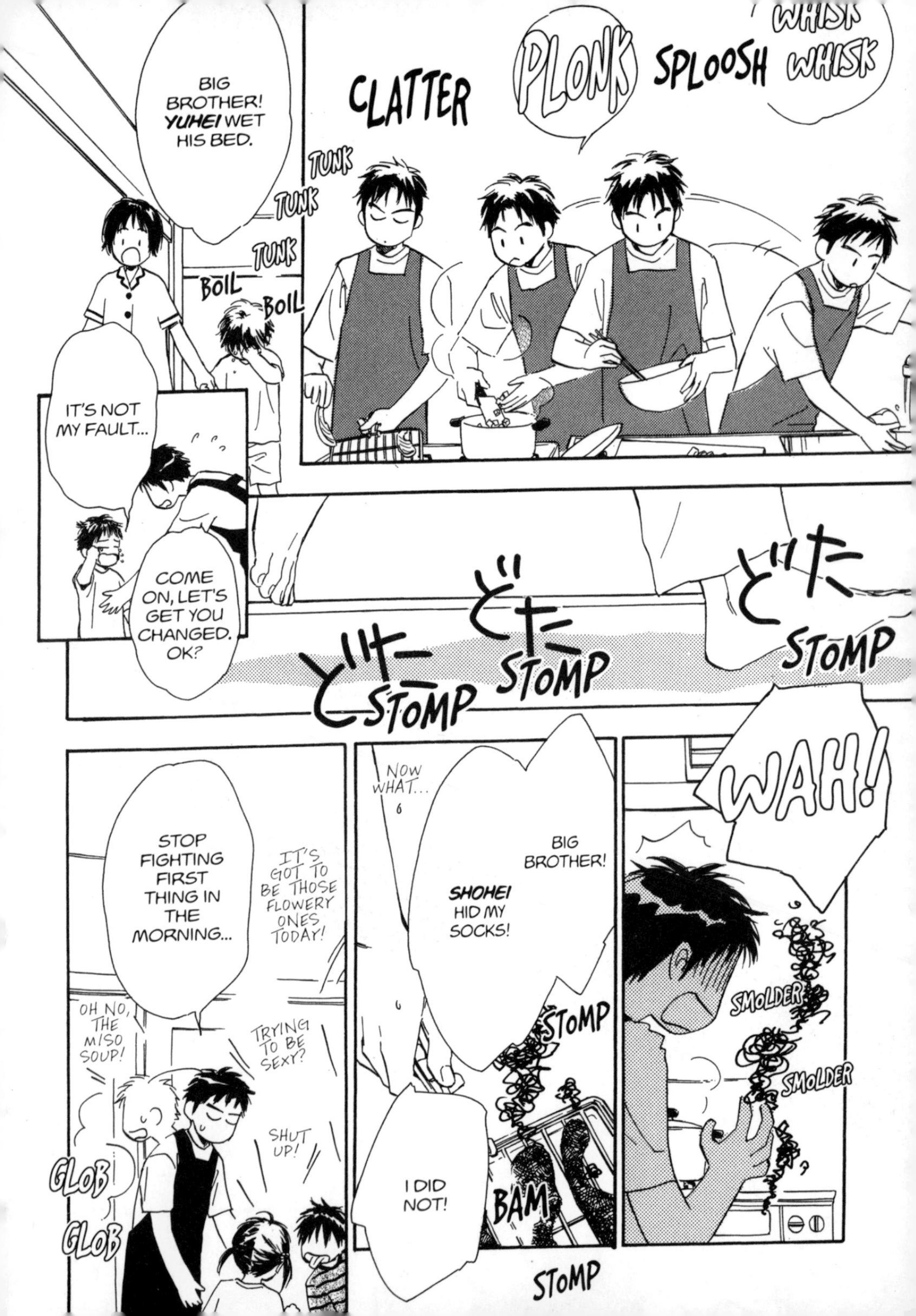
WHISK WHISK
SPLOOSH
PLONK
CLATTER
TUNK
TUNK
TUNK
BOIL
BOIL
BIG BROTHER! YUHEI WET HIS BED.
IT'S NOT MY FAULT...
COME ON, LET'S GET YOU CHANGED. OK?
どた
STOMP
どた
STOMP
どけー
STOMP
WAH!
SMOLDER
SMOLDER
NOW WHAT...
BIG BROTHER!
SHOHEI HID MY SOCKS!
STOMP
I DID NOT!
BAM
STOMP
STOP FIGHTING FIRST THING IN THE MORNING...
IT'S GOT TO BE THOSE FLOWERY ONES TODAY!
TRYING TO BE SEXY?
OH NO, THE MISO SOUP!
SHUT UP!
GLOB
GLOB

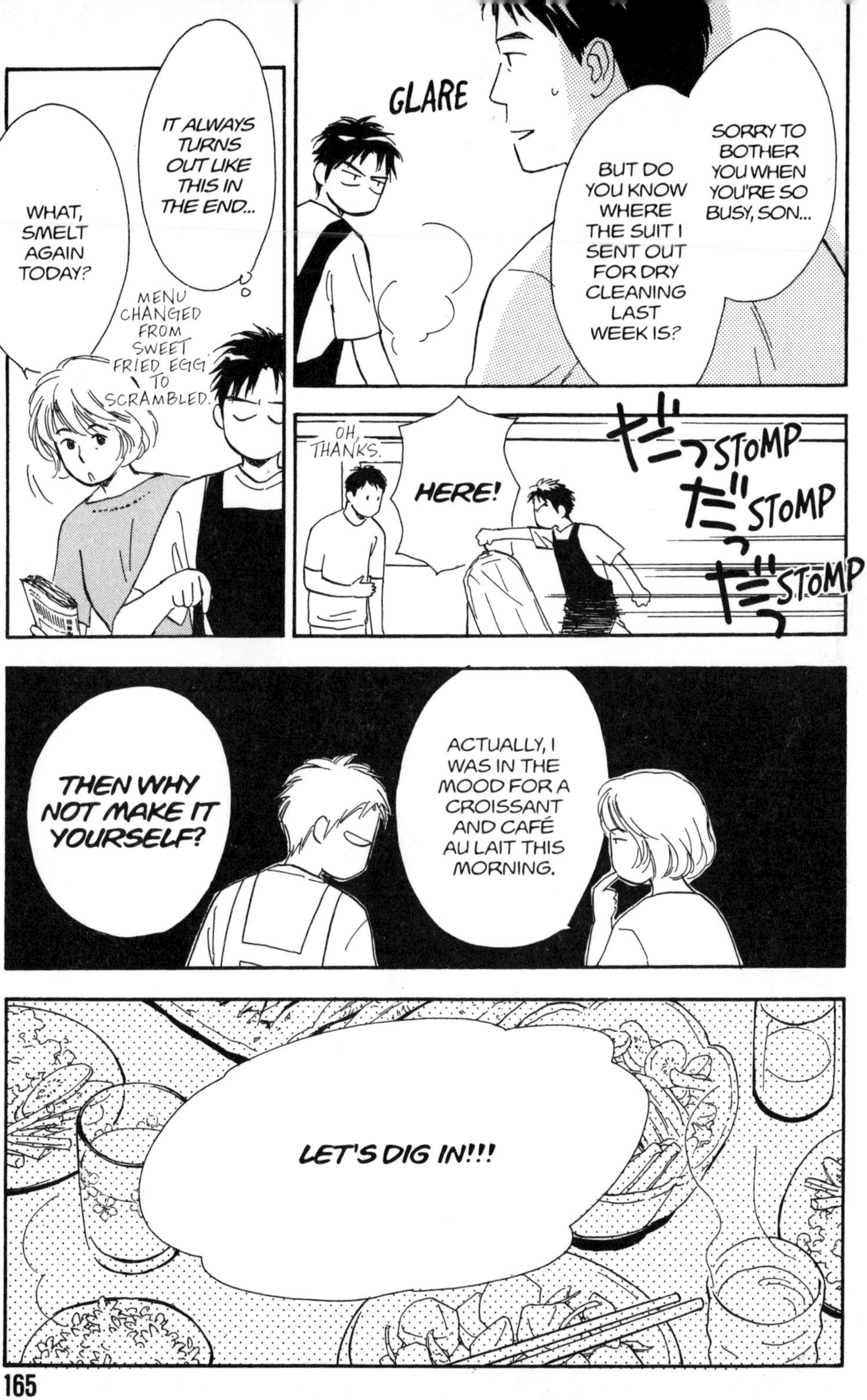
SORRY TO BOTHER YOU WHEN YOU'RE SO BUSY, SON...
BUT DO YOU KNOW WHERE THE SUIT I SENT OUT FOR DRY CLEANING LAST WEEK IS?
GLARE
だっ STOMP
だっ STOMP
だっ STOMP
HERE!
OH THANKS.
IT ALWAYS TURNS OUT LIKE THIS IN THE END...
WHAT, SMELT AGAIN TODAY?
MENU CHANGED FROM SWEET FRIED EGG TO SCRAMBLED.
ACTUALLY, I WAS IN THE MOOD FOR A CROISSANT AND CAFÉ AU LAIT THIS MORNING.
THEN WHY NOT MAKE IT YOURSELF?
LET'S DIG IN!!!

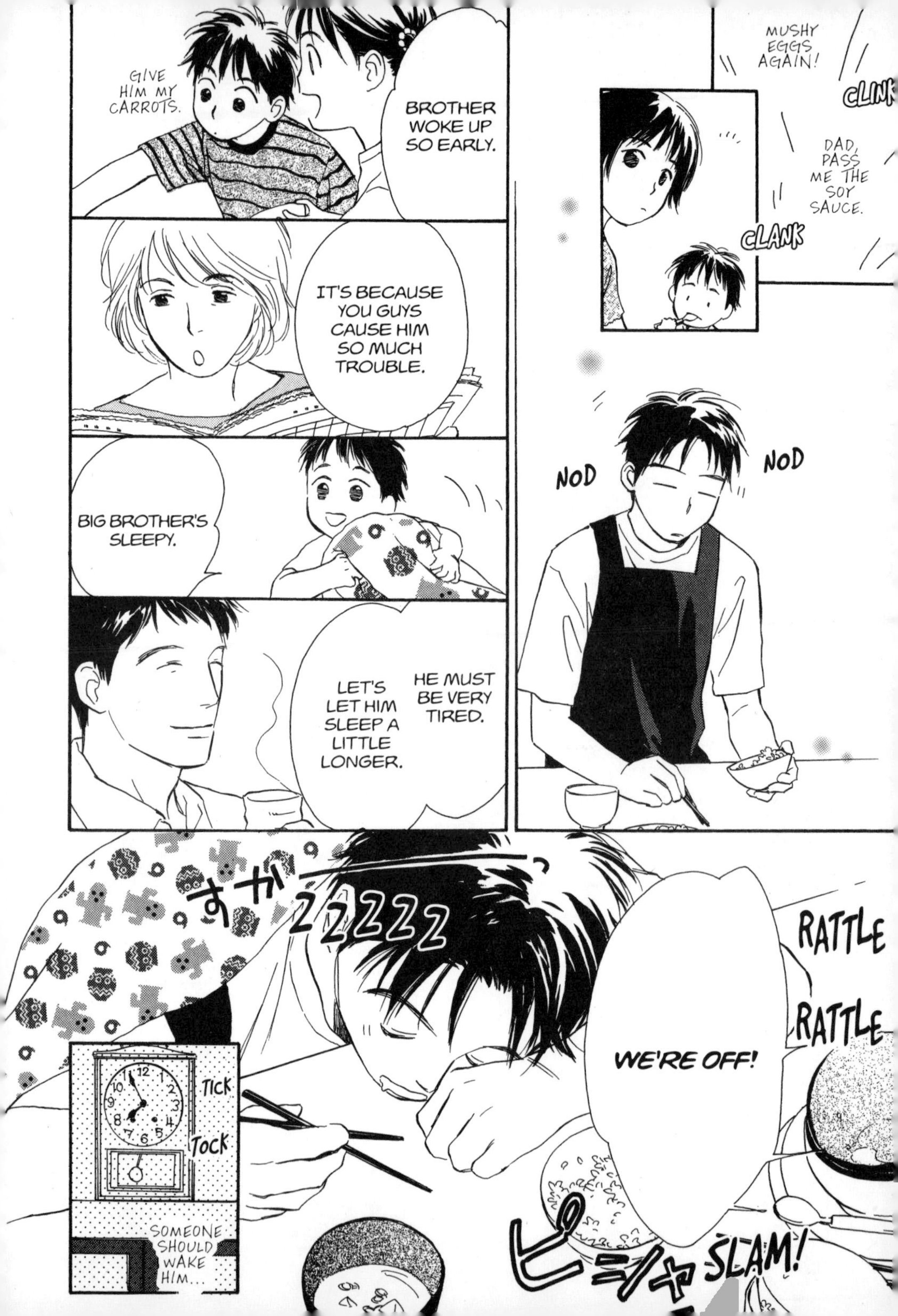
MUSHY EGGS AGAIN!
CLINK
DAD, PASS ME THE SOY SAUCE.
CLANK
NOD
NOD
BROTHER WOKE UP SO EARLY.
GIVE HIM MY CARROTS.
IT'S BECAUSE YOU GUYS CAUSE HIM SO MUCH TROUBLE.
BIG BROTHER'S SLEEPY.
HE MUST BE VERY TIRED.
LET'S LET HIM SLEEP A LITTLE LONGER.
RATTLE
RATTLE
WE'RE OFF!
すが ZZZZZ
TICK
TOCK
SOMEONE SHOULD WAKE HIM...
ピシャ SLAM!

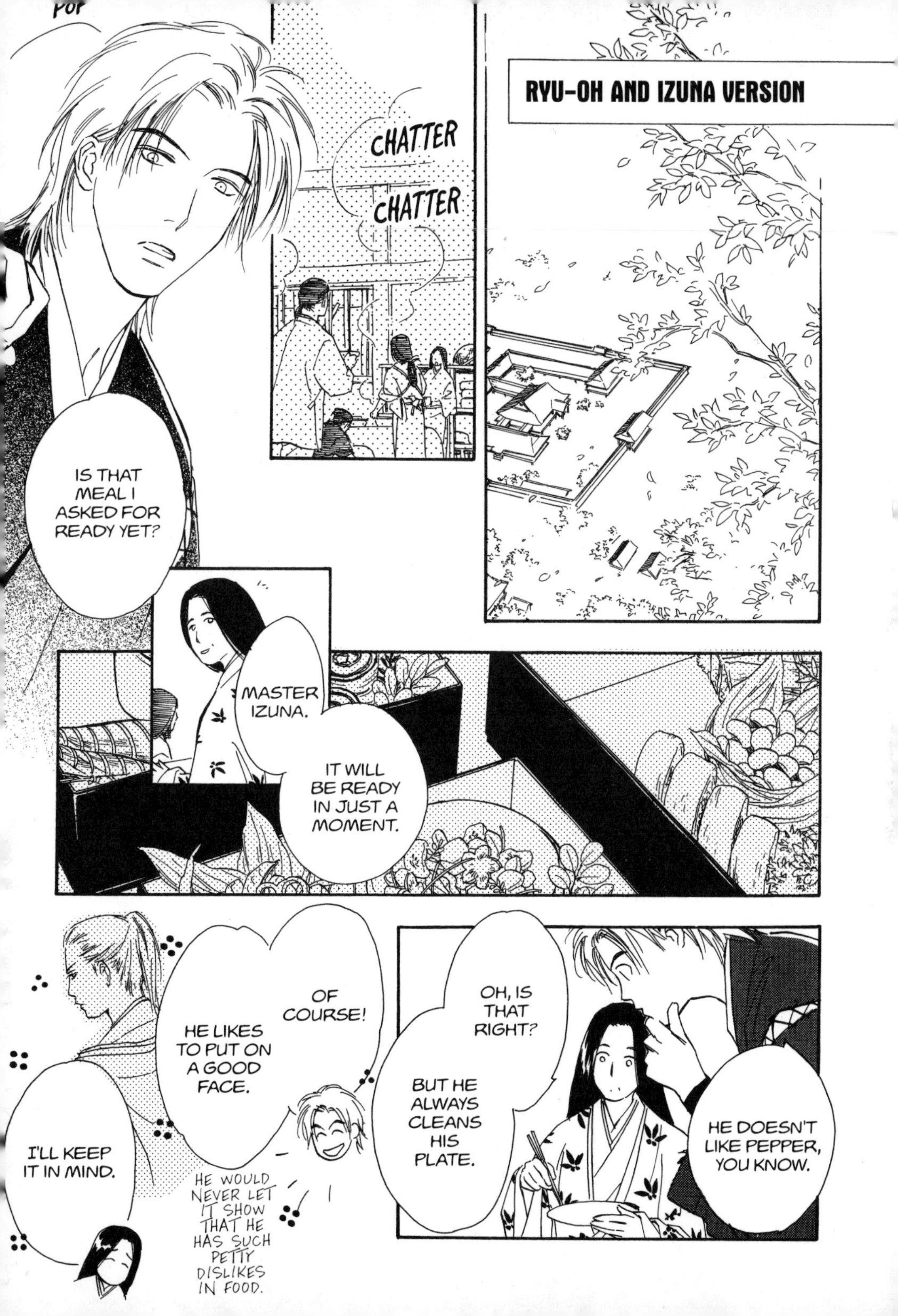
RYU-OH AND IZUNA VERSION
CHATTER
CHATTER
IS THAT MEAL I ASKED FOR READY YET?
MASTER IZUNA.
IT WILL BE READY IN JUST A MOMENT.
HE DOESN'T LIKE PEPPER, YOU KNOW.
OH, IS THAT RIGHT?
BUT HE ALWAYS CLEANS HIS PLATE.
OF COURSE!
HE LIKES TO PUT ON A GOOD FACE.
HE WOULD NEVER LET IT SHOW THAT HE HAS SUCH PETTY DISLIKES IN FOOD.
I'LL KEEP IT IN MIND.

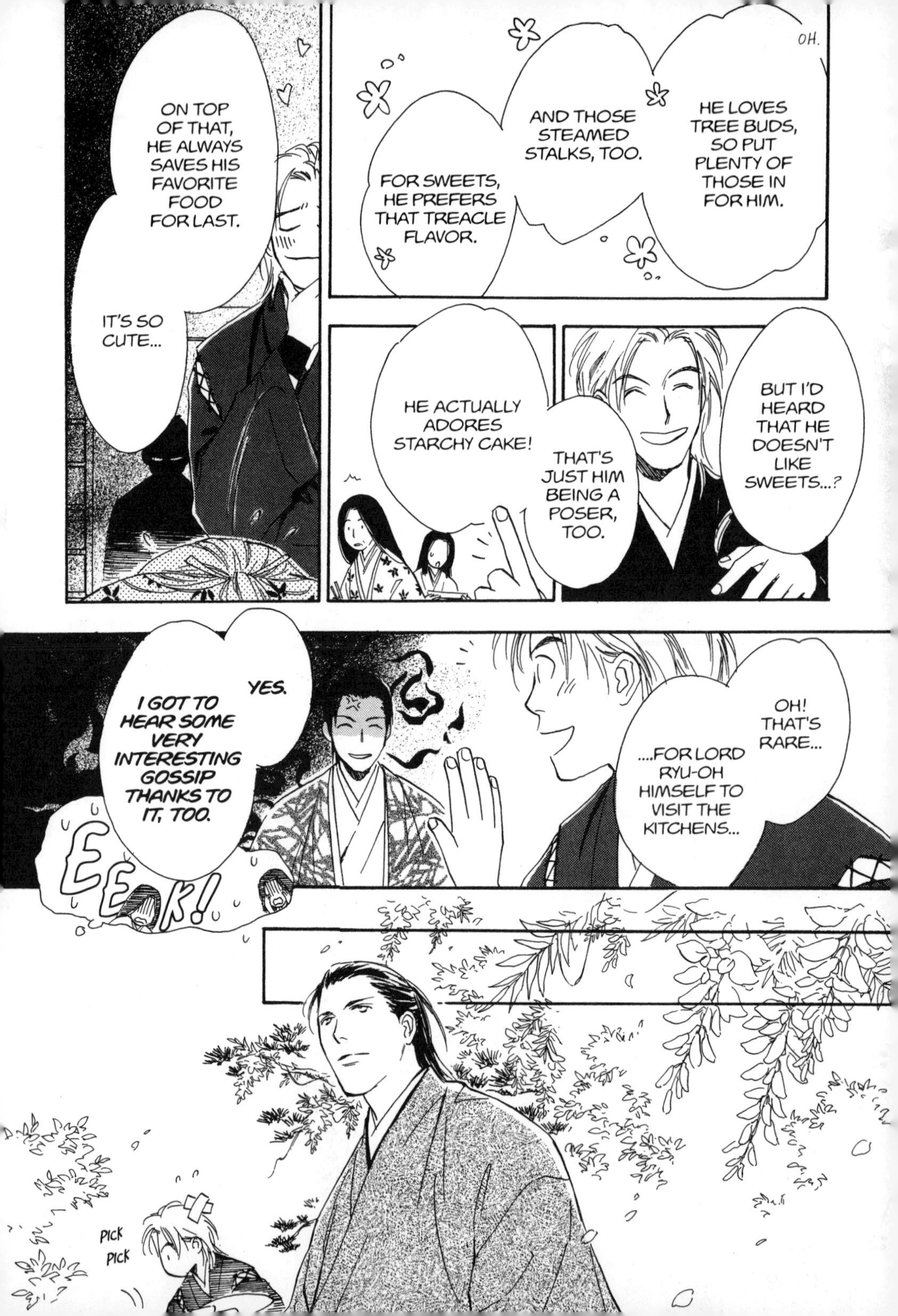
OH.
HE LOVES TREE BUDS, SO PUT PLENTY OF THOSE IN FOR HIM.
AND THOSE STEAMED STALKS, TOO.
FOR SWEETS, HE PREFERS THAT TREACLE FLAVOR.
BUT I'D HEARD THAT HE DOESN'T LIKE SWEETS...?
THAT'S JUST HIM BEING A POSER, TOO.
HE ACTUALLY ADORES STARCHY CAKE!
ON TOP OF THAT, HE ALWAYS SAVES HIS FAVORITE FOOD FOR LAST.
IT'S SO CUTE...
OH! THAT'S RARE...
....FOR LORD RYU-OH HIMSELF TO VISIT THE KITCHENS...
YES.
I GOT TO HEAR SOME VERY INTERESTING GOSSIP THANKS TO IT, TOO.
EEK!
PICK
PICK

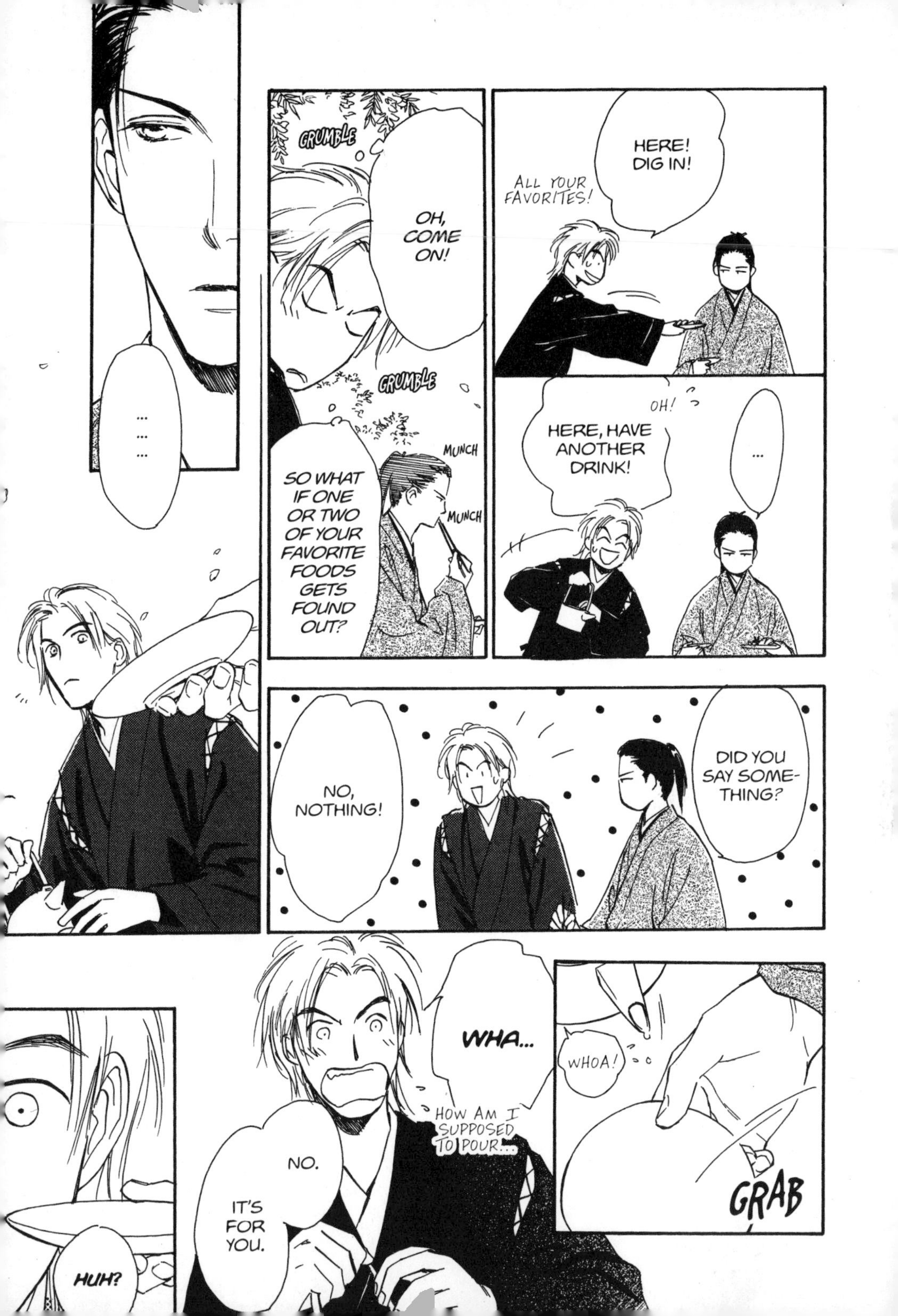
HERE! DIG IN!
ALL YOUR FAVORITES!
OH!
HERE, HAVE ANOTHER DRINK!
...
GRUMBLE
OH, COME ON!
GRUMBLE
MUNCH
MUNCH
SO WHAT IF ONE OR TWO OF YOUR FAVORITE FOODS GETS FOUND OUT?
...
...
...
DID YOU SAY SOME-THING?
NO, NOTHING!
WHOA!
GRAB
WHA...
HOW AM I SUPPOSED TO POUR...
NO.
IT'S FOR YOU.
HUH?

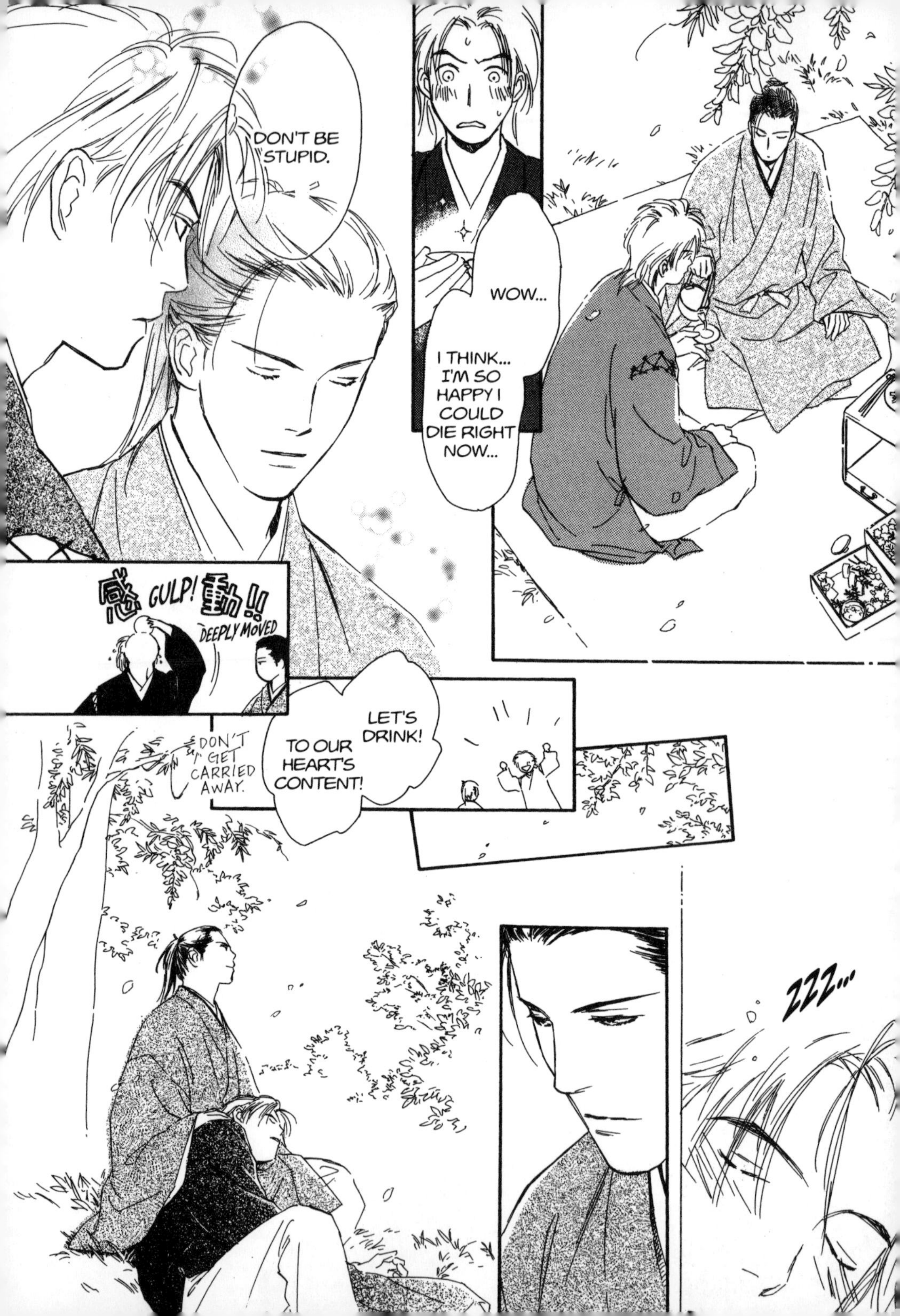
WOW...
I THINK... I'M SO HAPPY I COULD DIE RIGHT NOW...
DON'T BE STUPID.
感 GULP! 動!!
DEEPLY MOVED
LET'S DRINK!
TO OUR HEART'S CONTENT!
DON'T GET CARRIED AWAY.
ZZZ...

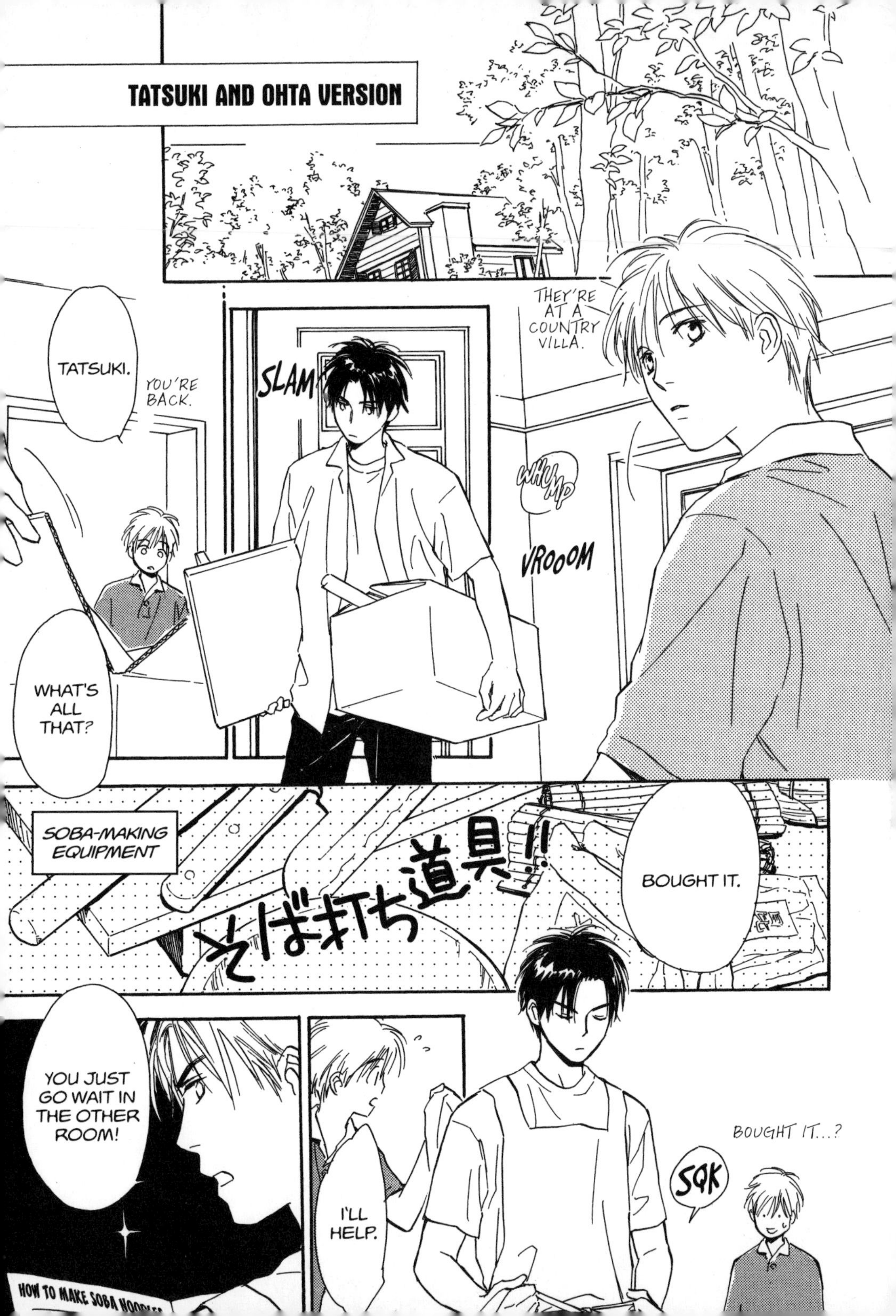

TATSUKI AND OHTA VERSION
THEY'RE AT A COUNTRY VILLA.
WHUMP
VROOOM
TATSUKI.
YOU'RE BACK.
SLAM
WHAT'S ALL THAT?
BOUGHT IT.
そば打ち道具!!
SOBA-MAKING EQUIPMENT
BOUGHT IT...?
SQK
I'LL HELP.
YOU JUST GO WAIT IN THE OTHER ROOM!
HOW TO MAKE SOBA NOODLES

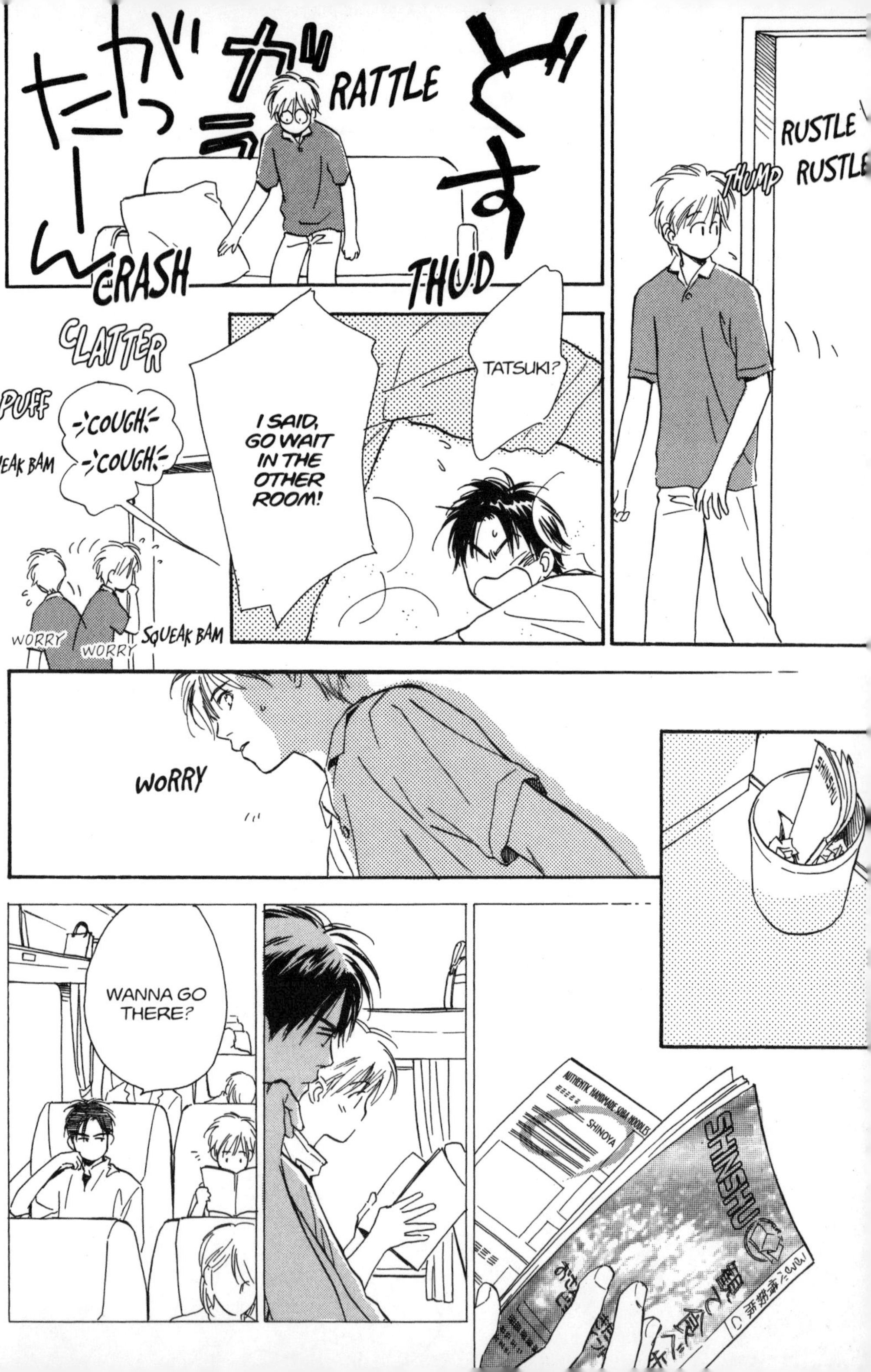

RUSTLE
THUMP
RUSTLE
どす
THUD
RATTLE
CRASH
TATSUKI?
I SAID, GO WAIT IN THE OTHER ROOM!
CLATTER
PUFF
COUGH
COUGH
SQUEAK BAM
WORRY
WORRY
SQUEAK BAM
SHINSHU
WORRY
AUTHENTIC HANDMADE SOBA NOODLES
SHINOYA
SHINSHU
WANNA GO THERE?

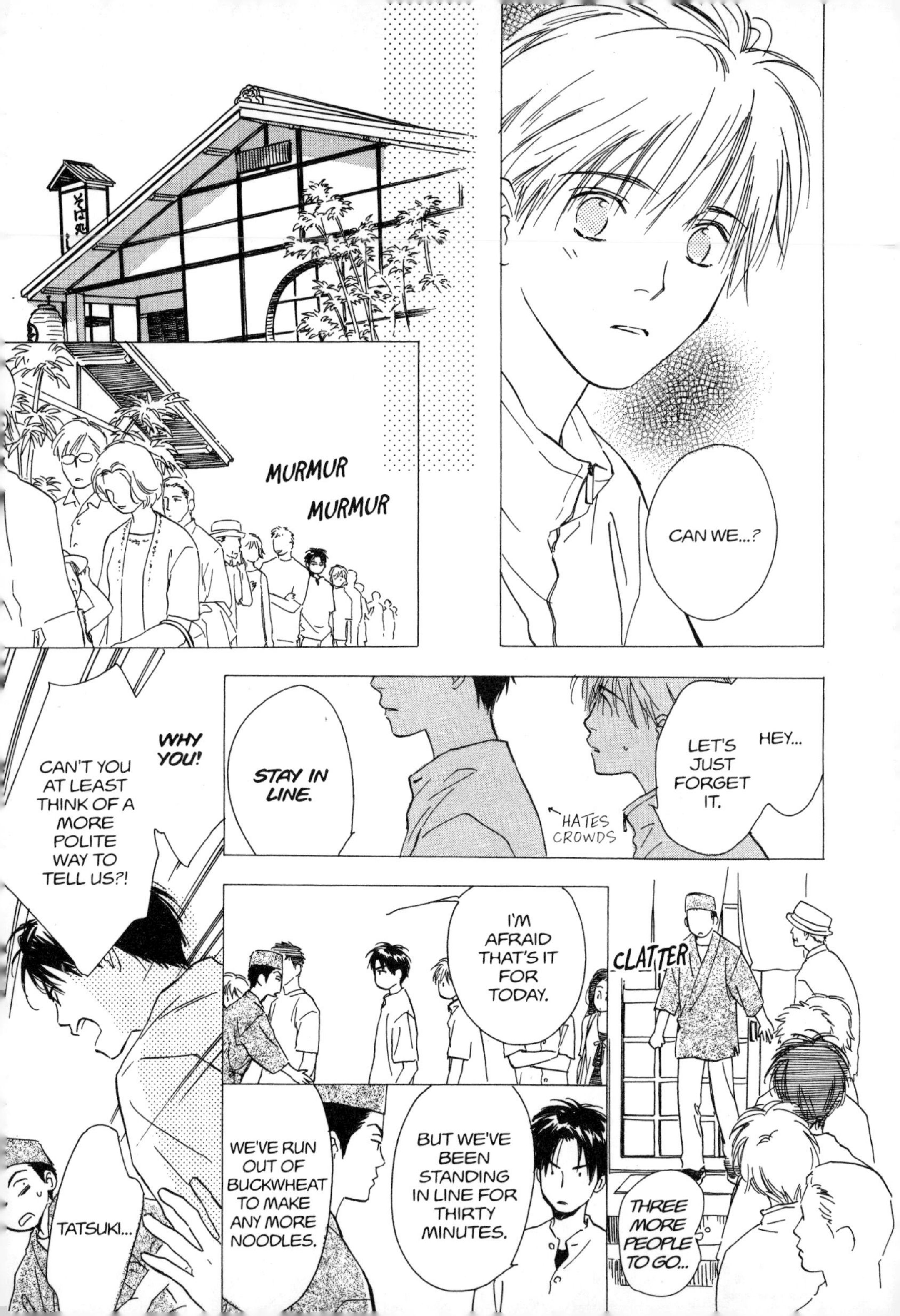
CAN WE...?
MURMUR
MURMUR
HEY...
LET'S JUST FORGET IT.
HATES CROWDS
STAY IN LINE.
CLATTER
THREE MORE PEOPLE TO GO...
I'M AFRAID THAT'S IT FOR TODAY.
BUT WE'VE BEEN STANDING IN LINE FOR THIRTY MINUTES.
WE'VE RUN OUT OF BUCKWHEAT TO MAKE ANY MORE NOODLES.
WHY YOU!
CAN'T YOU AT LEAST THINK OF A MORE POLITE WAY TO TELL US?!
TATSUKI...

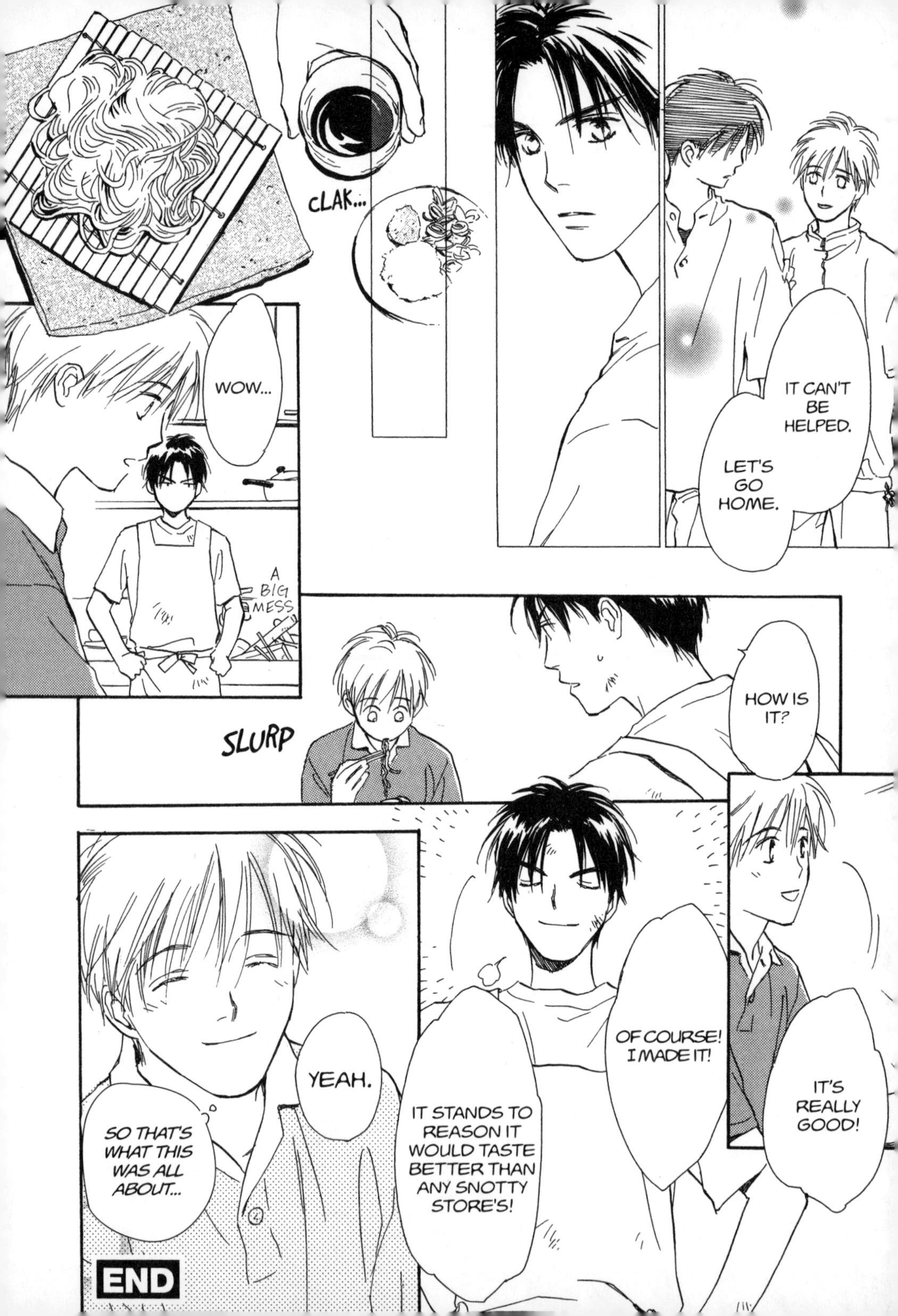
IT CAN'T BE HELPED.
LET'S GO HOME.
CLAK...
WOW...
A BIG MESS
HOW IS IT?
SLURP
IT'S REALLY GOOD!
OF COURSE! I MADE IT!
IT STANDS TO REASON IT WOULD TASTE BETTER THAN ANY SNOTTY STORE'S!
YEAH.
SO THAT'S WHAT THIS WAS ALL ABOUT...
END

SWEET REVOLUTION

HELLO, THIS IS *SERUBO SUZUKI.*

I DON'T EXPECT ANYONE TO BELIEVE ME WHEN I SAY THIS NOW, BUT THIS "SWEET" SERIES WAS ORIGINALLY SUPPOSED TO BE A "CUTE LITTLE SCHOOL STORY" IN WHICH TO FEATURE ARTIST *YUKINE HONAMI'S* ADORABLE DRAWINGS.

WHERE IT VEERED OFF THAT PATH, I DON'T KNOW...I TRY TO THINK BACK, BUT SINCE THE FIRST PUBLICATION CAME OUT BACK IN THE AUTUMN OF HEISEI YEAR 10, THERE'S NO WAY THAT MY DRIED-UP HUSK OF A BRAIN COULD RECALL SOMETHING FROM SO LONG AGO.

WHAT I DO REMEMBER IS THAT, AFTER READING THE SCRIPT FOR CHAPTER 5, "SWEET CRISIS", MY EDITOR CALLED UP TO ASK, "UMM...SO, IZUNA IS DEFINITELY THE 'PITCHER' IN THIS RELATIONSHIP, RIGHT?"

I FELT AS IF I'D RECEIVED A SHOCK TO THE BRAIN.

"HUH? BUT DOESN'T IZUNA SEEM MORE LIKE THE 'CATCHER' TO YOU?" PERHAPS MY EDITOR FELT A SIMILAR SHOCK AT MY ANSWER.

"ACTUALLY, NOW THAT YOU BRING IT UP, LORD RYU-OH REALLY FEELS MORE LIKE THE 'CATCHER'."

"BUT THE FACT THAT YOU ASKED ME IS BECAUSE YOU HAD AT LEAST A LITTLE BIT OF DOUBT ABOUT IT...RIGHT?"

THE CONVERSATION CONTINUED IN CIRCLES, UNTIL FINALLY, WE DECIDED TO LEAVE IT UP TO MS. HONAMI TO DECIDE.

THE RESULT IS IN THE STORY AS YOU SEE IT HERE. AS I LOOKED THROUGH THE ART THAT WAS FAXED TO ME, I BECAME AWARE, FOR THE FIRST TIME IN MY LIFE, OF THE SAD TRAVAILS OF MINOR SUB-CHARACTER COUPLES.

"WE SHOWED IT TO EVERYONE HERE IN THE EDITORIAL OFFICE, AND THEY ALL FEEL THAT IZUNA IS THE 'PITCHER'..."

MY EDITOR SOUNDED VERY APOLOGETIC INDEED, BUT I AM OF THE FIRM BELIEF THAT THE EXPRESSION ON THE FACE AT THE OTHER END OF THE PHONE WAS A TRIUMPHANT ONE.

BUT AS I READ AND RE-READ THE PUBLISHED SERIES, I WENT FROM THINKING, "SO IS THIS WHAT MAINSTREAM THINKING IS...?" TO, "YUP, IZUNA IS DEFINITELY THE 'PITCHER'," PROVING THAT I HAVE YET TO COMPREHEND THE TRAVAILS OF MINOR SUB-CHARACTER COUPLES.

I CAN'T HELP IT. THE LORD RYU-OH THAT MS. HONAMI ILLUSTRATES IS SUCH A DARLING "CATCHER". HIS FACE, HIS EXPRESSIONS, HIS MANNERISMS   IN MY MIND, THERE IS NO LONGER ANY OTHER VERSION OF RYU-OH BUT THIS ONE. SO NOW, THERE IS NO CHOICE BUT TO HAVE IZUNA BE THE "PITCHER".

ALTHOUGH THIS WORK HAS TURNED OUT TO BE A FAR CRY FROM THE "CUTE LITTLE SCHOOL STORY" IT WAS INTENDED TO BE, I THINK IT HAS TURNED INTO A "CUTE LITTLE FAIRYTALE" INSTEAD.

NOW THAT I HAVE THOUGHT ABOUT IT, I WOULD DEFINITELY LIKE TO SEE MS. HONAMI'S ADORABLE ILLUSTRATIONS RETELLING TALES OF HORROR SUCH AS *KONAKI JIJII, NURARIHYON,* AND *SUNAKAKE BABAA.* A "CUTE" *SUNAKAKE BABAA*...WHAT WOULD THAT BE LIKE? I'M INTRIGUED, IN A STRANGE WAY.

RIGHT NOW, MY HUMBLE WISH IS THAT THE WORD "FANTASY" WILL NEVER BE ATTACHED IN ANY WAY TO THIS STORY OF MINE. ON THE DAY THIS STORY IS EVER LABELED AS A "FANTASY," I WILL BE SO OVERCOME WITH FEELINGS OF EMBARRASSMENT AND ABJECT APOLOGY THAT I WON'T KNOW WHAT TO DO WITH MYSELF.

DURING THE SHORT SPAN OF A YEAR AND HALF, MY HAPPIEST EXPERIENCE HAS BEEN TO SEE MY CLUMSY LITTLE SCRIPT, IN THE TALENTED HANDS OF MS. HONAMI, TURN INTO A WONDERFUL MANGA. FOR AN AUTHOR, HAVING ILLUSTRATIONS ADDED TO HIS WORK IS LIKE A LITTLE "PRESENT" A REWARD FOR HAVING WORKED SO HARD TO PRODUCE THE STORY. SO WHEN THE STORY IS NOT ONLY ENHANCED BY ILLUSTRATIONS BUT TURNED INTO A FULL-BLOWN MANGA, THE EFFECT IS MUCH MORE THAN THAT OF A MERE LITTLE "PRESENT."

SO TO MS. HONAMI AND THE EDITORS WHO GAVE ME THIS HAPPINESS, I AM VERY THANKFUL. AND MY DEEPEST WISH IS THAT ALL OF YOU WHO HAVE BEEN GOOD ENOUGH TO TAKE THIS BOOK IN HAND FIND ENJOYMENT IN WHAT YOU READ...

NOTE: *KONAKI JIJII, NURARIHYON,* AND *SUNAKAKE BABAA*
ARE ALL NAMES OF CLASSIC JAPANESE *YOKAI* (MONSTERS).

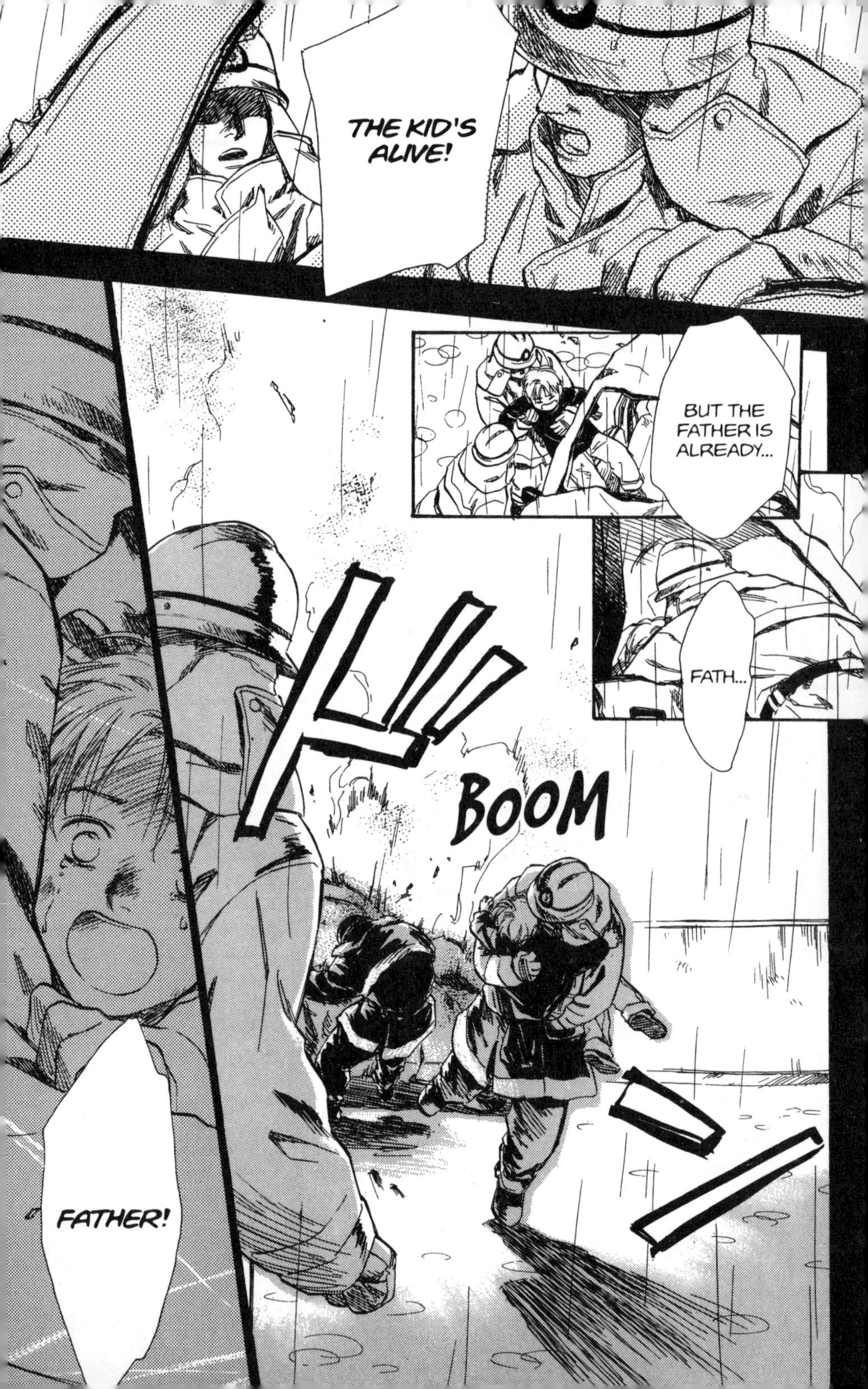
THE KID'S ALIVE!
BUT THE FATHER IS ALREADY...
FATH...
BOOM
FATHER!

みえないチカラ
AN UNSEEN FORCE

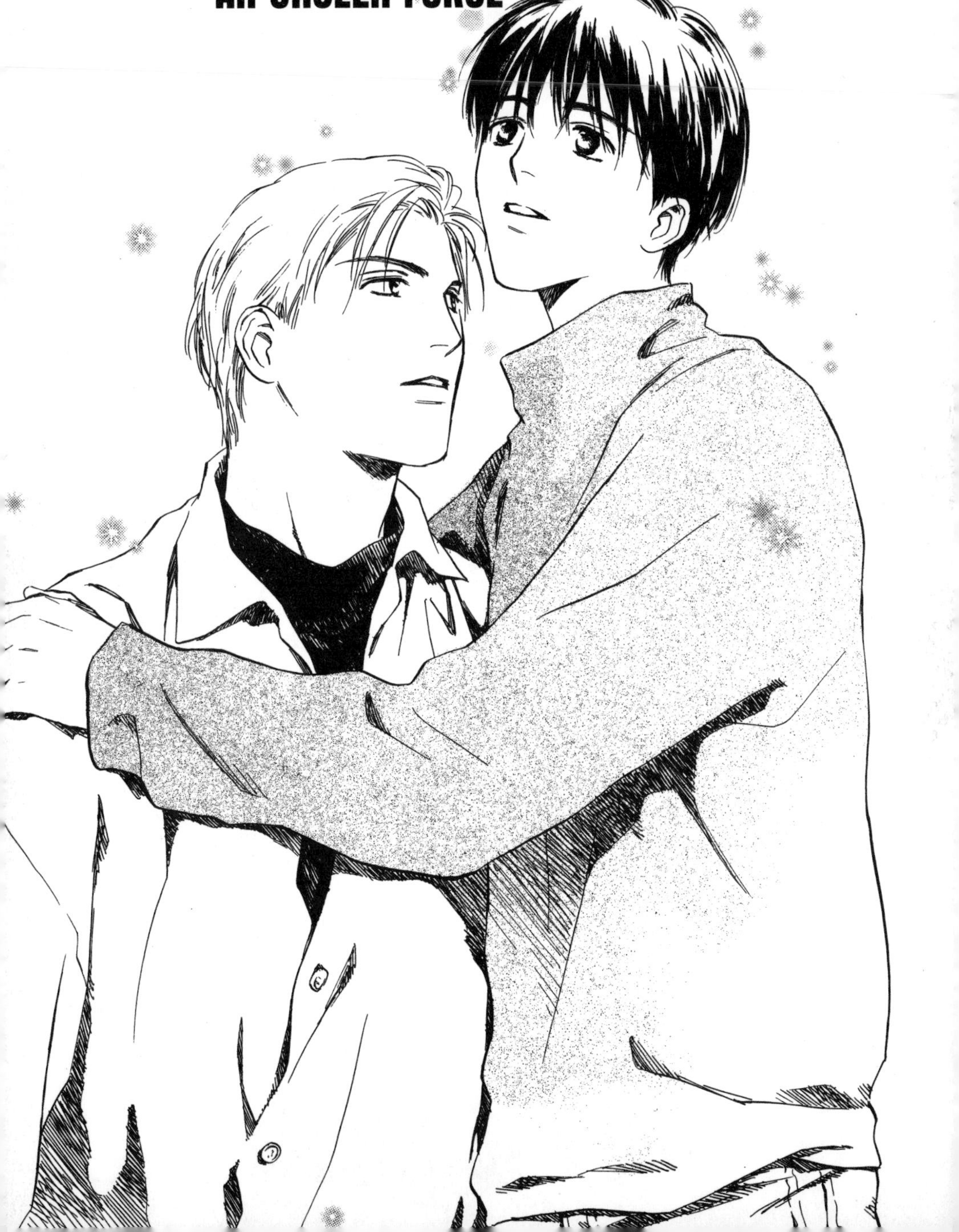

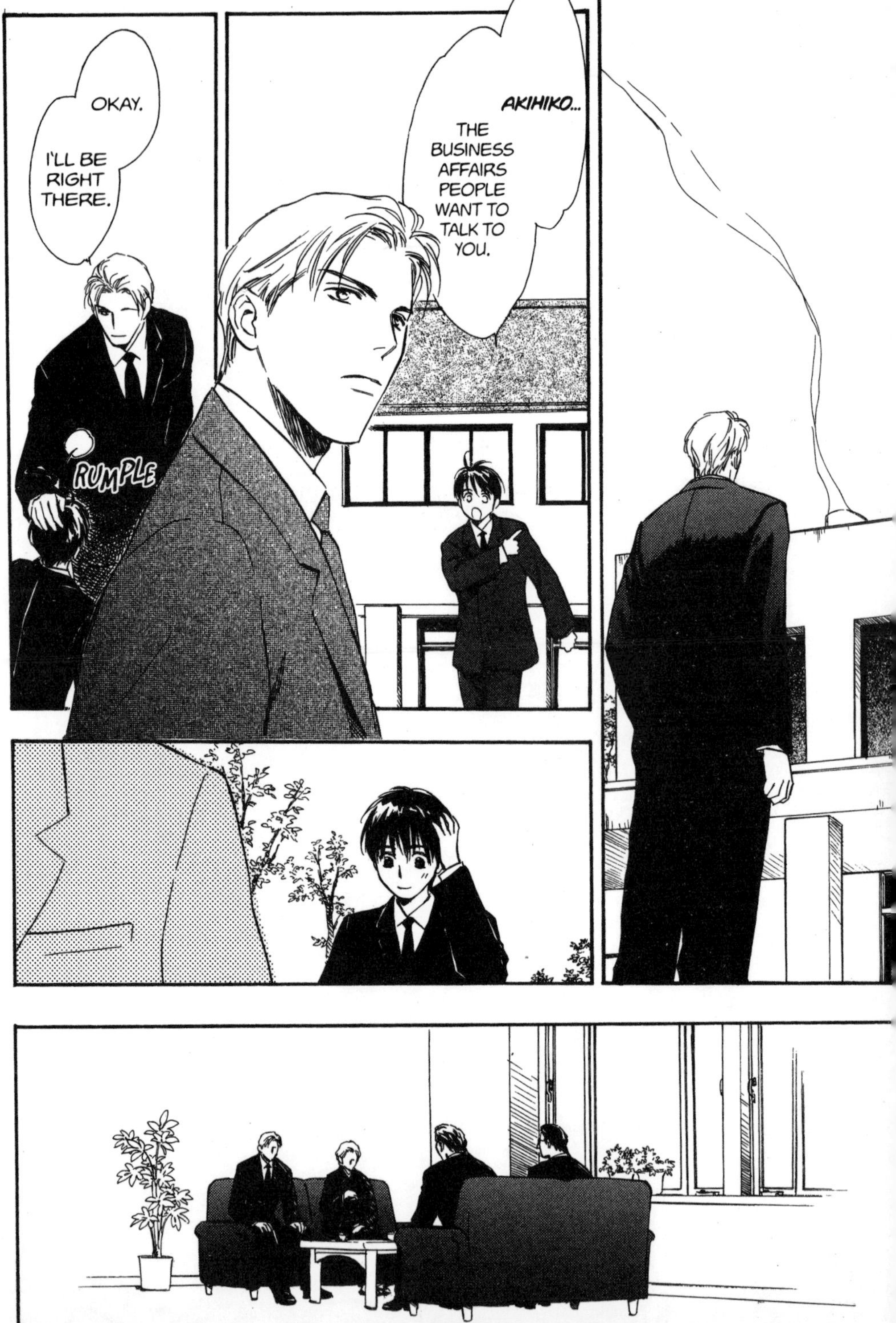
AKIHIKO...
THE BUSINESS AFFAIRS PEOPLE WANT TO TALK TO YOU.
OKAY.
I'LL BE RIGHT THERE.
RUMPLE

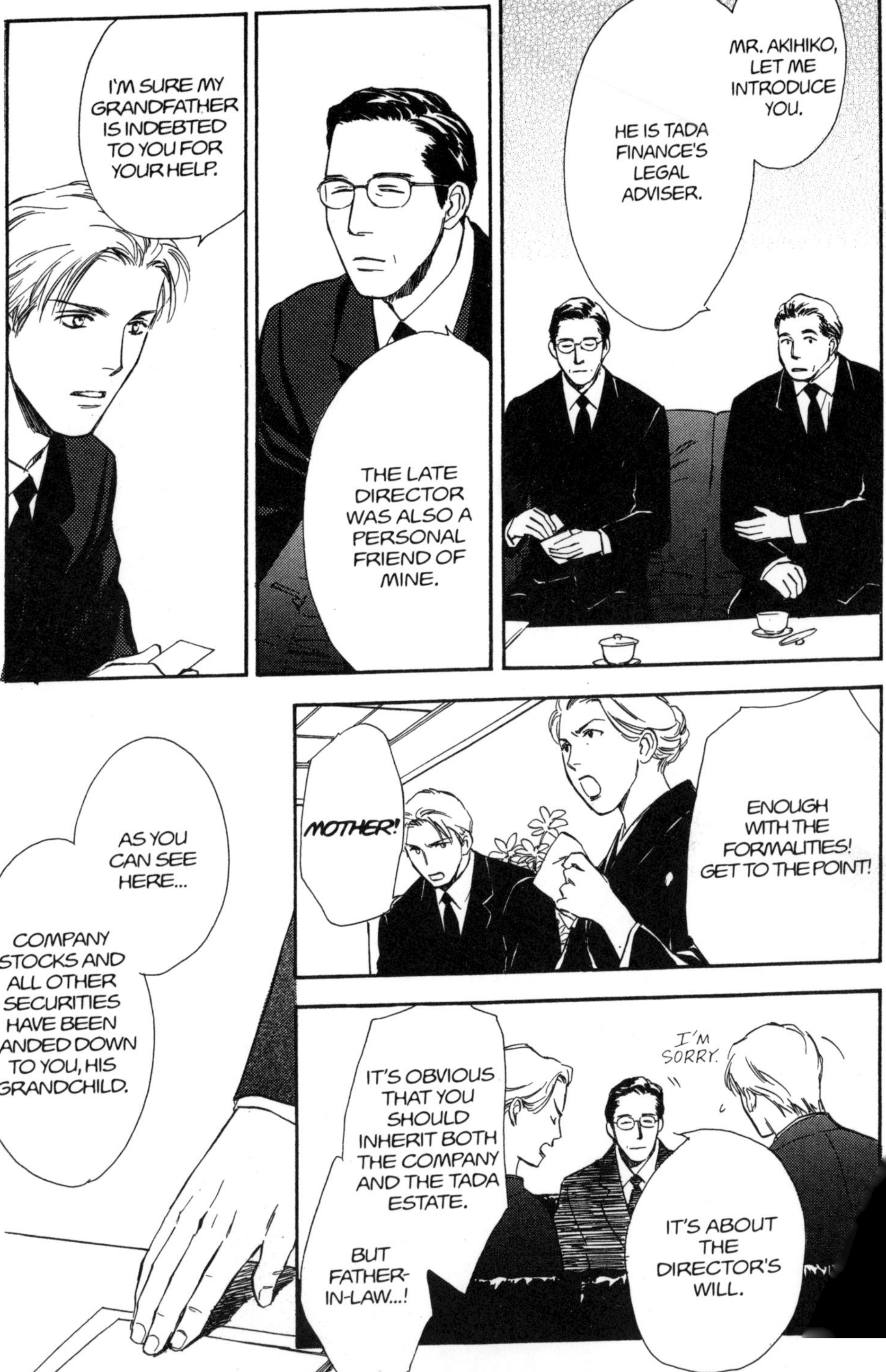
MR. AKIHIKO, LET ME INTRODUCE YOU.
HE IS TADA FINANCE'S LEGAL ADVISER.
THE LATE DIRECTOR WAS ALSO A PERSONAL FRIEND OF MINE.
I'M SURE MY GRANDFATHER IS INDEBTED TO YOU FOR YOUR HELP.
ENOUGH WITH THE FORMALITIES! GET TO THE POINT!
MOTHER!
I'M SORRY.
IT'S ABOUT THE DIRECTOR'S WILL.
IT'S OBVIOUS THAT YOU SHOULD INHERIT BOTH THE COMPANY AND THE TADA ESTATE.
BUT FATHER-IN-LAW...!
AS YOU CAN SEE HERE...
COMPANY STOCKS AND ALL OTHER SECURITIES HAVE BEEN HANDED DOWN TO YOU, HIS GRANDCHILD.

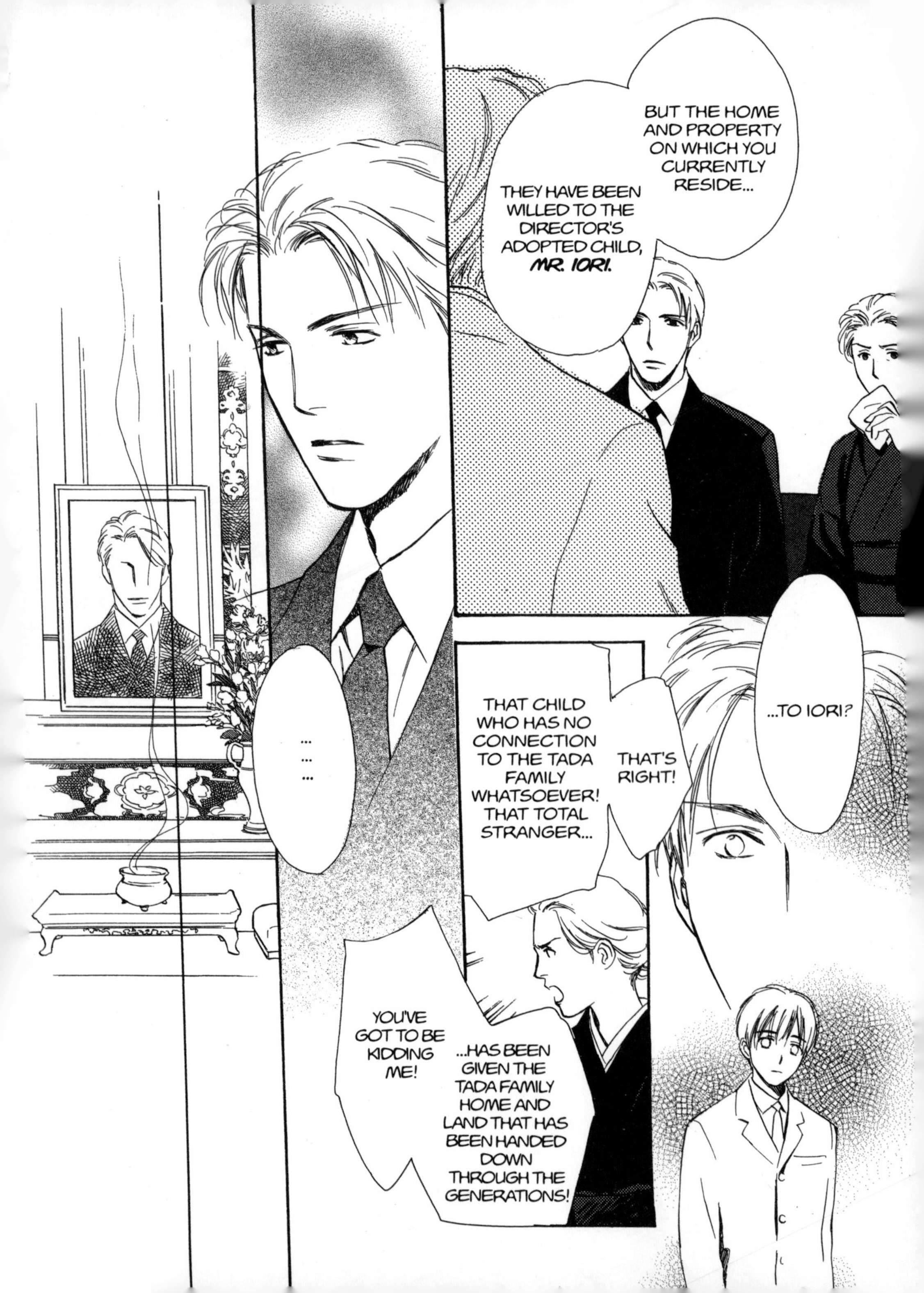
BUT THE HOME AND PROPERTY ON WHICH YOU CURRENTLY RESIDE...
THEY HAVE BEEN WILLED TO THE DIRECTOR'S ADOPTED CHILD, ***MR. IORI.***
...TO IORI?
THAT'S RIGHT!
THAT CHILD WHO HAS NO CONNECTION TO THE TADA FAMILY WHATSOEVER! THAT TOTAL STRANGER...
...HAS BEEN GIVEN THE TADA FAMILY HOME AND LAND THAT HAS BEEN HANDED DOWN THROUGH THE GENERATIONS!
YOU'VE GOT TO BE KIDDING ME!
... ...

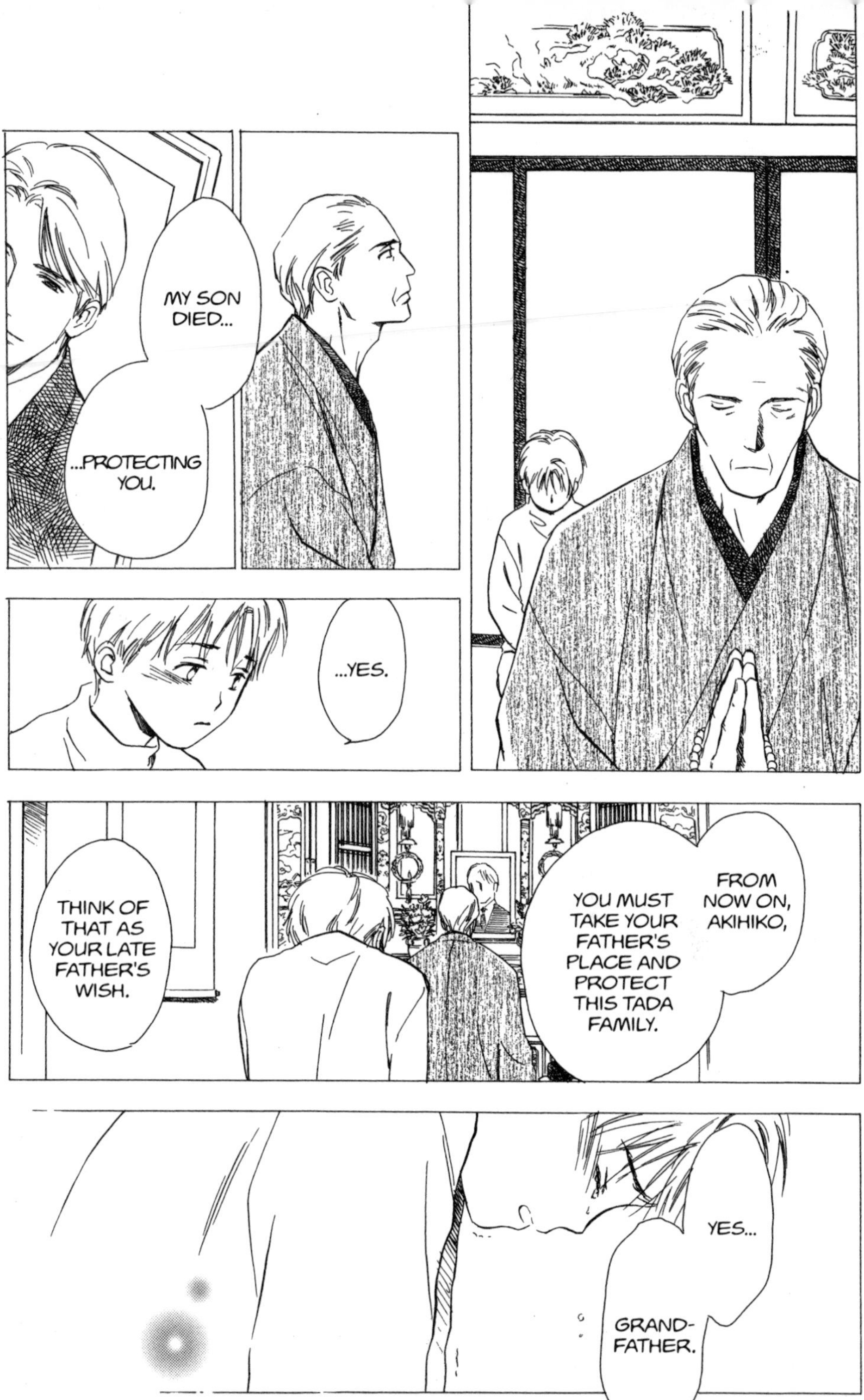
MY SON DIED...
...PROTECTING YOU.
...YES.
FROM NOW ON, AKIHIKO,
YOU MUST TAKE YOUR FATHER'S PLACE AND PROTECT THIS TADA FAMILY.
THINK OF THAT AS YOUR LATE FATHER'S WISH.
YES...
GRAND-FATHER.

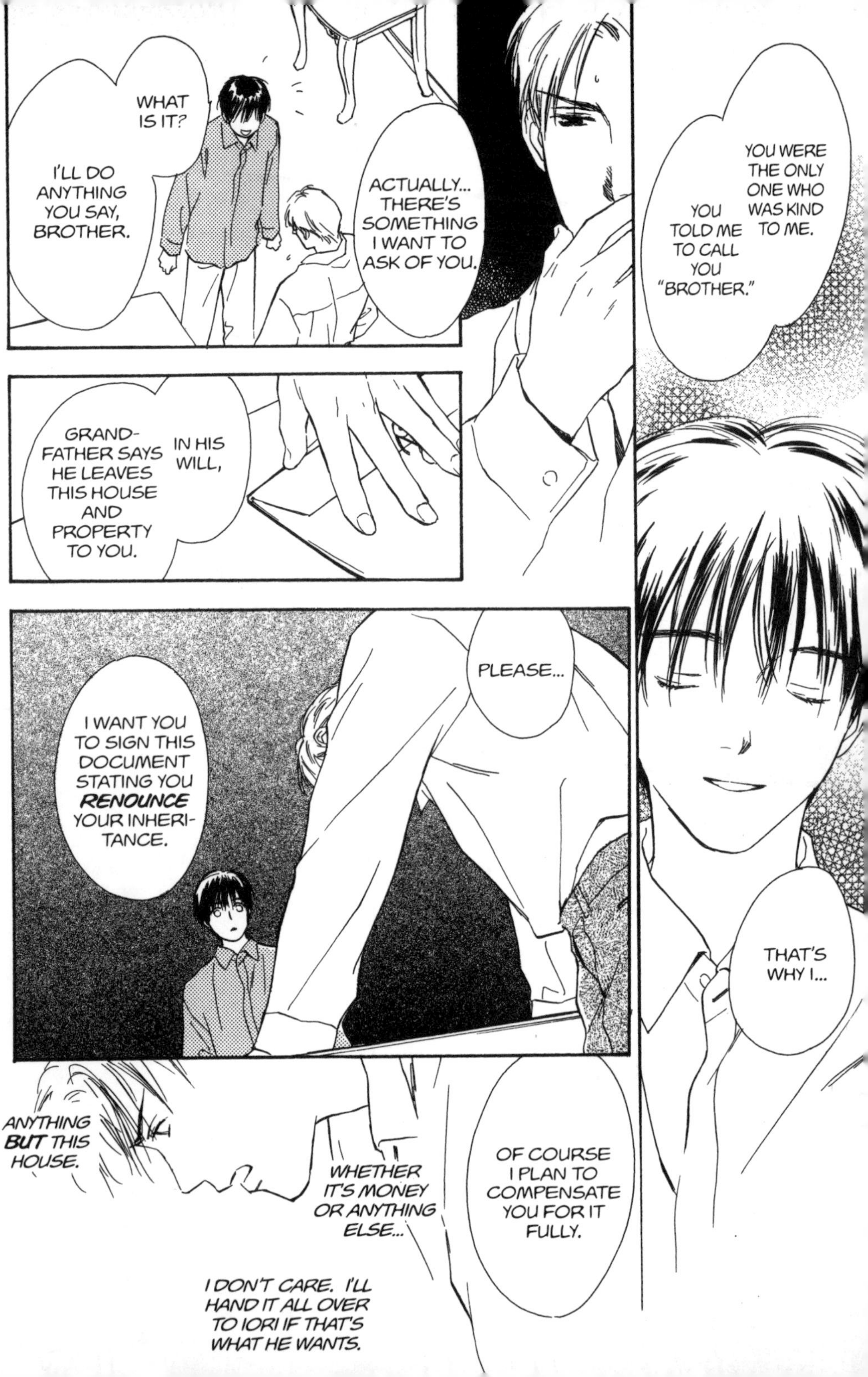
YOU WERE THE ONLY ONE WHO WAS KIND TO ME.
YOU TOLD ME TO CALL YOU "BROTHER."
THAT'S WHY I...
ACTUALLY... THERE'S SOMETHING I WANT TO ASK OF YOU.
WHAT IS IT?
I'LL DO ANYTHING YOU SAY, BROTHER.
IN HIS WILL,
GRAND-FATHER SAYS HE LEAVES THIS HOUSE AND PROPERTY TO YOU.
PLEASE...
I WANT YOU TO SIGN THIS DOCUMENT STATING YOU **RENOUNCE** YOUR INHERI-TANCE.
OF COURSE I PLAN TO COMPENSATE YOU FOR IT FULLY.
WHETHER IT'S MONEY OR ANYTHING ELSE...
ANYTHING **BUT** THIS HOUSE.
I DON'T CARE. I'LL HAND IT ALL OVER TO IORI IF THAT'S WHAT HE WANTS.

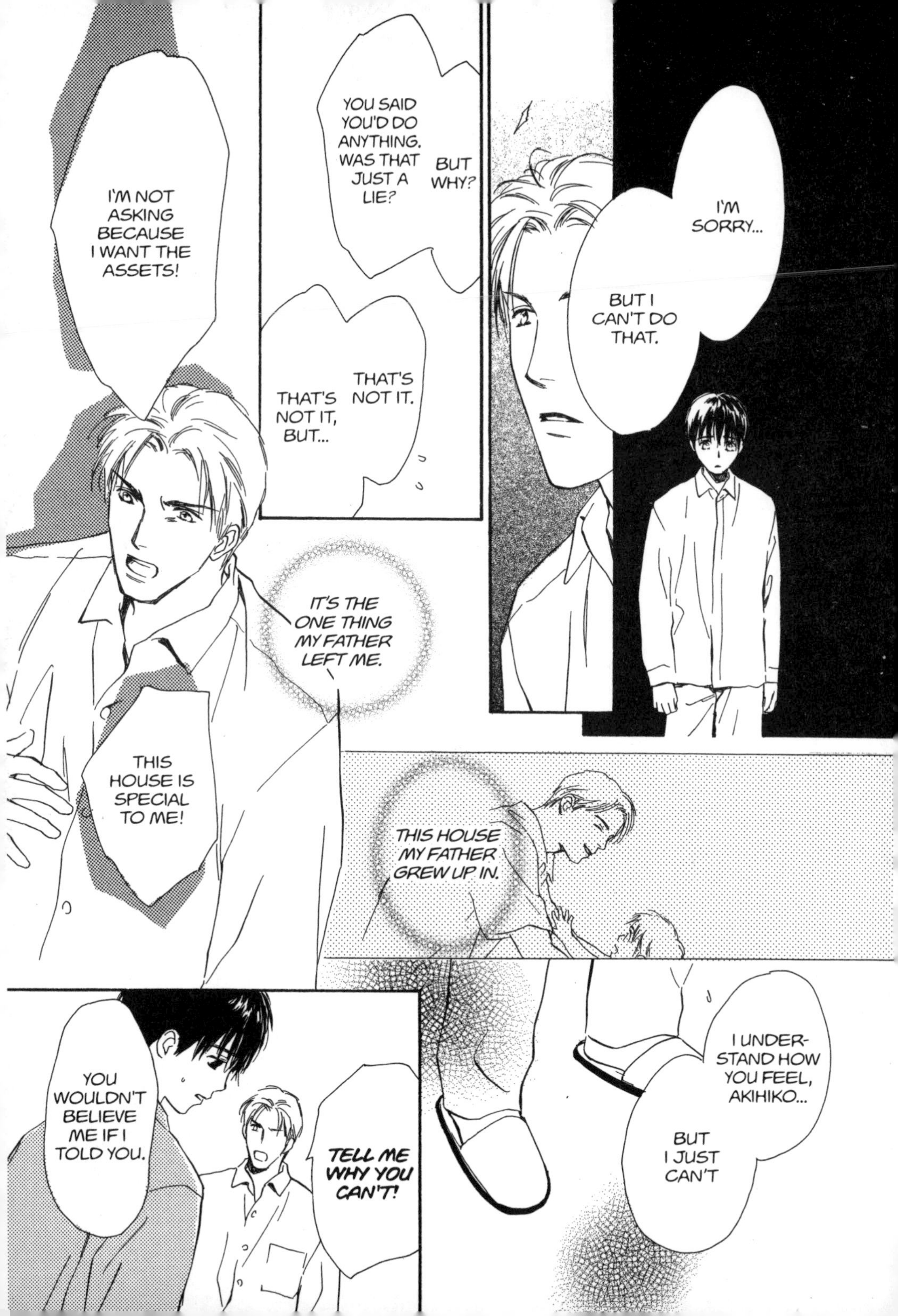
I'M SORRY...
BUT I CAN'T DO THAT.
BUT WHY?
YOU SAID YOU'D DO ANYTHING. WAS THAT JUST A LIE?
THAT'S NOT IT.
THAT'S NOT IT, BUT...
I'M NOT ASKING BECAUSE I WANT THE ASSETS!
IT'S THE ONE THING MY FATHER LEFT ME.
THIS HOUSE IS SPECIAL TO ME!
THIS HOUSE MY FATHER GREW UP IN.
I UNDER-STAND HOW YOU FEEL, AKIHIKO...
BUT I JUST CAN'T
TELL ME WHY YOU CAN'T!
YOU WOULDN'T BELIEVE ME IF I TOLD YOU.

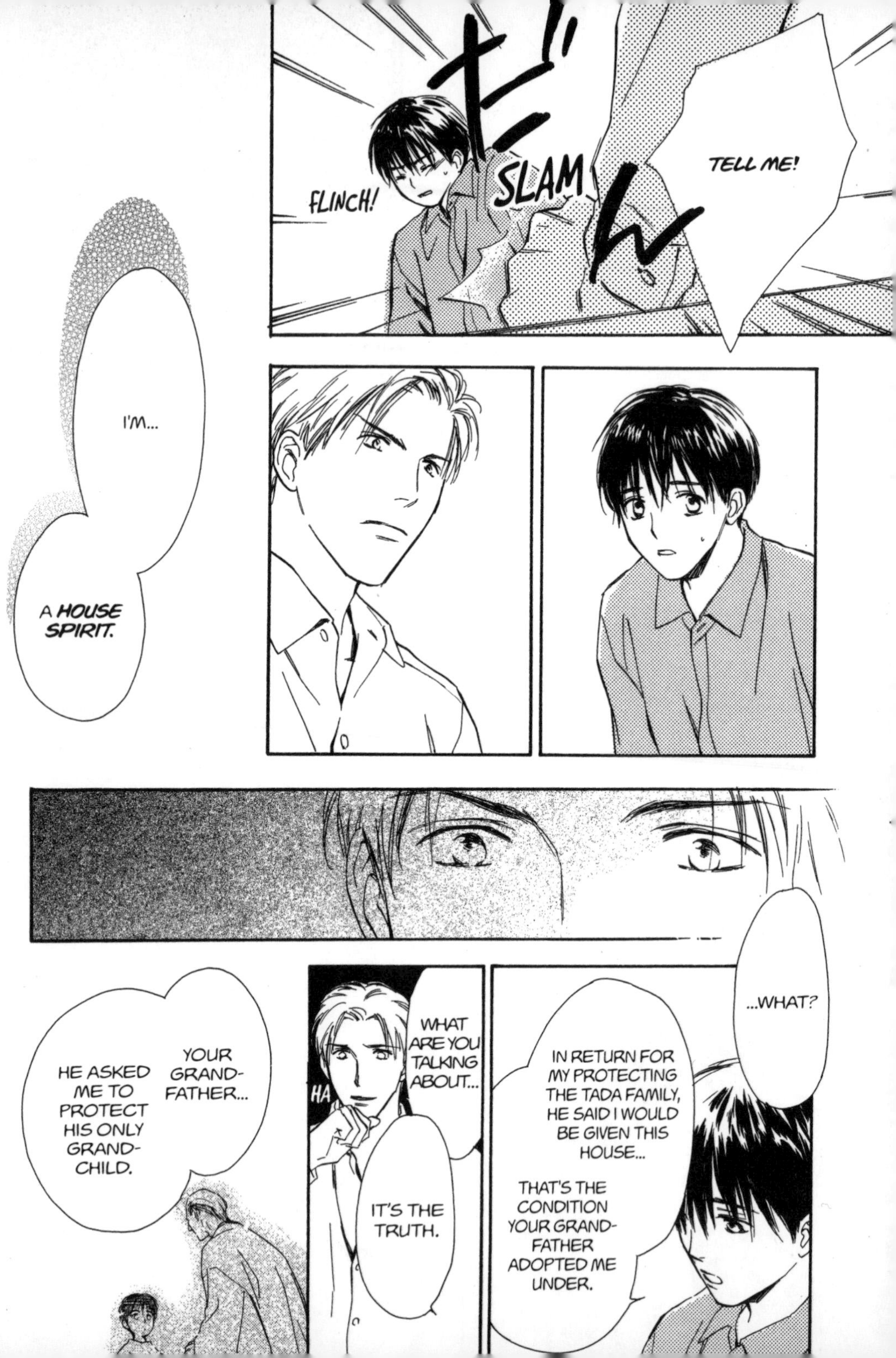
TELL ME!
ざん
SLAM
FLINCH!
I'M...
A HOUSE SPIRIT.
...WHAT?
IN RETURN FOR MY PROTECTING THE TADA FAMILY, HE SAID I WOULD BE GIVEN THIS HOUSE...
THAT'S THE CONDITION YOUR GRAND-FATHER ADOPTED ME UNDER.
WHAT ARE YOU TALKING ABOUT...
HA
IT'S THE TRUTH.
YOUR GRAND-FATHER...
HE ASKED ME TO PROTECT HIS ONLY GRAND-CHILD.

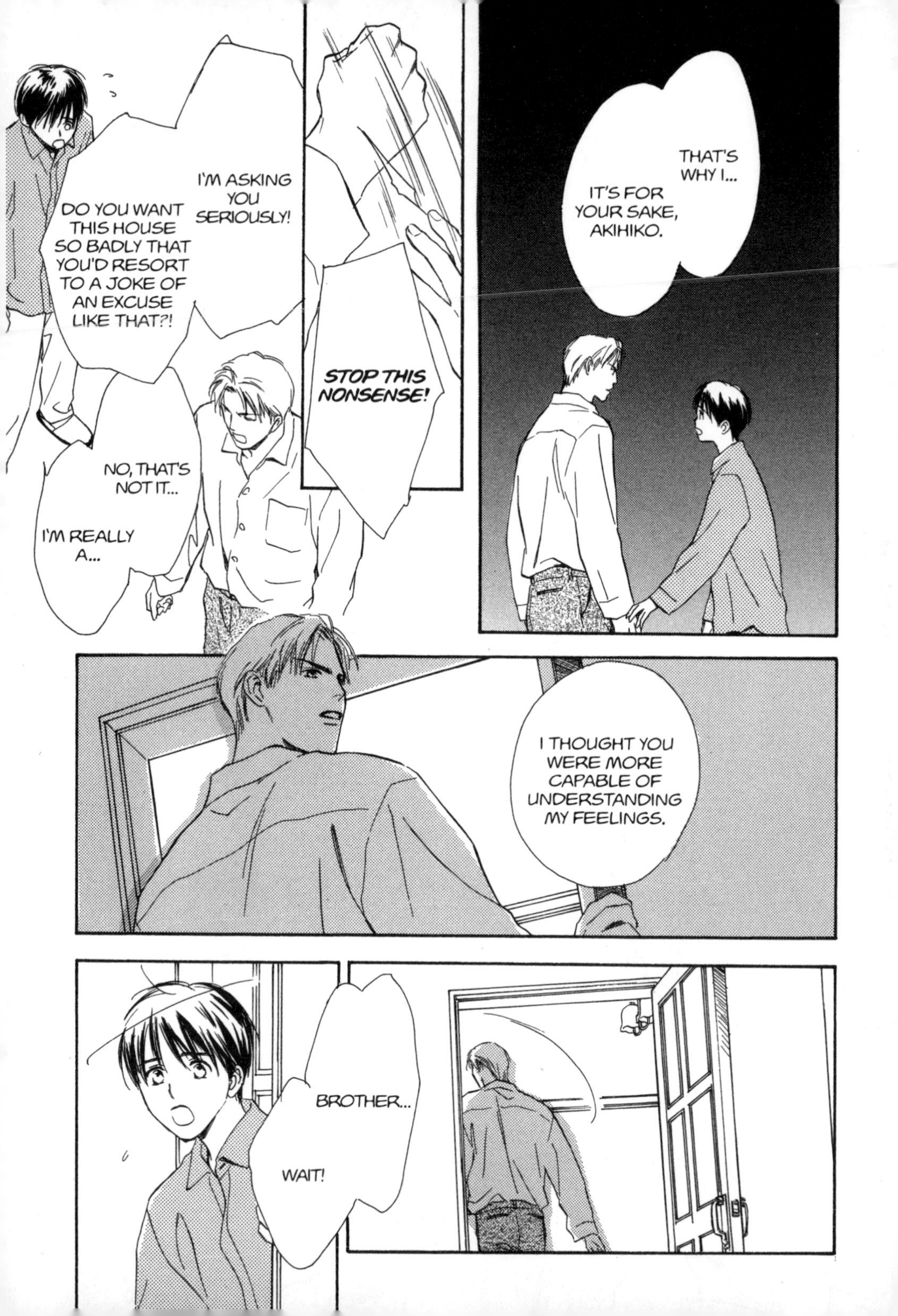
THAT'S WHY I...
IT'S FOR YOUR SAKE, AKIHIKO.
STOP THIS NONSENSE!
I'M ASKING YOU SERIOUSLY!
DO YOU WANT THIS HOUSE SO BADLY THAT YOU'D RESORT TO A JOKE OF AN EXCUSE LIKE THAT?!
NO, THAT'S NOT IT...
I'M REALLY A...
I THOUGHT YOU WERE MORE CAPABLE OF UNDERSTANDING MY FEELINGS.
BROTHER...
WAIT!

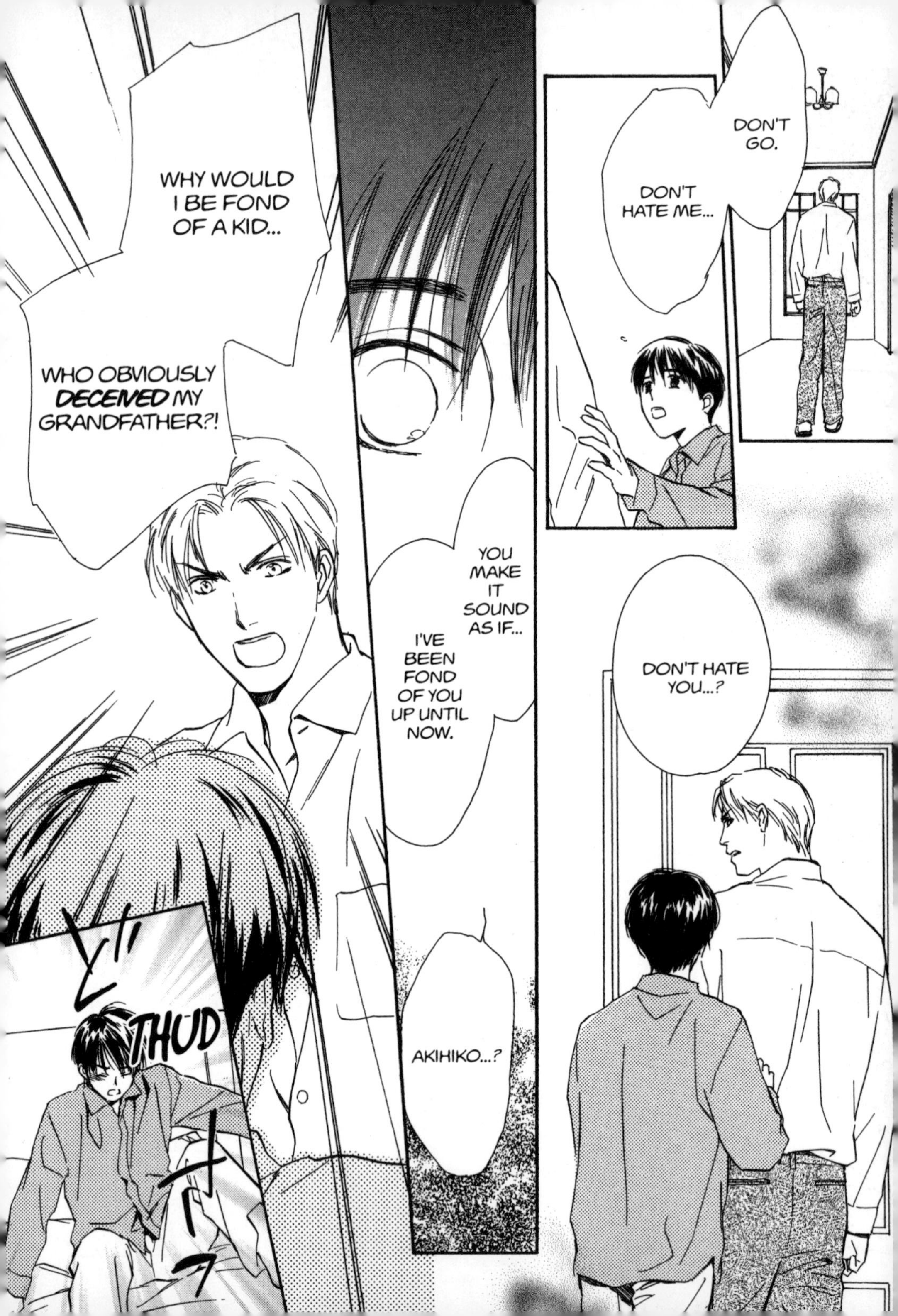
DON'T GO.
DON'T HATE ME...
DON'T HATE YOU...?
YOU MAKE IT SOUND AS IF...
I'VE BEEN FOND OF YOU UP UNTIL NOW.
AKIHIKO...?
WHY WOULD I BE FOND OF A KID...
WHO OBVIOUSLY DECEIVED MY GRANDFATHER?!
THUD

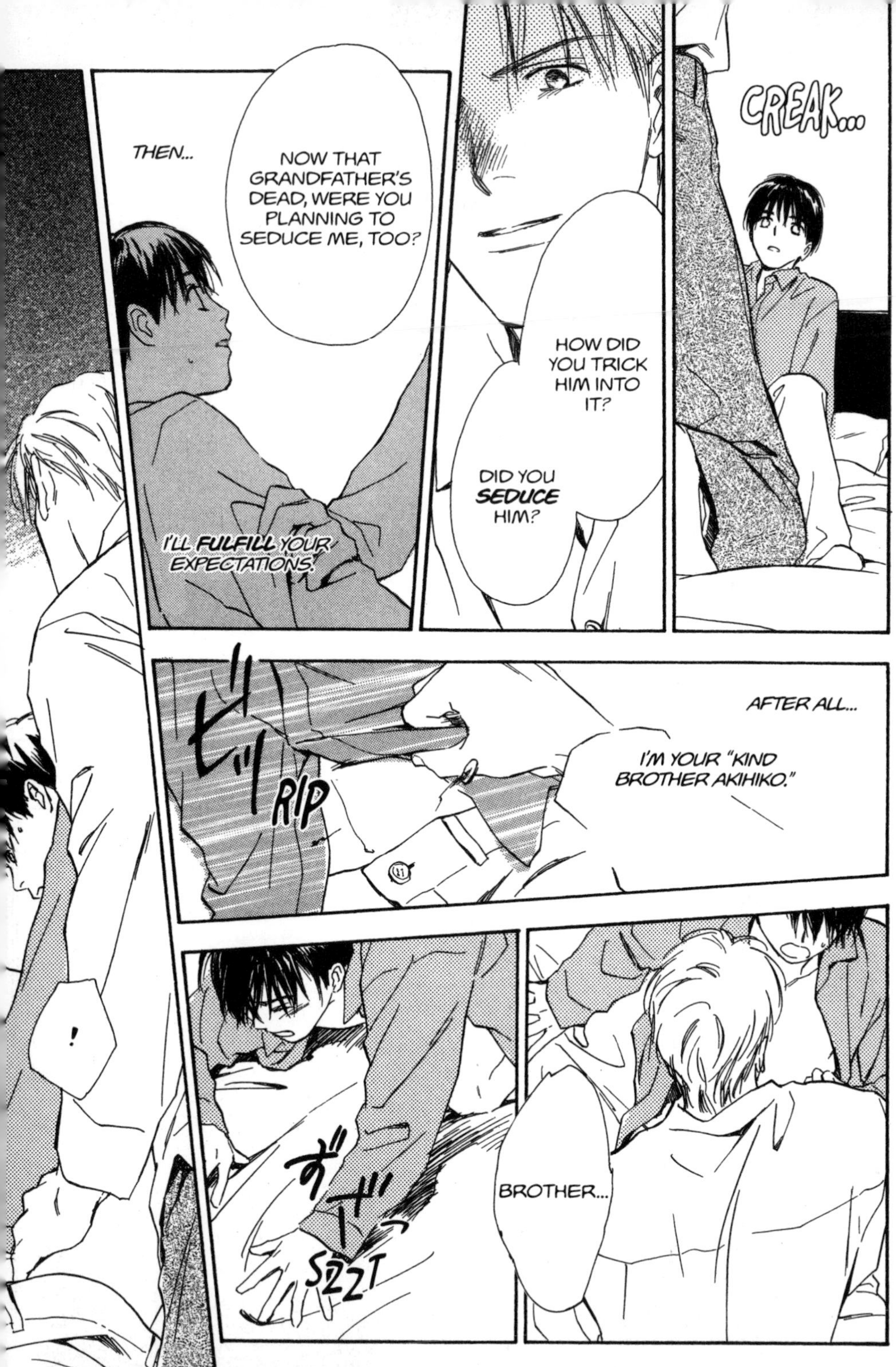
CREAK...
HOW DID YOU TRICK HIM INTO IT?
DID YOU **SEDUCE** HIM?
THEN...
NOW THAT GRANDFATHER'S DEAD, WERE YOU PLANNING TO SEDUCE ME, TOO?
I'LL **FULFILL** YOUR EXPECTATIONS.
AFTER ALL...
I'M YOUR "KIND BROTHER AKIHIKO."
ビリッ
RIP
BROTHER...
ずザーッ
SZZT
!

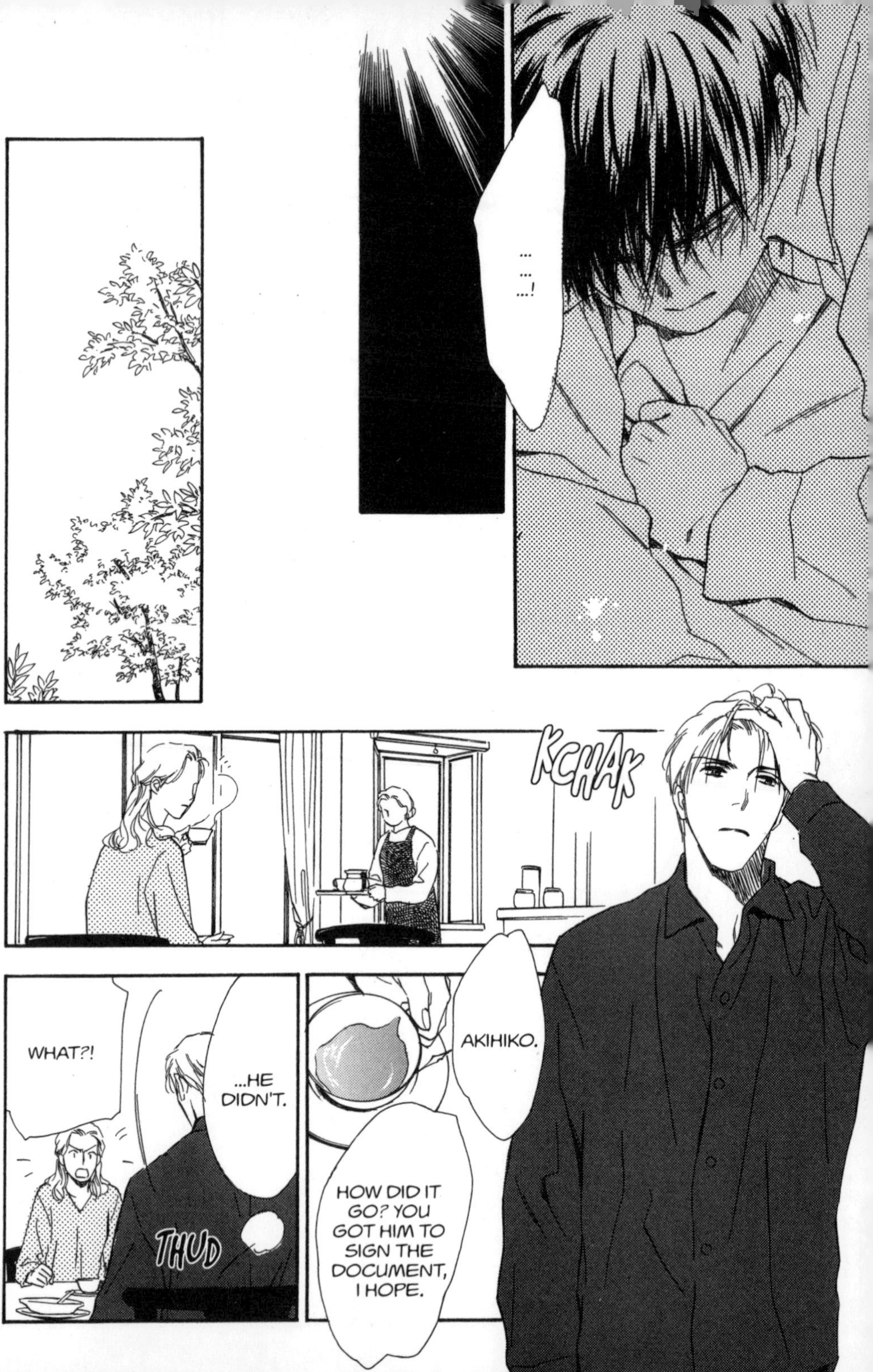
...
...
...!
KCHAK
AKIHIKO.
HOW DID IT GO? YOU GOT HIM TO SIGN THE DOCUMENT, I HOPE.
...HE DIDN'T.
WHAT?!
THUD

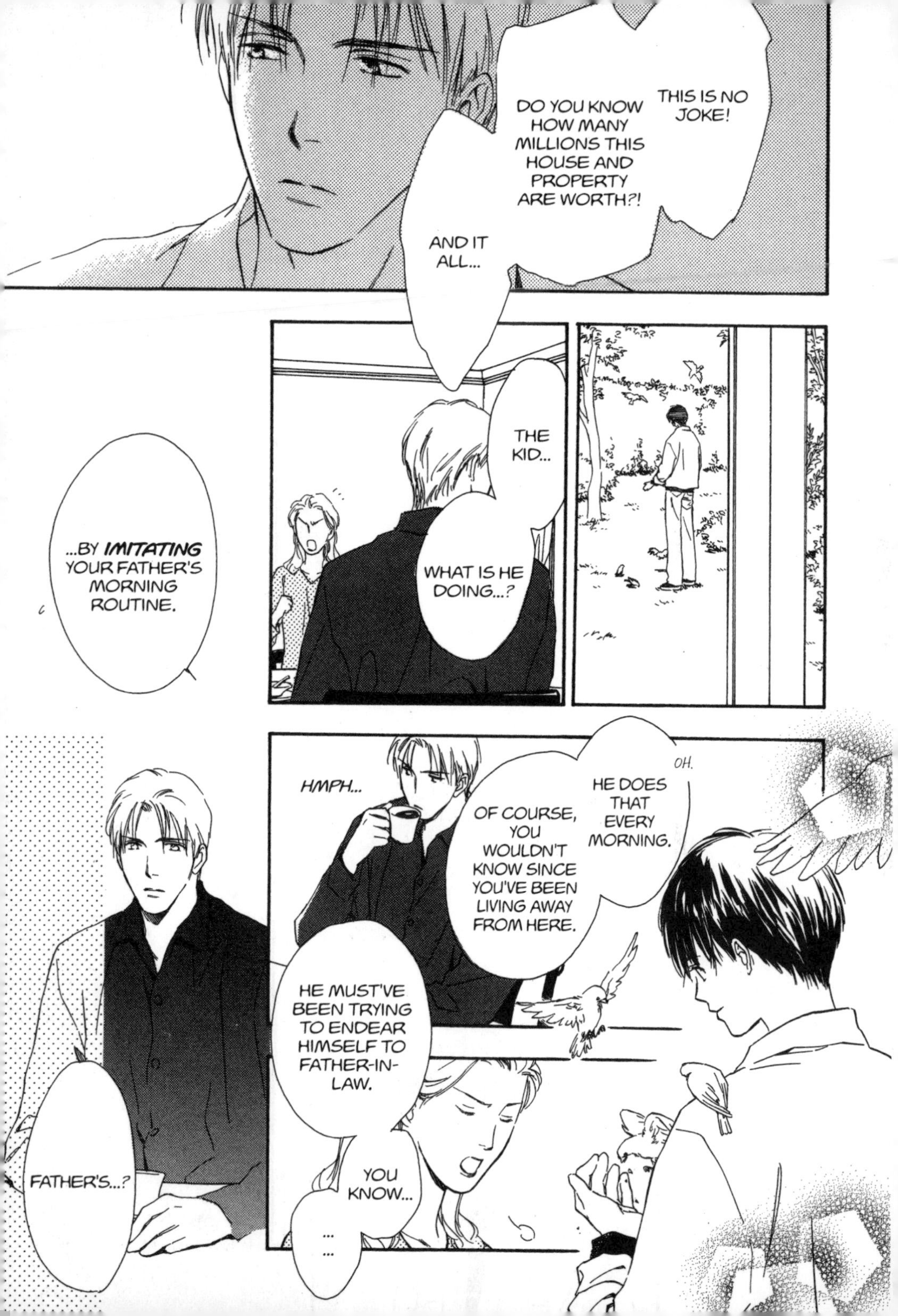
THIS IS NO JOKE!
DO YOU KNOW HOW MANY MILLIONS THIS HOUSE AND PROPERTY ARE WORTH?!
AND IT ALL...
THE KID...
WHAT IS HE DOING...?
...BY *IMITATING* YOUR FATHER'S MORNING ROUTINE.
OH.
HE DOES THAT EVERY MORNING.
OF COURSE, YOU WOULDN'T KNOW SINCE YOU'VE BEEN LIVING AWAY FROM HERE.
HMPH...
HE MUST'VE BEEN TRYING TO ENDEAR HIMSELF TO FATHER-IN-LAW.
YOU KNOW...
... ...
FATHER'S...?

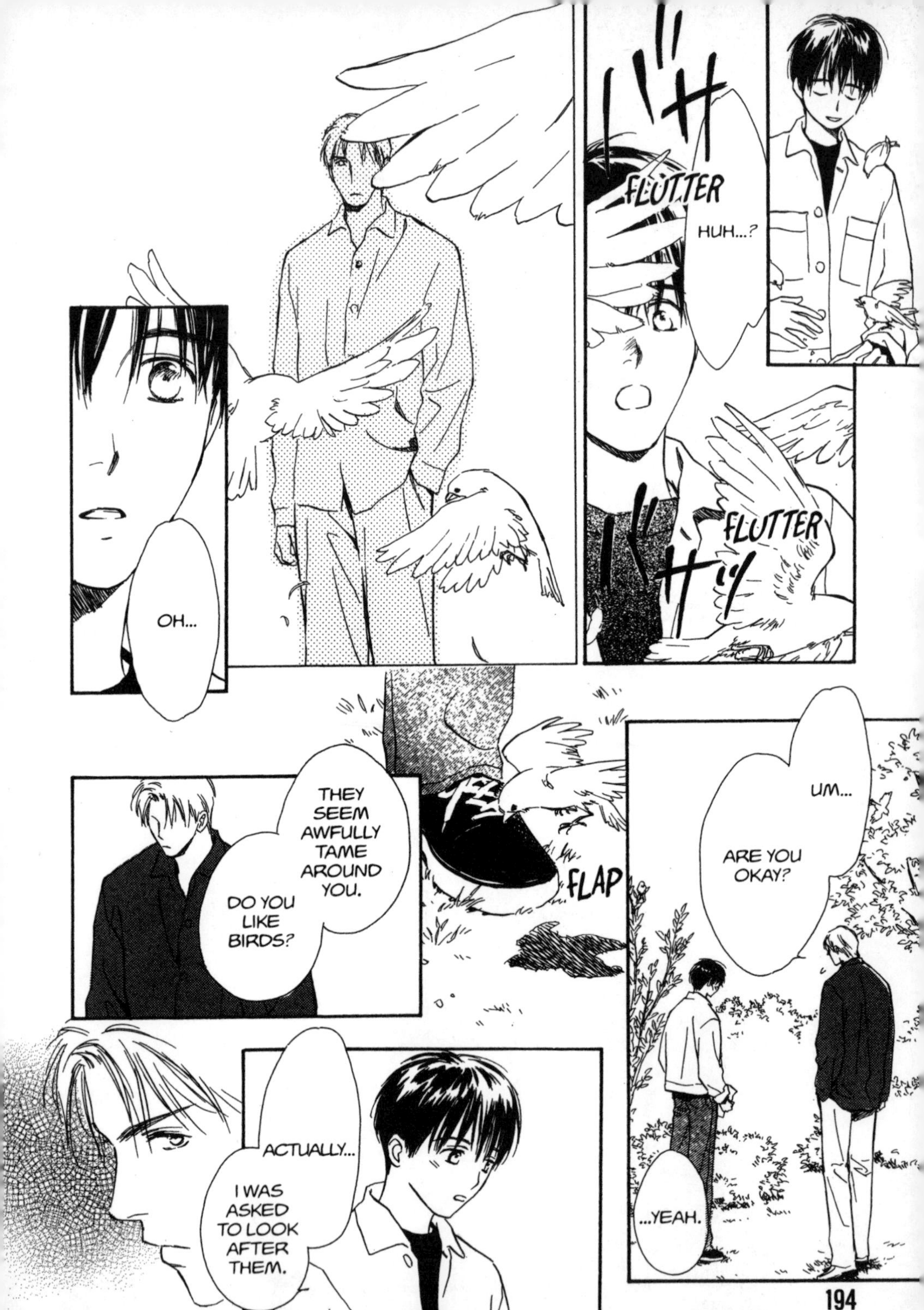
FLUTTER
HUH...?
FLUTTER
OH...
UM...
ARE YOU OKAY?
...YEAH.
FLAP
THEY SEEM AWFULLY TAME AROUND YOU.
DO YOU LIKE BIRDS?
ACTUALLY...
I WAS ASKED TO LOOK AFTER THEM.

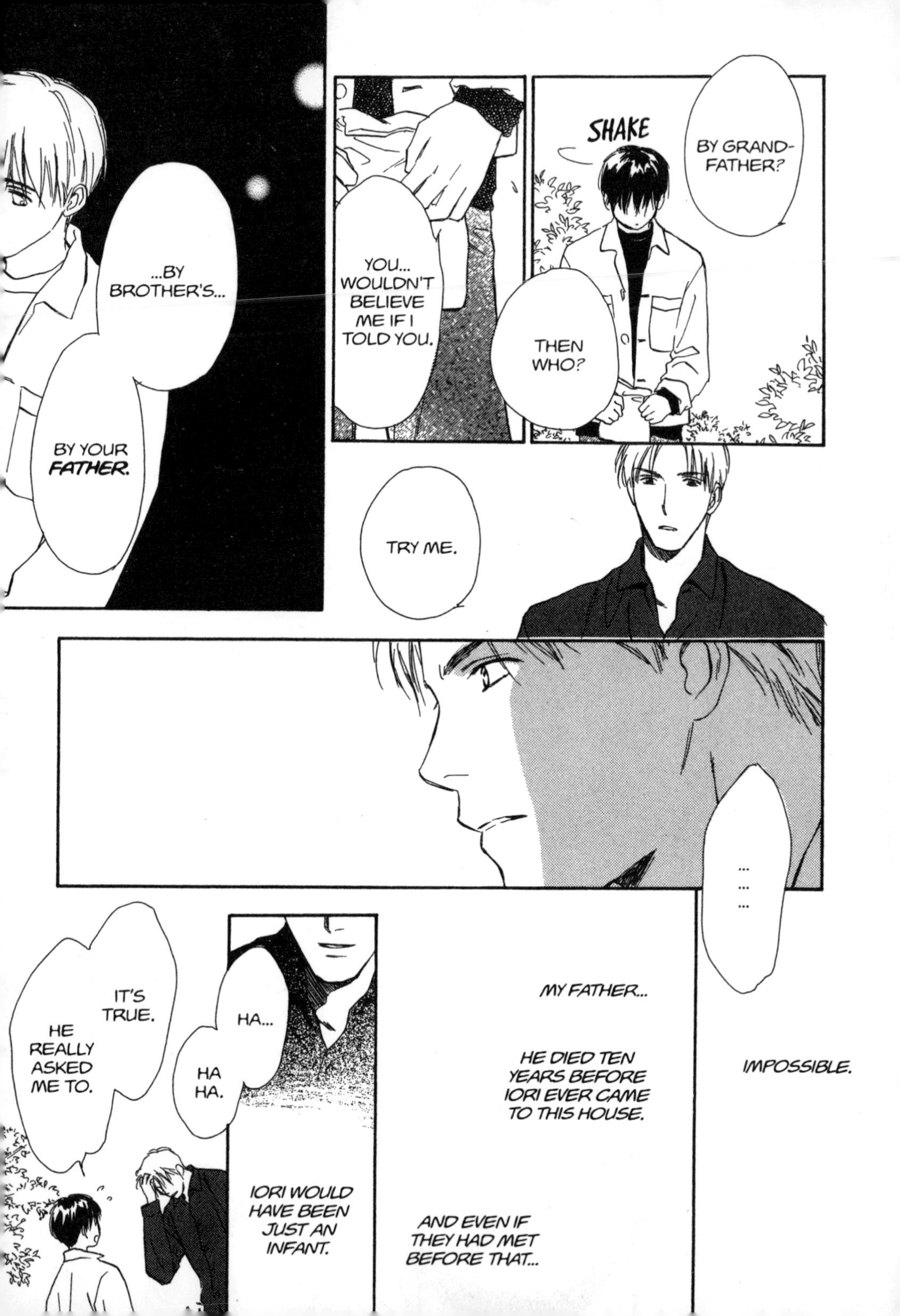
SHAKE
BY GRAND-FATHER?
THEN WHO?
YOU... WOULDN'T BELIEVE ME IF I TOLD YOU.
TRY ME.
...BY BROTHER'S...
BY YOUR *FATHER.*
...
...
...
IMPOSSIBLE.
MY FATHER...
HE DIED TEN YEARS BEFORE IORI EVER CAME TO THIS HOUSE.
AND EVEN IF THEY HAD MET BEFORE THAT...
IORI WOULD HAVE BEEN JUST AN INFANT.
HA...
HA HA.
IT'S TRUE.
HE REALLY ASKED ME TO.

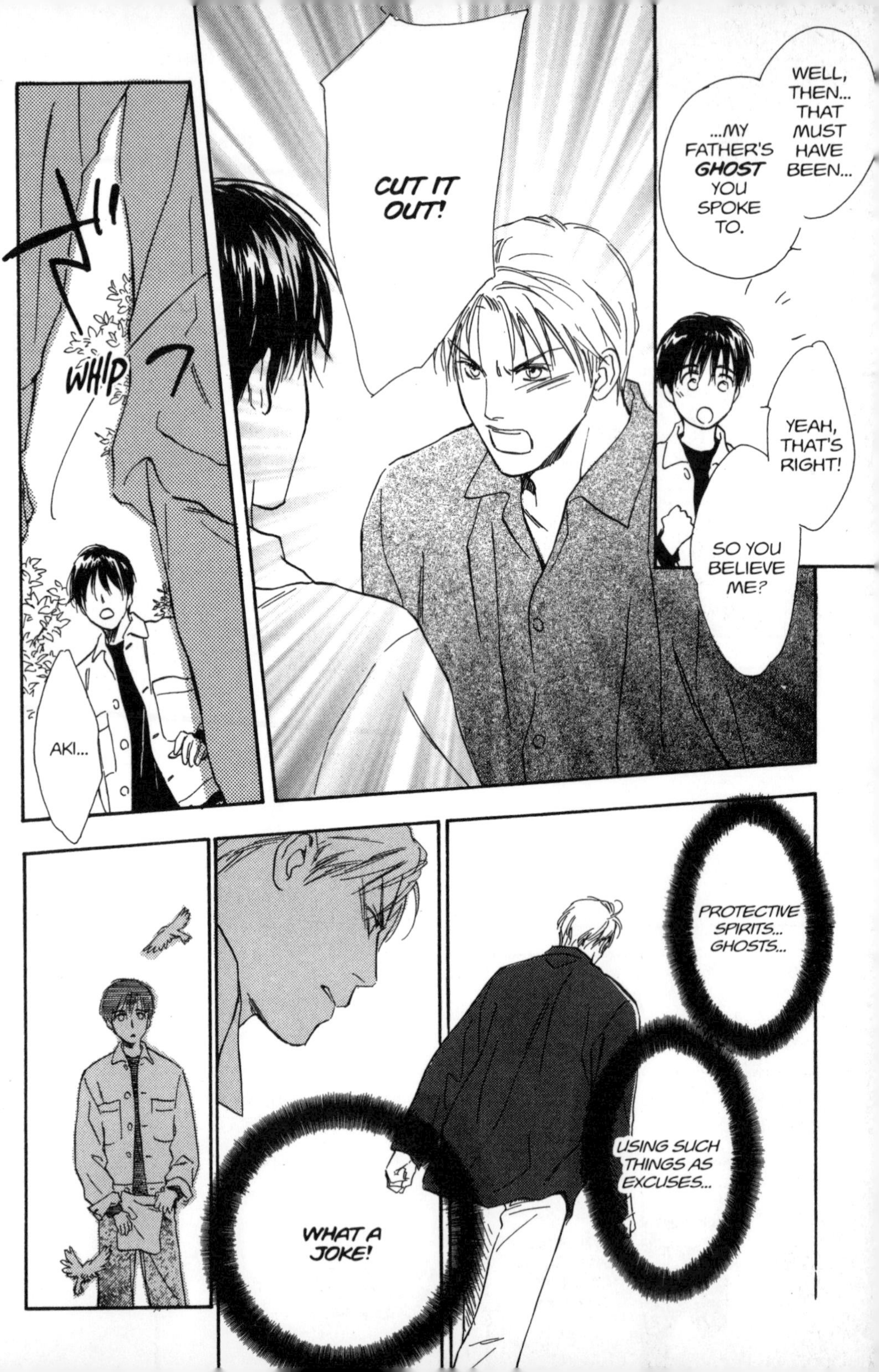
WELL, THEN... THAT MUST HAVE BEEN...
...MY FATHER'S GHOST YOU SPOKE TO.
YEAH, THAT'S RIGHT!
SO YOU BELIEVE ME?
CUT IT OUT!
WHIP
AKI...
PROTECTIVE SPIRITS... GHOSTS...
USING SUCH THINGS AS EXCUSES...
WHAT A JOKE!

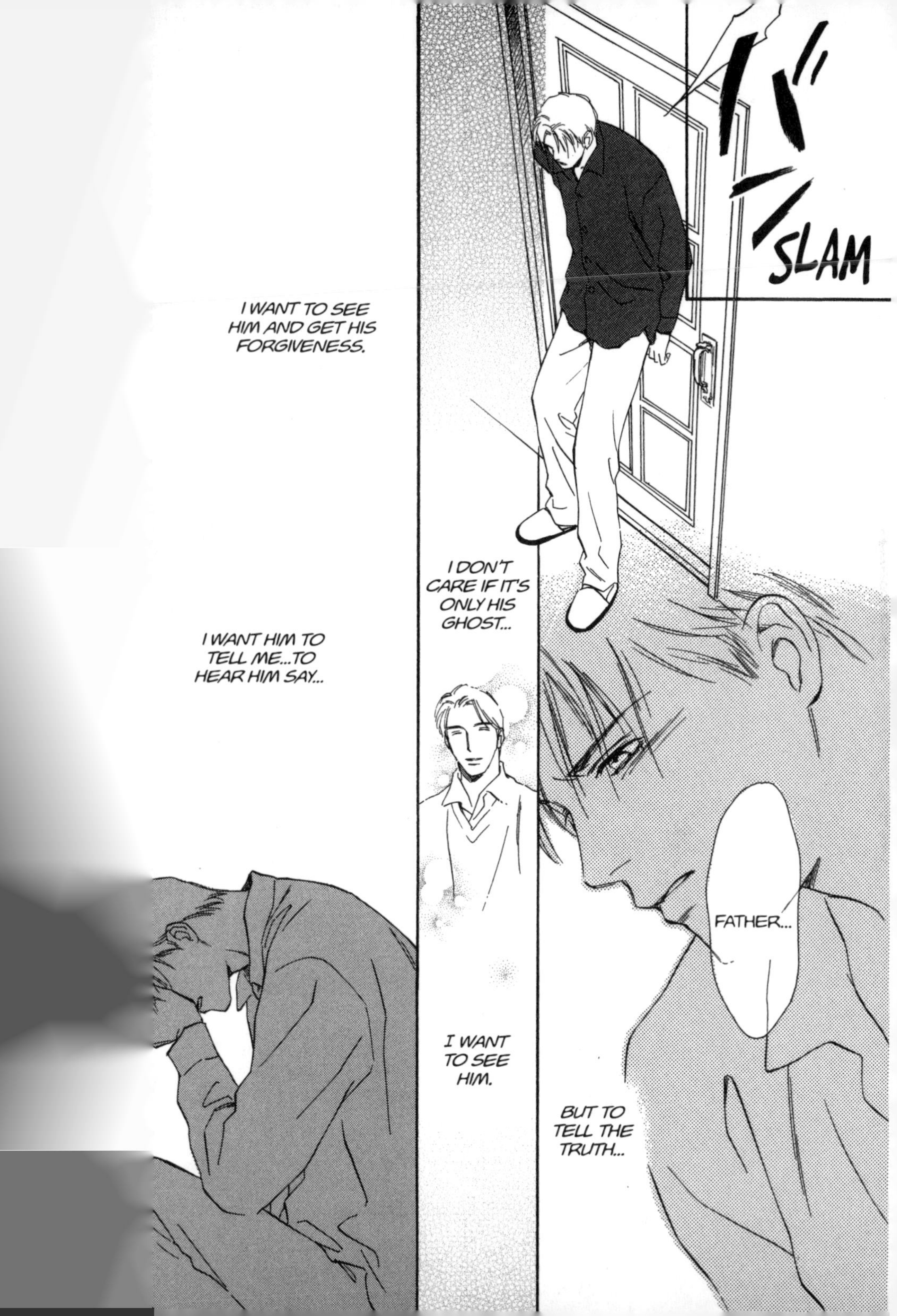
SLAM
FATHER...
BUT TO TELL THE TRUTH...
I DON'T CARE IF IT'S ONLY HIS GHOST...
I WANT TO SEE HIM.
I WANT TO SEE HIM AND GET HIS FORGIVENESS.
I WANT HIM TO TELL ME...TO HEAR HIM SAY...

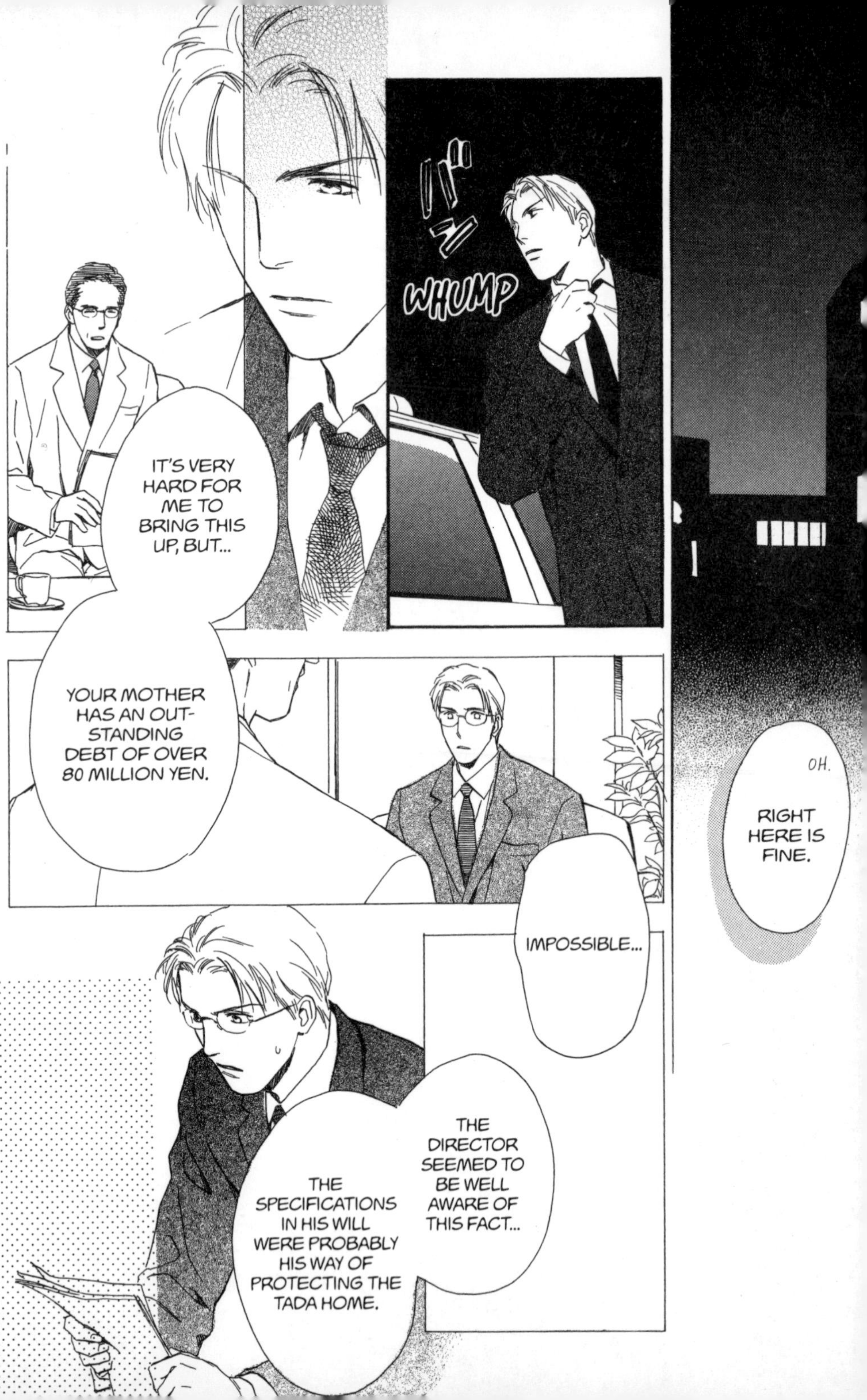
OH.
RIGHT HERE IS FINE.
WHUMP
IT'S VERY HARD FOR ME TO BRING THIS UP, BUT...
YOUR MOTHER HAS AN OUT-STANDING DEBT OF OVER 80 MILLION YEN.
IMPOSSIBLE...
THE DIRECTOR SEEMED TO BE WELL AWARE OF THIS FACT...
THE SPECIFICATIONS IN HIS WILL WERE PROBABLY HIS WAY OF PROTECTING THE TADA HOME.

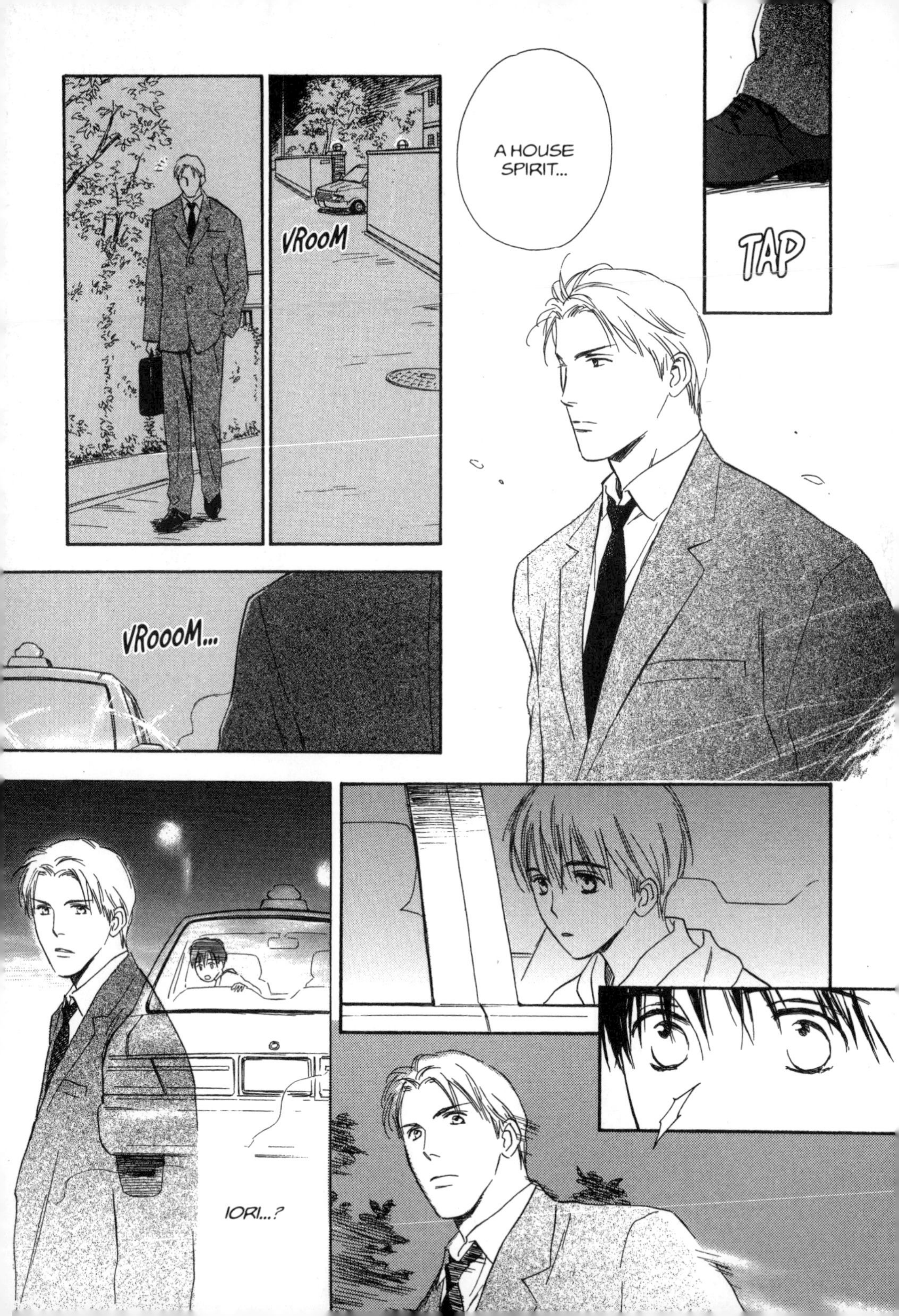
TAP
A HOUSE SPIRIT...
VROOM
VROOOM...
IORI...?

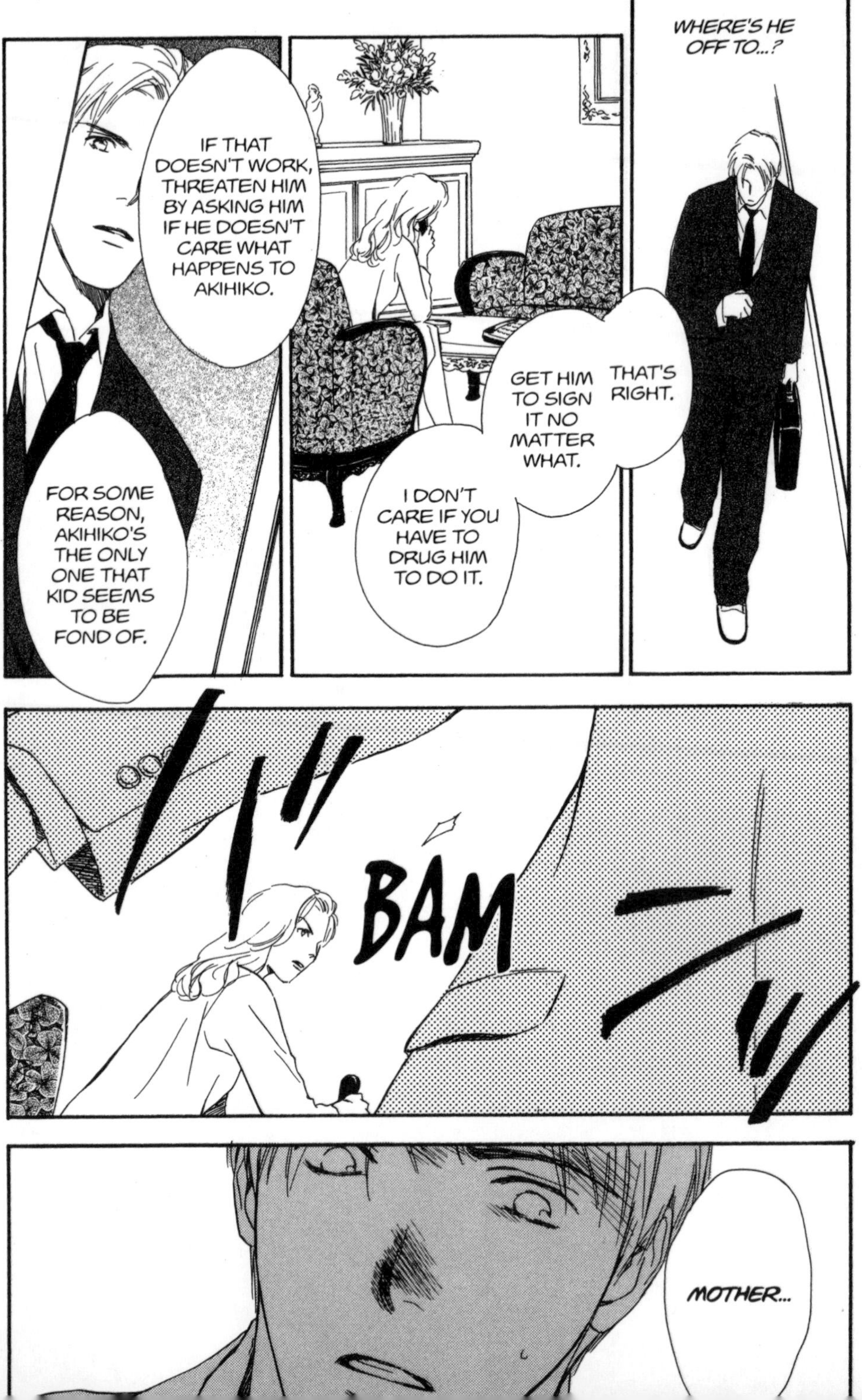
WHERE'S HE OFF TO...?
THAT'S RIGHT.
GET HIM TO SIGN IT NO MATTER WHAT.
I DON'T CARE IF YOU HAVE TO DRUG HIM TO DO IT.
IF THAT DOESN'T WORK, THREATEN HIM BY ASKING HIM IF HE DOESN'T CARE WHAT HAPPENS TO AKIHIKO.
FOR SOME REASON, AKIHIKO'S THE ONLY ONE THAT KID SEEMS TO BE FOND OF.
BAM
MOTHER...

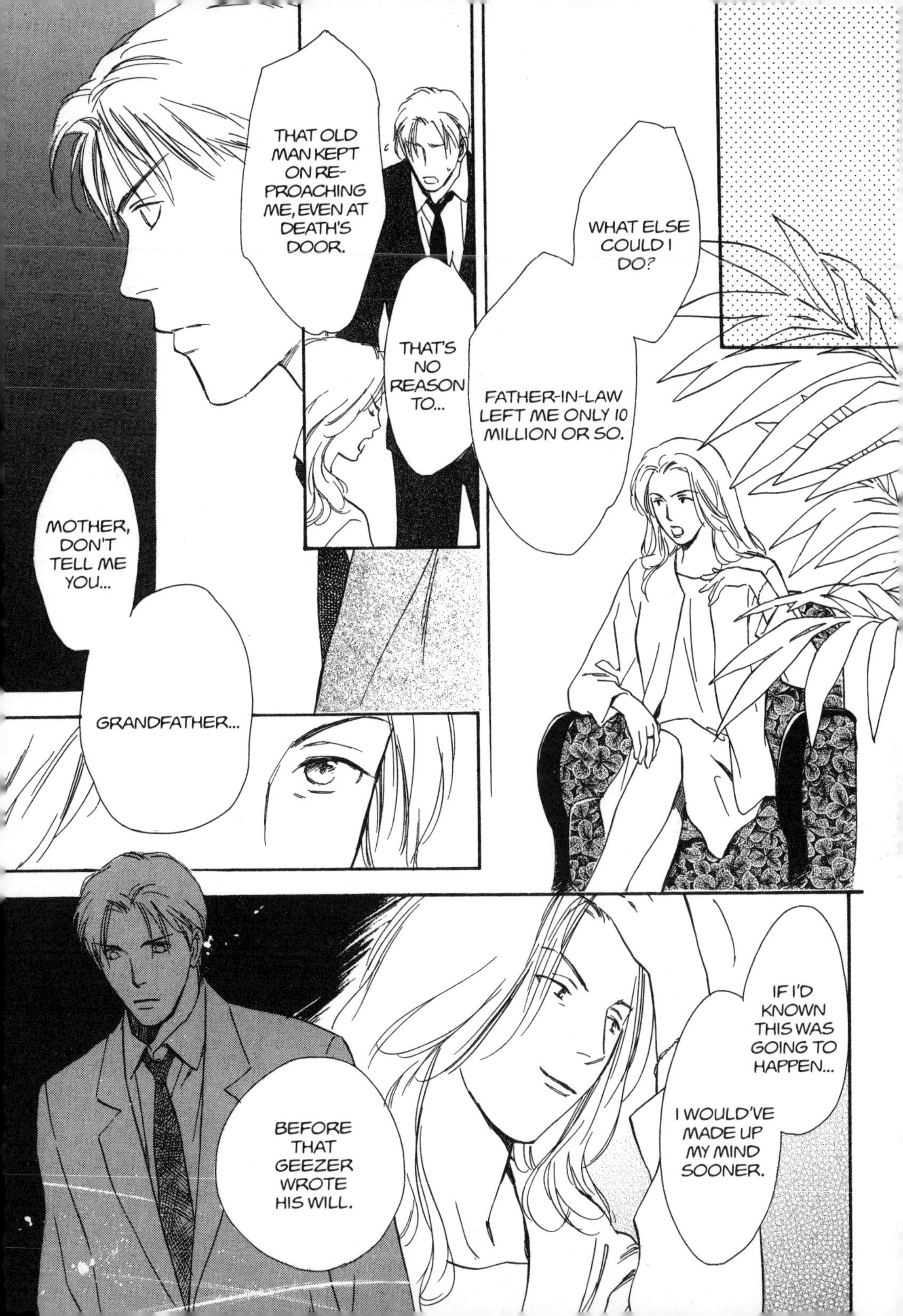
WHAT ELSE COULD I DO?
FATHER-IN-LAW LEFT ME ONLY 10 MILLION OR SO.
THAT'S NO REASON TO...
THAT OLD MAN KEPT ON RE-PROACHING ME, EVEN AT DEATH'S DOOR.
MOTHER, DON'T TELL ME YOU...
GRANDFATHER...
IF I'D KNOWN THIS WAS GOING TO HAPPEN...
I WOULD'VE MADE UP MY MIND SOONER.
BEFORE THAT GEEZER WROTE HIS WILL.

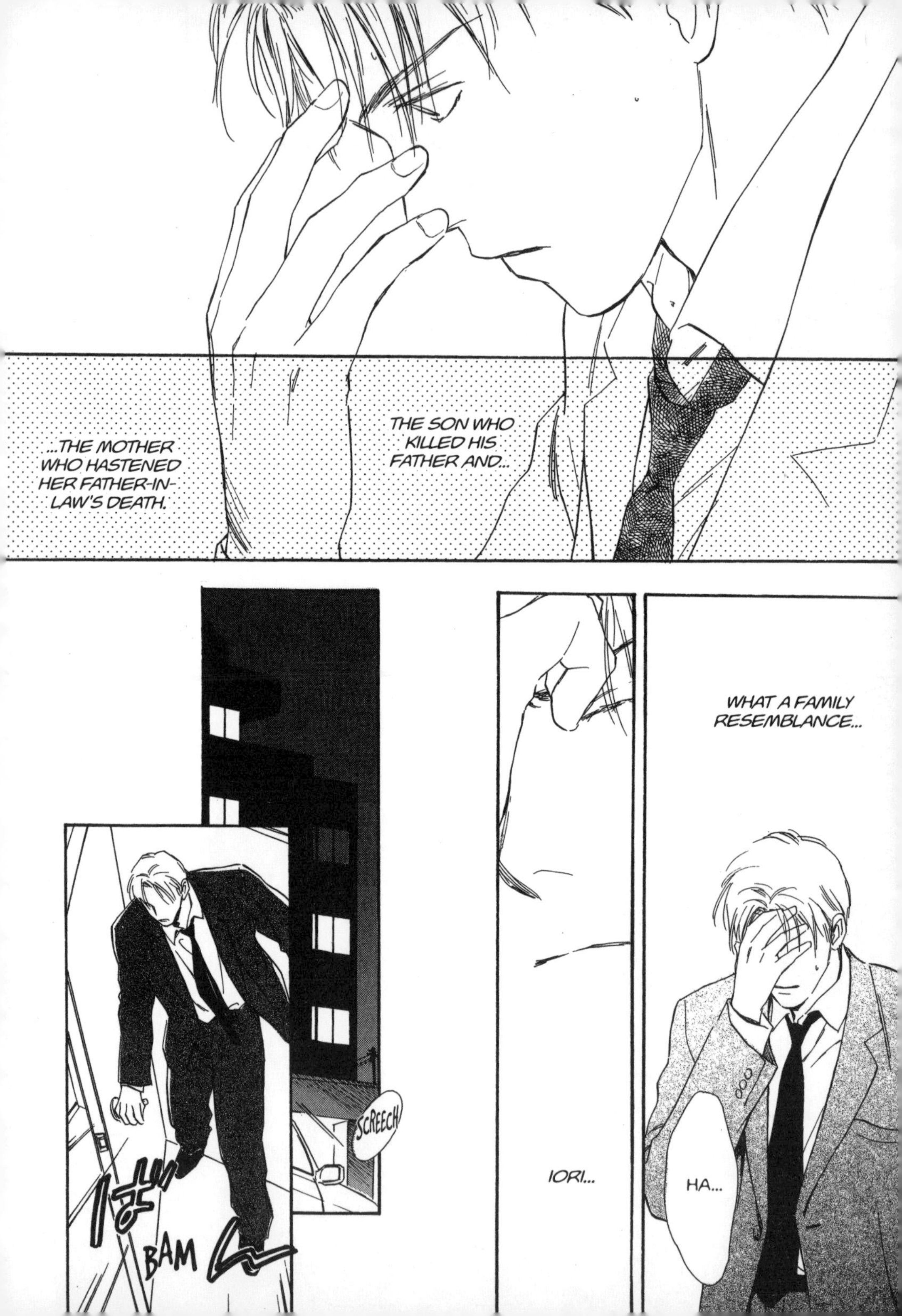
THE SON WHO KILLED HIS FATHER AND...
...THE MOTHER WHO HASTENED HER FATHER-IN-LAW'S DEATH.
WHAT A FAMILY RESEMBLANCE...
HA...
IORI...
SCREECH
BAM

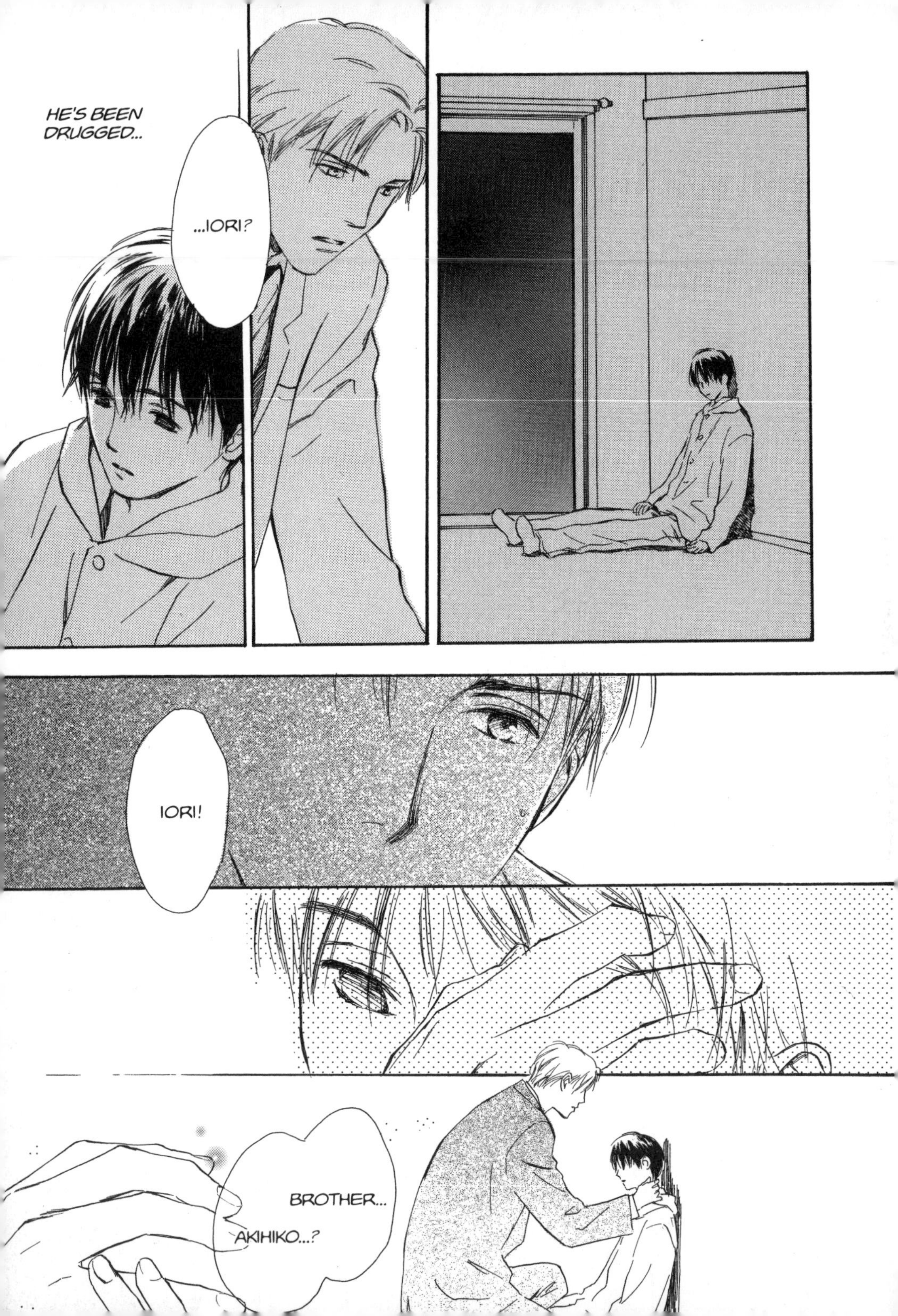
...IORI?
HE'S BEEN DRUGGED...
IORI!
BROTHER...
AKIHIKO...?

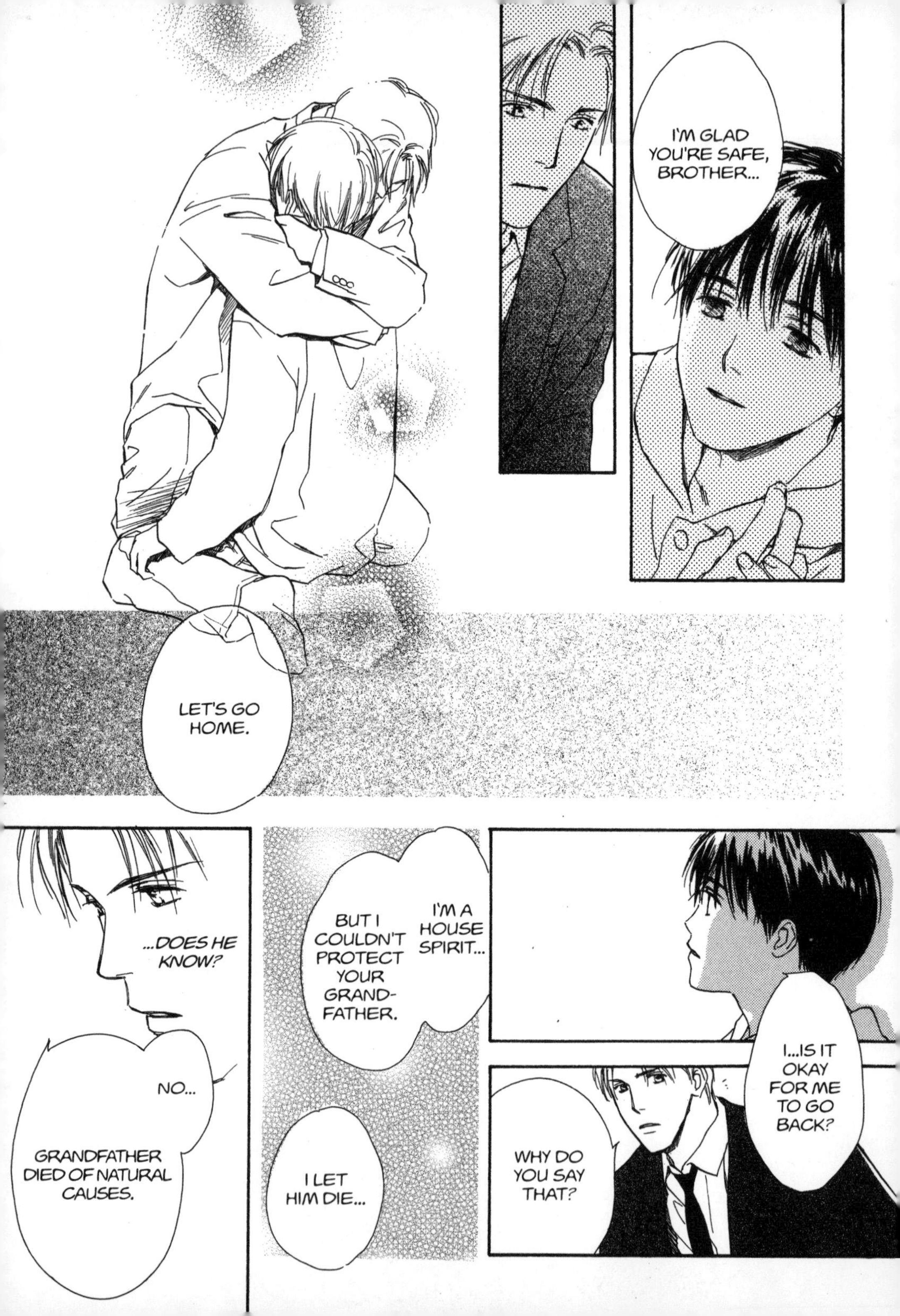
I'M GLAD YOU'RE SAFE, BROTHER...
LET'S GO HOME.
I...IS IT OKAY FOR ME TO GO BACK?
WHY DO YOU SAY THAT?
I'M A HOUSE SPIRIT...
BUT I COULDN'T PROTECT YOUR GRANDFATHER.
I LET HIM DIE...
...DOES HE KNOW?
NO...
GRANDFATHER DIED OF NATURAL CAUSES.

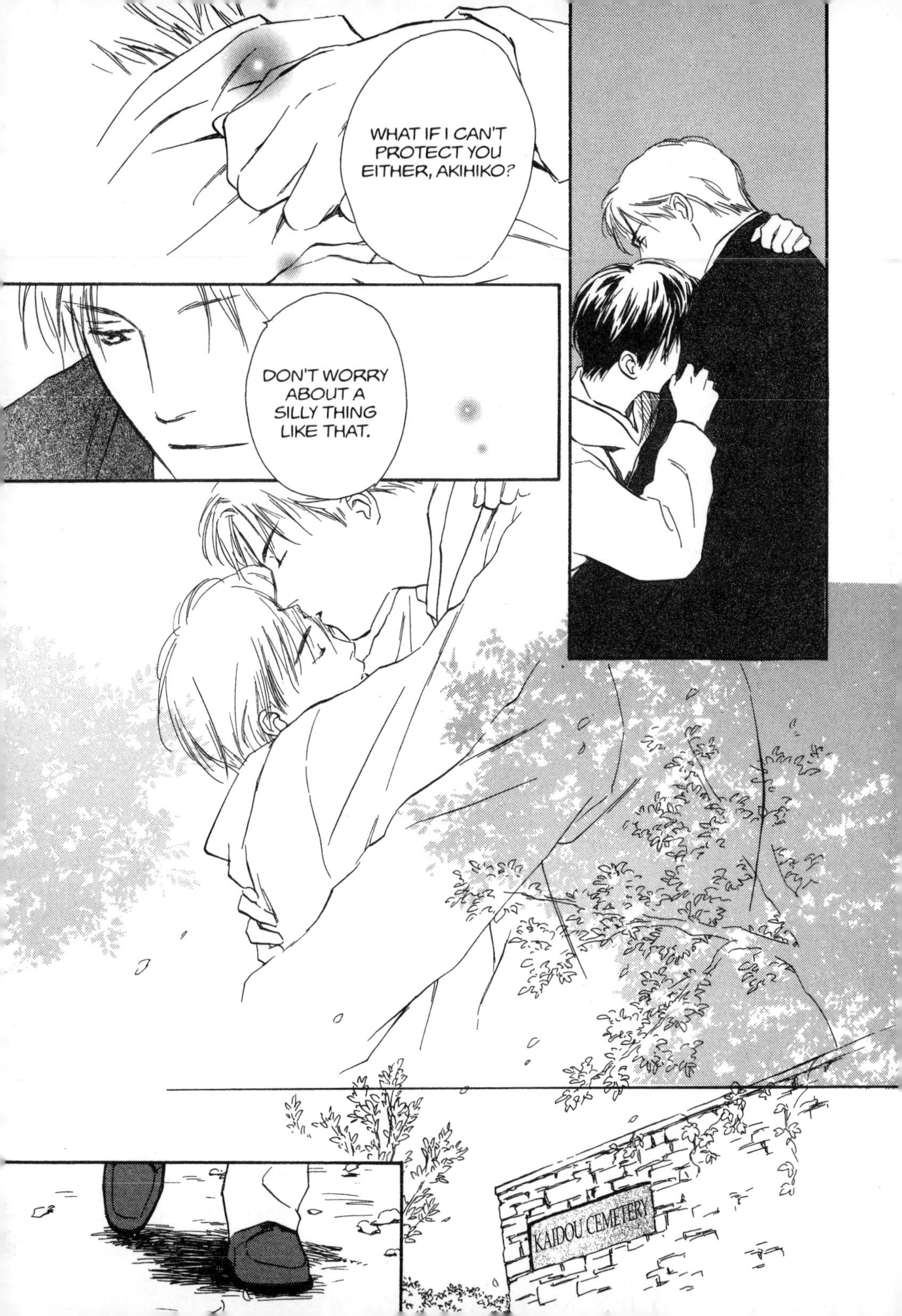
WHAT IF I CAN'T PROTECT YOU EITHER, AKIHIKO?
DON'T WORRY ABOUT A SILLY THING LIKE THAT.
KAIDOU CEMETERY

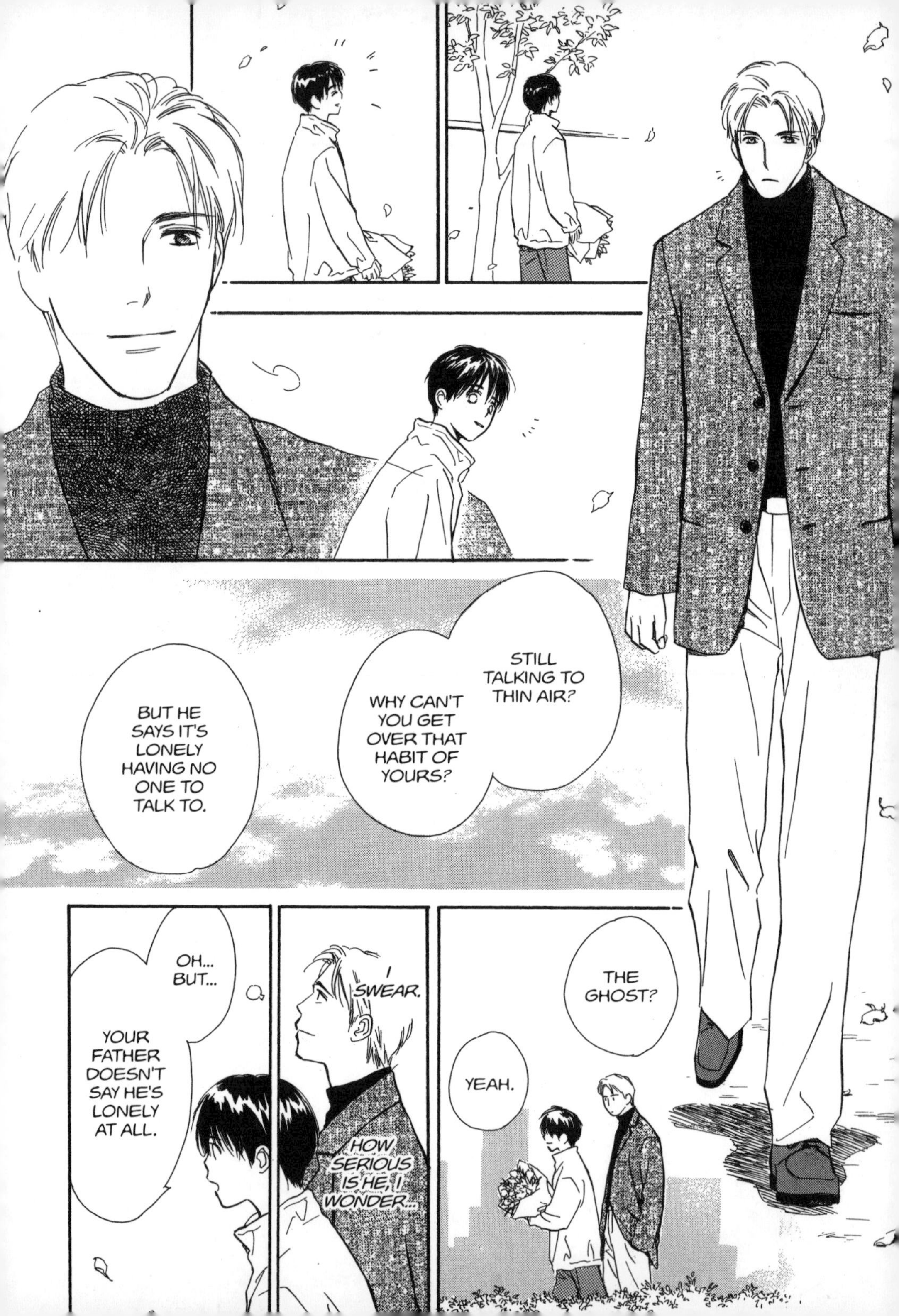
STILL TALKING TO THIN AIR?
WHY CAN'T YOU GET OVER THAT HABIT OF YOURS?
BUT HE SAYS IT'S LONELY HAVING NO ONE TO TALK TO.
THE GHOST?
YEAH.
I SWEAR.
HOW SERIOUS IS HE, I WONDER...
OH... BUT...
YOUR FATHER DOESN'T SAY HE'S LONELY AT ALL.

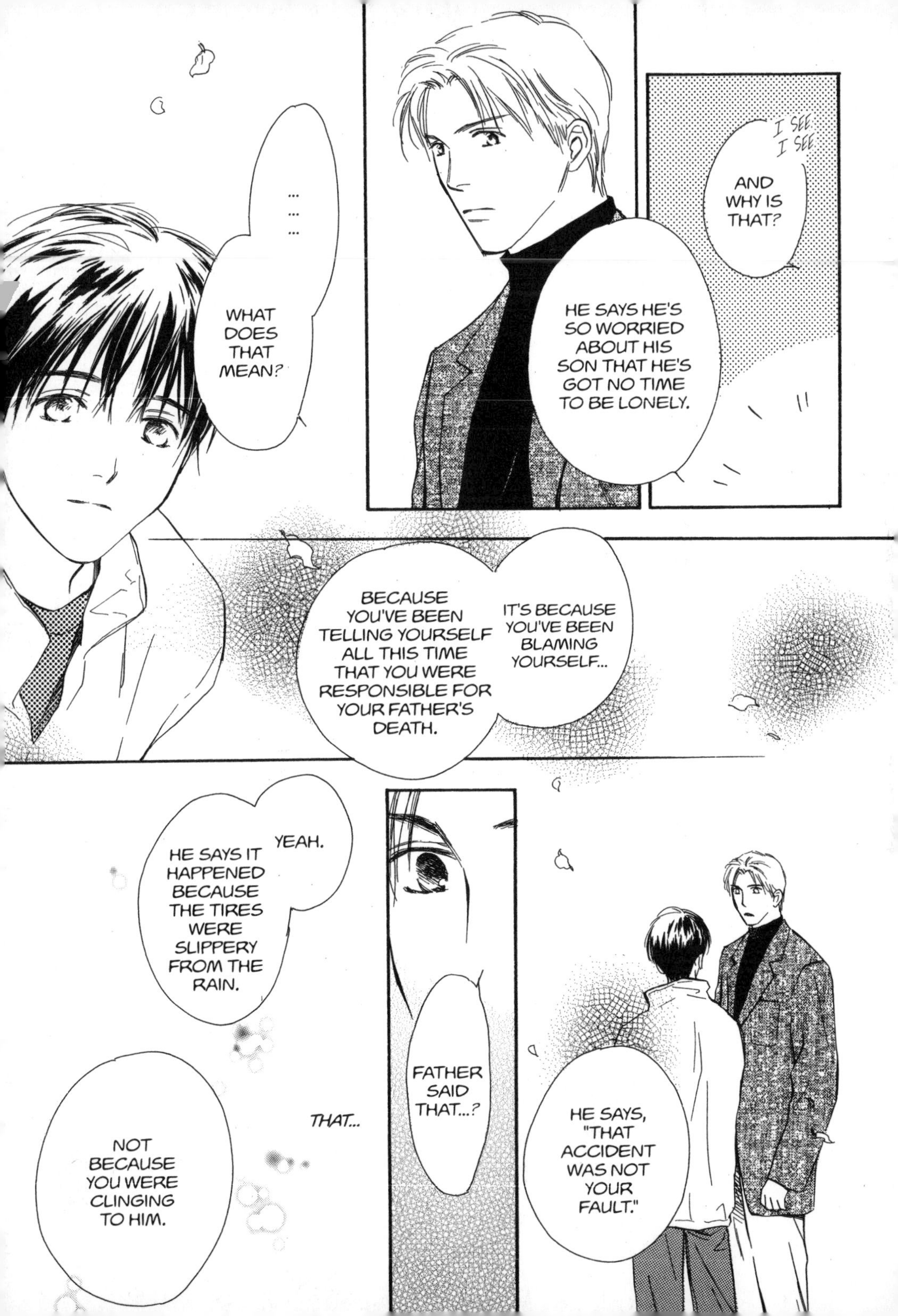
I SEE I SEE
AND WHY IS THAT?
HE SAYS HE'S SO WORRIED ABOUT HIS SON THAT HE'S GOT NO TIME TO BE LONELY.
... ...
WHAT DOES THAT MEAN?
IT'S BECAUSE YOU'VE BEEN BLAMING YOURSELF...
BECAUSE YOU'VE BEEN TELLING YOURSELF ALL THIS TIME THAT YOU WERE RESPONSIBLE FOR YOUR FATHER'S DEATH.
HE SAYS, "THAT ACCIDENT WAS NOT YOUR FAULT."
FATHER SAID THAT...?
YEAH.
HE SAYS IT HAPPENED BECAUSE THE TIRES WERE SLIPPERY FROM THE RAIN.
THAT...
NOT BECAUSE YOU WERE CLINGING TO HIM.

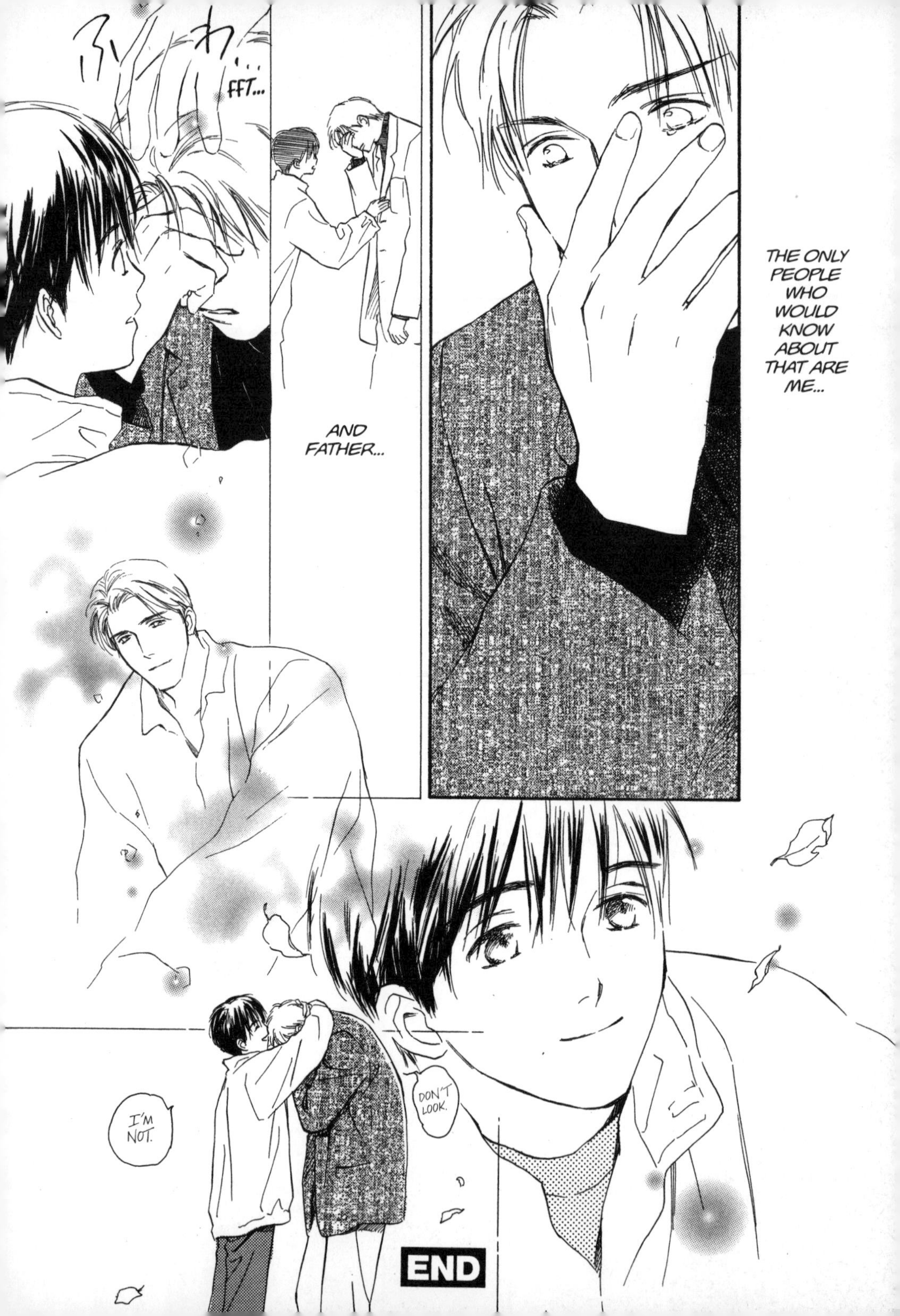
THE ONLY PEOPLE WHO WOULD KNOW ABOUT THAT ARE ME...
AND FATHER...
ふわ...
FFT...
DON'T LOOK.
I'M NOT.
END

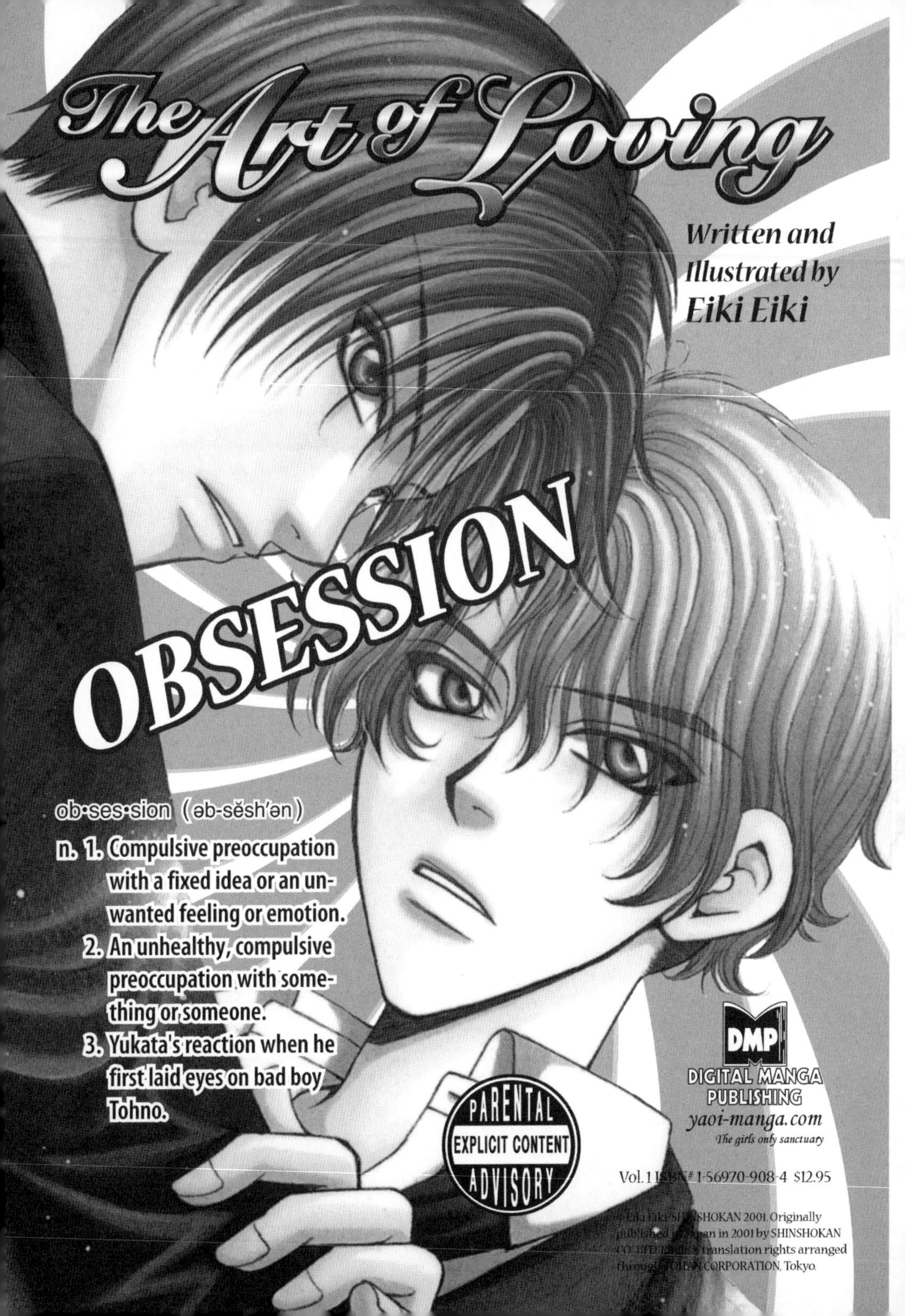
The Art of Loving
Written and Illustrated by Eiki Eiki
OBSESSION
ob·ses·sion (əb-sĕsh'ən)
n. 1. Compulsive preoccupation with a fixed idea or an unwanted feeling or emotion.
2. An unhealthy, compulsive preoccupation with something or someone.
3. Yukata's reaction when he first laid eyes on bad boy Tohno.
PARENTAL EXPLICIT CONTENT ADVISORY
DMP
DIGITAL MANGA PUBLISHING
yaoi-manga.com
The girls only sanctuary
Vol. 1 ISBN# 1-56970-908-4 $12.95
© Eiki Eiki/SHINSHOKAN 2001. Originally published in Japan in 2001 by SHINSHOKAN CO., LTD. English translation rights arranged through TOHAN CORPORATION, Tokyo.

You & Harujion

by Keiko Kinoshita

All is lost...

Haru has just lost his father,
Yakuza-esque creditors are
coming to collect on his
father's debts, and the
bank has foreclosed
the mortgage on
the house...

When things go from bad to worse,
in steps Yuuji Senoh...

ISBN# 1-56970-925-4 $12.95

DMP
DIGITAL MANGA
PUBLISHING

yaoi-manga.com
The girls only sanctuary

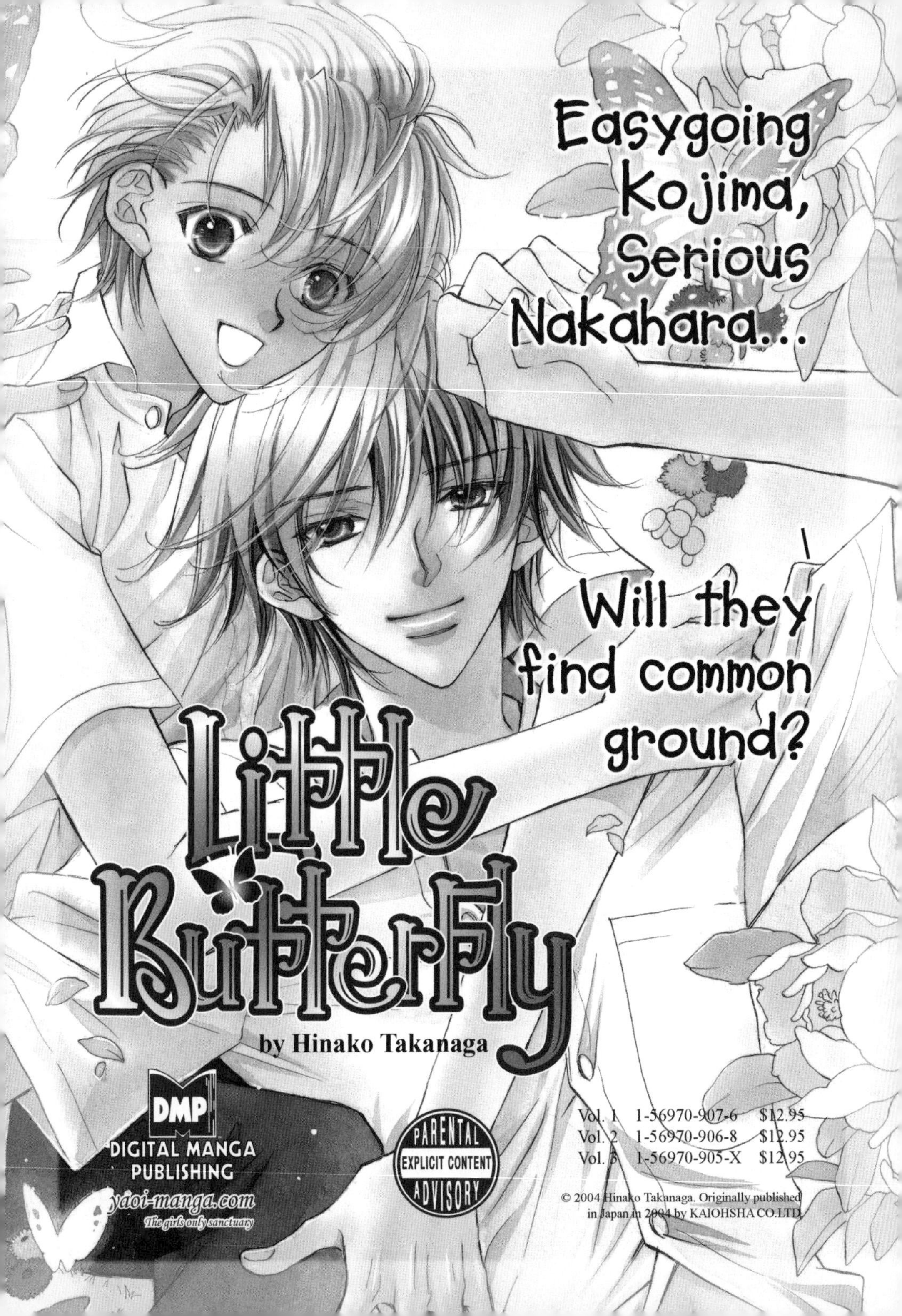
Easygoing Kojima, Serious Nakahara...
Will they find common ground?
Little Butterfly
by Hinako Takanaga
DMP
DIGITAL MANGA PUBLISHING
yaoi-manga.com
The girls only sanctuary
PARENTAL EXPLICIT CONTENT ADVISORY
Vol. 1 1-56970-907-6 $12.95
Vol. 2 1-56970-906-8 $12.95
Vol. 3 1-56970-905-X $12.95
© 2004 Hinako Takanaga. Originally published in Japan in 2004 by KAIOHSHA CO.LTD.

When the music stops...

love begins.

Il gatto sul G

Kind-hearted Atsushi finds Riya injured on his doorstep and offers him a safe haven from the demons pursing him.

By Tooko Miyagi

Vol. 1 ISBN# 1-56970-923-8 $12.95
Vol. 2 ISBN# 1-56970-893-2 $12.95

DMP
DIGITAL MANGA
PUBLISHING

yaoi-manga.com
The girls only sanctuary

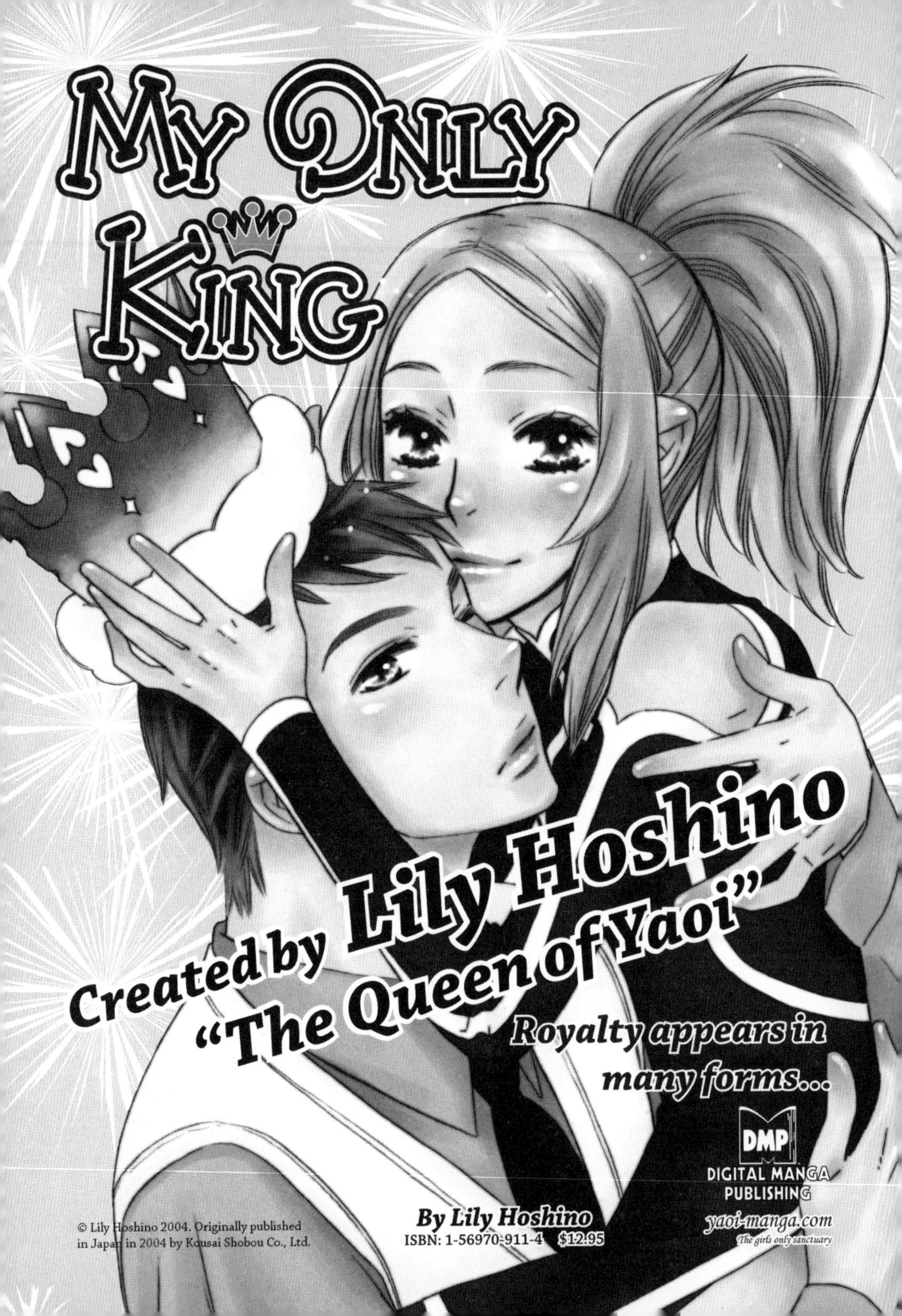
MY ONLY KING
Created by Lily Hoshino
"The Queen of Yaoi"
Royalty appears in many forms...
DMP
DIGITAL MANGA PUBLISHING
By Lily Hoshino
ISBN: 1-56970-911-4 $12.95
yaoi-manga.com
The girls only sanctuary
© Lily Hoshino 2004. Originally published in Japan in 2004 by Kousai Shobou Co., Ltd.

LOST BOYS

"Will you be our father?"

by Kaname Itsuki

A boy named "Air" appears at Mizuki's window one night and transports him to Neverland.

ISBN# 1-56970-924-6 $12.95

DIGITAL MANGA PUBLISHING

yaoi-manga.com
The girls only sanctuary

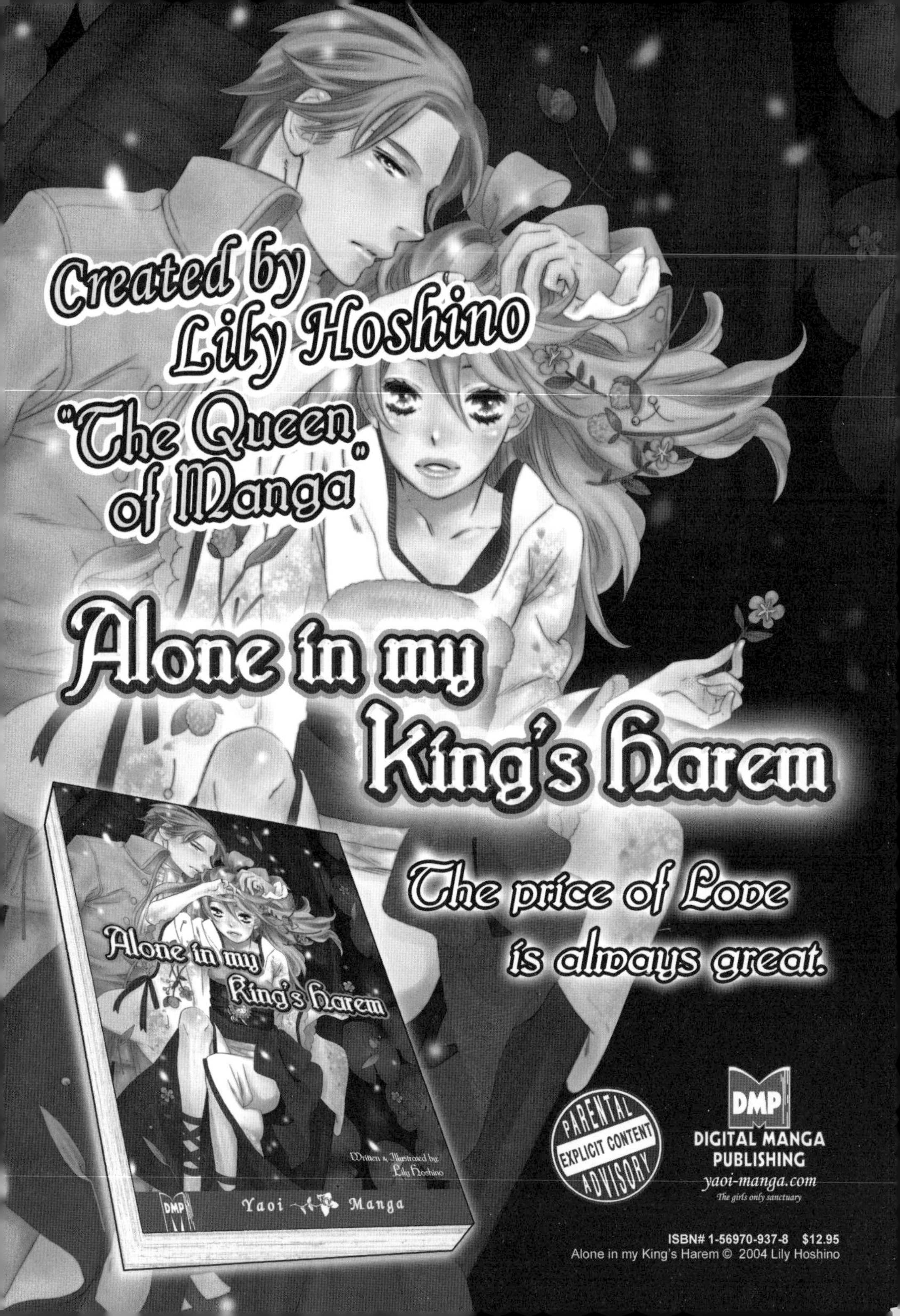
Created by
Lily Hoshino
"The Queen of Manga"
Alone in my King's Harem
The price of Love is always great.
Alone in my King's harem
Written & Illustrated by: Lily Hoshino
DMP
Yaoi Manga
PARENTAL ADVISORY
EXPLICIT CONTENT
DMP
DIGITAL MANGA PUBLISHING
yaoi-manga.com
The girls only sanctuary
ISBN# 1-56970-937-8 $12.95
Alone in my King's Harem © 2004 Lily Hoshino

STOP

This is the back of the book! Start from the other side.

NATIVE MANGA readers read manga from *right to left*.

1
2
1
3
2
3
5
4
4
6
5
8
7
6

*If you run into our **Native Manga** logo on any of our books... you'll know that this manga is published in it's true original native Japanese right to left reading format, as it was intended. Turn to the other side of the book and start reading from right to left, top to bottom.*

Follow the diagram to see how its done.
Surf's Up!

NATIVE MANGA
READ RIGHT TO LEFT